Emerging Innovations in Agile Software Development

Imran Ghani
Universiti Teknologi Malaysia, Malaysia

Dayang Norhayati Abang Jawawi
Universiti Teknologi Malaysia, Malaysia

Siva Dorairaj
Software Education, New Zealand

Ahmed Sidky
ICAgile, USA

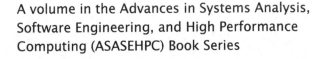

A volume in the Advances in Systems Analysis,
Software Engineering, and High Performance
Computing (ASASEHPC) Book Series

Information Science
REFERENCE
An Imprint of IGI Global

Published in the United States of America by
Information Science Reference (an imprint of IGI Global)
701 E. Chocolate Avenue
Hershey PA, USA 17033
Tel: 717-533-8845
Fax: 717-533-8661
E-mail: cust@igi-global.com
Web site: http://www.igi-global.com

Library of Congress Cataloging-in-Publication Data

Names: Ghani, Imran, 1975- editor. | Jawawi, Dayang Norhayati Abang, 1972-
  editor. | Dorairaj, Siva, 1972- editor. | Sidky, Ahmed editor.
Title: Emerging innovations in agile software development / Imran Ghani,
  Dayang Norhayati Abang Jawawi, Siva Dorairaj, and Ahmed Sidky, editors.
Description: Hershey, PA : Information Science Reference, an imprint of IGI
  Global, [2016] | Includes bibliographical references and index.
Identifiers: LCCN 2015046888| ISBN 9781466698581 (hardcover) | ISBN
  9781466698598 (ebook)
Subjects: LCSH: Agile software development--Technological innovations.
Classification: LCC QA76.76.D47 E465 2016 | DDC 005.1--dc23 LC record available at http://lccn.loc.gov/2015046888

This book is published in the IGI Global book series Advances in Systems Analysis, Software Engineering, and High Performance Computing (ASASEHPC) (ISSN: 2327-3453; eISSN: 2327-3461)

British Cataloguing in Publication Data
A Cataloguing in Publication record for this book is available from the British Library.

All work contributed to this book is new, previously-unpublished material. The views expressed in this book are those of the authors, but not necessarily of the publisher.

For electronic access to this publication, please contact: eresources@igi-global.com.

Advances in Systems Analysis, Software Engineering, and High Performance Computing (ASASEHPC) Book Series

Vijayan Sugumaran
Oakland University, USA

ISSN: 2327-3453
EISSN: 2327-3461

MISSION

The theory and practice of computing applications and distributed systems has emerged as one of the key areas of research driving innovations in business, engineering, and science. The fields of software engineering, systems analysis, and high performance computing offer a wide range of applications and solutions in solving computational problems for any modern organization.

The **Advances in Systems Analysis, Software Engineering, and High Performance Computing (ASASEHPC) Book Series** brings together research in the areas of distributed computing, systems and software engineering, high performance computing, and service science. This collection of publications is useful for academics, researchers, and practitioners seeking the latest practices and knowledge in this field.

COVERAGE

- Engineering Environments
- Storage Systems
- Computer System Analysis
- Performance Modelling
- Metadata and Semantic Web
- Distributed Cloud Computing
- Network Management
- Virtual Data Systems
- Human-Computer Interaction
- Parallel Architectures

IGI Global is currently accepting manuscripts for publication within this series. To submit a proposal for a volume in this series, please contact our Acquisition Editors at Acquisitions@igi-global.com or visit: http://www.igi-global.com/publish/.

Titles in this Series

For a list of additional titles in this series, please visit: www.igi-global.com

Emerging Research Surrounding Power Consumption and Performance Issues in Utility Computing
Ganesh Chandra Deka (Regional Vocational Training Institute (RVTI) for Women, India) G.M. Siddesh (M S Ramaiah Institute of Technology, Bangalore, India) K. G. Srinivasa (M S Ramaiah Institute of Technology, Bangalore, India) and L.M. Patnaik (IISc, Bangalore, India)
Information Science Reference • copyright 2016 • 460pp • H/C (ISBN: 9781466688537) • US $215.00 (our price)

Advanced Research on Cloud Computing Design and Applications
Shadi Aljawarneh (Jordan University of Science and Technology, Jordan)
Information Science Reference • copyright 2015 • 388pp • H/C (ISBN: 9781466686762) • US $205.00 (our price)

Handbook of Research on Computational Simulation and Modeling in Engineering
Francisco Miranda (Instituto Politécnico de Viana do Castelo and CIDMA of University of Aveiro, Portugal) and Carlos Abreu (Instituto Politécnico de Viana do Castelo, Portugal)
Engineering Science Reference • copyright 2016 • 824pp • H/C (ISBN: 9781466688230) • US $420.00 (our price)

Intelligent Applications for Heterogeneous System Modeling and Design
Kandarpa Kumar Sarma (Gauhati University, India) Manash Pratim Sarma (Gauhati University, India) and Mousmita Sarma (SpeecHWareNet (I) Pvt. Ltd, India)
Information Science Reference • copyright 2015 • 407pp • H/C (ISBN: 9781466684935) • US $255.00 (our price)

Achieving Enterprise Agility through Innovative Software Development
Amitoj Singh (Chitkara University, Punjab, India)
Information Science Reference • copyright 2015 • 349pp • H/C (ISBN: 9781466685109) • US $225.00 (our price)

Delivery and Adoption of Cloud Computing Services in Contemporary Organizations
Victor Chang (Computing, Creative Technologies and Engineering, Leeds Beckett University, UK) Robert John Walters (Electronics and Computer Science, University of Southampton, UK) and Gary Wills (Electronics and Computer Science, University of Southampton, UK)
Information Science Reference • copyright 2015 • 519pp • H/C (ISBN: 9781466682108) • US $225.00 (our price)

Emerging Research in Cloud Distributed Computing Systems
Susmit Bagchi (Gyeongsang National University, South Korea)
Information Science Reference • copyright 2015 • 446pp • H/C (ISBN: 9781466682139) • US $200.00 (our price)

www.igi-global.com

701 E. Chocolate Ave., Hershey, PA 17033
Order online at www.igi-global.com or call 717-533-8845 x100
To place a standing order for titles released in this series, contact: cust@igi-global.com
Mon-Fri 8:00 am - 5:00 pm (est) or fax 24 hours a day 717-533-8661

Editorial Advisory Board

Table of Contents

Detailed Table of Contents

    Shane Hastie, Software Education, New Zealand

A number of agile brands downplay the need for business analysis and requirements management on agile projects, putting large store in the role of the Product Owner. This paper tackles some of the problems this misconception can result in and shows how effective product ownership almost always requires a team with a variety of skills and backgrounds to be effective. Product Ownership requires clarity of vision, alignment with organizational strategy, understanding of the development process and the ability to communicate with a wide variety of stakeholders across all levels both inside and outside the organization. The complexity of the role is most often more than a single person can (or should) cope with – effective product ownership requires a teamwork approach covering a variety of skills and knowledge.

    Taghi Javdani Gandomani, Islamic Azad University – Boroujen, Iran
    Mina Ziaei Nafchi, Islamic Azad University – Boroujen, Iran

Prevalence of Agile methods in software companies is increasing dramatically. Software companies and teams need to employ these methods to overcome the inherent challenges of traditional methods in software development. However, transitioning to Agile approach is a topic of debate. This is mainly because software companies are facing with many challenges, obstacles, and hindrances when leaving traditional methods and moving to Agile methods, as shown in previous research studies. Conducting a large-scale research study showed that Agile transformation need to be supported by several facilitators and identified its most important facilitators. The main aim of this chapter is to present two hidden facilitators of Agile transition, Agile coaches and Agile champions, which rarely have been taken into consideration. Both of these facilitators directly impress the people involved in the transition. People-intensive nature of Agile methods and critical role of the people in the transition process reflect the importance of these facilitators when a software company doing its transition.

Although agile development promises better customer response and quality, not all who attempt agile seem to get such desired results. The issue is context – understanding the context in which agile is being adopted and choosing the right practices. Our research question is how agile-coaches can best elicit and communicate the agile adoption context with development teams and organizations. In this paper, we propose capturing and describing agile adoption context visually using a set of architectural views. This is analogous to describing architectures, but now applied to the context of agile adoption. We propose a set of views and applied it in the agile adoption of a company's internal social network system (SNS). Our experiences taught us that context evolves as agile coaches interact with development organization and teams, and the context description evolves and converges to the team's desired way of working after the agile coach leaves the scene. It is also the basis for drawing upon past experiences and building experiences for the next agile adoption engagement.

In this chapter, a report containing the author's many years of experience in software development together with a discussion of software engineering are presented. The report begins with the software crisis and includes different projects following the traditional waterfall model with heavy documents. In a re-engineering project of a legacy IT system by modernizing COBOL applications, we established an agile and model driven approach to software development. This approach which has been successfully applied in 13 projects since 2004 is presented. The key factors required for our success will also be discussed. Both the good and bad experiences of the last ten years will be summarized. The chapter will be finalized with a vision of a new architecture for agile software development.

This chapter describes the agile transformation of an IT organization in China with about 4000 people including contractors. In the span of one year, 47 teams and 1700 engineers moved from traditional to agile way of working. There was a 44% reduction in development lead-time, 5% reduction in production defects and 22% reduction in production incidents. This agile transformation occurred at two levels. At the organization level, adoption speed was crucial, as we wanted to reach critical mass in rapid time with limited coaching resources. This was very much an entrepreneur startup problem, where customers in our case are teams and members in the IT organization. At the team level, a practice architecture provided a roadmap for continuous improvement. A theory-based-software-engineering approach facilitated deeper learning. Beyond the usual factors for leading successful change, this transformation exemplified the use of a startup mentality, social networks, practice architecture, simulation, gamification, and more importantly integrating theory and practice.

The sustainability of agile transformations is deeply linked to how the organization "transforms" to agile. Sustainable, effective agile transformations affect all the elements of culture such as, leadership style, leadership values, work structures, reward systems, processes, and of course the work habits of people. How to affect that culture shift is the key question we will present in this chapter. The author will present two different common transformation approaches (organizational-led and process-led) and then describe a hybrid version called culture-led transformation that is designed to change critical organizational and personal habits to improve and sustain organizational agility.

While many existing Agile product development methodologies like SCRUM, Extreme Programming (XP), Dynamic Systems Development Method (DSDM), Feature Driven Development (FDD) etc. cover aspects related to developing & delivering a product solution, they are not meant to provide an end to end framework for an organization to transition / embrace and adopt agile way of software development. For an organization's agile journey to be successful we should consider several organizational elements like how to do a business case for agile, how to build agile leadership qualities for staff at all levels (especially Managers), how to setup & govern an agile organization, how to assess an agile organization etc.

Nowadays, since business environment is highly dynamic, software necessities are continuously being improved in order to meet the needs of modern industrialized world. Therefore, IT organizations seek for a quick way of software delivery and for adapting to the necessary technological changes. From this ideal viewpoint, traditional plan-driven developments lag behind to overcome these conflicts. The purpose of this chapter is to present the existing models and frameworks which guide organizations to adopt agile methods. This may help organizations to follow professionals' suggestions during their migration from traditional systems to agile development.

Agile methods are widely used in software companies in recent years. Many software companies are replacing their traditional development methods with agile methods. Nonetheless, measuring agility that they have achieved has been a topic of debate. Software teams and companies need to know how agile they are or how much is the agility degree of their organization. Unlike traditional methods in software development, there is no standard or universal model (like CMM/CMMI) to measure maturity of agile teams and software companies. So far, only a few methods and tools have been proposed to measure the agility of software companies. The main aim of this chapter is introducing the structure and main features of the existing agile assessment methods and providing a brief discussion on drawbacks of these methods. This chapter tries to elucidate the actual position of agility measurement methods in measuring agility degree of companies who are trying to adapt to agile methods and practices.

The first part of this chapter presents the results of a systematic literature review on Agile Software Development (ASD) challenges as are reported in implementation and adoption cases. The data only considers the concrete evidences of surfaced problems mainly according to work experience and case study articles. The results are analyzed so that types, nature and intensity of the problems are determined and, compared to each other, within three major classifications of "large organizations", "distributed settings" and "both large and distributed environments". The analysis reveals that, in ASD, common organizational and managerial issues have been replaced by communication and collaboration problems. The second part uses the results of the part one as a frame of analysis to render more interpretations e.g. signifying that non-agility preconceptions are the root of a majority of problematic projects. Besides, mediating between agile projects and traditional forms of management, and, economic governance are two major rival approaches that are emerging in response to these challenges.

As the popularity and acceptance of agile software development methodologies increases, the need to integrate usability engineering in the design and development processes is imperative. While, agile the focus is on technical and functional requirements not on end-user interaction, usability is usually only dealt with on the side. Combining this two in practice will go a long way in development of better product. Since the success and acceptance of software product depends not only on the technologies used but how well it integrates user-oriented methods. Therefore, this chapter puts together works on how usability engineering has been integrated with agile processes.

Chapter 12
Anuradha Chaminda Gajanayaka, Exilesoft (Pvt) Limited, Sri Lanka

Agile software development has established as a reliable alternative to waterfall software development model. Unfortunately the use of agile software development has been limited to time based contracts and not for time limited contracts. The main reason for this limitation is the "Agile manifesto" itself. The forth value of the manifesto states that agile believers find more value in "Responding to change over following a plan". This is the one of the main reasons why agile software development methods are not preferred for a fixed priced contract or time limited contract. The following case study provides an example on how the agile software development can be used for fixed priced software development contracts even when operating in offshore context. The agile software development concepts were used throughout to plan, execute, monitor, report, etc. for the project documented in this case study.

Chapter 13
Praveen Ramachandra Menon, Independent Researcher, Singapore

This chapter highlights a crucial problem seen often in software development that is bridging the communication gap between business and technical language and that it can be addressed with "Behavior Driven Development" (BDD) methodology supplemented with "Specification By Example" approach of delivering the right software that matters. Effective communication has always been a challenge between clients, business stakeholders, project managers, developers, testers and business analysts because a "ubiquitous" language that every one can easily understand and use does not exist. Specification By Example serves as that ubiquitous language for all, helps build right software that matters through effective communication. Specifications are written in plain English language using the Gherkin syntax to describe various behaviors of software. BDD tools help write software specification using gherkin language and also create a living documentation that is automatically generated by programming language reflecting the current state of software at any given point of time.

Chapter 14
Deshinta Arrova Dewi Dewi, INTI International University, Malaysia
Mohana Muniandy, INTI International University, Malaysia

This paper presents the review of literatures that shows the contribution of the agile methodology towards teaching and learning environment at university level. Teaching and learning at university has since migrated from traditional learning to active learning methodology where students are expected to learn by doing rather than listening passively to lectures alone. The agile methodology naturally has promoted the active participation of team members during system development phases. Some literature have proposed ways of adopting agile into active learning to improve teaching and learning processes and have highlighted this method as a great success. We would like to highlight how efficient the agile concept is in tackling several situations in academic learning as shown by an interesting mapping of agile principles to the classroom environment. We also offer options for the agile evaluation framework to consider academic environment as a tool to obtain the agile performance feedback.

Foreword

In today's dynamic, fast-paced, creative economy, to seize new and emerging market opportunities before their competitors do, organizations need to have business and technical agility. To achieve sustainable business and technical agility, most organizations are in the process of planning or executing some level of an "Agile Transformation".

The words "Agile" and "transformation" are often greeted with a mixed bag of emotions and cultural implications across the software industry and more so in the business world.

It is important to clarify that Agile is neither a process nor a methodology; it is a mindset. Many people may think that Agile is just another software development process. Although that is true to a degree, there is a lot more to Agile than just a process or just a set of practices. Agile (or agility) is a way of thinking grounded in the realities of learning, adapting, and continuous growth that happen naturally with creative work and creative workers. Once adopted, the Agile mindset forces people to think in a value-driven approach about numerous things in their lives, including of course their work. On the same note, the purpose of an Agile Transformation is to positively influence organizations towards a culture governed by the Agile mindset.

This is an unprecedented time for businesses all around the world. Shifting their organizational strategies, structures, processes and more importantly their leaders and people to be inline with what is needed for a creative economy is not a trivial matter by any stretch of the imagination. Therefore we are living in a time when learning and sharing how organizations are making these cultural changes and scaling Agile is critical.

This book provides a great deal of innovations and insights about how organizations are assessing their readiness for Agile, scaling Agile across their organizations, designing Agile transformations and reaching business agility.

There are a number of chapters in the book that share stories and experiences from large-scale Agile transformations. When I lead Agile transformations for a number of Fortune 100 companies, stories were an important tool for executives and leaders of the organization to see what other organization are doing and to reassure them that while the journey may be hard and long it is worth the investment.

This book also does a fantastic job at exploring various Agile transformation approaches. This is very important since most organizations end-up creating a custom Agile approach for them. Learning not one, by many approaches, broadens an organization's understanding of what is possible and as a natural consequence helps the organization craft an approach that is most suitable for it. I have constantly been amazed with how organizations can learn and extract the most suitable elements from each Agile approach to make something that will give them their utmost agility.

There are many complex challenges organizations face on their Agile journey. Some of them are related to selecting an adoption approaches or methodology, other challenges stem from having the right personnel to lead such a transformation. Many organizations are also exploring how Agile will affect other parts of the business that are less technical in nature like Talent, Finance or Learning and Development.

If you are looking for the latest research or comparative analysis, this book includes the work of great academicians. If you want to read about cutting-edge innovations great thought-leaders in the Agile space have shared their insights in a couple of different chapters throughout this book. And if you are looking for experience from the trenches the book highlights the works of a number of expert practitioners. This book is a great collection and has something for everyone, wherever you are on your Agile journey. Enjoy.

Ahmed Sidky
ICAgile, USA

Ahmed Sidky *is the founder of the International Consortium for Agile (ICAgile), and the author of the publication Becoming Agile in an Imperfect World.*

Preface

Agile is a relatively recent methodology used in the development process of a project. Therefore, it is important to share new emerging knowledge with the audiences interested in adopting an Agile mindset. The upcoming book, Emerging Innovations in Agile Software Development, focuses on the use of agile methodologies to manage, design, develop, test and maintain software projects. This book consists of fourteen chapters.

In "Design of a Framework to Implement Agility at Organizational Level: Organizational Agile Transformation" Jagadeesh Balakrishnan highlights compatibility problems with existing agile product development methodologies for companies laying foot for the first time in agile domain. To assist in such situation, He has provided guidelines for each phase of agile adoption respectively.

In "Rapid Agile Transformation at a Large IT Organization" Pan-Wei Ng describes agile transformation of an IT organization in China with 4000 people including contractors. At the team level, a practice architecture provided a roadmap for continuous improvement. This transformation had 44% reduction in development lead-time, 5% reduction in production defects and 22% reduction in production incidents and proved to be a win-win situation for everyone.

In "A Canvas for Capturing Context of Agile Adoption" Pan-Wei Ng identifies the reasons for which companies are not able to gain better customer response and quality using agile practices. To address this problem they propose capturing and describing agile adoption context visually using a set of architectural views.

In "Agile Software Development Challenges in Implementation and Adoption: Focusing on Large and Distributed Settings - Past Experiences, Emergent Topics" Abbas Moshref Razavi, Rodina Ahmad present the results of systematic literature review on agile software development challenges and identify mediating between agile projects and traditional forms of management, and, economic governance as major rival approaches that are emerging in response to these challenges.

In "Fixed Priced Projects in Agile: Fixed Projects in Agile Software Development Environments" Anuradha Chaminda Gajanayaka points out that why agile software development has been limited to time based contracts and not for time limited contracts. Issues were further explained using case studies which used agile software development concepts throughout planning, execution, monitoring, reporting, etc. for the project documentation.

In "A Transformation Approach for Scaling and Sustaining Agility at an Enterprise-Level: A Culture-Led Agile Transformation Approach" Ahmed Sidky explain how Sustainable, effective agile transformations affect all the elements of corporate culture such as, leadership style, leadership values, work structures, reward systems, processes, and of course the work habits of people.

In "Agile Assessment Methods and Approaches" Mina Ziaei Nafchi, Taghi Javdani Gandomani introduce the structure and main features of the existing agile assessment methods and providing a brief discussion on drawbacks of these methods.

In "A Survey of Agile Transition Models" Imran Ghani, Dayang Abang Jawawi, Naghmeh Niknejad, Seung Ryul Jeong and Murad Khan present a survey on existing models and frameworks available to guide organizations for agile transition. These models and frameworks may help the organizations to follow professionals' suggestions during their migration from traditional environment to agile environment.

In "10 Years of Experience with Agile and Model Driven Software Development in a Legacy Platform" Chung-Yeung Pang discuss an agile and model driven approach to software development established while re-engineering project of a legacy IT system by modernizing COBOL application. This approach has been successfully applied in 13 projects since 2004 is presented.

In "Usability Engineering in Agile Software Development Processes" Muhammad Aminu Umar, Sahabi Ali Yusuf, Salami Sheidu Tenuche, Aminu Onimisi Abdulsalami, Aliyu Muhammad Kufena point out While, in agile the focus is on technical and functional requirements not on end-user interaction, usability is usually only dealt with on the side. Combining this two in practice will go a long way in development of better product. Hence chapter puts together works on how usability engineering has been integrated with agile processes.

In "Agile Coaches and Champions: Two Hidden Facilitators of Agile Transition" Taghi Javdani Gandomani, Mina Ziaei Nafchi Conducted a large-scale research study showing that agile transformation need to be supported by several facilitators and identify its most important facilitators. Hence they present two hidden facilitators of agile transition, Agile coaches and Agile champions, which rarely have been taken into consideration. Both of these facilitators directly impress the people involved in the transition.

In "Product Ownership is a Team Sport" Shane Hastie describes that product ownership requires clarity of vision, alignment with organizational strategy, understanding of the development process and the ability to communicate with a wide variety of stakeholders across all levels both inside and outside the organization

In "Behavior-Driven Development Using Specification by Example: An Approach for Delivering the Right Software Built in Right Way" Praveen Ramachandra Menon highlights a crucial problem seen often in software development that is bridging the communication gap between business and technical language and that it can be addressed with "Behavior Driven Development" (BDD) methodology supplemented with "Specification By Example" approach of delivering the right software that matters.

In "The Agility of Agile Methodology for Teaching and Learning Activities" Deshinta Arrova Dewi Dewi, Mohana Muniandy present review of literatures that shows the contribution of the agile methodology towards teaching and learning environment at university level. Later they offer options for the agile evaluation framework to consider academic environment as a tool to obtain the agile performance feedback in academic environment.

In the preparation of this book, we received many high quality contributions in response to our call for chapters. The number of contributors indicates that Agile Software Development is a promising technique transforming software industry. We are very grateful for the contributions and would like to thank all the authors for their efforts.

Imran Ghani
Universiti Teknologi Malaysia, Malaysia

Dayang Norhayati Abang Jawawi
Universiti Teknologi Malaysia, Malaysia

Siva Dorairaj
Software Education, New Zealand

Ahmed Sidky
ICAgile, USA

Chapter 1
Product Ownership
Is a Team Sport

Shane Hastie
Software Education, New Zealand

ABSTRACT

A number of agile brands downplay the need for business analysis and requirements management on agile projects, putting large store in the role of the Product Owner. This paper tackles some of the problems this misconception can result in and shows how effective product ownership almost always requires a team with a variety of skills and backgrounds to be effective. Product Ownership requires clarity of vision, alignment with organizational strategy, understanding of the development process and the ability to communicate with a wide variety of stakeholders across all levels both inside and outside the organization. The complexity of the role is most often more than a single person can (or should) cope with – effective product ownership requires a teamwork approach covering a variety of skills and knowledge.

INTRODUCTION

A number of agile brands downplay the need for business analysis and requirements management on agile projects, putting large store in the role of the Product Owner. This paper tackles some of the problems this misconception can result in and shows how effective product ownership almost always requires a team with a variety of skills and backgrounds to be effective.

Product Ownership requires clarity of vision, alignment with organizational strategy, understanding of the development process (Methodology, 2014) and the ability to communicate with a wide variety of stakeholders across all levels both inside and outside the organization. The complexity of the role is most often more than a single person can (or should) cope with – effective product ownership requires a teamwork approach covering a variety of skills and knowledge (Andrea, 2005).

In this chapter we examine various aspects of Product Ownership, the characteristics needed in the team for successful product ownership, look at the capabilities needed in a product ownership team, examine the difference between value and velocity and provide some practical tools which can be used for product ownership in agile and non-agile projects (Currim, Mintz, & Siddarth, 2015).

DOI: 10.4018/978-1-4666-9858-1.ch001

PRODUCT OWNERSHIP IN CONTEXT

The Product Owner Role

The Product Owner is one of the three roles defined in Scrum, and is referenced in many of the agile brands. The term Product Owner has become almost ubiquitous yet there is a lot of confusion and lots of misinformation about what the role is and what it actually entails.

The Scrum Guide defines the Product Owner role as follows:

The Product Owner is responsible for maximizing the value of the product and the work of the Development Team. How this is done may vary widely across organizations, Scrum Teams, and individuals. (Education, 2014)

The Product Owner is the sole person responsible for managing the Product Backlog. Product Backlog management includes:

- Clearly expressing Product Backlog items;
- Ordering the items in the Product Backlog to best achieve goals and missions;
- Optimizing the value of the work the Development Team performs;
- Ensuring that the Product Backlog is visible, transparent, and clear to all, and shows what the Scrum Team will work on next; and,
- Ensuring the Development Team understands items in the Product Backlog to the level needed. (Schwaber, 2013)

Extreme Programming talks about needing the Customer onsite all the time:

One of the few requirements of extreme programming (XP) is to have the customer available. Not only to help the development team, but to be a part of it as well. All phases of an XP project require communication with the customer, preferably face to face, on site. It's best to simply assign one or more customers to the development team. (Programming, 2014)

This puts a huge demand on the individual taking the Product Owner or Onsite Customer role, one which for the vast majority of real-world projects is beyond the skills and capabilities of any one individual.

Project Types

The nature of knowledge work is that it is inherently unpredictable, especially in complex environments such as software development projects. The typical software development project today requires interfacing with a number of existing systems both internal to and outside of the control of the organization building the product, solving problems for a variety of stakeholders from different business units or divisions spread across multiple locations in different time zones (Hastie, 2014).

Add to this complexity the nature of product development projects – often the problem to be solved is unclear and unknowable until the solution.

The Cinderella Project

In September 2005, Jennitta Andrea (Andrea, 2005) described what she called the Cinderella Project, one for which the agile shoe fits perfectly. She described the characteristics of the Cinderella Project as:

- *A team is small enough to fit within a collocated space—ideally less than ten people but no more than twenty.*
- *SMEs are a permanent part of the team.*
- *SMEs have a clear vision for the system requirements and can effectively communicate this to developers.*
- *SMEs can express the requirements in the form of functional tests.*
- *Either the problem domain has a short learning curve or the developers have deep experience in a more complex domain.*

In that environment the Product Owner would be the SME (subject matter expert) able to provide the team with absolute clarity of direction and define clearly what success looks like for every aspect of the project.

Unfortunately this project doesn't happen often today, and almost never in the large corporate environment where agile practices are gaining greater and greater adoption.

Your Project

The reality of the project environment today is much more complex and uncertain.

Projects are defined with vague goals, where the problem itself is not clearly understood, the business domain is in a state of flux, the technology environment is rapidly evolving (think mobile devices and platforms), the stakeholders have competing needs and the team is distributed across many time zones.

In many organizations today team members are expected to work on multiple projects at the same time, architectures and interfaces are constrained and options restricted, timelines are unrealistic and inflexible and the product being worked on may have 20 years of accumulated technical debt (Education, 2014).

This is the modern reality of product development and project management. It helps to have a framework to at least begin to understand what the elements of complexity are.

The Octopus Model

Philippe Kruchten (Kruchten, 2011) describes the eight aspects of context as follows (see Figure 1):

1. **Size:** How big is the system to develop (in SLOC, function points, or person-months).
2. **Criticality:** How many people die if the system fail, or how many billions of euros are lost.
3. **Age of the System:** Greenfield development, brownfield, evolution of legacy system, maintenance
4. **Business Model:** How is the project remunerated for its effort; in-house development, commercial product, software embedded in another product or system, open source development, research.
5. **Team Distribution:** Collocated, geographical distributed (outsourcing, etc.).
6. **Volatility:** Of the environment: how stable are the requirements and the surrounding business environment.

Figure 1. The Octopus Model

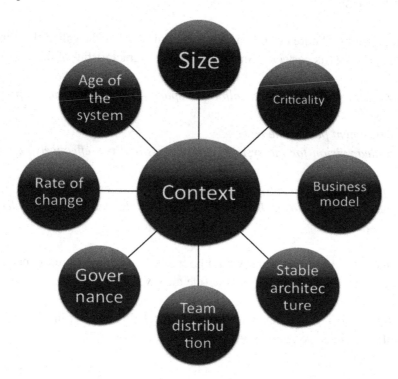

7. **Stable Architecture:** How much of a stable architecture exist at the start of the project.
8. **Governance:** What are the external rules imposed to the project to control its trajectory and how formal are they.

He says that these elements impact on the approach that is needed to product delivery in roughly descending order of importance, and that they are in addition to the overriding factors of business domain and organizational culture.

Given the very real complexity of the product development environments we work in today, the Product Owner simply can't be the single voice defining value in what is to be built, it needs Product Ownership.

Product Ownership Requires a Broad Range of Skills and Knowledge

Product ownership encompasses a variety of areas of the organization and requires bringing together many voices including:

- Product Management
- Marketing
- Business Advocacy
- Customer Advocacy
- End User Advocacy
- Domain Subject Matter Knowledge

- Business and Technical Analysis
- User Experience and Graphic Design
- Innovation
- Communications
- Legal and Compliance

No one individual can represent all these aspects, nor can they hold all these considerations in their mind – there is simply too much happening for one individual to provide the clarity of understanding and direction needed. It truly requires a team. This team is responsible for jointly identifying the elements of value, identifying the overall goals and objectives of the initiative being undertaken and for progressively elaborating the backlog to ensure the right product is built.

The Value Team is responsible for managing the backlog, under the direction and guidance of the Value Facilitator, acting as the team captain. The Value Facilitator acts as the team captain for the value team – they provide the overall guidance and keep the team focused on delivering the right value at the right time. As with a sports team, individual team members are expected to know what is needed to win their game and they do not defer to the captain for every decision, rather they understand the captain's goals and work collaboratively to achieve these goals.

The Value Team

This image shows the likely knowledge and skills needed on a Value Team (see Figure 2).

Figure 2. Composition of an Agile Value Team

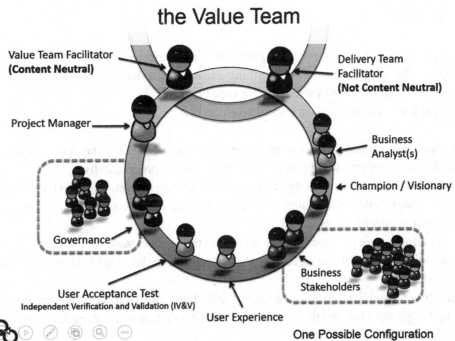

- **Value Facilitator:** Someone who leads this team, engages with others to reach consensus and provides overall direction, stands up for value and the product vision.
- **Project Management:** Focused on time and money, understands the tradeoffs that need to be made to achieve the project's goals within the constraints imposed.
- **Governance:** Focused on ensuring the right processes are followed and compliance needs are communicated to the team.
- **Business Analysis and Subject Matter Expertise:** Bring domain knowledge and an understanding of who knows what, able to reach out to the wider stakeholder community to elicit needs and validate solutions, acting as the voice of the customer in specific areas.
- **User Experience/Graphics:** Where there is a high degree of interaction in the required product these skills are necessary to help make the product useful and useable for the target audience, and to ensure the right aesthetic values (such as corporate branding) are incorporated in the product.
- **User Acceptance Test/I V&V:** Able to check the delivered product against user needs and (if required) validate it against legal or other external criteria and show compliance.
- **Delivery Team Facilitator:** Brings the voice of the delivery team to the product conversations – ensuring the feasibility and sustainability of the delivered product, advocating for sustainable pace and technical qualities.

These are roles not job titles – in some environments there may be just one or two people playing these roles, in others there may be many divergent jobs represented on the team (Thomsett, 2001).

The key is that the team has everything they need to identify and prioritize business value increments, scope the smallest solution that might possibly deliver on the business value increment, to prepare the runway for the delivery teams by gathering all the details needed by the delivery team to deliver a feature/story and .getting the backlog items to a READY state.

The Delivery Team

As with the Value Team, these are roles not job titles – it is feasible that one person will play multiple roles in the team. The delivery team has everything and everyone they need to deliver a working increment of tested, documented, deployable software (see Figure 3).

The typical roles in a delivery team encompass:

- **Team Facilitation:** The process conscience of the team, looking out for team health, process workability and usefulness and removing obstacles to the product delivery.
- **Analysis:** Bring domain knowledge and an understanding of who knows what, able to reach out to the wider stakeholder community to elicit needs and validate solutions, acting as the voice of the customer in specific areas.
- **Testing:** Helping to define and measure quality in the product, assessing and advocating for quality in the delivered product, examining and communicating the state of the various quality aspects in the product.
- **Architecture:** Providing advocacy, guidance and clarity of direction from a technical viewpoint, ensuring the product fits into the broader technical ecosystem of the organization.

Figure 3. Composition of an Agile Delivery Team

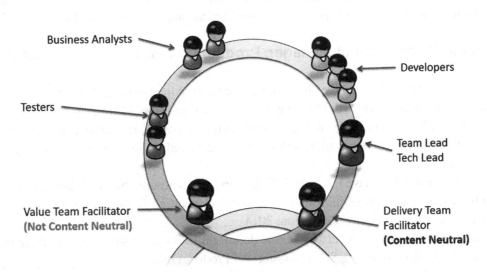

The Delivery Team: has everything and everyone they need to deliver a working piece of tested, documented, deployable software.

- **Development:** The team members with the skills needed to deliver the product backlog items to fully production-ready state.

The whole team are *Generalizing Specialists* someone who (Ambler, 2014):

1. Has one or more technical specialties (e.g. Java programming, Project Management, Database Administration, ...)
2. Has at least a general knowledge of software development
3. Has at least a general knowledge of the business domain in which they work
4. Actively seeks to gain new skills in both their existing specialties as well as in other areas, including both technical and domain areas

The Delivery Team are responsible for taking the product backlog items which have been made READY and getting them to a fully deliverable, production-ready DONE state.

Depending on the complexity of the environment and the nature of the initiative being undertaken the Value Team and Delivery Team may be working tightly coupled and largely overlapping with the same cadence and very little visible differentiation between members of the two groups or they may be loosely coupled with aspects of their work offset by up to a whole iteration. It is strongly recommended that the maximum offset in the flow of work between the two groups is no more than one iteration, ideally it is a matter of hours to days, with a Three Amigo's workshop or equivalent being held to ensure the story is READY shortly before the delivery team members get it to DONE.

One Overlapping, Collaborative Team

The reality of this "two-team" view is that there is actually a high level of overlap and tight collaboration between the roles on the team, and the view is more like this image (see Figure 4).

Relating the Roles: Project Manager, Product Owner, and Scrum Master

It is frequently necessary to clarify the distinction in the leadership roles on agile teams. In the Cinderella Project referred to earlier there will likely be a high overlap in responsibilities with the boundaries of the various roles blurring and different team members taking on different activities as the needs arise. In more complicated environments there will normally be a need to clarify some of the responsibilities more explicitly.

Mature agile teams will have far more T-Shaped people who are able to tackle multiple different roles and there will be a natural diminishing in reliance on specific role titles as the team becomes more self-organising and self-directing (Education, 2014).

Early teams tend to need more clarity in role definition, and three roles which are often the subject of confusion are Project Manager, Scrum Master and Product Owner.

- **Project Manager:** This is an externally focused, highly collaborative, cross-team/cross-initiative role. Very small, stand-alone initiatives will most likely not need this role as the initiative is iso-

Figure 4. Whole team

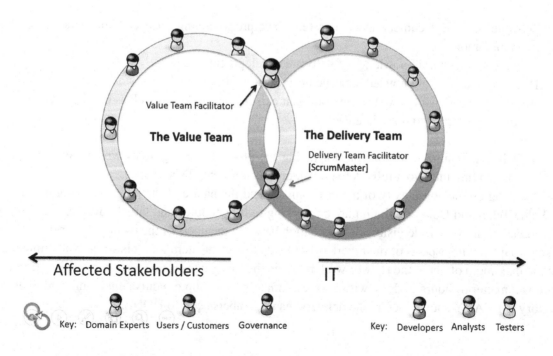

lated from the larger organizational context. The Project Manager is shown in the diagrams above as a member of the Value Team – providing the interface to the larger organization, building relationships across many areas/departments and using their knowledge of organization structures, goals and strategy to influence the broader ecosystem and help the initiative be successful. This role often "holds the purse-strings" and is acts as the time & money conscience for the initiative (Dillon, 2015). Project management in agile environments is substantially different to the traditional perception of the role as being one of task allocation and daily monitoring – self-organization empowers the team members to take on those responsibilities themselves, freeing project managers to be impediment removers and diplomats acting on behalf of the initiative in the larger playing field.

- **Product Owner:** This is one title for the Value Facilitator in the Value Team. They play the role of Value Conscience for the initiative, ensuring the Value Team are focused on the right backlog items, keeping the flow of value through the pipeline is steady, making the hard decisions regarding the many tradeoffs that need to be made and leading the value definition activities. The Product Owner acts as the team captain for the value team – they provide the overall guidance and keep the team focused on delivering the right value at the right time. As with a sports team, individual team members are expected to know what is needed to win their game and they do not defer to the captain for every decision, rather they understand the captain's goals and work collaboratively to achieve these goals.

- **Scrum Master:** This is one title for the delivery Team Facilitator described above. They act in the best interests of the team's ongoing sustainability, monitor the health of the process, guide the team towards more and more self-organization, encourage the constant learning needed to improve their processes and generally act as the Process Conscience for the team (Hastie, 2014). This role is often shared across multiple team members as the team matures, although there is an argument for keeping the role a full-time responsibility.

These three roles are complimentary, with some activities overlapping but a general separation of concerns in the three areas is recommended – combining these roles leads to internal conflict as the same individual is asked to balance quite distinctly separate concerns. While it is possible to have one person play multiple roles it is not advised (Jacobson, 2014).

Putting Value Front and Centre

Product ownership requires that decisions are made with a value-based focus – what is the smallest piece of work we can do that will validate the assumptions being made, and deliver real useful value to our organization and delight our customers.

Value is not related to velocity – velocity is a measure of the cost of producing the product, not the value to the organization of having the backlog item built (see Figure 5).

The first few iterations the team will pull work from the backlog based on confirming or disproving some assumptions, addressing some of the important areas of uncertainty and risk and occasionally doing small experiments and spike solutions to reduce uncertainty risk through the rapid feedback cycle that agile projects allow – the early delivery will enable the value manager to validate the concepts and confirm or deny the early assumptions made about the customer needs. There will be a lot of learning about the capability of the team, the uncertainty in the project, the way people work together and many

Figure 5. Value vs. velocity

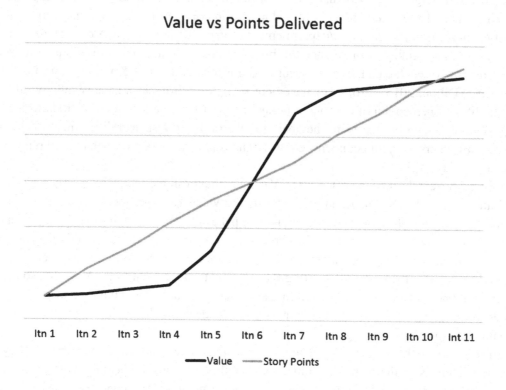

other aspects which need to be exposed early in a product lifecycle. There will definitely be velocity, but the delivered velocity will not be directly proportional to the value derived from the stories.

The likelihood is that these first few iterations will not produce enough of the product for it to be truly valuable in the marketplace until enough of the stories have been delivered to cross the MVP threshold – the Minimum VIABLE Product which can be utilized beyond a select and limited group of early-adopter or test customers, something that actually does start generating at least a subset of the planned benefits.

Once the MVP has been delivered there is often a sharp upturn in value delivered – as new stories are added to the product they make it more attractive to the customers. For a while this sharp increase in value continues as the most useful stories are delivered. The iterative feedback nature allows the team to learn what the customers REALLY want, and that is likely to be quite different to what was originally planned. As new stories are identified they need to be added to the backlog in value-based prioritized order.

At some point the rate of value delivery tapers off – the team has built the features and capabilities which are of the most interest to the customers, and adding new capabilities does not significantly increase the usefulness of the product to the customers. This is the point where the value facilitator needs to be ruthless about cutting the remaining work – yes there are plenty of epics and stories left in the backlog, yes there is more budget money in the pot, yes some people want those stories too, but is adding additional capabilities to this product actually the best thing to do with the remaining funding?

Evidence from studies of products seems to indicate that stopping work early is a very good thing. Depending on which study you look at, somewhere between 50% and 70% of the features in a typical software product are never used. Now, a portion of those features are built in the hope that they will

Figure 6. Knowing when to stop

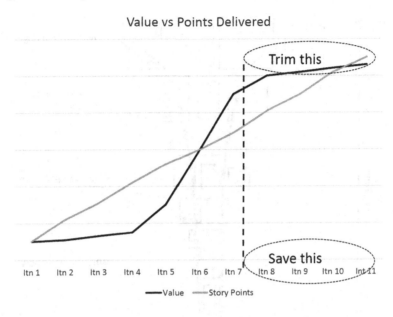

never be needed – these are often the disaster recovery and security protection features which hopefully won't be exercised. However these do NOT account for half of the work in a typical product. Surely it will be better to stop work rather than build features which no one will ever use in the wild (see Figure 6).

The Shape of a Healthy Backlog

A Backlog should not just be a list of hundreds of user stories waiting to be delivered – that approach simply results in lengthy wait times for individual stories to be delivered, a large queue of work which becomes a bottleneck and source of waste.

Once an item has been added to a backlog there is tendency for it to take on a life of its own (no matter how small or large it is), someone who matters wants it to be included in the delivered product and they are prepared to argue for it whenever it gets looked at in a grooming or forward planning session. The "someone who matters" could be a value manager, product owner, a technical member of the team, a subject matter expert, or any other interested party.

We know that one of the benefits of using an Agile approach is the ability to move items in and out of the backlog easily which is a great capability, enabling us to ensure that the product we build meets the customers' needs effectively through always focusing in the next most important piece of business value.

The normal, and generally correct, approach is for the value manager to work with the team to produce a prioritized backlog with clarity on the high priority items and accepted uncertainty in the items which are further away (see Figure 7).

The stories which come out of the bottom of the grinder are small enough for the team to deliver using their agile development practices (Adolph, 2014), progressively elaborated to a Ready state, able to be built and ideally they should be fully implementable (as per the agreed Definition of Done) in half an iteration or less – the smaller our stories when they are being implemented the better our ability to predict and plan work (Jacobson, 2014).

Figure 7. The shape of a healthy backlog

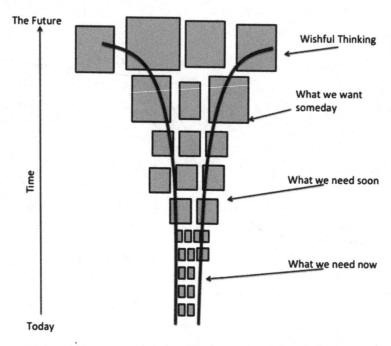

So far we have looked at product ownership in concept, in terms of the roles who contribute and the value-based focus which is needed. Next we explore some of the tools used for product ownership, with a particular focus on the activities undertaken when starting an initiative.

PRODUCT OWNERSHIP IN PRACTICE

One of the most important tasks of the Value Facilitator is to ensure that we build the right product, and this needs clarity of vision regarding the goals and outcomes desired from the initiative, the alignment with organizational strategy and a clear understanding of the value to be delivered (Construx, 2014).

What follows is a discussion of some of the tools which can be used to gain this clarity of vision. The tool is not the goal, but these tools can help in articulating the different aspects which are needed to convey the desired results. Generally these tools will be used in collaborative workshops which the Value Facilitator will facilitate and ensure the results are recorded in an appropriate format (with a bias towards low-tech and ease of access/use).

Value Stream Mapping

Value Stream Mapping (VSM) is a technique to help identify the steps in a process and to focus on solving the right problem. It looks at elements in a process to identify waste – anything that causes delay, requires double handling, results in rework, could result in mistakes being made or in any other way detracts from delivering value to the customer of the process (Ambler, 2014).

VSM uses a fairly extreme definition of the word 'waste' and you might be surprised or shocked to learn how much of your daily work tasks are considered waste when looking at them through a VSM lens. Another way of looking at it is to ask the question 'would the customer for this value stream be happy to pay for the work I'm currently doing?' If you think the answer is yes (i.e. the customer can see how the work being done is valuable to them), then the work is probably a value add to the customer: otherwise, it's waste (see Figure 8).

The whiteboard snapshot of the value stream map shown here is a great example of how simple and quick this process should be.

- Identify extra steps, duplicates, delays or waste.
- Revise the process to achieve the outcome with less delay or dependencies.
- Focus on outcome value not specific artefacts.
- Does this simplify the feature?
- Above all, think lo-tech and quick!

Purpose Alignment Model

This model provides a way to decide what approach to addressing a business need based around the level of importance to the business that the outcomes will have (see Figure 9).

Figure 8. A low-tech value stream map

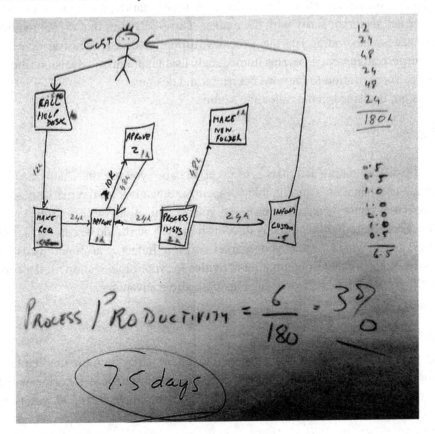

Figure 9. The Purpose alignment model

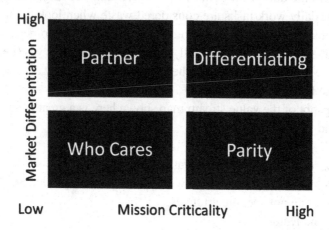

Kent McDonald presents a detailed discussion of when and how to use this model on his website: http://www.beyondrequirements.com/purpose-based-alignment-model/.

What It Is

The Purpose Based Alignment Model, created by Niel Nickolaisen (Pixton et al, 2009), is a method for aligning business decisions and process and feature designs around purpose. The purpose of some decisions and designs is to differentiate the organization in the market; the purpose of most other decisions is to achieve and maintain parity with the market. Those activities that do not require operational excellence either necessitate finding a partner to achieve differentiation or do not deserve much attention.

In practice, purpose alignment generates immediately usable, pragmatic decision filters that you can cascade through the organization to improve decisions and designs.

The quadrants are explained in the following sections.

Differentiating

The purpose of the differentiating activities is to excel. Because you use these activities to gain market share and to create and maintain a sustainable competitive advantage in the marketplace, you want to perform these activities better than anyone else. For your organization, these activities are or should be its claim to fame. These activities link directly to your strategy. You should be careful to not under-invest in these activities, as that would weaken your market position. In fact, you should focus your creativity on these processes. What are the differentiating activities for your organization? It depends. It depends on the specific things you do to create sustainable competitive advantage.

Parity

The purpose of the parity activities is to achieve and maintain parity with the marketplace. Stated differently, your organization does not generate any competitive advantage if it performs these activities better than its competitors. However, because these activities are mission critical, you must ensure that you do not under-invest in or perform these activities poorly. These activities are ideal candidates for simplification and streamlining, because complexity implies that you are likely over-investing. While there might be value in performing the differentiating activities in a unique way, performing the parity activities in a unique way will not generate value and could actually decrease the organization's value if your over-investment in parity processes limits the resources you can apply to differentiating processes.

Partner

Some activities are not mission critical (for your organization) but can nevertheless differentiate the organization in the marketplace. The way to exploit these activities—and generate increased market share—is to find a partner for whom those activities are differentiating and combine efforts to create this differentiation.

Who Cares

Finally, some business activities are neither mission critical nor market differentiating. The goal for these activities is to perform them as little as possible. We refer to these activities as the "who cares" processes. Because these activities are neither market differentiating nor mission critical, you should spend as little time and attention as possible on them. Who really cares?

Expressing Project Scope and Goals

The Focusing Question or Elevator Statement

A one or two sentence statement that conveys the goals and objectives of the project.

The "elevator statement" is something that will enable any team member to explain the purpose of the project in the time it takes to ride between floors in an elevator (imagine you get into the elevator with the CEO of your company and are asked to explain what the project is you are working on before the elevator gets to their floor).

During the workshop this is one of the first things that should be produced, and written up for all to read – it provides focus for the rest of the workshop activities.

One possible template for expressing the vision in a single statement is to use a structure such as the following:

For *(customer),* **who** *(statement of need),* **the** *(product name)* **is a** *(product category)* **that** *(key benefit, compelling reason to buy).* **Unlike** *(primary competitor),* **our product** *(statement of primary differentiation).*

The Vision Box

A Vision Box presents the features and benefits of the project as a box of cereal – the front has a name and branding, along with a list of the key benefits the product will convey to its buyers (the customers who will eventually use the product, be they internal to the organization or real paying customers) (Cockburn, 1999). The back of the box contains operating instructions (high level design decisions) and a list of the key features the product will have.

Building a vision box is a creative activity that helps the team articulate what they are thinking about. It can be useful to break into smaller groups and have the groups each build a vision box that they then "sell" to the remainder of the team. After the separate presentations a shared vision box should be produced that conveys the ideas of the whole team.

Business Benefits Matrix

A simple matrix which articulates the strategic value that the product is intended to provide. The matrix looks like the following table (see Table 1).

The goals of the project are expressed against the strategic drivers, there should only be one primary driver and there might be a number of secondary or tertiary goals. Where there is more than one goal in a column then they need to be ranked to avoid the "everything's critical" conflict.

Preparing this as a group activity helps the team to understand the clear and explicit focus for the project.

Sliders

A tool for showing the priorities for the team across multiple dimensions.

The sliders range from Fully On to Fully Off – if an element is On then it will be the strongest factor that drives the decision making as the project continues. No two sliders can be set at the same level, and the more sliders there are on the "On" side of the grid the higher the risk of catastrophic failure this project accepts. Where there is little leeway in the project sliders then the choice becomes deliver everything or deliver nothing, whereas more leeway allows for partial delivery that contributes to the organizations goals (see Figure 10).

Rob Thomsett describes the Slider tool in his book Radical Project Management.

Table 1.

	Primary	Secondary	Tertiary
Increase Revenue	(25% revenue increase within 12 months of launch)		
Reduce/Avoid Costs			(n/a)
Improve Service		(Increase customer satisfaction rating by 20% based on quarterly satisfaction survey results)	
(Other)			(Reduce staff turnover in call centre because of customer satisfaction)

Figure 10. Thomsett's sliders

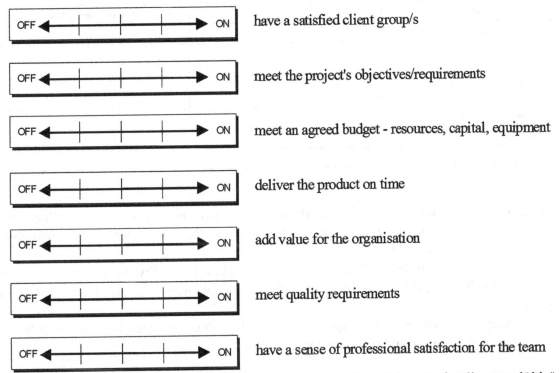

OFF ← ⊢—⊢—⊢ → ON	have a satisfied client group/s
OFF ← ⊢—⊢—⊢ → ON	meet the project's objectives/requirements
OFF ← ⊢—⊢—⊢ → ON	meet an agreed budget - resources, capital, equipment
OFF ← ⊢—⊢—⊢ → ON	deliver the product on time
OFF ← ⊢—⊢—⊢ → ON	add value for the organisation
OFF ← ⊢—⊢—⊢ → ON	meet quality requirements
OFF ← ⊢—⊢—⊢ → ON	have a sense of professional satisfaction for the team

Off - Success Factor is not relevant. It is measured however. On - Success Factor is relevant. Degree of relevance is indicated by position of "slider".

Scope Matrix

The "in/out list" is a simple tool that conveys clearly what will be done as part of this project, what will not be done and where there is uncertainty about deliverables (see table 2).

Where a topic is "in" the project team is responsible for delivery of this component.

Where something is explicitly out of scope the team will not spend any time or effort on this component. If an "out" topic is something that the broader program of work is dependent on then it is important that the responsibility for undertaking this work is clearly defined, the project stream and person taking responsibility for ensuring this is delivered.

Where there is uncertainty about a topic being in scope or not then it goes into the "Undecided" area. The team will not work on his piece and the product owner or project manager needs to investigate further to identify if the piece of work is in or out of scope.

This tool is also explained in Radical Project Management, by Rob Thomsett (Thomsett, 2001).

Cost/Benefit Matrix

This should convey the level of uncertainty surrounding the estimates of both cost and benefit the organization will get from the project. Early in the project the costs will have a large Cone of Uncertainty and as the project progresses this will get narrower and narrower. It is likely that the benefits also have

Table 2. Scope in/out/undecided matrix

Topic	In	Out (Responsibility)
(Taking service calls)	X	
(Assigning service calls to support technicians)	X	
(New product promotions via service centre)	X	
(Debtor follow-up via service desk)		X
Undecided		
(Web-based self service capability)		

a wide range of uncertainty. Uncertainty in both costs and benefits is not necessarily a problem on a project provided the range is correct. Both costs and benefits should be shown at three levels – optimistic, likely and pessimistic. For example see table 3.

This project should be considered high risk, as there is a distinct possibility that the organization will lose money on it. There might be other drivers which warrant the investment and the reward profile if things go well is significant.

Undertaking cost/benefit analysis on a project is primarily a management level responsibility, but the financial goals and drivers should be shared with the team.

Articulate the Vision

These tools can help teams gain a clear understanding of the goals and objectives that have driven the selection of this project to be worked on. Together they form a Project Charter or Vision Document which distils the why and what if the initiative being undertaken.

Preparing the product vision is a very important starting point for the project. This provides the focus for the work the team will undertake as the project continues. The wallware[1] artefacts produced during the workshop(s) should form part of the team environment so anyone working on the project can see at a glance the project drivers and goals. It may also be valuable to produce a formal document that summarizes the product vision. Remember that the value lies only partly in the document but in the shared understanding that the team has achieved in producing the vision.

Table 3. Cost/benefit matrix

		Minimum Benefit	Likely Benefit	Maximum Benefit
		$1M	**$5M**	**$12M**
Maximum Cost	**$2M**	-$1M	$3m	$10M
Likely Cost	**$1.5M**	-$0.5M	$3.5M	$10.5M
Minimum Cost	**$1M**	$0	$4M	$11M

The figure in each cell is the net of benefit minus the cost.

Having a clear statement of why and what we are aiming to build clearly visible and articulated in terms such as this give the team clarity on what and why they are working on, and provides a measuring rod for decisions later in the initiative – every activity can be measured against the goals and objectives and the optimum approach taken to maximize the value delivered.

If the team who will work on the product are distributed they should be brought together for the production of the product vision – this will help to create a "one team" culture and help with the ongoing communication when they are dispersed.

Team members who join after the vision has been created need to be walked through the project charter by someone who was present at the workshop(s) to help them understand the drivers behind the work being undertaken.

If during the execution of the initiative the environment changes and the vision is no longer achievable or the organization goals/drivers change such that the initiative no longer delivers on them then the initiative should be stopped and reassessed. Changes in the product vision are often evidence of massive change in the organization ecosystem.

Kano Analysis

The Kano model offers some insight into the product attributes which are perceived to be important to customers. The purpose of the tool is to support product specification and discussion through better development of team understanding (see Figure 11). Kano's model focuses on differentiating product features, as opposed to focusing initially on customer needs.

Figure 11. The Kano Model

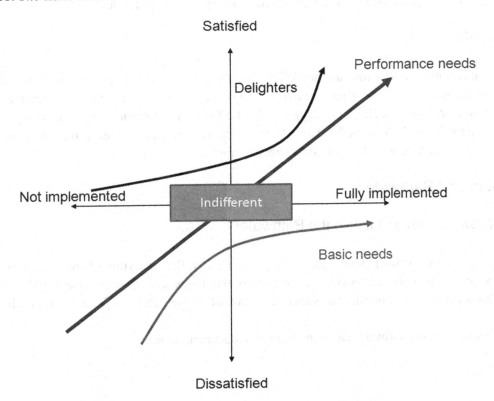

According to the Kano Model (Cockburn, 1999), a product or service can have three types of attribute (or property):

- **Basic Needs:** Which customers expect to be present in a product.
- **Performance Attributes:** Which are not absolutely necessary, but which are known about and increase the customer's enjoyment of the product. Higher performance in these aspects tends to result in higher satisfaction, low performance can be a cause of dissatisfaction
- **Delighters:** Which customers don't even know they want, but are delighted when they find them.

Basic Needs affect customers' satisfaction with the product or service by their absence: If they're not present, customers are dissatisfied. And even if they're present, if no other attributes are present, customers aren't particularly happy (you can see this as the bottom curve on the graph above).

To use Kano Model Analysis, follow these steps:

- Brainstorm all of the possible features and attributes of your product or service, and everything you can do to please your customers.
- Classify these as "Basic", "Performance", "Delighters" and "Not Relevant".
- Make sure your product or service has all appropriate Basic Attributes. If necessary, cut out Performance Attributes so that you can get these – you're going nowhere fast if these aren't present.
- Where possible, cut out attributes that are "Not Relevant".
- Look at the Delighters, and think how you can build some of these into your product or service. Again if necessary, cut some Performance Attributes, so that you can "afford" your Delighters.
- Select appropriate Performance Attributes so that you can deliver a product or service at a price the customer is prepared to pay, while still maintaining a good profit margin.

Other Tools

There are many other tools which are needed in the ongoing activities of progressively refining and elaborating the product backlog. These are beyond the scope of this chapter but include techniques such as Agile Modelling, Agile UX, Story Mapping, INVEST criteria, Behavior Driven Development and Specification by Example, to name but a few. The reader is encouraged to examine these techniques and explore how they may be useful in your own specific context.

Of Babies and Bathwater

Don't Throw the Baby Out with the Bathwater

Another misconception that plagues agile projects is the idea that everything is new – we no longer use the analysis techniques and tools that have been used in the past because in some way they are "not agile". This is often a result of misunderstanding the second Value statement from the Agile Manifesto:

- We value working software over comprehensive documentation.

The language of the Manifesto was very carefully crafted, and the word in the middle of that phrase is "over" – not "instead of"!

We can and should still make use of those tools which will add clarity and value to uncovering the real business needs without adding waste to the process. Not everything old is bad. Some of the tools mentioned above are indeed new, but most are derived from ideas which have been around for many years.

CONCLUSION

This chapter has examined the role of the Product Owner and shown that while Product Ownership is a crucial and critical aspect of product delivery, the "single wringable neck" individual product owner who has all the skill and knowledge needed to make all the important decisions about priority and business value is not attainable except in a very small subset of project types.

The majority of projects undertaken today are complicated or complex, falling into areas where innovation is needed, where the problem and the solution are both uncertain and in which a single individual cannot know everything, nor should they be expected to.

Product Ownership truly is a team sport – it requires a multi-skilled group who collaborate and work together to identify what constitutes value in each aspect of the initiative, and who then constantly refine and adapt the product backlog based on the emergent learning and discovery that happens as work continues. This Value Team are collaboratively responsible for getting the product backlog items to a Ready state, following which the Delivery Team gets them to Done. The Value Team and Delivery Team are a tightly collaborative group working together closely with shared focus on maximising the value delivered to our organisation and delight to our customers. There is no "one-size-fits-all" approach, each initiative has a different context in which it is being undertaken, the business drivers, customer needs, local environment and team makeup are unique and need a unique approach to the delivery process.

Selecting the right initiative to fund, bringing the right people together, identifying and refining the product backlog require skills that draw on techniques which have been around for a long time in the creative industries, and also demand some new ways of thinking. Knowing when to stop is one of the hardest and most important aspects of truly maximising value delivery.

REFERENCES

Adolph, S. (2014). *Agile BA in Practice: Using Cadence to Leave Things to the Last Responsible Moment*. Retrieved from http://www.developmentknowledge.com/index.php/blog/141-agile-ba-in-practice-using-cadence-to-leave-things-to-the-last-responsible-moment

Ambler, S. (2014). *Generalizing Specialists: Improving Your IT Career Skills*. Academic Press.

Andrea, J. (2005). If the Shoe Doesn't Fit – Agile Requirements for Stepsister Projects. Better Software Magazine. *Molecular Pharmacology*. doi:10.1124/mol.105.020230

Cockburn, A. (1999). A Methodology per project. Academic Press.

Construx. (2014). *The Cone of Uncertainty*. Retrieved from http://www.construx.com/Thought_Leadership/Books/The_Cone_of_Uncertainty/

Currim, I. S., Mintz, O., & Siddarth, S. (2015). Information Accessed or Information Available? The Impact on Consumer Preferences Inferred at a Durable Product E-commerce Website. *Journal of Interactive Marketing*, *29*, 11–25. doi:10.1016/j.intmar.2014.09.003

Dillon, R. (2015). *Ready*. Singapore: Springer Singapore.

Hastie, S. (2014). *Knowing When to Stop – trim that tail ruthlessly*. Academic Press.

Jacobson, M. S. (2014). Scrum Master Allocation: The Case for a Dedicated Scrum Master. Academic Press.

Kruchten, P. (2011). The Frog and the Octopus – A Conceptual Model of Software Development. Academic Press.

Pixton, P., Nickolaisen, N., Little, T., & McDonald, K. (2009). *Stand Back and Deliver, Accelerating Business Agility*. Boston: Addison-Wesley.

Programming, E. (2014). *Extreme Programming: A Gentle Introduction*. Retrieved from http://www.extremeprogramming.org

Schwaber, K., & Sutherland, J. (2013). The Scrum Guide. Academic Press.

Software Education. (2014). *Agile Product Ownership course*. Wellington, New Zealand: Author.

Thomsett, R. (2001). *Radical Project Management*. Upper Saddle River, NJ: Prentice Hall.

KEY TERMS AND DEFINITIONS

Agile Software Development: Agile software development is a group of software development methods in which requirements and solutions evolve through collaboration between self-organizing, cross-functional teams. It promotes adaptive planning, evolutionary development, early delivery, continuous improvement, and encourages rapid and flexible response to change.

Product Owner: In Scrum, the product owner is typically a project's key stakeholder. Part of the product owner responsibilities is to have a vision of what he or she wishes to build, and convey that vision to the scrum team.

Software Component: A software unit of functionality that manages a single abstraction.

User Stories: User stories are part of an agile approach that helps shift the focus from writing about requirements to talking about them. All agile user stories include a written sentence or two and, more importantly, a series of conversations about the desired functionality.

User-Centered Design (UCD): User-centered design is a process (not restricted to interfaces or technologies) in which the needs, wants, and limitations of end users of a product, service or process are given extensive attention at each stage of the design process. User-centered design can be characterized as a multi-stage problem solving process that not only requires designers to analyse and foresee how users are likely to use a product, but also to test the validity of their assumptions with regard to user behaviour in real world tests with actual users. Such testing is necessary as it is often very difficult for the designers of a product to understand intuitively what a first-time user of their design experiences, and what each user's learning curve may look like.

Waterfall Model: A sequential design, used in software development processes, in which progress is seen as flowing steadily downwards (like a waterfall) through the phases of Conception, Initiation, Analysis, Design, Construction, Testing, Deployment and Maintenance.

ENDNOTE

[1]   Wallware refers to flipcharts, graphs, story cards and other artifacts that are prominently displayed in and around the team space, they provide a visual record of the project, serving as reminders of key decisions and visible to anyone who has an interest in the project. Other commonly used terms are Information Radiators and Big Visible Charts.

Chapter 2
Agile Coaches and Champions:
Two Hidden Facilitators of Agile Transition

Taghi Javdani Gandomani
Islamic Azad University – Boroujen, Iran

Mina Ziaei Nafchi
Islamic Azad University – Boroujen, Iran

ABSTRACT

Prevalence of Agile methods in software companies is increasing dramatically. Software companies and teams need to employ these methods to overcome the inherent challenges of traditional methods in software development. However, transitioning to Agile approach is a topic of debate. This is mainly because software companies are facing with many challenges, obstacles, and hindrances when leaving traditional methods and moving to Agile methods, as shown in previous research studies. Conducting a large-scale research study showed that Agile transformation need to be supported by several facilitators and identified its most important facilitators. The main aim of this chapter is to present two hidden facilitators of Agile transition, Agile coaches and Agile champions, which rarely have been taken into consideration. Both of these facilitators directly impress the people involved in the transition. People-intensive nature of Agile methods and critical role of the people in the transition process reflect the importance of these facilitators when a software company doing its transition.

INTRODUCTION

Agile software development as a reaction to disciplined software development, known as traditional software development, has been introduced to software industry by creating Agile manifesto (Beck, Cockburn, Jeffries, & Highsmith, 2001). Agile methods in software development have focused on different values compared to the traditional methods, including early and frequent releases, light-weight documentation, higher quality, customer satisfaction, embracing changes in user requirement, low ceremonies and so forth (Cohen, Lindvall, & Costa, 2004).

Unlike traditional methods, Agile methods mainly focus on people and human interactions. People-centric nature of these methods has led to some difficulties when software companies are changing their

DOI: 10.4018/978-1-4666-9858-1.ch002

development style from traditional to Agile (Gandomani, Zulzalil, Ghani, Sultan, & Nafchi, 2013). Agile transition requires involvement and collaboration of all of the software practitioners such as developers, business experts, project and department managers, senior managers, customers, etc.

Various problems and challenges are faced by software companies during their Agile transition (Gandomani, Zulzalil, Ghani, Sultan, & Nafchi, 2013; Nerur, Mahapatra, & Mangalaraj, 2005). Most of the problems and challenges have roots in the people's behaviours and mindsets as well as their roles in development process. Most often people prefer to do their roles as they are trained previously and adopted for a long time. So, most often resistance to change is a common challenge, as reported by many scholars. Clearly, changing traditional mindset of such people is not easy and needs enough time and effort (Cockburn & Highsmith, 2001; Conboy, Coyle, Wang, & Pikkarainen, 2011). Providing appropriate facilitators and supporters would help software companies and development teams to adapt to their new roles and responsibilities (Gandomani, Zulzalil, Abd Ghani, Sultan, & Sharif, 2014).

The previous studies identified several facilitators, enablers, and success factors to support Agile transition (Bayona, Calvo-Manzano, & San Feliu, 2012; Misra, Kumar, & Kumar, 2009; Pikkarainen, Salo, Kuusela, & Abrahamsson, 2012; Vijayasarathy & Turk, 2012). However, most the identified facilitators are straightforward and it seems that there are more serious facilitators which are not clearly identified yet. This chapter presents a small part of large-scale empirical study on Agile transformation. This research studied the whole process of Agile transformation and tried to explore its various aspects and dimensions and showed that although several supporters and change facilitators can be taken into consideration, Agile coaches and Agile champions as two hidden facilitators play a critical role in pushing the transition process forward. These facilitators directly impress the people involved the transformation and can highly support them when facing a challenge during the change process. This chapter solely describes the role of aforementioned facilitators in Agile transition and identify responsibilities of these roles in real environments.

Adopted research methodology advised the researcher against conducting an up-front major literature review (B. Glaser, 1992). This mainly helps to reduce the researchers' biases in data collection and analysis. However, tying the results with literature review reflects the importance of the findings and brings more benefits for readers. To adhere to the applied research methodology, this chapter presents the literature after presenting the research results by providing a discussion on them.

AGILE TRANSITION CHALLENGES

Agile transition process is considered as an organizational mutation in which all aspects of the organization will be affected. Changing the software development style as expected by Agile approach, is a socio-technical change (Conboy et al., 2011). This fact makes the transition more difficult than expected. Software companies need to be aware of the transition challenges and provide appropriate strategies to cope with the challenges and barriers.

The main problems and challenges are related to the people involved in the transition. After several years using traditional methods, software practitioners are accustomed to disciplined methods and their processes. All the involved people really adapted to their roles and activities. Hence, they may resist against Agile transition. For instance, Agile methods emphasize on self-organizing teams and shared-decision making, but 'command and control' approach has been used widely as management style in traditional methods. In this case, managers (such as senior managers and project manager) prefer to decide singly and at the same time, team members are not enough confident to collaborate in decision making (Moe, Aurum, & Dybå, 2012). Such problems act as vital barriers of the transition. It seems that while software practitioners are motivating to employ Agile methods, they prefer to retain their previous roles, responsibilities, and behaviours.

People and organizational culture are other problems in the transition process. People culture affects the transition and makes it more difficult than expected. Also, strict organizational processes are inconsistent with Agile approach that gives the people enough authority in performing their jobs (Iivari & Iivari, 2011).

Technical problems are other transition challenges. However, they are not as critical as the others (Gandomani, Zulzalil, Ghani, Sultan, & Nafchi, 2013). Finally, customers in several case studies have been reported as the transition challenges (R. Hoda, Noble, & Marshall, 2011b; Angela Martin, Robert Biddle, & James Noble, 2009). Customer involvement is one of the underpinnings of Agile software development. Customer collaboration and participation are highly required by many Agile practices. For instance, Scrum and XP have several roles in which customers play a great role. Therefore, lack of customer collaboration is a serious risk for successful Agile transition and adoption (Misra et al., 2009; Tsirakidis, Köbler, & Krcmar, 2009).

Agile and disciplined methods are different in nature, so, those who have experience in disciplined methods, normally could not adapt themselves easily with Agile processes and practices. There are various human aspects to be considered in Agile transformation (Gandomani, Zulzalil, Abdul Ghani, Sultan, & Sharif, 2014). This fact makes the transition a multi-dimensional and complicated process which needs to be supported by appropriate and in-time facilitators.

To sum up, Agile transition is subject to the various problems and barriers, and software companies and teams strongly need to provide effective facilitators to deal with the possible challenges.

RESEARCH METHODOLOGY

Grounded Theory (GT) was employed to conduct a large-scale research study to explore various aspects of Agile transition process. GT proposes a systematic process to help the researchers to discover a grounded theory (the outcome of GT) using substantive data (B. Glaser, 2005). GT is a suitable research methodology to study people behaviours and human-related issues (B. Glaser, 1992). Hence, application of GT in a people-centric process like Agile transition process assists GT researchers to achieve valuable results. Furthermore, employing GT while there is no up-front hypothesis is really helpful (B. Glaser, 1992). In this study, there was no preconceived problem or hypothesis too. Therefore, GT was a good choice for the researchers. Moreover, conducting several high quality research studies in context of Agile software development using GT, motivated the researchers to choose GT for this study (Adolph, Hall, & Kruchten, 2011; Coleman & O'Connor, 2007; Dorairaj, Noble, & Malik, 2012; R. Hoda, Noble, & Marshall, 2011a; A. Martin, R. Biddle, & J. Noble, 2009; Treccani & De Souza, 2011). The previous GT studies in context of Agile software development have led to valuable results. The authors have explained how well GT can assist researchers to study the context of Agile software development (Gandomani, Zulzalil, Ghani, Sultan, & Sharif, 2013).

Data Collection

This study was started with data collection as recommended by GT instructions (B. Glaser & Strauss, 1967). The recruitment process was started by publishing several online invitations in Agile professional on-line communities over the internet. Those Agile experts who had experience in at least one Agile transition process were eligible to attend the study. Forty nine (49) Agile practitioners from different companies in 13 countries voluntarily participated in this study. The participants had various roles in their companies. About half of them, however, were Agile coaches and mentors who helped many companies to do their Agile transition. Also, most of the participants were from US and Europe and a few from Asia and Australia. Agile transition was an ongoing project in about half of them and it was a good opportunity for the researchers to collect fresh data. In this study, we addressed the participants by their number and role, if necessary.

Several interviews have been conducted using semi-structured and open-ended questions. Since most of the participants were out of the country, online media were used to conduct the interviews. The initial questions were about the participants' backgrounds and general concepts of Agile transition. The next questions were about the challenges they faced with during the transition, their suggested solutions and strategies, steps of the transition, etc. Following GT guidelines, all the questions covered only general concepts and issues, and data collection was continued up to reaching data saturation which means no new concepts appear in the interviews (B. Glaser, 1992).

Due to space limitation, list of the participants has not been provided.

GT PROCEDURE

Typically, GT starts with data collection and ends with theory building (B. Glaser, 1998). Figure 1 shows GT steps and artefacts. Once some data were collected, data analysis or data coding was started. The transcribed data were reviewed line by line and key points were extracted. Once a key point was extracted, a code, called open code was assigned to it. Then, immediately, the new code was compared to existing open codes in the same and previous transcribed. This process is known as constant comparison technique. Then, employing constant comparison method on all open codes led to emergence of concepts, a higher level abstraction in the coded data. Again, constant comparison method was run on the emerged concepts and led to emergence of categories. Finally, theoretical coding was employed to develop a grounded theory. In this study, Glaser's Process coding family was used to describe the process of Agile transition and adoption.

The emergent theory reflects the main concerns of the Agile practitioners in real environment when moving to Agile software development. Such a theory is grounded in data which has been collected directly from the real environments. Data analysis discovered all aspects of Agile transition including its challenges, its facilitators, its prerequisites and so on.

Obviously, presenting all findings of such a large-scale study needs enough time and space. Indeed, the researchers need to report the emerging concepts, categories, grounded theory or some parts of it. This chapter solely presents two emergent concepts regarding to Agile transition facilitators. Furthermore, since commonly, GT papers often include quotes from interviews to highlight certain points; this chapter does provide a few verbatim quotes, primarily to support the findings of the study (see figure 1).

Figure 1. GT steps and its artefacts

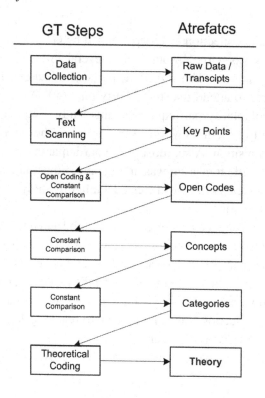

AGILE COACH AS A TRANSITION FACILITATOR

Agile coaches play a significant role in Agile transition process. The participants explained the role of Agile coaches as transition facilitators.

Our coach helped us to overcome lots of challenges during the transformation. Even now, after 6 months, I really believed that he should be with our team for the rest of our project [transformation]... (P25, Agile Developer)

After 10 months dealing with lots of challenges, an experienced Agile coach was added to our team. After that our progress increased significantly. He was a great Agile expert. ... Then, we adapted several Agile practices in a short while. (P29, Project Manager)

The role of an Agile coach is highlighted in various points as follows.

1. **Preparation Phase:** Preparation phase is the initial step of the transition, when the company is providing the transition prerequisites and gets ready to start the transition.

I've run Agile transformations for a number of companies since then [first transformation]. I would say that companies that are willing to embrace change and who have undergone good training and coaching to understand the true impact of Agile, are best prepared for transformation (P6, Agile Consultant)

In this phase, Agile coach can help managers in the following items:

- Guiding the managers in defining the transition goals and success criteria.
- Guiding the managers in defining business goals.
- Guiding the managers in training needs analysis.
- Teaching Agile principles and expected values.
- Conducting a pre-start up assessment to check whether company is ready for the change or not.
- Motivating customers to involve and collaborate in the transition process.
- Preparing an action plan or framework for Agile transition.
- Identifying the potential risks of pilot project and raising them before starting the transition.
- Collaboration with HR department to select the most qualified team members for the initial adoption.
- Help in preparing a transition plan, from preparation phase to fully adoption.

Based on the above items, it seems that Agile coach should be hired before starting the transition to manage or handle the preparation phase.

2. **Adaptation Phase:** While development team members, managers, and customers are adapting to their new roles and Agile practices, having enough access to an Agile coach is very helpful. The participants stressed on having an on-site full-time coach during the transition. Since most of the challenges stem from adapting people to new roles, such a supportive coach, can help them to change themselves with less effort and time.

[I] strongly advise you to hire a full-time coach. We were faced with many problems and no one was available to help us. Hiring a full time coach could help us, one who was able to feel our situation, look ahead, and help us. An experienced coach or trainer should be involved in transition process. (P7, Agile Developer)

Also, in this stage, an Agile coach can help the team members to be familiar with the Agile practices, in a practical manner.

An Agile coach must make sure that Agile transformation is on track. To do this, he/she can make sure that team members are following the desired Agile practices. He/she also should consider the ground conditions and make the winning strategy.

An Agile coach needs to answer the questions related to Agile approach, methods, or practices during the transition. This is also another reason why a coach is better to be on the ground to answer the raised questions quickly.

Beside the above roles, Agile coach need to have a plan for gradual adaptation. In this case, the transformation will be easier and more effective. Encouraging people to the changes, especially when facing problems, is also another duty of the Agile coach that facilitates the transition.

An expert coach provides lots of valuable service during your project [transformation]. He may help with long-term strategy across the entire organization before the pilot project. Then, he can help periodically check up on teams, help them stay on track with Agile techniques, and fine-tune behaviour as needed... (P39, Agile coach)

3. **Adjustment:** During the transition or even after adoption, an adjustment phase or step can be defined, if necessary. In this step, Agile coach can suggest some adjustment activities in order to better adaptation to the Agile practices. Sometimes, the adjustment is necessary to cope with the company's limitations or weaknesses. Handling the required adjustments is one of the Agile coach's responsibilities.

An experienced Agile coach is able to provide objective guidance, the real thing that companies need during the transformation, without political or personal considerations. (P43, Agile Coach)

Sometime fully adoption is not possible. In this case, software companies need to do some development tasks or activities in non-Agile ways. Although in such cases most often some parts of companies remain non-Agile, but they can do some modifications in Agile practices in order to employ them based on their limitations.

Beside the above roles and responsibilities, this study also discovered that an Agile coaches need to have some specific characteristics. Because of the critical role of an Agile coach, he/she needs to be patient when doing his job. Most often, an Agile coach needs to deal with many people with different culture, background, and mindset. Therefore, having such characteristic help him/her to effectively interact with the transition participants.

In many organizations, sometimes coaches are also responsible for training; in this case, they should be patient and feel people's problems. (P8, Project Manager)

AGILE CHAMPION AS A TRANSITION FACILITATOR

Agile champion was addressed as another facilitator that directly impresses the people involved in Agile transition. A champion in Agile transformation was referred to as a person who can adjust Agile practices to suit environment and also support other members in the change process.

The participants claimed that existence of champions in Agile teams can facilitate transformation and motivate the others to follow required changes as defined in the transition framework or plan.

In transition process, champions play a critical role. I totally agree with the idea that having at least to champions on the teams during Agile transformation gets people to herald its adoption. In my opinion, changes with more champions come to fruition easier. I believe that any successful Agile transformation has a champion, even he would not be known with that name. (P23, Agile Coach)

The participants declared that most often Agile champions are those with the most enthusiasm, while rest of team member are almost indifferent to Agile. Agile champion was referred to as 'Agile hero' too, who is exemplar for the other members. Such an expert can motivate others to go forward when they are exhausted or disappointed.

Companies should hire an expert; they should have their own champion. Champions can reduce side effects of change, lead and inspire the change and lead people to next level. (P16, Project Manager)

Agile champions can drive the internal changes, and expand or even break the borders that Agile practices face in their environment. The changes with more Agile champions come to fruition easier.

They [Agile champions] also try to find the better ways of working with the others around them. They really help organizations in transformation process. (P6, Agile Consultant)

Some of the participant addressed "dark champions" as those who "fight for status quo". They believed that Agile coach should focus on dark champions more than indifferent members. They argued that most of the barriers and obstacles stem from "dark champions". They continued that if the transition fails or faces with critical problems in initial stages, "dark champions" impress the indifferent members.

Agile champions are a member of an Agile team (pilot team), so, they are completely close to other members and feel the real challenges the pilot team is facing. Therefore, Agile champions are direct contributors to success to the success of pilot teams.

Some of the participants stated that Agile champions can overcome the "it won't work here" symptom. As they expressed, Agile champions strongly can facilitate achieving initial successes and encouraging indifferent and opponent members.

Furthermore, Champions can reduce side effects of changes, lead and inspire the change and lead people to next levels. This is also very critical, especially to help other people in new technical tasks.

As participant expressed, an Agile champion can be a developer, project manager, Scrum master, etc. and it does not matter what is the technical role of an Agile champion.

DISCUSSION

After presenting the findings of the GT, reviewing the literature is helpful to strengthen the position of the research results.

Coaching in Agile methods is slightly different from coaching in traditional methods. Good coaching can bring leadership concept to Agile methods (Augustine, 2005). Augustine (Augustine, 2005) explained that such coaching is meant to demonstrate "light touch" leadership. Ganesh and Thangasamy (Ganesh & Thangasamy, 2012) described personal characteristics of an Agile coach by explaining importance role of Agile coaches and their effects on the transition.

Beck and Andres (Beck & Andres, 2004) suggested to hire experienced Scrum masters and Agile coaches to help team members for adapting to Scrum practices, especially those which have focused on individuals and interactions.

Poppendieck (Anderson et al., 2003) in a panel emphasized on the role of Agile leaders and coaches in Agile migration and expressed that for helping people in the transition, Agile coaches and leaders are required while managers are optional. Hoda (Rashina Hoda, 2011) described the role of Agile coach and mentor and focused on the role of coach on self-organizing team as one of the important Agile concepts. On the other hand, there are some reports on lack of effective and good coaching and its effects on Agile transformation (Hajjdiab & Taleb, 2011; Srinivasan & Lundqvist, 2010; Sureshchandra & Shrinivasavadhani, 2008).

The authors also in (Gandomani, Zulzalil, Abd Ghani, et al., 2014; Gandomani, Zulzalil, Ghani, Sultan, & Parizi, 2015) explained facilitators of Agile transition and explained how well a good coaching and mentoring service can help Agile teams and organization to cope with problems during Agile transition. Role of the Agile coach in training also has been emphasized.

Some roles in Agile teams may impress other members significantly during the transition. Agile champions are those who play a hidden role to facilitate the changes and persuade others to change themselves. Hoda et al. (R. Hoda, Noble, & Marshall, 2010) explained the role of champions in self-organizing teams. They stressed on the role of champions in understanding business drivers and also their effects on other members. They also showed that champions are necessary for securing senior management support, propagating more teams, convincing top management, and establishing pilot team. However, they believed that sometime Agile coach or a developer play the role of champion.

Senapathi and Srinivasan (Senapathi & Srinivasan, 2012) discovered that champions and senior managers are the roles that have significant influence on usage and adoption of Agile practices. Earlier, Kum and Law (Kum & Law, 2006) discovered that Agile champion (a member or a team), is one of the success factors in Test Driven Development methodology. Also, the findings of the current study discovered that Agile champions make Agile transition easier and help other team members to adapt their new roles. Yet, it seems that it can be studied further.

Literature review supported the important role of the Agile coaches and Agile champions in facilitating of the transition. Both of the roles encourage the persons involved to adapt their activities to what Agile expects. Furthermore, this study showed the responsibilities of Agile coach and champion during Agile transformation.

This study has some implications and recommendations for theory and practice. The main implication of this study for theory is related to human-centric nature of Agile approach. While Agile manifesto simply explains Agile values, Agile adoption is not a straightforward and smooth process. This is mainly because successful Agile transition requires changing in people's mindset. Accordingly, the change is not easy and needs considerable supports. For this purpose, considering some roles to direct and encourage pilot teams is extremely helpful. Agile coaches and champions are those who directly and indirectly impress other members during Agile transition and adoption.

The first recommendation for practice is that software company have to hire Agile coach(es) and Agile champion(s) before starting their transition. Managers should empower Agile coaches and Agile champions to really do their jobs as expected. Agile coaches can help company from preparation phase, when company is preparing to change its development process. Software companies need to consider Agile coach's viewpoints in many stages of Agile transition such as hiring competent members, team set up, preparing an action plan, creating progress criteria, defining business goals, etc.

Also, this study recommends hiring a full-time on-site coach rather than an external coach. Since pilot teams most often are faced by various challenges, a full-time coach can help them in the right time. Such a coach can train team members can train team members and help them in case of problems.

Furthermore, hiring some Agile experts as Agile champions in various roles will facilitate the transition. Especially in software companies with many years' experience in disciplined methods, Agile champions can strongly facilitate the change process. They can overcome the resistance against change and negative perceptions about Agile approach and its usefulness.

Moreover, Agile champions can facilitate some successes in early stages of the transition. Reaching early success in Agile transformation process is a success key for fully adoption. Early successes can encourage indifferent team members or even Agile opponents to effectively collaborate with other members and follow the change process by following the Agile processes.

While there are many potential challenges and problems during Agile transformation, hiring competent Agile coaches and champions can reduce the challenges and increase the chance of success.

CONCLUSION

This chapter explained two critical roles in Agile transition process. Agile coaches and Agile champions are the transition facilitators which directly impress the people involved the change process. Agile coaches have a distinguished role in the transition in many stages. They can facilitate providing the prerequisites of the transition. Also, they can be helpful in direct coaching the people who involved in the transition by teaching them what they need to be familiar with their new roles and responsibilities. Also, they can facilitate the adaptation by proposing the required adjustments. Totally, they can help all the practitioners to overcome their problems during the transition process and facilitate the change process.

Agile champions like Agile coaches can significantly facilitate the transition. They can adjust Agile practices to suit environment. Also, they act as exemplar for other members, encourage them to accept their new roles, and adapt to Agile activities in a practical manner.

REFERENCES

Adolph, S., Hall, W., & Kruchten, P. (2011). Using grounded theory to study the experience of software development. *Empirical Software Engineering, 16*(4), 487–513. doi:10.1007/s10664-010-9152-6

Anderson, L., Alleman, G. B., Beck, K., Blotner, J., Cunningham, W., Poppendieck, M., & Wirfs-Brock, R. (2003). *Agile management - an oxymoron?: who needs managers anyway?* Paper presented at the Companion of the 18th annual ACM SIGPLAN conference on Object-oriented programming, systems, languages, and applications, Anaheim, CA. doi:10.1145/949344.949410

Augustine, S. (2005). Managing agile projects. Prentice Hall.

Bayona, S., Calvo-Manzano, J. A., & San Feliu, T. (2012). Critical success factors in software process improvement: A systematic review. In A. Mas, A. Mesquida, T. Rout, R. V. O'Connor, & A. Dorling (Eds.), *Vol. SPICE 2012, CCIS 290* (pp. 1–12). Palma. doi:10.1007/978-3-642-30439-2_1

Beck, K., & Andres, C. (2004). *Extreme Programming Explained: Embrace Change* (2nd ed.). Boston, MA: Addison-Wesley Professional.

Beck, K., Cockburn, A., Jeffries, R., & Highsmith, J. (2001). *Agile manifesto*. Retrieved May 2014, from http://www.agilemanifesto.org

Cockburn, A., & Highsmith, J. (2001). Agile software development: The people factor. *Computer, 34*(11), 131–133. doi:10.1109/2.963450

Cohen, D., Lindvall, M., & Costa, P. (2004). An introduction to Agile methods. *Advances in Computers, 62*, 1-66. doi: 10.1016/S0065-2458(03)62001-2

Coleman, G., & O'Connor, R. (2007). Using grounded theory to understand software process improvement: A study of Irish software product companies. *Information and Software Technology, 49*(6), 654–667. doi:10.1016/j.infsof.2007.02.011

Conboy, K., Coyle, S., Wang, X., & Pikkarainen, M. (2011). People over process: Key challenges in agile development. *IEEE Software, 28*(4), 48–57. doi:10.1109/MS.2010.132

Dorairaj, S., Noble, J., & Malik, P. (2012, May 14-15). *Understanding lack of trust in distributed agile teams: A grounded theory study*. Paper presented at the 16th International Conference on Evaluation and Assessment in Software Engineering, EASE 2012, Ciudad Real, Spain. doi:10.1049/ic.2012.0011

Gandomani, T. J., Zulzalil, H., Ghani, A. A. A., Sultan, A. B. M., & Sharif, K. Y. (2013). How Grounded Theory can facilitate research studies in context of Agile software development. *Science International-Lahore, 25*(4), 1131–1136.

Gandomani, T. J., Zulzalil, H., Abdul Ghani, A. A., Sultan, A. B. M., & Sharif, K. Y. (2014). How human aspects impress Agile software development transition and adoption. *International Journal of Software Engineering and its Applications, 8*(1), 129-148. doi: 10.14257/ijseia.2014.8.1.12

Gandomani, T. J., Zulzalil, H., & Ghani, A. (2013). Obstacles to moving to agile software development; at a glance. *Journal of Computer Science, 9*(5), 620–625. doi:10.3844/jcssp.2013.620.625

Gandomani, T. J., Zulzalil, H., & Ghani, Abdul, A. A., Sultan, A. B. M., & Sharif, K. Y. (2014). Exploring Facilitators of Transition and Adoption to Agile Methods: A Grounded Theory Study. *Journal of Software, 7*(9), 1666–1678. doi:10.4304/jsw.9.7.1666-1678

Gandomani, T. J., Zulzalil, H., Ghani, A. A. A., & Sultan, A. B. M., & Parizi, R. M. (2015). The impact of inadequate and dysfunctional training on Agile transformation process: A Grounded Theory study. *Information and Software Technology, 57*, 295–309. doi:10.1016/j.infsof.2014.05.011

Ganesh, N., & Thangasamy, S. (2012). Lessons learned in transforming from traditional to agile development. *Journal of Computer Science, 8*(3), 389–392. doi:10.3844/jcssp.2012.389.392

Glaser, B. (1992). *Basics of Grounded Theory Analysis: Emergence Vs. Forcing*. Mill Valley, CA: Sociology Press.

Glaser, B. (1998). *Doing Grounded Theory: Issues and Discussions*. Mill Valley, CA: Sociology Press.

Glaser, B., & Strauss, A. (1967). *The Discovery of Grounded Theory: Strategies for Qualitative Research*. Chicago: Aldine Transaction.

Glaser, B. G. (2005). *The Grounded Theory Perspective III: Theoretical Coding*. Mill Valley, CA: Sociology Press.

Hajjdiab, H., & Taleb, A. S. (2011). *Agile adoption experience: A case study in the U.A.E.* Paper presented at the IEEE 2nd International Conference on Software Engineering and Service Science, ICSESS 2011, Beijing, China. doi:10.1109/ICSESS.2011.5982247

Hoda, R. (2011). *Self-Organizing Agile Teams: A Grounded Theory.* (PhD Thesis). Victoria University of Wellington, New Zealand.

Hoda, R., Noble, J., & Marshall, S. (2010). *Organizing self-organizing teams.* Paper presented at the 32nd ACM/IEEE International Conference on Software Engineering, ICSE 2010, Cape Town, South Africa. doi:10.1145/1806799.1806843

Hoda, R., Noble, J., & Marshall, S. (2011a). Developing a grounded theory to explain the practices of self-organizing Agile teams. *Empirical Software Engineering, 17*(6), 609–639. doi:10.1007/s10664-011-9161-0

Hoda, R., Noble, J., & Marshall, S. (2011b). The impact of inadequate customer collaboration on self-organizing Agile teams. *Information and Software Technology, 53*(5), 521–534. doi:10.1016/j.infsof.2010.10.009

Iivari, J., & Iivari, N. (2011). The relationship between organizational culture and the deployment of agile methods. *Information and Software Technology, 53*(5), 509–520. doi:10.1016/j.infsof.2010.10.008

Kum, W., & Law, A. (2006). *Learning effective test driven development: Software development projects in an energy company.* Paper presented at the 1st International Conference on Software and Data Technologies, ICSOFT 2006, Setubal, Portugal.

Martin, A., Biddle, R., & Noble, J. (2009). *XP customer practices: A grounded theory.* Paper presented at the Agile 2009 Conference, Chicago, IL.

Martin, A., Biddle, R., & Noble, J. (2009). *The XP Customer Team: A Grounded Theory.* Paper presented at the 2009 Agile Conference. doi:10.1109/AGILE.2009.70

Misra, S. C., Kumar, V., & Kumar, U. (2009). Identifying some important success factors in adopting agile software development practices. *Journal of Systems and Software, 82*(11), 1869–1890. doi:10.1016/j.jss.2009.05.052

Moe, N. B., Aurum, A., & Dybå, T. (2012). Challenges of shared decision-making: A multiple case study of agile software development. *Information and Software Technology, 54*(8), 853–865. doi:10.1016/j.infsof.2011.11.006

Nerur, S., Mahapatra, R., & Mangalaraj, G. (2005). Challenges of migrating to agile methodologies. *Communications of the ACM, 48*(5), 72–78. doi:10.1145/1060710.1060712

Pikkarainen, M., Salo, O., Kuusela, R., & Abrahamsson, P. (2012). Strengths and barriers behind the successful agile deployment-insights from the three software intensive companies in Finland. *Empirical Software Engineering, 17*(6), 675–702. doi:10.1007/s10664-011-9185-5

Senapathi, M., & Srinivasan, A. (2012). Understanding post-adoptive agile usage: An exploratory cross-case analysis. *Journal of Systems and Software, 85*(6), 1255–1268. doi:10.1016/j.jss.2012.02.025

Srinivasan, J., & Lundqvist, K. (2010). *Agile in India: Challenges and lessons learned.* Paper presented at the 3rd India Software Engineering Conference, ISEC'10, Mysore, India. doi:10.1145/1730874.1730898

Sureshchandra, K., & Shrinivasavadhani, J. (2008). *Moving from waterfall to agile.* Paper presented at the Agile 2008 Conference, Toronto, Canada.

Treccani, P. J. F., & De Souza, C. R. B. (2011). *Collaborative refactoring: Results of an empirical study using grounded theory* (Vol. 6969). Paraty: LNCS.

Tsirakidis, P., Köbler, F., & Krcmar, H. (2009). *Identification of success and failure factors of two agile software development teams in an open source organization.* Paper presented at the 4th IEEE International Conference on Global Software Engineering, ICGSE 2009, Limerick. doi:10.1109/ICGSE.2009.42

Vijayasarathy, L., & Turk, D. (2012). Drivers of agile software development use: Dialectic interplay between benefits and hindrances. *Information and Software Technology, 54*(2), 137–148. doi:10.1016/j.infsof.2011.08.003

KEY TERMS AND DEFINITIONS

Scrum: Scrum is one of the popular agile methodologies which aims to address the challenges of projects involving complex scope of work using a simple process dependent on a small team who are motivated, collaborative and highly focused on producing working software every 2-4 weeks.

Feature Driven Development: Feature Driven Development (FDD) is an agile method that focuses on delivering working software in a timely manner by using simple, client focused and practical software process. This method works well without tailoring to both small (< 8 team size) and large teams (> 30 team size).

Extreme Programming: Extreme Programming (XP) is an agile methodology that specifically emphasizes the use of agile technical practices (e.g. Test Driven Development) for the success of an agile project. Practical experience shows that XP complements Scrum well and both the methods work well together.

Refactoring: Refactoring aims to have a cleaner "code" by restructuring the code without changing its external behaviour. The idea is to improve the design of the code with the intention of making it easy to use.

Agile Software Development: A software management and development approach that helps to create software quickly while addressing the issue of requirement change.

Chapter 3
A Canvas for Capturing Context of Agile Adoption

Pan-Wei Ng
Ivar Jacobson International, Singapore

ABSTRACT

Although agile development promises better customer response and quality, not all who attempt agile seem to get such desired results. The issue is context – understanding the context in which agile is being adopted and choosing the right practices. Our research question is how agile-coaches can best elicit and communicate the agile adoption context with development teams and organizations. In this paper, we propose capturing and describing agile adoption context visually using a set of architectural views. This is analogous to describing architectures, but now applied to the context of agile adoption. We propose a set of views and applied it in the agile adoption of a company's internal social network system (SNS). Our experiences taught us that context evolves as agile coaches interact with development organization and teams, and the context description evolves and converges to the team's desired way of working after the agile coach leaves the scene. It is also the basis for drawing upon past experiences and building experiences for the next agile adoption engagement.

1. INTRODUCTION

1.1 Context! Context! Context!

The fundamental challenge is that software development is complex and success depends on a large number of context factors. Dyba (T. Dybå, Dag IK Sjøberg, and Daniela S. Cruzes., 2012) pointed out the importance of context when it comes to empirical studies. Indeed, some development is very complex. Clarke and Connors (Clarke & O'Connor, 2012) found 8 classifications, 44 factors and 170 sub-factors. Jones (Kotter, 1995) identified 121 factors affecting quality alone. The large number of factors poses serious challenges to practitioners. Teams need to evaluate which factors are more important them and understand when certain factors be emphasized or downplayed.

DOI: 10.4018/978-1-4666-9858-1.ch003

Before moving further, we want to clarify the context for our discussion in this paper. Indeed our discussion about context requires a context. The context of our discussion is about agile adoption, the transition from a less agile approach to a more agile one. Kruchten (P. Kruchten, 2007) highlighted that successful agile adoption depended on context.Hoda, Kruchten, Noble, and Marshall (Hoda, Kruchten, Noble, & Marshall, 2010) conducted a Grounded Theory study and argued that development methods and practices must be adapted to fit their contexts.For example, agile adoption in a highly regulated context would be different from a less regulated one as reported by Fitzgerald, Stol, O'Sullivan, and O'Brien(Fritscher & Pigneur, 2010). Chow and Cao (Chow & Cao, 2008)found 36 factors affecting the success of agile adoption.Today, empirical studies (Begel, 2007; T. Dybå & Dingsøyr, 2008; Li, 2010) on agile methods are plentiful and easily accessible by practitioners. However, there is still very little work to provide a systematic approach to describe the context in which agile methods and adoption took place.

1.2 Objective and Overview of Paper

The challenge for practitioners, especially agile coaches, ishow to get an accurate understanding of the agile adoption context comprehensively and quickly and from there, help teams choose the appropriate course of action.Note that while being able to consolidate empirical data and make generalizations is a useful by-product, our primary goal is to make concrete actionable recommendations and steer clear of potential pitfalls for the specific case we are involved in.

We propose using an architecture centric approach to capturing agile adoption context. Osterweil noted that software processes are software too(Osterweil, 1987). Accordingly, just as software architecture descriptions help us understand the nature of complex software systems, software processes need architecture descriptions too. In software itself, architecture descriptions with agreed viewpoints are often used to communicate the complexities of a software system (Hofmeister et al., 2007). As pointed out by Ambler (Ambler, 2002), the use of architecture descriptions should be agile and lightweight. Lightweight models of businesses such as the business model canvas (Fritscher & Pigneur, 2010) used in Lean Startup (Blank, 2013) are gaining popularity. It follows naturally that some kind of lightweight informal architecture description with agreed viewpoints would be useful to describe and communicate agile adoption context, to identify potential improvements to current way of working, and where barriers and roadblocks to adoption might be.

Our proposed agile adoption canvas builds upon our earlier works on modeling analyzing process improvement context (Pan-Wei Ng, 2014; Ng, 2013; Pan-Wei. Ng, 2014). The agile adoption canvas answers three questions:

1. How a team is developing and delivering software.
2. What the team has tried.
3. What the team should try next and why.

The agile adoption canvas comprises a number of viewpoints, namely: the timeline, value-stream-activity, software system, stakeholder-and-team, work-management, and objectives-and-practices viewpoints. We propose using an agile approach to capture these views through an informal canvas, which is a whiteboard that participants can doodle and comment on. As such we call this context description an agile adoption canvas.

In this paper, we describe our experiences applying the agile adoption canvas to the agile adoption in a company's internal social network service (SNS) product. Section 2 shows the kind of context information each of the above-mentioned views captures. In Section 3, we give examples showing what each view contains by documenting our experiences in an industrial setting. Section 4 of this paper describes our lessons learnt. We recognize that capturing the context of agile adoption is not an easy task. It involves communicating back to the team (adopting agile methods) and getting confirmation. It is at least a two-way street as an agile coach interacts with the team. Observations either validate or invalidate past observations and assumptions. Finally, in Section5, we discuss the generality of our proposed approach and draw conclusions and future work.

2. AGILE ADOPTION CANVAS

As agile development become main stream, its application has extended beyond small-scaled development to larger-scale (more people), broader scope (involving more kinds of activities) and more novel situations. Our work with a large scale IT organization involving about 4000 developers and contractors was one such situation. The author was the lead-coach and advisor of this agile transformation. This IT organization had many product teams with staffing ranging from tens to hundreds. Agile adoption had to go beyond simple scrum and XP inspired practices like continuous integration and refactoring. It became necessary and even critical to understand the adoption context and how agile principles can address their challenges, as emergent and novel practices were needed. Moreover, this large-scale enterprise agile adoption endeavor involved 10 external and internal coaches with each coach was responsible for the agile adoption of separate product teams and some level of consistency amongst coaches was important.

Existing approaches like checklists, maturity models (McAvoy, 2009) and root-cause-analysis approaches (Lehtinen, 2011) needed pre-requisite steps to first understand what product teams are doing. This inspired the invention of the agile adoption canvas. Having agreed viewpoints help coaches be thorough and consistent when collecting and communicating contextual information about the product teams. It provided crucial inputs for recommending and tracking improvements.

The agile adoption canvas comprises a set of viewpoints that highlight elements about the way teams develop and deliver software and provides the inputs to discuss challenges faced and explore solutions.

We classify elements into context elements and adoption elements. Context elements describe how a team is currently developing and delivering software and adoption elements describe the challenges it faces and the new practices it should adopt. Context elements are further classified into time elements and structural elements. Time elements comprise major events that have impact on adoption. Structural elements are elements about the way the team conducts development.

Timeline Viewpoint: The timeline viewpoint provides shows significant time elements such as major events and lifecycle milestones that have impact on the way the team develops software or impact agile adoption (see Figure 2). It addresses our concern about when the team tried something, whether it worked and why. For example, a team might have tried using some agile practices without getting desired benefits. In such as situation, an agile coach has to be sensitive to the challenges the team had faced, instead of proposing the same practices. The timeline view also highlights upcoming milestones and deadlines that a team has to keep up with. These milestones impose time limits and constraints as to the practices that can be introduced. For example, a team might have completed their traditional "requirements" face

Figure 1. Agile Adoption Canvas viewpoints and elements

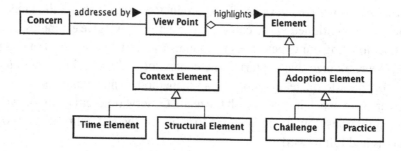

Figure 2. Timeline context elements and viewpoint

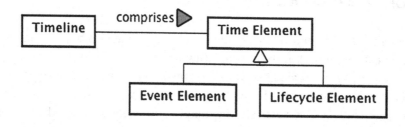

and are now working towards an impending release. In such a case, it does not make sense suggesting the team to rewrite their requirements from a traditional approach to one that uses user stories. Instead, the focus should be on practices that help the team achieve their delivery.

Structural context viewpoints and elements describe the way a team develops and delivers software. Figure 3 shows the different types of structural elements and their containing. These structural context viewpoints serve as a background for product teams and coaches to identify challenges and practices to overcome them.

Value Stream Activity Viewpoint: The value-stream-activity viewpoint describes major activities and periodic activities of a software development endeavor. Development value streams often include stages like conceiving a requirement or a feature to its analysis, development, testing and release. More complicated value streams would include feedback and collaboration between teams and departments.

Figure 3. Structural context elements and viewpoints

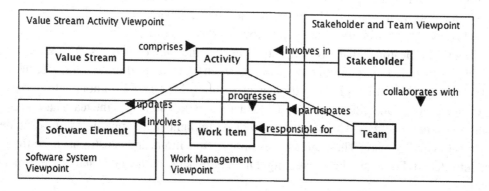

This viewpoint is useful for understanding development lead-times, wastes and bottlenecks. Frequently, we find software development lifecycles in traditional organizations work with large batches that hinders early feedback. Agile and lean methods however, advocate having fixed cadence and managing scope to maximize value (Reinertsen, 2009).

Software System Viewpoint: The software system viewpoint describes the software system structure and highlight technical debts (P. Kruchten, 2007) that may hinder the adoption of agile methods. Kruchten's 4+1 (P. B. Kruchten, 1995) is a popular approach for software development. However, we find logical views and implementation views most relevant when considering agile adoption. Logical views highlight component complexities and dependencies between components. Implementation views highlight branch-and-merge strategies. Both have significant impact on development velocity and quality.

Stakeholder and Team Viewpoint: The stakeholder and team viewpoint describes the participants of the development process, their relationships and where problems occur. Agile development emphasizes collaboration and engagement. This view helps us understand how well various parties collaborate and where collaborations breakdown and silos occur. This viewpoint also highlights the attitudes participants have towards agile principles and practices (Power, 2010).

Work Management Viewpoint: Large-scale and complex agile development requires some kind of tooling for teams to manage their work. The work management viewpoint describes the kind of work-items and work-products that the teams are responsible for, how the teams track and manage these items. Poor work management, prioritization and alignment lead to unnecessary delays and bottlenecks.

Objectives and Practices Viewpoint: Teams who adopt agile approaches want to achieve some objectives such as increased customer satisfaction, higher productivity, better staff engagement, better quality, or to overcome specific weaknesses in their development approach. The objectives-and-practices viewpoint links the agreed objectives to the challenges and practices identified from earlier viewpoints. This viewpoint further highlights factors affecting the adoption of these practices. Examples of such factors include business orientation, organization culture, mindset, executive involvement, etc. as discussed by Dyba (Power, 2010) and Chow and Cao (Chow & Cao, 2008).

3. APPLYING THE AGILE ADOPTION CANVAS

This section describes our experiences applying the agile adoption canvas to above-mentioned company's internal social network service (SNS) development team. Our purpose here is to exemplify the kind of contents that are communicated through the canvas. We use an informal free-form approach to describe each view to encourage creative and novel use of the canvas. We annotate negative (i.e. hinder-

Figure 4. Adoption elements

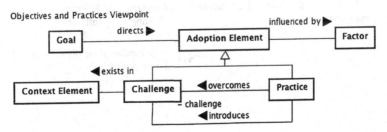

ing agile) factors and challenges with an explosion icon and positive (i.e. supporting agile) factors with a star. Neutral facts had no adornment. Solid arrows show influence, while dashed arrows anchor text to diagram elements.

Timeline View: Three months before our engagement (see Figure 5), the SNS team experimented with agile approaches. As there was little executive support, little changed. One month before starting to engage with this team, there an organizational level agile adoption strategy was established. This included agreeing a candidate set of practices to introduce, designating of internal and external coaches, coaching roles and responsibilities, targeting candidate product teams who would be the first batch of early adopters, executive expectations from these teams, agreed measurements and their baselines. The SNS team had to report their achievements 4 months later for executive review. This created a push to make agile adoption successful.

Value Stream and Activity View: Prior to agile adoption, SNS development cycles took on average 2.5 months (see Figure 6). The time when an agreed requirement was received to the time it went to production usually took 5 months. Moreover, large numbers of incidents frequently followed each production release. These problems were the motivation for the SNS product team to adopt agile methods. They wanted to move from a 2.5-month cadence to a 1-month cadence by adopting agile practices.

Software System View: The left hand side of Figure 7 shows the logical view of the SNS software system. The SNS product comprised several social network channels running on top of an SNS platform. The channels had integration with an external search engine and other products in the IT department. SNS codes were relatively well structured and did not pose any threat to agile adoption.

Figure 5. SNS: Timeline view

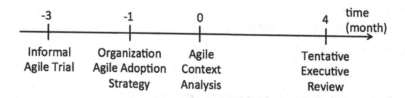

Figure 6. SNS: Value stream and activity view

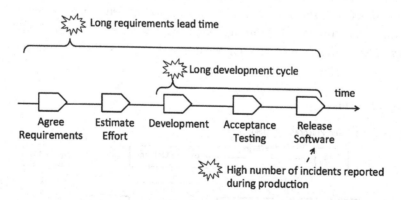

Figure 7. SNS: Software system view

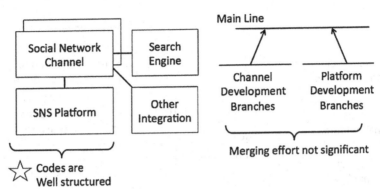

The right-hand-side of Figure 7 shows the implementation view of the SNS software system focusing on its branching strategy. Development teams work on different branches that are merged to the main branch on a weekly basis. This merging effort was not significant and did not pose any immediate threat to their agile adoption.

Stakeholder and Team View: The SNS core development team consists of a project manager, one business analyst, one software architect, five design engineers and one test manager. This core team was staffed by the companies IT department. Development teams carried out the actual development work. Each development teams were staffed from two separate contractor companies. Each had an on-site manager responsible for their staff. There was a total of about 50 contracted staff.

The relationships that the SNS team had with other stakeholders are rather complicated (see Figure 8). Requirements originated from stakeholder representatives, one for each social network channel. Frequent requirement changes occurred with the sales channel representatives, which created much disturbance to the development teams, which were roughly aligned with the social network channels. In addition, there was heavy and complicated governance procedures to ensure quality before a release of the SNS was allowed to go "live".

Furthermore, to prevent impact to users, any software deployment to production was only permitted during weekends (Saturday 10pm at the earliest). The SNS product had tight integration with a search engine developed by a separate product team. Fortunately, the latter was also adopting agile methods and was willing to abide by the SNS product team's new cadence.

Work Management View: There were two main kinds of work-items for SNS development, namely: enhancements that were expressed in requirement documents and defects that were captured using an in-house defect-tracking tool (see Figure 9). No work-item tracking tool was used to track the progress of enhancements.

Majority of the enhancements could be implemented within 10 man-days. Enhancements were small and conformed to the INVEST (Independent, Negotiable, Valuable, Estimable, Small, Testable) criteria for user stories (Dyba, 2005).

Objectives and Practices View: The key challenges were due to a number of factors, such as poor collaboration between teams, poor collaboration between developers and testers and outdated processes and governance procedures (see Figure 10). The candidate practices that for the SNS product team to adopt are depicted as hexagons, the notation from the OMG Essence specification (Wake, 2003). Planning agile adoption involved prioritizing and introducing these practices. The different shades represented

Figure 8. SNS: Stakeholder and team view

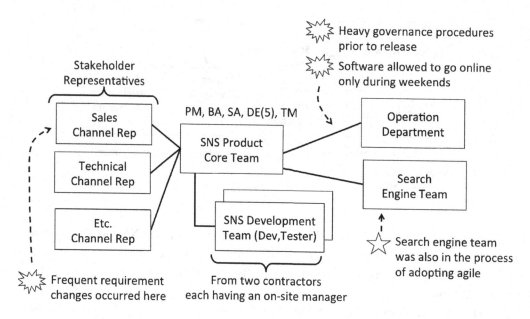

Figure 9. SNS: Work management view

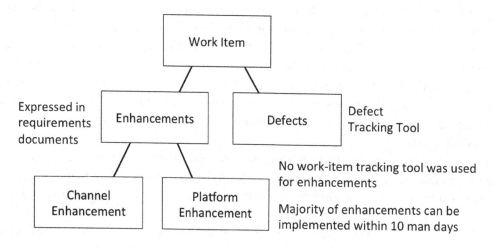

whether they are standard vanilla practices that could be acquired from books, or had to be adapted, or they were novel and had to be invented to meet the specific challenges at hand. The different types of practices highlighted the preparation work needed before the practice can be made fit-for-purpose.

The identified practices included scrum, lean-startup inspired requirements management, super-scrum (a simple large scale instantiation of scrum, incident analysis (finding root causes of incidents and defects), acceptance test driven development (ATDD) (Rubin, 2012), automated testing, agile governance (Gärtner, 2012) and DevOps (Qumer, 2007).

Figure 10. SNS: Objectives and practices view

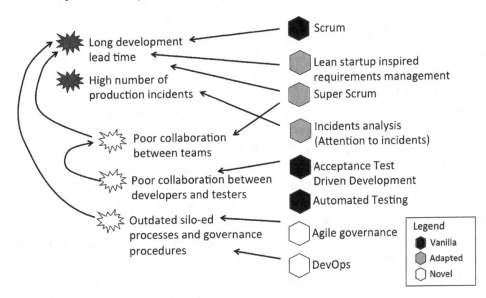

4. EXPERIENCES WITH THE ADOPTION CANVAS

During the four months that we coach the SNS product team, the agile adoption canvas evolved and served as an input for determining actions and their priorities. It was a shared reference between external and internal coaches and the SNS project manager. Our experiences yield the following observations:

Write it down. The first rule-of-thumb is "write it down immediately and organize gradually". We found that physical facts are quite easy to capture, but physiological and cultural facts were much harder to detect and document. For example, erroneous generalizations occurred frequently leading to capability traps and self-confirming attribution errors highlighted by Repenning, and Sterman (Gene Kim, 2013).

Context canvas evolves. It is not easy to capture all contextual information at once, but instead takes a while. Even then context evolves as the software development endeavor progress. Much of the context information about the SNS agile adoption was gathered over a period of time. For example, events like department restructuring was something we knew only 2 months into the adoption after investigating why it was difficult to arrange progress meetings. The impact of the business analyst's strong personality was confirmed after a series of events. The product team's heavy workload generated much inertia for introducing automated testing.

Context canvas requires and facilitates engagement. For the context canvas to work, participants need to actively provide information. This could be achieved by having regular retrospective meetings and it takes time and effort. However, we also found that making the contents of the canvas visible to participants of the agile adoption also served to get them engaged.

Context canvas is a training and facilitation tool. The context canvas serves as a useful two-way communication tool. It drives team members to highlight their existing challenges in a way understandable to an agile coach. It is also provides a way for an agile coach to describe how agile approaches are different from or similar to current approaches. For example, the development and delivery view gave us the opportunity to discuss the value of working in small batches and to explain how the SNS team could work in small batches.

Desired development approach emerges from the context canvas. As mentioned, the context canvas was always evolving. It began by describing the current development approach highlighting the problem areas. Each month of the adoption period, we update the context canvas with new information and changed work processes. As such, it was always describing the SNS's specific development approach at the point in time, albeit at a high level. Moreover, the history view also captured what we tried and did not work and why, which set the stage for agile adoption for the next month. Gradually, the context description converges, the team's desired agile way of working emerges, and the team now have an architecture centric description of their specific agile process.

Context canvas provides transparency. As mentioned, the SNS agile adoption was part of a much larger. There were about 4000 software engineers (in-house and contracted) in theIT organization that the SNS product belonged to. Five external coaches were engaged who worked closely with designated product teams. The context canvas provided a means to the organizational level agile adoption team a clear and transparent picture of what was going on in the field.

Context canvas requires effort and discipline. Keeping the context canvas updated required effort. We first used whiteboards for discussion, but this was quickly replaced by PowerPoint files to permit sharing electronically. We believe this effort was worthwhile because it provided inputs for reflection and analysis.

5. CONCLUSION AND FUTURE WORK

During the 4 calendar months of agile adoption, the SNS product team reduced their development and delivery cycle by 50%. There was significant decrease in defects reported. Business representatives collaborate with the SNS product team to prioritize their product backlog. Automated testing was introduced. Such a positive report like the paragraph above would raise different response from different readers. Agile advocates would cite this as a confirmation of agile benefits. Skeptics would dismiss it as an exaggeration and say, "It will not work here." Or at the very least, an expected response would be "Our situation is different." The truth lay on an adequate understanding of the adoption context. In this paper, we had demonstrated the application of the agile adoption canvas on the SNS case. This demonstration also serves as an exemplary guide to describe the reader's case.

Evaluation

At the beginning of this paper, we have mentioned that the goal of the canvas is to clarify the context for a specific case, i.e. the SNS. As coaches we needed to the due diligence for acquiring sufficient inputs to make choose the correct course of action and to recommend the right practices.

However, we have not evaluated the generality of our approach. We had not evaluated (1) if the list of views are complete, (2) whether the views are too few or many for small and large scale agile adoption, and, (3) the kind of pre-requisite knowledge to effectively make use of the context canvas.

Future Work

Clearly, more needs to be done. Empirical evaluation of the generality of the canvas is clearly needed, as are guidelines for using the canvas, especially the kind of context information for each view.

Software development is challenging and making the right decision and taking the right course of decision requires consideration into the development context and goals. Adopting agile methods is also complex, and perhaps even more complex because it involved organizational changes. In their review of a decade of agile methods, Dingsøyr et al. (Repenning, 2002) recommended a more theory-based approach to research. Dyba° and Dingsøyr (T. Dybå & Dingsøyr, 2008) surveyed research for empirical evidence of agile software development and found that different reporting content hinders analysis. Jedlitschka, Ciolkowski, and Pfahl (Dingsøyr, Nerur, Balijepally, & Moe, 2012) also pointed out that a major problem for integrating software engineering research results into a common body of knowledge is the diversity of reporting styles. It is difficult to locate relevant information; and important information is often missing. Petersen and Wohlin (Andreas Jedlitschka, 2008) found that studies investigating a similar object do not agree on which context facets are important to mention and provided a checklist that aims to help researchers make informed decisions on what to include and not to include. Clearly, an agreed approach or domain model to capture agile development context is important.

REFERENCES

Abrahamsson, P., Conboy, K., & Wang, X. (2009). 'Lots done, more to do': The current state of agile systems development research. *European Journal of Information Systems, 18*(4), 281–284. doi:10.1057/ejis.2009.27

Ambler, S. (2002). Agile modeling: effective practices for extreme programming and the unified process. Academic Press.

Begel, A., & Nagappan, N. (2007). Usage and perceptions of agile software development in an industrial context: An exploratory study. In *Empirical Software Engineering and Measurement*, (pp. 255-264). doi: 10.1109/esem.2007.84

Blank, S. (2013). Why the lean start-up changes everything. *Harvard Business Review, 91*(5), 63–72. doi:10.4324/9780203104569

Brooks, F. (1995). The Mythical Man-Month. *IEEE Software, 12*(5), 57–60. doi:10.1109/MS.1995.10042

Chow, T., & Cao, D.-B. (2008). A survey study of critical success factors in agile software projects. *Journal of Systems and Software, 81*(6), 961–971. doi:10.1016/j.jss.2007.08.020

Clarke, P., & O'Connor, R. V. (2012). The situational factors that affect the software development process: Towards a comprehensive reference framework. *Information and Software Technology, 54*(5), 433–447. doi:10.1016/j.infsof.2011.12.003

Dingsøyr, T., Nerur, S., Balijepally, V. G., & Moe, N. B. (2012). A decade of agile methodologies: Towards explaining agile software development. *Journal of Systems and Software, 85*(6), 1213–1221. doi:10.1016/j.jss.2012.02.033

Dyba, T. (2005). An empirical investigation of the key factors for success in software process improvement. *IEEE Transactions on Software Engineering, 31*(5), 410–424. doi:10.1109/TSE.2005.53

Dybå, T., Sjøberg, & Cruzes. (2012). *What works for whom, where, when, and why?: on the role of context in empirical software engineering* Paper presented at the ACM-IEEE international symposium on Empirical software engineering and measurement. doi:10.1145/2372251.2372256

Dybå, T., & Dingsøyr, T. (2008). Empirical studies of agile software development: A systematic review. *Information and Software Technology, 50*(9-10), 833–859. doi:10.1016/j.infsof.2008.01.006

Fritscher, B., & Pigneur, Y. (2010). *Supporting Business Model Modelling: A Compromise between Creativity and Constraints*. Academic Press.

Gärtner, M. (2012). *ATDD by example: a practical guide to acceptance test-driven development*. Addison-Wesley.

Glass, R. L. (2004). Matching methodology to problem domain. *Communications of the ACM, 47*(5), 19–21. doi:10.1145/986213.986228

Hoda, R., Kruchten, P., Noble, J., & Marshall, S. (2010). Agility in context. *ACM SIGPLAN Notices, 45*(10), 74. doi:10.1145/1932682.1869467

Hofmeister, C., Kruchten, P., Nord, R. L., Obbink, H., Ran, A., & America, P. (2007). A general model of software architecture design derived from five industrial approaches. *Journal of Systems and Software, 80*(1), 106–126. doi:10.1016/j.jss.2006.05.024

Jedlitschka, A., Ciolkowski, M., & Pfahl, D. (2008). Reporting experiments in software engineering. *Guide to Advanced Empirical Software Engineering, 232*(3), 201–228. doi:10.1007/978-1-84800-044-5_8

Kim, G., Behr, K., & Spafford, G. (2013). The Phoenix Project: A Novel about IT, DevOps, and Helping Your Business Win. IT Revolution Press. doi:10.1524/hzhz.2013.0149

Kotter, J. P. (1995). Leading change: Why transformation efforts fail. *Harvard Business Review, 73*(2), 59–67.

Kruchten, P. (2007). Voyage in the agile memeplex. *Queue, 5*(5), 38. doi:10.1145/1281881.1281893

Kruchten, P. B. (1995). The 4+1 View Model of architecture. *IEEE Software, 12*(6), 42–50. doi:10.1109/52.469759

Lehtinen, T. O. A., Mäntylä, & Vanhanen. (2011). Development and evaluation of a lightweight root cause analysis method (ARCA method) – Field studies at four software companies. *Information and Software Technology, 53*(10), 1045–1061. doi: 10.1016/j.infsof.2011.05.005

Lethbridge, Diaz-Herrera, LeBlanc, & Thompson. (2007). Improving software practice through education: Challenges and future trends. *Future of Software Engineering*, 12–28. doi: 10.1109/fose.2007.13

Li, J., Moe, N. B., & Dybå, T. (2010). Transition from a plan-driven process to Scrum: a longitudinal case study on software quality. In *Proceedings of the 2010 ACM-IEEE international symposium on empirical software engineering and measurement*. doi:10.1145/1852786.1852804

Maurer, F., & Melnik, G. (2007). *Agile methods: Crossing the chasm*. Paper presented at the Companion to the proceedings of the 29th International Conference on Software Engineering.

McAvoy, J., & Butler, T. (2009). A Failure to Learn in a Software Development Team: The Unsuccessful Introduction of an Agile Method. *Information Systems Developmen, 5*, 1–13. doi:10.1007/978-0-387-68772-8_1

Ng, P.-W. (2014). Framework for Describing and Analyzing Context and Factors for Software Engineering Research. *Applying the SEMAT Kernel Lecture Notes on Software Engineering, 2*(4), 179–196. doi:10.1007/978-1-62703-721-1_10

Ng, P.-W. (2014). Theory based software engineering with the SEMAT kernel: preliminary investigation and experiences. In *Proceedings of the 3rd SEMAT Workshop on General Theories of Software Engineering.* doi:10.1145/2593752.2593756

Ng, P-W., Huang, & Wu. (2013). On the value of essence to software engineering research: A preliminary study. *Software Engineering, 10*(3), 51-58. doi: 10.1002/rcs.1534

Osterweil, L. (1987). *Software processes are software too* Paper presented at the 9th international conference on Software Engineering.

Power, K. (2010). *Stakeholder identification in agile software product development organizations: A model for understanding who and what really count.* Paper presented at the Agile conference. doi:10.1109/AGILE.2010.17

Qumer, A. (2007). Defining an Integrated Agile Governance for Large Agile Software Development Environments. *Defining an Integrated Agile Governance for Large Agile Software Development Environments Agile Processes in Software Engineering and Extreme Programming, 4536*, 157–160. doi:10.1007/978-3-540-73101-6_23

Reinertsen, D. G. (2009). The principles of product development flow. *Second Generation Lean Product Development, 62.* doi: 10.1787/dcr-2009-graph12-en

Repenning, N. P., & Sterman, J. D. (2002). Capability traps and self-confirming attribution errors in the dynamics of process improvement. *Administrative Science Quarterly, 47*(2), 265–295. doi:10.2307/3094806

Rubin, K. S. (2012). Essential Scrum: A practical guide to the most popular Agile process. *Journal of Functional Programming, 22*(03), 375–377. doi:10.1017/s0956796812000123

Vijayasarathy, L. E. O. R., & Turk. (2008). Agile Software Development: A survey of early adopters. *Journal of Information Technology Management, 19*(2), 1–8. doi:10.1080/1097198x.2008.10856469

Wake, W. C. (2003). *INVEST in Good Stories, and SMART Tasks.* Retrieved from www.xp123.com

KEY TERMS AND DEFINITIONS

Agile Software Architecture: A software architecture that lays out blue prints of the organization and structure of software components as well as well-defined mechanism on how components can be tested and integrated into the system that would sustain the agile approach throughout the software development life cycle.

Agile Software Development Process: An evolutionary and iterative approach to software development with focuses on adaptation to changes.

Continuous Integration: Continuous integration is a prescribed software engineering practice which advocates merging the developer working copies with a central, shared mainline several times a day.

Refactoring: Refactoring aims to have a cleaner "code" by restructuring the code without changing its external behaviour. The idea is to improve the design of the code with the intention of making it easy to use.

Waterfall Model: A sequential design, used in software development processes, in which progress is seen as flowing steadily downwards (like a waterfall) through the phases of Conception, Initiation, Analysis, Design, Construction, Testing, Deployment and Maintenance.

Chapter 4
Ten Years of Experience with Agile and Model–Driven Software Development in a Legacy Platform

Chung-Yeung Pang
Seveco AG, Switzerland

ABSTRACT

In this chapter, a report containing the author's many years of experience in software development together with a discussion of software engineering are presented. The report begins with the software crisis and includes different projects following the traditional waterfall model with heavy documents. In a re-engineering project of a legacy IT system by modernizing COBOL applications, we established an agile and model driven approach to software development. This approach which has been successfully applied in 13 projects since 2004 is presented. The key factors required for our success will also be discussed. Both the good and bad experiences of the last ten years will be summarized. The chapter will be finalized with a vision of a new architecture for agile software development.

INTRODUCTION

Computer technology has evolved at a rapid rate. It was inconceivable that my current notebook has more computer power than the huge IBM 370 machine that ran my first program in my university days. It is a real joke when someone still uses hardware components from the good old days for today's business. On the other hand, what about software? Many COBOL programs developed in the 1970s are still in operation. In fact, enterprise IT systems usually undergo a long period of evolution. This decade long, the software projects evolved into some of the most complex software systems. For large corporations, mainframe applications programmed in COBOL often form the backbone of the IT structure. Despite their obsolescence, legacy systems continue to provide a competitive advantage through supporting unique business processes and containing invaluable knowledge and historical data.

DOI: 10.4018/978-1-4666-9858-1.ch004

Maintaining and upgrading legacy systems is one of the most difficult challenges many companies currently face. They struggle with the problem of modernizing these systems while keeping the day-to-day operation intact. As reported later in this chapter, many large corporations have tried but failed to re-build their legacy systems using object-oriented language like Java or Smalltalk. At the same time, new applications developed in Java do not seem to provide significant advantages in terms of performance or enhancement in business agility. On the other hand, with a proper approach to software development, one can build flexible, maintainable, agile applications in a legacy platform with a language like COBOL. The approach was first reported in 2012 (Cockburn & Highsmith, 2001; Pang, 2012) and its solution framework includes the following features:

- Modular and pluggable for architecture business and system component integration.
- Reuse in terms of design and code patterns.
- Use model driven approach and code generation in the development process.
- Test infrastructure for unit testing, component integration testing and service testing.
- Adapt agile development process.

The development approach is based on practical experience from a re-engineering project of a legacy IT system in a large corporation. It was first applied in 2004. During the last 10 years, the approach has been applied in 13 projects. Although some projects were under significant pressure with time and budget constraints, all projects were completed on time and within budget.

In this chapter, I report my many years of experience in software development, particularly the last ten years of using the development approach. The chapter is organized as follows. In the background section, my experience of the software crisis, software development process based on the waterfall model, challenges and success of software projects are elaborated. In the next section I discuss the agile development process with the agile manifesto and its critiques. Software architecture, which in my experience is crucial to the agile process for enterprise application development is also elaborated. In the following section the history and evolution of the agile architecture for our development approach are presented. The architecture, model driven approach, tools and framework are discussed. Following that is a section on project experience. Then a section on the experience with developers, development teams and managers is presented. Following is a section about overall experience and lessons learnt. The acceptance, positive and negative experience as well as the findings are presented in this section. The chapter is finalized with future research directions and conclusions.

BACKGROUND

As background I present my personal experience with the software crisis, various software development processes, as well as challenges and successes of software projects.

Software Crisis

In the early days of software history, programmers tended to develop their programs in an ad hoc style with no documentation. A result of this was the software crisis of the 1960s, 1970s and 1980s. Typical phenomena of the software crisis are (Crisis, 2010):

- Many problems have arisen in software development.
- Software projects tend to run over budget and are late or completely fail to deliver.
- Mission critical programs become obsolete and not maintainable.
- Enterprise IT systems have become increasingly complex and they cannot easily be managed.

I gained personal experience of the software crisis in the mid-1980s when I started my career as a software developer. My first job involved maintaining and extending a software package developed by 12 developers over a period of 5 years. All the developers had left the company. The only documents left behind were a few sketches on two scraps of paper. In this job, I had to go through thousands of lines of code written in different styles and structures and I tried to understand the algorithms of the whole software package. I fully understood the problems related to the software crisis after this experience. It also gave me a strong incentive to carry out research in software engineering. I would never support code centric approach to software development, although it is still common practice for most programmers.

Software Engnieering (Jackson, 2010) is a discipline that provides solutions to counter a software crisis. It defines standards, disciplines, methodologies and processes for software development. In the past decades, many new methodologies, standards, programming languages and paradigms have been developed. Programming styles like structural programming, object-oriented programming, etc. have been introduced. Programming languages such as ADA, C++, Smalltalk, Java, Prolog, etc. have been evolved to enable developers to program using better structures and to adapt to new programming styles like object-oriented programming as well as concepts of artificial intelligence and expert systems. Various CASE tools have become available to assist software development through modeling. The Unified Modeling Language (UML) has also evolved. Developers can build different software artifacts in different phases of a software development process in the form of UML models. For the software development life cycle (SDLC), we have the waterfall model, spiral development model, rational unified process (RUP), agile development process, etc. Extreme programming, rapid application development (RAD) with prototyping and SCRUM, etc. provide different programming paradigms. There has been a great evolution of software technologies since the period of the software crisis.

Despite the advances in software technologies, the problems related to software crisis do not seem to have been solved. The Standish Group's 2009 CHAOS report (Collier, 2009) shows only 32 percent of software projects are completed successfully. 44% are challenged which are late, over budget and/or have less than the required features and functions and 24% failed which are cancelled prior to completion or delivered and never used. "These numbers represent a downtick in the success rates from the previous study, as well as a significant increase in the number of failures", says Jim Crear, Standish Group CIO, "They are a low point in the last five study periods. This year's results represent the highest failure rate in over a decade".

I have personally observed similar statistics as those provided by the CHAOS report. Ambler challenged the CHAOS report in a LinkedIn debate and argued that the agile approach to software development has a far more successful rate (S.W. Ambler, 2013). In a vote, many participants shared that their projects had been successful (Ambler, 2013). However, most of them faced great challenges in their projects. Recently a friend celebrated the success of a software project in his company. The project was originally planned for two years; however it took four years to complete and costed three times the original budget. To the team it was a success as they argued that the final product has many functionalities that are different to the original concept of the product. It is difficult to define success. However, software development remains a challenge to date. More examples will be provided in a later sub-section.

Software Development Process

In 1970, (Royce, 1970) presented the first formal description of the waterfall model, although he did not use the term waterfall. The earliest use of the term "waterfall" may have been in a 1976 paper by Bell and Thayer (Bell & Thayer, 1976). As shown in Figure 1, the waterfall model provides a simple and logical structure of different activities involved with clear deliverables in a software development process. It is still popular today.

Despite its popularity, the linear sequential flow of activities in the waterfall model has many flaws. One major flaw relates to the concept that the requirements specification must be fully completed before the design and implementation activities start. This concept is in the mindset of many project managers, analysts and developers. "We can't start the development unless we know exactly what we are going to develop". One always hears such a sentence in a development project. Unless the project is very small, I personally have never come across the fact that any requirements specifications can be made up front and remain unchanged throughout the development life cycle. In the late 80s I went for a job interview. The project was to develop a new version of a radio phone system. The project was originally planned for two years. During my interview, I was told that they had been in the phase of specifying the requirements for one and a half years. Development had not started yet. Later on I took a job to develop a mobile communication system. We spent three quarters of a year trying to come up with the system specification. I requested to develop some prototypes but was turned down by the project manager. We ended up spending too much of the budget with no signs of progress. The higher management did not agree to fund the project further and the project was ended. The final product of the project was a heap of documents that nobody would ever read.

There is a tendency to try to come up with a requirement specification for a perfect system that can solve all problems. This was the case for the two projects previously mentioned. In fact, in my drawer, there is still a set of CDs containing documents that had cost a financial institute many tens of millions

Figure 1. Waterfall model for software development process

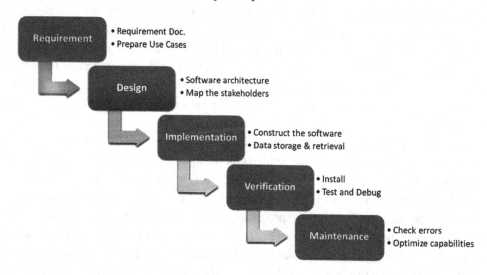

to develop in the late '90s. The documents contain the concepts and specifications of a dream financial system which was never completely developed. Those CDs have been in my drawer for over 15 years and I have not looked at them since.

In October 2007, we were going to develop a new version of our code generator. My original plan for the project was to have the first prototype in January and a new version in May 2008. A new project team took over the job. A couple of developers tried to come up with the requirement specification and we had meetings every two weeks to review this. There were many discussions on what the code generator should be able to do. In April 2008, we had still not completed the specification or got past the inception phase (the new term for the requirement specification phase). Then came the financial crisis and all projects were ended. Until now we have not had a new version of the code generator.

Requirement is often a moving target, as we see that most software packages have different versions. It is not a good idea to come up with a complete and thorough requirement before embarking on the next phase of development. It is the same as design. To complete a software design down to the final details before implementation starts is not advisable. Often we find that it is not feasible to implement the detailed design. Design should be constantly verified with prototypes. In short, the life cycle of software development is usually an iterative and incremental process.

Despite its flaws, the waterfall model has laid out a foundation for the software development process. In the meantime, lots of new models based on the waterfall model have evolved. As software development is actually an iterative process, Boehm (B. Boehm, 1986; B. W. Boehm, 1988) came up with a spiral model. The prototyping model is another approach that emphasizes the development of prototypes to allow users of the software to evaluate developers' proposals for the design of the eventual product by actually trying them out. Prototyping also serves the purpose of verifying the feasibility of implementation for architectural design. The incremental model is yet another model that applies the waterfall model incrementally. A recent approach is the agile software development methodology. This approach will be elaborated on in further detail in a later subsection. The different approaches of the software development life cycle (SDLC) have been well presented in many literatures (Johnson & Robinson, 2001).

Challenges in Software Projects

Advances in software technologies have made numerous promises. Back in the late '80s, software scientists claimed that OO languages were for programming on the whole (Wegner, 1989). The OO paradigm with polymorphism and inheritance was a solution to resolve and control the complexity of enterprise applications. Corporation executives have been led to believe that if they could port all their legacy applications to a new platform using programming languages such as Java and Smalltalk, they would have business agility and a great reduction in operating costs. In real practice, this often turns out to be an illusion.

A few years ago there was a project to port all the COBOL applications from the IBM z/OS system to the UNIX platform using Java as the main programming language. The project team had two and a half years time with substantial funding. The company executives were so committed to the project that they terminated all the software licenses of their legacy system at the time the project was scheduled to be completed. The project failed to complete and the company ran into so many problems that its survival was in question.

Enterprise IT systems involve a complex interplay of people and processes. Technologies alone do not provide solutions for managing the complex IT landscape. Development style, budget pressures and project deliverables followed by the need to deliver short-term results in an over-constrained environment led to the rapid creation of huge amounts of proprietary code. Figure 2 shows a typical outline of Java packages' inter-dependencies in a real enterprise project. Classes are developed as required. Cross references are made between objects when extensions of existing classes for new functionalities are required. This results in a "mountain-of-spaghetti" of Java code. The maintenance and operation of such a system represents a logistic nightmare just like COBOL based programs in legacy IT systems. The re-engineering of current IT systems turns into a process of continuous cycles.

Another example of failure was the development of a new general ledger system in a large corporation in the mid-90s. The system was based on a client server architecture. Smalltalk was the language for GUI development for the front end, while the existing mainframe back end system would act as a server to

Figure 2. Illustration of Java packages' inter-dependencies of an application

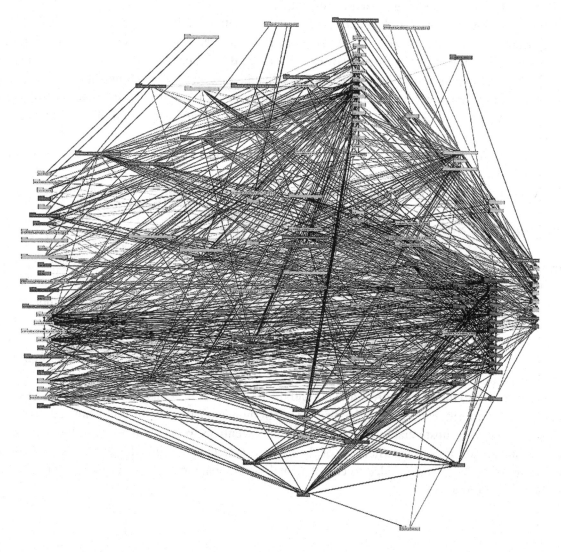

provide the data requested by the front end. Many hundreds of millions were invested in the project. The major problem with the project (in my opinion) was the implementation of the architecture. Populating a field would normally involve sending a query to the server. Eventually there were too many transactions involved in the mainframe system just to populate one screen. The system performance was absolutely not acceptable and operation costs would be too high. The last announcement by the management in that project was that they could not manage OO and client server technology. The project was ended.

A couple of years ago the Swiss government announced the complete failure of a software project for tax management after an investment of the equivalent to over one hundred million USD. In the press we were informed that the central office divided the whole project into the development of many software packages and subcontracted these packages to different contractors. These software packages did not work together.

For all the examples described so far, they show that software development is still a challenge 40 years after the start of the software crisis period. The causes of failure in software projects vary. They could be flaws in the development process such as consuming most of the budget in requirement specifications, flaws in architectural design and implementation like the project with the general ledger system, unable to handle the complexity of the software system, particularly when a huge system should be developed in one go, or poor project management and understanding of what is really required to manage a software project.

Success in Software Development

In 2006 the Standish Group put forward the following top ten success factors for IT projects (Hartmann Preuss, 2006; Krigsman, 2006).

1. User involvement
2. Executive management support
3. Clear business objectives
4. Optimizing scope
5. Agile process
6. Project management expertise
7. Financial management
8. Skilled resources
9. Formal methodology
10. Standard tools and infrastructure

In addition to the factors listed above, an additional key factor is the ability to resolve and control complexity. Staying focused on the essentials and proper architectural design are also important factors.

The above list provides a set of check points for IT projects. Descriptions of these factors can also be found in the 2001 online article by (Johnson & Robinson, 2001). It is interesting that the factor "firm basic requirements" in this article has been replaced by "agile process".

In the late '80s, I was involved in a telecommunication project. In this project we had a framework written in Modula 2. The framework was based on architecture with a plug and play mechanism for the modules. The whole framework provided a frame for every application with an infrastructure for all the basic system functions in place. When new requirements came in, we carried out some analyses and quickly developed prototypes to verify the requirements as well as the design. The development process was evolutionary and iterative and we were able to estimate the effort required for each requirement. Applications were developed on time and within budget.

From the late '90s to the early 2000s, I experienced success in a number of projects that had solid architectures and used an iterative and incremental development process. The 13 projects of the last 10 years that used the approach presented in this chapter are also examples of successful stories.

AGILE DEVELOPMENT PROCESS AND SOFTWARE ARCHITECTURE

In this section, I present the concept of agile development process together with its critics and problems. A subsection focused on the agile software architecture which I consider rather important to the success of software projects is also included

Agile Manifesto and Development Process

The agile software development process has become very popular in the software industry over the past few years. This process takes the evolutionary and iterative approach to software development (S.W. Ambler, 2010; Larman, 2003) and focuses on adaptation to changes. The concept fits well with any re-engineering project to improve business and IT agility. As previously mentioned the Standish Group removed "firm basic requirements" as a success factor and replaced it with "agile process". To establish firm basic requirements requires a detailed analysis of the business process and how it should function at the start of the project. In the agile development process, on the other hand, concrete requirements are identified along with the development process through successive implementations of prototypes.

In an agile development process, requirements and solutions evolve through collaboration between self-organizing, cross-functional teams. It promotes adaptive planning, evolutionary development, early delivery, continuous improvement and encourages a rapid and flexible response to change. The *Agile Manifesto*, which first laid out the underlying concepts of Agile development, introduced the term in 2001. The manifesto items within the agile software development context are:

- Individuals and interactions over processes and tools: In agile development, self-organization and motivation are important, as are interactions such as co-location and pair programming.
- Working software over comprehensive documentation: Working software will be more useful and welcome than just presenting documents to clients in meetings.
- Customer collaboration over contract negotiation: Requirements cannot be fully collected at the beginning of the software development cycle, therefore continuous customer or stakeholder involvement is very important.
- Responding to change over following a plan: Agile development focuses on quick responses to change and continuous development.

The Agile Manifesto is based on 12 principles:

1. Customer satisfaction through the rapid delivery of useful software.
2. Welcomes changing requirements, even late in development.

3. Working software is delivered frequently (weeks rather than months).
4. Close, daily cooperation between business people and developers.
5. Projects are built around motivated individuals, who should be trusted.
6. Face-to-face conversation is the best form of communication (co-location).
7. Working software is the principal measure of progress.
8. Sustainable development, able to maintain a constant pace.
9. Continuous attention to technical excellence and good design.
10. Simplicity—the art of maximizing the amount of work not done—is essential.
11. Self-organizing teams.
12. Regular adaptation to changing circumstances.

There is extensive literature on the topic of the agile development process and practices(S.W. Ambler, 2013; Larman, 2003; McGovern, 2003). Some of the most common practices include SCRUM, test-driven development (TDD), the user story driven approach, agile modeling, etc. The Agile Alliance has provided a comprehensive online collection with a map guide to applying agile practices (S.W. Ambler, 2010). We do not adhere to just a single practice published in literature. Rather we basically break tasks into small increments with minimal planning. Iterations have short time frames. An iteration can involve a team working through a full software development cycle, which includes planning, requirements analysis, design, coding, unit testing and acceptance testing when a working product is demonstrated to stakeholders. This helps to minimize overall risk and lets the project adapt to changes quickly.

Critics and Problems Related to Agile Development Process

The agile approach to software development eliminates the heavy documents that result from the waterfall model and hence reduces the significant effort invested in the requirements specification. The process also forces the development team to stop dwelling on the very high level concepts about what the system should do by getting the development down to the ground with early prototyping. It has numerous advantages over the conventional waterfall model.

Despite its many advantages, there are also many critics against the agile approach (Bogard, 2012; Harlow, 2014). Rakitin, (2001) criticized the agile approach as an attempt to undermine the discipline of software engineering. The concept of "Working software over comprehensive document" leads to "We want to spend all our time coding. Remember, real programmers don't write documentation." In fact, most programmers do love the code centric style of development. I have come across development teams that carry out a purely code centric style of development while claiming that they use the agile approach.

A similar critique was raised by Gualtieri (Gualtieri, 2011). In his blog, Gualtieri found that "working software as the measure of progress" is narcissistic. Rushing to write code is oft the translation of this misguided principle. Another critique he put forward is related to "business people and developers working together daily". He did not agree that meeting together with the business people every day would get the requirement right. Often business people are not the same as the users. The development team must understand the business and the users. Gualtieri commented that software is not code and development teams are not coders. Great developers must be design and domain experts. He also pointed out that design is essential. One gets what one designs, so one better get the design right.

Moczar (Moczar, 2013) pointed out the following three flaws in agile methodology:

1. "Delivery over quality" recasts the agile principle of "early and continuous delivery" of valuable software. Focusing on continuous delivery has the effect of creating an unmanageable defect backlog.
2. "Development over planning" hits the agile principle of "responding to change over following a plan". This principle encourages poor and irresponsible planning while hiding its effects.
3. "Collaboration over management" with emphasis on self-organizing teams that do the right thing in some sort of group evolutionary manner. While self-organizing agile teams are also self-managing, they are not self-leading. An agile team needs the type of leadership that provides a vision to work towards and motivation for achieving that vision. A strong agile leader, often in the form of a product owner, knows how to motivate a team with a description of an extremely desirable product that is just beyond what the team may think it can do. Freed to pursue that goal and provided with ongoing guidance from a product owner, an agile team can become truly high performing.

Big projects using the agile approach like Universal Credit (Saravanan, 2013) and Surrey Police System (Murphy, 2014) have failed. Experts argued that the agile methodology was not properly adapted in these projects. This leads to the point that it is not at all easy to adapt the agile approach to software development for large projects in large organizations. Kiggundu (Kiggundu, 2014) presented a scenario that the user of an application from the National Health System in the USA is the entire population of the country. It is not possible to adapt to the principles of Agile when there are millions of stakeholders along with their complex interactions at individual, political and organization levels. In the various large organizations I have been involved in, the development teams are spread across different countries. It is not possible to have co-location of a development team in those organizations. In general, the larger the project and organization, the higher the complexity in both managerial and technical aspects. It is much harder for a large project to adapt a new technology than a smaller one. The failure rate is also higher. McKinsey (Blocher, 2012) reported that on average, large IT projects exceeding $15 million run 45 percent over budget and 7 percent over time, while delivering 56 percent less value than predicted.

In the Agile Manifesto 10th Anniversary, Kruchten (Kruchten, 2011) made the following comment:

The agile movement is in some ways a bit like a teenager: very self-conscious, checking constantly its appearance in a mirror, accepting few criticisms, only interested in being with its peers, rejecting en bloc all wisdom from the past, just because it is from the past, adopting fads and new jargon, at times cocky and arrogant. But I have no doubts that it will mature further, become more open to the outside world, be more reflective, and also therefore more effective. I got a hint of what's up for the future at the Snowbird meeting, which produced much more than our side meeting on elephants.

Throughout human history, whenever there was a complete turnover of government through a revolution, the state was in chaos afterwards. I feel that this applies to the software development process being carried out in large organizations. A complete turnover of an established process to software development in a large organization and enforcing the agile approach can easily lead to chaos. I tend to agree with Moczar's idea (Moczar, 2013) as he wrote:

Think of agile as the ability to take the input of all the variable elements of the project—budget, time, design patterns, reusability, customer needs, corporate needs, precedents, standards, technology innovations and limitations—and come up with a pragmatic approach that solves the problem at hand in such a way that the product is delivered properly.

In adapting to the agile approach, we need to change the mindset of developers gradually and introduce various techniques out of the agile methodology that would clearly bring benefits to the overall software development process. One must not undermine the software engineering principles that have evolved after so many years of experience.

Agile Software Architecture

In our modern days, nobody would gather carpenters, electricians, ironworkers, plumbers, masons, etc. and ask them to build a house without proper planning and architectural design. In software development, we still have this trend that programmers are gathered and start developing software without planning and design. A very experienced programmer once told me that they have never needed architecture. The architecture would appear after they build the software. Some developers using the agile approach would also argue that the software architecture would appear after the first few iterations. Software architecture design has been seen by many as a prime example of "big design up front" that is in contrast to general agile practices.

To program a single module for a set of independent functions is not a difficult task. In fact an experience programmer can write a lot of code within a short time. Problems arise when thousands of programs need to collaborate to perform the business functions. In a complex system (like the one illustrated in figure 2), it is almost impossible to keep an overall view of all the modules. Functions of an individual module and the parts it plays in the system are no longer transparent. At the start of the project, one may observe very fast progress. As the system grew, adding new modules into the system would increase its complexity and make the whole situation worse. Maintenance becomes a very difficult task.

Programming a single module for a set of independent functions is not a difficult task. In fact, an experienced programmer can write a lot of code within a short time. Problems arise when thousands of programs need to collaborate to perform the business functions. In a complex system (like the one illustrated in Figure 2), it is almost impossible to have an overall view of all the modules. The functions of an individual module and the part it plays in the system are no longer transparent. At the start of the project, one may observe very quick progress. As the system grows, adding new modules to the system will increase its complexity and make the whole situation worse. Maintenance becomes a very difficult task.

To provide business and IT agility, one must be able to resolve and control the overall complexity of the IT system. Proper software architecture is required (Ali Babar, 2014) . Netherwood states that architecture is important because it (Malan, 2010):

- Controls complexity.
- Enforces best practice.
- Gives consistency and uniformity.
- Communicates skill needs.
- Reduces risk.
- Enables re-use.

Architecture is defined as the rules, heuristics and patterns governing:

- Partitioning the problem and the system to be built into discrete pieces.
- Techniques used to create interfaces between these pieces.
- Techniques to manage overall structure and flow.
- Techniques used to interface the system to its environment.
- Appropriate use of development and delivery approaches, techniques and tools.

Architecture includes the methods, standards, tools, frameworks, policies and management directives. A proper architectural design with its supporting infrastructure is critical to the success of an IT project. The architecture provides a blue print on how software components should be structured and developed as well as the way continuous integration should work. It ensures the agility of the overall system which allows the agile approach to development to be carried out throughout the whole software life cycle with no or few technical debts. It must reduce and not increase the complexity of the IT system. Software tools and standards must simplify the development process and not make it more complicated.

Using the infrastructure of a complex integrated technical architecture requires highly trained and experienced programmers. The Standish Group's research shows that 70% of application code is infrastructure (Johnson & Robinson, 2001). Applications are usually coded by programmers who have great knowledge of the technical structure. They are also responsible for programming the business rules and logic in the applications.

There should be a clear separation of the implementation of the business and technical aspects. Technical infrastructure is generally stable and the same for all applications. We can develop code segments and patterns that can be parameterized according to what is required. Application developers should just concentrate on the business related aspects and include the infrastructure code segments and patterns in their programs whenever needed. The application developers should not have to master the infrastructure. The effort of writing 70% of the infrastructure related application code can also be spared.

HISTORY AND EVOLUTION OF AGILE ARCHITECTURE

In this section, the history and evolution of our agile architecture are presented. The section starts with the history of a project to reengineer a legacy IT system. The agile and model driven development approach is presented in a following subsection.

Reengineering of a Legacy IT System

In 1998, I was engaged in the rebuilding of the legacy IT system of a large corporation. The system had evolved since the 1970s and contained thousands of COBOL programs. The new system should be based on an architecture with CORBA with front and back ends. Java was the programming language for the object oriented style of programming. We started off with some basic applications as prototypes, and programmed and deployed them in work stations. The final code should be ported and deployed in the mainframe host system.

Our prototypes were complicated enough to involve different development groups responsible for different components for both the front and back ends. During the development, we found it very troublesome to keep the interfaces for the remote procedure calls in CORBA in sync between different development groups. Hence we moved from a fixed record remote procedure call style to document style messaging with XML and took a step into component based service oriented architecture (SOA). Each component would extract the required data from the document model and put the output data in the document model when it has completed the processing. In this way, any changes in any component would only need to coordinate with those who are affected but not others, although they may share the same service interface. This was a kind of refactoring process of the architecture during prototyping.

In 2000 our prototypes were ready to be ported to the mainframe host system. The CORBA infrastructure, on the other hand, was not ready. Despite the promises of the vender, we could not deploy our Java programs in the mainframe host system. In addition, we also saw that we could not replace the working system with a big bang. Whatever we developed needed to interoperate with the existing COBOL programs but we were not in a position to do this. The management finally decided that the front end applications with GUI could be used as they were but the back end applications should stay in COBOL.

The back end applications could not be programmed in Java but we wanted to keep our component based SOA architecture. Our first question was if we could use XML since no commercial XML parser was available in 2000. A few of us gathered and tried to develop an XML parser in COBOL. After a few weeks we managed to create our first prototype of an XML parser in COBOL. XML was parsed and transformed into a tree structure via link lists. Within months we managed to put the infrastructure in place so we could program our applications in COBOL in our SOA.

Towards Agile and Model Driven Approach

Despite the use of SOA, application development in COBOL remained a challenge. In late 2003 I was called in to look at the problems from a project. The development for this project had been carried out for one and three quarter years and most of the budget had been used up with no signs of completion. When I inspected the project, I found that there were many COBOL modules and they were all tightly coupled in a fashion, as illustrated in Figure 3. None of the modules could be unit tested on their own. The whole application was driven by a set of control flags. These control flags as well as the state data were passed from one module to another and updated in an uncontrolled way. Nobody had any architecture overview and any change could affect many modules. A developer showed me through the debugger how the state data were changed unexpectedly after calling another module that involved a chain of further actions. He was not able to program his module to produce the expected outcome.

At the beginning of 2004 I took up the technical lead of the project. The task was a real challenge. The goal was to complete the project within five months using the remaining budget. I had the option of fixing the current implementation and tried to make it work. If I made this choice, and even if I could succeed in getting the application to work, it would not be maintainable. Alternatively, I could re-design the whole architecture and start again. The pressure would be very high but I chose to start again.

One thing I realized was that in the COBOL program, a lot of code was just to handle the tree structure of the input and output messages. COBOL programmers did not like the tree structure. They were familiar with the COBOL data structure. My first effort was to come up with an infrastructure to carry out the mapping between the XML and COBOL records. At that time the service message interfaces were very well documented in UML class diagrams by a business analyst. The one responsible for the UML tool said that he could extract the meta data from the UML class diagrams. We made our first prototype of a code generator that was based on the meta data of the UML class diagrams, we generated the XML and

Figure 3. Illustration of tightly coupled COBOL module

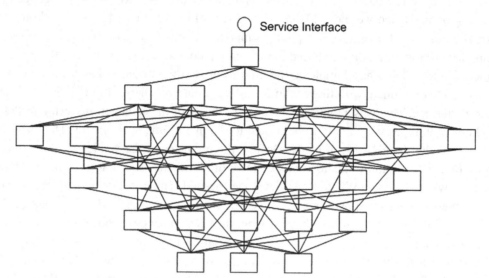

DTD structures, the COBOL copy books which contain the COBOL data records, and the data object descriptors. A data object descriptor is basically a COBOL program that contains meta information for the mapping between the XML and COBOL record structure. A separate COBOL module was developed to carry out the mapping using this data object descriptor. An illustration of the UML class model and the generated software artefacts are shown in Figure 4. The whole set of prototypes were completed within three weeks. It reduced the effort made by all COBOL programmers to handle the incoming and outgoing service messages.

I have always been convinced of the agile approach with an iterative incremental process and continuous integration. The question was how I could put it in to action in the project. If the COBOL programmers were to start coding again the way they had done, we would just end up with the same state as before. We all realized that we must eliminate the strong coupling and interdependencies of the COBOL modules. I had a couple of discussions and brain storming sessions with the project architect and we made the following decisions:

- Process control must be centralized.
- COBOL modules must be independent autonomous units with well-defined contracts to fulfil.
- Apart from an invocation of external services offered by other business components, COBOL modules are not supposed to make direct calls to other COBOL modules.
- A plug and play architecture is required so that a COBOL module can be plugged in at any time for continuous integration.
- All state data will be held in a context container.
- State data in the COBOL structure can be deposited in the context container with a given logical name and it can be retrieved via the logical name.
- Each module will fetch the required state data from the context container and put new or updated state data in the context container.

Figure 4. Class model and software artefacts generation

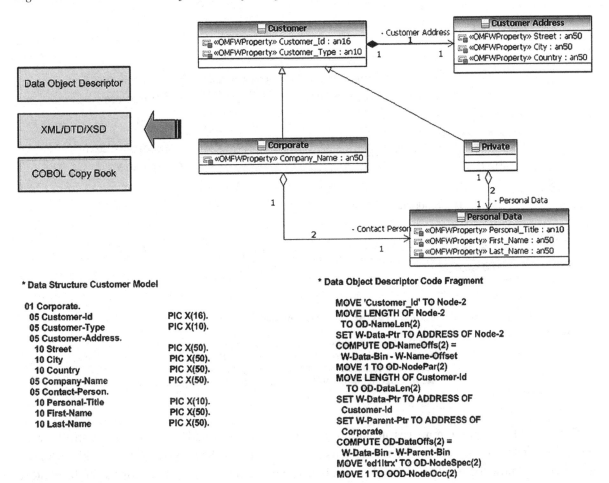

* Data Structure Customer Model

```
01 Corporate.
   05 Customer-Id              PIC X(16).
   05 Customer-Type            PIC X(10).
   05 Customer-Address.
      10 Street                PIC X(50).
      10 City                  PIC X(50).
      10 Country               PIC X(50).
   05 Company-Name            PIC X(50).
   05 Contact-Person.
      10 Personal-Title        PIC X(10).
      10 First-Name            PIC X(50).
      10 Last-Name             PIC X(50).
```

* Data Object Descriptor Code Fragment

```
MOVE 'Customer_Id' TO Node-2
MOVE LENGTH OF Node-2
   TO OD-NameLen(2)
SET W-Data-Ptr TO ADDRESS OF Node-2
COMPUTE OD-NameOffs(2) =
   W-Data-Bin - W-Name-Offset
MOVE 1 TO OD-NodePar(2)
MOVE LENGTH OF Customer-Id
   TO OD-DataLen(2)
SET W-Data-Ptr TO ADDRESS OF
   Customer-Id
SET W-Parent-Ptr TO ADDRESS OF
   Corporate
COMPUTE OD-DataOffs(2) =
   W-Data-Bin - W-Parent-Bin
MOVE 'ed1ltrx' TO OD-NodeSpec(2)
MOVE 1 TO OOD-NodeOcc(2)
```

The same business analyst who modelled the service message interfaces in class diagrams also modelled the process flow in UML state charts. We refined the state charts and made each action a COBOL module. We made some standard code patterns for COBOL modules on how to use the context container, standard error handling and an additional requirement that each module must deliver the outcome of its action with an event.

With the UML state charts, we extract the meta information and generate COBOL modules for centralized control of the process flows. These modules are called process controllers. The process controller is a finite state machine that calls a COBOL module based on an event. Figure 5 illustrates the state chart with a code segment of a process controller. In this figure, the process is a bit simple, as each action results in just one event. In normal cases, actions can result in a number of different events that would branch out into different process flows. A standard flow pattern is used for technical error handling which does not need to be included in the process flow model. If it is a technical error and not a business error, an exception will be raised and the process would terminate with error messages being sent back to the service consumer.

Figure 5. State model and code generation of a process controller

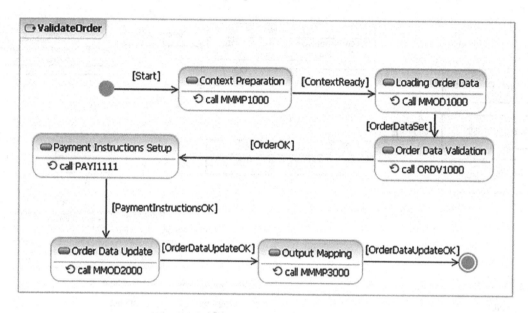

```
* Process Controller Descriptor Code Fragment

MOVE "OrderDataSet" TO  CP-Event(2)
MOVE "Loading Order Data" TO  CP-State(2)
MOVE C-Decision TO  CP-Activity-Name(2)
MOVE "Order Data Validation" TO  CP-Next-State(2)
```

Each module was programmed as an autonomous unit. It was activated by the process controller with the passing of the context container. It retrieved its required data from the context container without knowing where and how these data were made available. The output data would be deposited in the context container. An event would be generated by the module depending on the outcome of its action. In the modelling of the process flow we needed to ensure that each module would find its required data in the context container. For the testing of the flow we could plug in the dummy modules that just generated the events and updated the state data in the context container. These dummy modules could be replaced by real modules successively in our iterative process.

We managed to complete the infrastructure, code patterns and generators within the first month and a half. Application development turned out to be rather straight forward. The whole project was completed within five months using just the remaining budget.

After the success of the first project, we were allowed to use the same approach in a second project. We also extended our tools. First we developed a tool for the unit testing of the COBOL module. The tool contains a COBOL module with the following functions:

- Parses XML input and maps the data to the COBOL structure based on object descriptors.
- Creates the context container and puts the input data in context with a pre-defined logical name.
- Activates the module.
- Fetches the output data structure from the context container and generates XML output based on data object descriptors.

The design of a test tool is illustrated in Figure 6.

The business analysts used to specify each module in WinWord documents. I suggested that they specify the data with UML class diagrams and the flow with activity diagrams to avoid ambiguities. They followed my suggestion. We then found that if we put in enough meta information in these diagrams, we could generate the whole COBOL module. The next stage of our generator included the COBOL module generation based on class and activity diagrams. Figure 7 shows an example of the activity diagram and the generated code. The activity model has the following features:

- Program rules and logic can be modelled in the UML activity diagram.
- Each action in the model can contain code or a link to code pattern with parameters.

Figure 6. COBOL unit test tool architecture

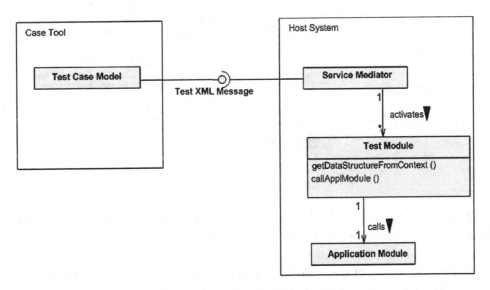

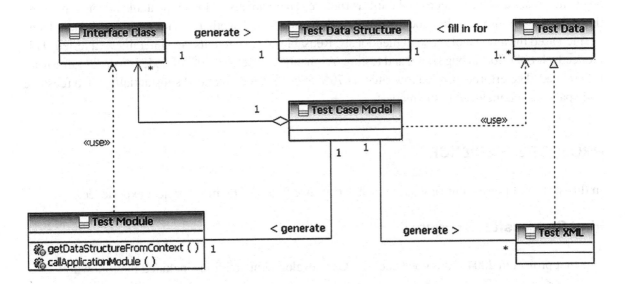

Figure 7. Activity modeling of module logic and code generation

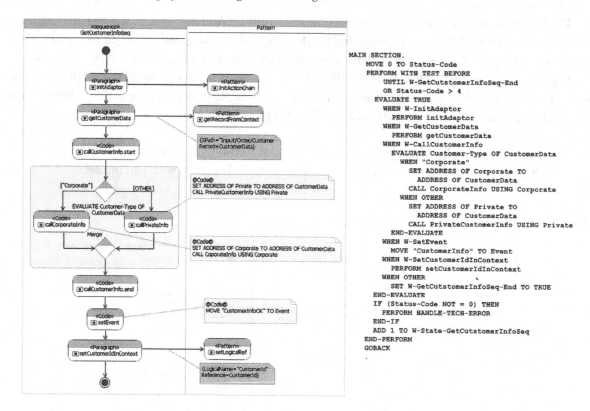

- Different structures are used by the code generator for different actions with different stereotypes.
- Various code templates are also used for the generation of COBOL modules for different purposes.

We found that all usages of the infrastructure can be put into a set of code patterns that can be parameterized. Hence, developers can just use these patterns in the model and set the parameters without any concern about the code behind the infrastructure. There are also a lot a repeatable business patterns that can be built into reusable code patterns with parameters. Together with reusable code templates, we increased the amount of reuse tremendously. Reusable code segments are generally well tested. This reduced a lot of effort in bug fixing and testing. As mentioned before, 70% of code is usually infrastructure related. The effort expended to write this 70% of code can be reduced substantially when reusable code patterns are included in the model.

PROJECT EXPERIENCE

In this section, I present our first successful experience followed by more project experience.

First Successful Experience

Our first project in 2004 was a great success. Our development activities included the following:

- Re-design of the processes.
- Specification of the activities to be realized in modules.
- Development of the context container, code templates and code generators.
- Programming of the modules.
- Final integration and testing.

The first release of the application, including the code generators, was within five months and only the remaining budget was used up. During our development process, we had daily morning coffee meetings that usually lasted around 15 to 20 minutes when we discussed our activities and the issues we faced within the whole team. On the other hand, only I, the project architect and the business analyst who did most of the UML modeling were involved in the design of the new architecture and infrastructures. We had pretty much the same team, except that the former project leader and the technical lead were dismissed.

The business requirement specification was reviewed, signed off and frozen long before I got involved in the project. After the first release and the business users started to experiment with the new application, we had 800 change requests. All change requests were implemented in the same fashion iteratively with specifications and modeling. The application was only in production after all the change requests had been implemented. Again this confirmed that specification is a moving target and one cannot expect to get it all right at the beginning of the development phase.

In our second project, we had the same project architect and business analyst. In this project we extended the code generator to generate COBOL modules from class and activity diagrams. We moved more into modeling instead of coding. The business analyst was very enthusiastic about modeling and code generation. On the other hand, the COBOL programmers were not very excited about the idea. Most of the code they wrote was mainly for code segments in the models. Some were also engaged in creating code patterns and templates. The majority of them did not like the changes from conventional programming to modeling. The project was completed more successfully than the management expected.

Prior to using our development approach and infrastructure, we must allow at least two weeks for a COBOL programmer to complete a module. Programmers used to spend a lot of time figuring out how to do things and how things worked. Testing and debugging also required a lot of effort. With the model driven approach, a great deal of effort was eliminated. To give an example, I once observed that the IBAN (International Bank Account Number) was interpreted with different algorithms in two different modules within an application. The programmer would not have to know the structure of an IBAN when a code pattern to interpret the IBAN was available for modeling. With our approach and framework, a business analyst can work closely with a programmer to complete a module, including testing, within two to three days.

More Project Experience Examples

In one of our projects, there were special requirements on how to display and log errors. We could not use our standard error handling pattern. I joined the project in February and code freeze should have been at the end of June. There were seven different chains of business process flows. At the start we spent a lot of time designing and prototyping the error handling pattern. By the time the first and most simple chain was completed, it had taken almost two months. The majority of the project team claimed that we would take a lot longer to complete the project using our approaches. The project manager turned to me and asked what I thought. I simply said no problem and asked who would pay for the feast when we had finished. The project manager asked me to give him a detailed plan of the development and I simply replied "six chains in three months, one chain per half a month". The project manager was not happy about this. We implemented all the chains by the end of June and the project was completed successfully. Ironically, the requirements specification was completed two weeks before code freeze.

In another project, there was a major change in the business requirement towards its end phase because the whole process flow must be modified with new business rules. We actually made the modifications in our autonomous modules and re-modeled the process descriptor. After we received the specification, we had a new version of the application ready for testing in two days. The agility and able to adapt changes came from our architecture. I do believe that an agile software architecture is important for the agile development process.

Since 2004, we have completed 13 projects using the approach and framework presented in this chapter. All projects were completed on time and within budget. In two projects I experienced we over-ran the budget and time. Both projects rejected the agile approach to software development and insisted on using the waterfall model with heavy documentation.

DEVELOPERS, DEVELOPMENT TEAM, AND MANAGERS

In this section, I show the skill required for a developer using our development approach in the first subsection. In the following subsections I present my experience with development teams and managers.

A Skillful Developer

One of the success factors of the Standish Group is "skilled resources". The question is what skills we need. We certainly need very skillful architects to design the architecture and framework. We also require skillful system programmers to implement the framework and infrastructure. They should build infrastructure related code patterns. However, they should support the application developers but they should not be the main application developers. The application developers are people who can analyze and model the business logic.

In 2005, a lady called Gaby joined our team as a business analyst. She had never written a program before. After a few months she was able to develop applications through modeling independently. In the meantime Gaby picked up some COBOL knowledge which allowed her to write the code segments required in the model and she followed the interactive debugger to debug the applications. After one year Gaby developed 80% of the required programs for a project that would normally need a team of 5 to 6 developers. She usually engaged business analysts and users to go through her models. At one time a COBOL developer claimed that he could develop programs as fast as Gaby modeled them and have them generated. Gaby used her models to discuss with the business analysts and the end users. The programmer, on the other hand, could not show his code to the business analysts and end users in a meeting.

Gaby's skills are:

- Logical thinking and able to analyze problems.
- Able to master abstractions and formulate them into rigorous models.
- Good communication skills and friendly manner.
- Responsible, works independently and committed to the projects.

"Gaby's skill" covers five of the ten Standish Group success factors such as user involvement, agile process, skilled resources, formal methodology and standard tools and infrastructure. The paradigm puts emphasis on business modeling rather than coding. Gaby and her colleagues can test and demonstrate the usability of our architecture and framework.

The idea of Gaby, a non-COBOL developer who managed to develop 80% of all the COBOL programs has not been well accepted. Even an expert in model driven architecture commented that the idea of Gaby doing the job of an experienced COBOL programmer was not acceptable. If I say my son, who does not know anything about HTML and Java Script can develop flashy websites and blogs with Tumblr (2014), I wonder if this software expert would also dismiss the idea.

The mindsets of many software experts are that application development requires in depth knowledge of the system infrastructure and programming language. In the project to port all the COBOL applications from the IBM z/OS system to the UNIX platform I reported previously, they recruited application programmers who had in depth knowledge of Eclipse plugins. Does this mean that one needs to go deep into Eclipse plugins in order to program business logic?

It is still a common practice to mingle business logic with infrastructure related logic. Back in the late '90s, aspect-oriented programming (AOP) (Kiczales et al., 1997) was evolved to tackle this problem. AOP is a programming paradigm that aims to increase modularity by allowing the separation of cross-cutting concerns. It includes programming methods and tools that support the modularization of concerns at the level of the source code. The programming approach entails breaking down program logic into distinct parts, so-called concerns, which are cohesive areas of functionality. Some concerns "cut across" multiple parts in a program, and defy these forms of implementation. AOP implementations use cross-cutting expressions known as aspects that encapsulate each concern in one place. Tools are provided so that such expressions can be implemented in separate classes or modules. The technique allows us to separate business logic related code from infrastructure related code. Code that deals with infrastructure can be implemented as aspects to be included in the programs as expressions. In our modeling approach, the templates and patterns provide a mechanism similar to AOP. Patterns that can be parameterized are dragged into the application models. During code generation, the code segments of these patterns would be included in the final programs.

Social network platforms like (Ning, 2014) offer customers the ability to create a community website and blogs with a customized appearance and feel. In general users have no programming knowledge or experience. In most large corporations, application programming still adheres to the traditional approach with requirements specifications done by the analysts and implementation being done by programmers. There can be a lot of tools to support the different phases of SDLC such as those for requirement specifications and coding. Tools with very high levels of abstractions in any form that enable skillful analysts like Gaby to formulate the business logic and generate programs are usually not available. With our experience, we can build such tools. They can be very useful for fast prototyping in an agile development process. Developers in general are rather skeptical about such tools. General acceptance is rather difficult to achieve.

Development Team

In most large corporations, there are strong hierarchies among the employees according to their job functions. For application development, different groups are involved as shown in figure 8. The groups are described in the following list:

Figure 8. Example of groups involved in application development in a corporation

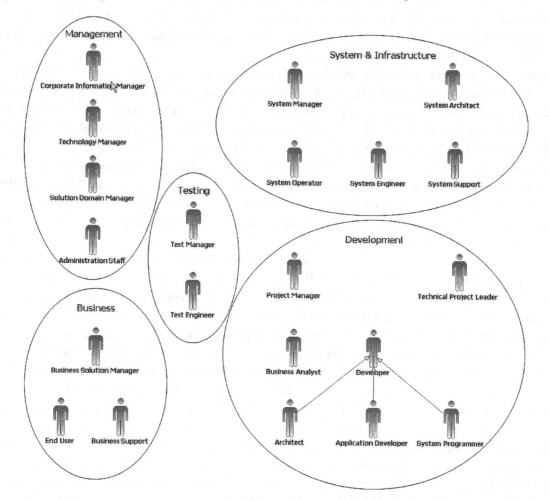

- **Management Group:** This group includes the different kinds of managers and administrative staffs. The responsibility of this group entails many of the basic management functions, like budgeting, staffing, change management, and organizing and controlling.
- **Business Group:** Proposals for new project or new features of existing applications are generally put forward by this group. They are also responsible for the functional specifications, final testing and acceptance of the applications. For some applications like E-Banking, end users are mostly clients of the corporation. End users for applications like the ones for teller in a bank are those who work in the counters. There are usually thousands of them. For these applications, developers do not have much direct interactions with the end users. Usually business solution managers or business support staffs act as user representatives. They write the business specifications, interact with developers, test the end products and carry out the acceptance process. Business solution managers or solution domain managers are usually stakeholders of application development projects.
- **System and Infrastructure Group:** This group is responsible for IT infrastructure that includes the composite hardware, software, network resources and services required for the existence, operation and management of the enterprise IT environment. To this group, system stability is one

of the most important aspects. Thus any new and change requests to this group would take a long time to be put into place. If any new system setup is required in an application, the development team should make the request at the early stage of the development cycle.

- **Testing Group:** The testing group verifies that the software complies with the functional specification. The group ensures that quality is built into the applications. Test engineers need to come up with test cases according to the business specification. In many companies, testing groups are parts of the development groups. In large corporations, testing groups are often separate groups. They work closely with the application developers. They should be involved in development projects at early stage.

- **Development Group:** The development group is responsible to the delivery of the applications. For a project, we usually have a project manager or project leader. Often there is also a technical project leader (also referred to as lead programmer). The technical project leader would mainly be responsible to the technology, development process, methodology, etc. to be used in the development. Often the architect is also the technical project leader. Architect is also a kind of developer. Following the concept described in the previous subsection, I make a distinction between system programmer and application developer. System programmers are responsible for the implementation of the framework and infrastructure. Application developers are the ones who analyze, model and program the business logic.

My former manager used to say that I always chose the same people for the development team in my projects. Indeed I did not want to work with others when I could have my dream team to do the job. Our dream team was self-organized and extremely efficient. The development would make such fast progress that we could meet extremely tight time schedules. The problem was that I could not have my dream team all the time.

I was regularly called to help out with projects that were in trouble. There were projects that were way behind schedule and I was asked to help them deliver the product on time. One of these projects had the problem that a team had been working on the project for a year. The plan was to have code freeze and be ready for production testing within four months. The development team claimed that it was an impossible task. My manager asked me to take over the project leadership and to make it possible. What was the reaction of the team when a new project leader came with a new approach and tools for development? How would they respond when the new project leader tried to establish a goal that the rest of the team was convinced was not possible? In one of my first meetings with the team members, a tall lady yelled at me so loud that many people came in to the meeting room to see what was happening. They were afraid that the lady would throw me out of the window. It was hard. I faced resistance from almost every team member. I had to model with the analysts and programmed the various code segments and patterns with the programmers side by side. After a month we started to make rapid progress and most of the team members, but not all of them, were convinced about the approach. The lady who had yelled at me actually became a very good colleague and she was very efficient. The team started to organize itself.

On another occasion a colleague suggested I should take up the technical leadership of a project she was working on. The project had started two years prior and had not made much progress. I joined the project in January and the code freeze should have been in June. Our approach was made known to the team through my colleague. When I joined the project and insisted on the development approach, there was a split between the team members. Three of them were absolutely against it, they even insulted others who agreed with me. It was a terrible atmosphere with a constant escalation of the situation. One of them even went as far as to sabotage the project in order to prove that we were on the wrong track. Being supported by the higher management, we managed to get rid of two of them at a later stage. We were only able to work harmoniously for two months.

I joined a relatively big project in November 2006. The goal was to deliver the first version of the product in June 2007. In the first two months we had a meeting every two weeks to discuss what should be developed. In January 2007 I went to the project manager and told him that we could not carry on the way we were working. He said that I could not fit into the team and my reply was that he was correct. If I did fit in, all my projects would drag on and never meet their deadlines. He dismissed me from the project. The project did not meet the deadline and the first release was changed to May 2008. At the time when the project was about to complete the coding, the financial crisis arrived. The management ended all projects and changed the IT strategy over night. The project was never completed. During that time, I was lucky to be involved with another project that was completed just before the financial crisis.

Recently I had a conversation with a course leader of agile development and scrum. She emphasized that a self-organized team is essential to agile development. She told me that I should have tried to get the buy in from all team members regarding my approach before starting the project. When I had my dream team together, I did not have any problems with this. In many other projects, I do not think that I would get too far by trying to get buy in from all the team members. My experience was that some would start to get enthusiastic about the development approach. This happened with a number of analysts who realized that modeling was not a difficult task and that the implementations would come directly from models. Many of them would just get along as we proved that the technique worked. Some of these would still be convinced that the approach was not a proper development process, while others did not want to have anything to do with our approach at all.

Management

In 2004, we were given a chance to carry out our first project by the management under great pressure. After our first success we were allowed to continue with more projects. Between 2006 and 2008 we had very strong support from senior management. Some senior managers would like to make our approach a strategy for the whole corporation and support us to develop it further. In fact, if we had not received such strong support, some of our projects would never have worked out because of the resistance we faced.

Everything changed when the financial crisis arrived as many senior managers left the company. Also, numerous developers were laid off or they left the company themselves. There were only a couple of us left behind. Our approach was greatly criticized by some senior developers and software architects. They claimed that our architecture and tools were proprietary and home grown. The new management was not happy about the decisions that were made by the former senior managers. While 13 key applications are based on our architecture and modeling tools, we are still needed to maintain these projects. The current management is upset that our know-how is still needed. We can still use our approach for the extension and maintenance of our applications but our approach is forbidden for any new development. Proprietary and home grown tools are still developed in the company and they are geared towards the traditional style of SDLC.

In one of the business domains in the company, applications have all been developed using our approach and tools. A few of us are required to do the maintenance and provide user support for this business domain. In another similar business domain with applications of the same nature and complexity developed with traditional SDLC, their group is three times as big. There was a time when we needed to make our applications available in a global international environment and the other group had to expand to 90 analysts and developers. There were huge problems which received lots of attention from the management. They received great complements and acknowledgement from the management when they solved the problems. In our group, we took up the job without too many problems. The job was done as usual and business ran the way it should. We did not receive any attention from the management nor was our effort acknowledged.

OVERALL EXPERIENCE AND LESSONS LEARNT

In this section, I present the acceptance, positive and negative experience of using our development approach. The section is completed with a subsection on lessons learnt.

Acceptance Experience

From our experience, we have the following statistics:

- Programmers:
  - 70% rejected the development approach.
  - 20% accepted the development approach.
  - 10% are excited about the development approach.
- Business analysts:
  - 40% learned the modelling techniques and have generated code with the help of programmers (number of analysts like Gaby who had no prior programming experience managed up to 70% of the development work on an application).
  - 60% still prefer to write documents.
- Software architects:
  - Those who had been involved are excited about the development approach and techniques.
  - All architects from other projects resisted trying the development approach and techniques.
- Managers:
  - Managers who experienced success in their projects would fully support the development approach.
  - Managers who do not have personal experience usually do not support the development approach being used.

Positive Experience

The most positive experience we had was our technical achievement. This can be summarized in the following list:

- Provided an agile architecture with a plug and play mechanism for modules and continuous integration.
- Standardized code style and structure and enhanced code quality (e.g. standard error handling).
- Focused on business logic rather than infrastructure and the interactions of different modules.

- Maximized reuse with patterns, templates and modules.
- Architect and analyst driven instead of an ad hoc style of development.
- Models that reflect current implementation are used as documents as well as a means of communication.
- Reduced redundancies with an observable improvement in performance (e.g. resources are loaded into the context once and are used by multiple modules; a kind of caching).
- Reduced development effort by factors and enhanced software maintainability.
- Agile software development with rapid prototyping.

As presented in the above list, one of our achievements was the improvement in the performance of our applications. One would expect that programs with generated code are less efficient. Our experience has been that the generated code does not reduce performance by any noticeable figure. Our architecture, on the other hand, has helped to improve performance. In one of the projects I was involved in, we needed to improve the performance of an existing application. The developers tried to optimize the SQL statements they used in the programs. When I looked at the performance figures, DB access only took 10% of the overall transaction CPU time. Even if we reduce this time by 50%, the overall performance would only be improved by 5%. I found that the major issues of performance problems were the repetitions of fetching resources and data during the transaction. When a module requires client information, financial instruments, etc., the module was programmed to activate the responsible components to fetch these data. With the introduction of the context container, we limited the activation of components for common resources to once. The performance was improved by 35%.

Negative Experience

The major critiques we have faced are as follows:

- Proprietary home grown modelling technique and code generators.
- Domain specific language (DSL) rather than universal standard approach.
- Special skills and mindsets required that do not fit the skill sets and experience of programmers.

There has been strong resistance to our approach from developers. Some senior developers consider that modeling with code generation is fundamentally a wrong approach. The architectural model with centralized process control and the separation of business rules from infrastructure has been considered unnatural to many developers. It is very difficult to convince the project team members to follow our approach. The "not invented here and not applicable in our projects" phenomenon stops the spreading of the development approach across IT groups. A common remark of developers is: "the paradigm works for their cases but not for our cases because our problems are far more complicated". The question remains how they would tackle the complexity of their problems.

When the financial crisis arrived in 2008, many developers involved in the application development using our approach left the company. Since then a number of new developers have joined to maintain the applications. Most of them have no experience with the concepts of agile and MDSD (Model Driven Software Development). We observed that programmers made modifications directly in the code without updating the models. They also created nested modules without models or integration in the process controller. This started to get quite messy in a lot of applications. With the lack of management support, it is difficult to maintain the standard and rules of our development approach.

Our Findings

The best practices in our experience include the following:

- Autonomous components and modules are easy to develop and maintain.
- Architecture that allows the plug and play of components with continuous integration is essential to the agile development process for enterprise applications.
- Modelling with code generation provides great benefits in application development:
  - Enhance communication and resolving of problems.
  - Provide useful documents and enhance understanding of implementation.
  - Maximize reuse.
  - Reduce effort in development and maintenance.
  - Improve code quality, adhesion to architecture and integration of standards.
  - Use and reuse of patterns, templates, modules, models have a great impact on new application development (e.g. reduce finding how-to processes).
- The agile development approach can eliminate lengthy requirements specification as well as speed up decision-making and requirement verification.
- The development approach must have management support and form part of the development strategy.

FUTURE RESEARCH DIRECTIONS

Although further development of our tools and modeling technique officially ended due to the financial crisis, I have continued with the research and prototyping of more advanced techniques. One thing I have observed is that the business processes of different business domains within a large corporation tend to have very similar patterns. For example, all payment and trading transactions in a financial institute require the retrieval of client and account information, availability and credit checks, the generation of client position movement, debit or/and credit of accounts, booking of the transaction in the general ledger, etc. There have been various activities to come up with standards for business applications by organizations such as OMG stated in Business Architecture, 2010. A research direction is to come up with standard model templates for the high level abstractions of business applications. They are used to construct rigorous business process model patterns. These model patterns can be tailored to different infrastructures and business components by providing the code segments and wrappers. Programs can then be generated from these models. Thus, we can have standard models for business processes that can be used for different business domains.

The business of an enterprise does not usually change. On the other hand, the applications must constantly be adjusted to the new regulations and products. Most of these changes are related to business rules. A new product usually just resembles the characteristics of old products with new flows. I found that a good tool for the maintenance and extensions of applications is a rule based engine that collaborates with existing software components and low level modules. Another potential big change is to migrate legacy applications to a new platform. A big bang approach to migrate all legacy applications to a new platform in one go is rather risky. A graduate migration would require interoperations between software components in the new platform and software components in the legacy platform. Out of personal interest, I am building a framework with a cross platform architecture. The framework contains the following features:

- A cross platform architecture which utilizes SOA, enterprise service bus (ESB), agent technology, and service integration is being designed.
- Uses rule based engines in both decentralized and host systems to tackle the fast evolution and changes in business rules.
- Process flow is driven by a combination of business rules and the state data within the context controlled by the rule based engine.
- Allow dynamic business rules, services and process flows composition based on meta-data that can be interpreted by rule based engines.

The concept of the architectural framework utilizing an ESB for application integration is illustrated in Figure 9. It has the following characteristics:

- The service bus is used for the integration of different enterprise applications.
- The legacy host system can provide services for its existing applications.
- The Central Intelligent Agent controls the business process and distributes the data processing to different software components in different platforms.
- Integration of Web service, mobile systems, community and social network systems, host systems and external systems in the cloud.

I have also enhanced the modeling technique with the following features:

- Models for code generation are platform and language independent.
- Formalize domain specific models for business rules, process flow and services with the generation of meta-data to be interpreted by rule based engines.

Prototypes have been built for the rule based engines in Java and COBOL, as well as the code generator for Java. The activities are ongoing.

CONCLUSION

In this chapter I have reported my many years of experience in software development, particularly the last ten years of using the agile and model driven approach. My first project of maintaining a large package of code with no documentation gave me the experience of a software crisis. Later on I had the opposite experience, with heavy documents resulting in a traditional waterfall approach to software development. In my opinion, these approaches have major flaws. My best experience is with the agile and the model driven approach. Agile coupled with MDSD allows us to put forward an iterative and

Figure 9. Design of a cross platform architecture

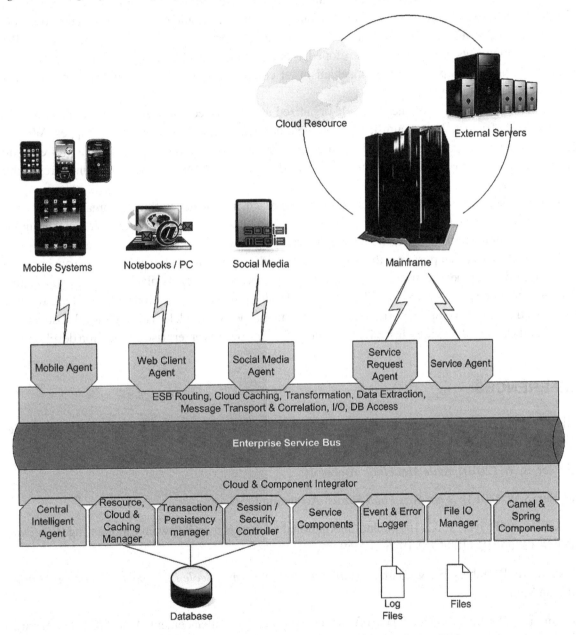

incremental development process with fast delivery of useful software and continuous integration. It eliminates the heavy documents but provides useful documentation through models. Programming can also start at the earlier stage parallel to requirements specification. The approach has been applied to 13 projects that were all completed successfully, on time and within budget.

The software architecture and the modeling framework with code generation tools have been the main contributors to our success. In my opinion, particularly for enterprise applications, the design of the software architecture is crucial to ensure the agile approach can be applied throughout the whole development life cycle. The software architecture should provide a foundation for the fast development of individual software components and continuous integration. It should ensure changes and extensions can be made relatively easily. We designed a software architecture with a central process controller. Software components or modules are developed as autonomous units that can be unit tested. The architecture also provides a plug and play mechanism for components and modules. It makes changes and extensions rather straight forward tasks.

The agile manifesto recommends a self-organized and motivated team. A dream team can be very effective and efficient. The circumstances, on the other hand, may not permit this to happen. We cannot rely on a dream team or even the buy in of the team members to our approach, as a pre-requisite. In some cases, we must persist with the way we work even though there is great resistance from other team members.

Despite the track records of projects using our approach, acceptance within our organization is only moderate. We face a lot of resistance from experienced architects and programmers. We had the support of management to start off; but as the management changed with time, the support disappeared.

Despite the lack of support from the management, I will continue to explore and improve our approach to software development. Currently I am building a prototype for a cross platform architecture which utilizes SOA, enterprise service bus (ESB), agent technology, service integration and a rule based engine. I am also trying to develop platform independent domain specific models with high level abstractions. Together they should provide a fast, effective and agile way towards enterprise application development.

REFERENCES

Ali Babar, M., Brown, A. W., & Mistrik, I. (2014). Agile Software Architecture. *Communication Design Quarterly Review*, *2*(2), 43–47. doi:10.1145/2597469.2597477

Ambler, S. W. (2010). *Agile Modeling*. Ambisoft.

Ambler, S.W. (2013). *What Was Final Status*. Academic Press.

Bell, T. E., & Thayer, T. A. (1976). 2nd International Conference on Software Engineering. *Computer*, *9*(8), 9–12. doi:10.1109/C-M.1976.218669

Blocher, M., Blumberg, S., & Laartz, J. (2012). *Delivering Large-Scale IT Projects on Time, on Budget. And on Value.*

Boehm, B. (1986). A spiral model of software development and enhancement. *ACM SIGSOFT Software Engineering Notes, ACM*, *11*(4), 22–42. doi:10.1145/12944.12948

Boehm, B. W. (1988). A spiral model of software development and enhancement. *Computer*, *21*(5), 61–72. doi:10.1109/2.59

Bogard, J. (2012). Why I'm done with Scrum. In Combining Kanban and Scrum -- Lessons from a Team of Sysadmins (pp. 99–102). LosTechieshoughtWorks.

Cockburn, A., & Highsmith, J. (2001). Agile software development, the people factor. *Computer*, *34*(11), 131–133. doi:10.1109/2.963450

Collier, M. J. (2009). CHAOS Summary 2009, The Standish Group. *Negotiation and Conflict Management Research, 2*(3), 285–306. doi:10.1111/j.1750-4716.2009.00041.x

Gualtieri, M. (2011). Agile Software is A Cop-Out; Here's What's Next. *Forrester, 36*(6), 529–531. doi:10.1097/SHK.0b013e318239235a

Harlow, M. (2014). Molecular biology: RNA retrieved from intact tissue. *Nature, 505*(7483), 264. doi:10.1038/505264d

Hartmann Preuss, D. (2006). Interview: Jim Johnson of Standish Group. *Info, Q*(289), 253. doi:10.2307/20632978

Jackson, M. (2010). Engineering and Software Engineering. Academic Press.

Johnson, J., Boucher, K. D., Connors, K., & Robinson, J. (2001). *Collaborating on Project Success.* SOFTWAREMAG.

Kiczales, G., Lamping, J., Mendhekar, A., Maeda, C., Videira Lopes, C., Loingtier, J., & Irwin, J. (1997). *Aspect-Oriented Programming.* Paper presented at the European Conference on Object-Oriented Programming ECOOP'97, Berlin, Germany. doi:10.1007/BFb0053381

Kiggundu, A. (2014). Agile – Theory vs. Practice. ThoughtWorks. *Nature, 505*(7483), 264. doi:10.1038/505264d

Krigsman, M. (2006). *Management of Critical Success Factors.* ZDNet.

Kruchten, P. B. (2011). Agile's Teenage Crisis. *InfoQ, 10*(4), 363–364. doi:10.1080/15332691.2011.6 13313

Larman, C. (2003). *Agile and Iterative Development: A Manager's Guide.* Routledge.

Malan, R., & Bredemeyer, D. (2010). Software Architecture and Related Concerns. *Resources for Software Architects, 6285,* 352–359.

McGovern, J., Ambler, S. W., Stevens, M. E., Linn, J., Sharan, V., & Jo, E. K. (2003). A Practical Guide To Enterprise Architecture. Upper Saddle River. *Business Communication Quarterly, 66*(1), 108–111. doi:10.1177/108056990306600116

Moczar, L. (2013). *Why Agile Isn't Working: Bringing Common Sense To Agile Principles.* Academic Press.

Murphy, M. (2014). Agile Project Failure kills £15m Surrey Police System. *Computerworld UK, 283.* doi:10.1163/9789004266827_013

Ning. (2014). . *BMJ (Clinical research ed.), 348,* g1585. doi: 10.1136/bmj.g1585

Pang, C. Y. (2012). *Improve Business Agility of Legacy IT System.* Paper presented at the Information Systems Reengineering for Modern Business Systems: ERP, SCM, CRM, E-Commerce Management Solutions, Hershey, PA.

Rakitin, S. R. (2001). *Manifesto Elicits Cynicism: Reader's Letter to the Editor.* Paper presented at the IEEE.

Royce, W. (1970). *Managing the Development of Large Software Systems.* Paper presented at the IEEE WESON.

Saravanan, G. (2013). Why Software Engineering Fails! (Most of the Time). *Software Engineering Notes, 38*(6), 1–4. doi:10.1145/2532780.2532802

Software Crisis. (2010). In *Wikipedia.* Retrieved July 26, 2010, from http://en.wikipedia.org/wiki/Software_crisis

Wegner, P. (1989). Concepts and Paradigms of Object-Oriented Programming. Academic Press.

ADDITIONAL READING

Agile Manifesto Group. (2001). Manifesto for Agile Software Development. *Agile Manifesto.* http://agilemanifesto.org

Ali Babar, M., Brown, A. W., & Mistrik, I. (2014). *Agile Software Architecture.* Waltham, MA: Morgan Kaufmann.

Ambler, S. W. (2010). Agile Modeling. *Ambysoft.* Retrieved July 26, 2010, from http://www.agilemodeling.com/

Arlow, J., & Neustadt, I. (2004). *Enterprise Patterns and MDA: Building Better Software with Archetype Patterns and UML.* Reading, MA: Addison-Wesley.

Bass, L., Clements, P., & Kazman, R. (2003). *Software Architecture in Practice* (2nd ed.). Reading, MA: Addison-Wesley.

Coplien, J., & Bjornvig, G. (2010). *Lean Architecture for Agile Software Development.* West Sussex, UK: John Wiley & Son.

Erl, T. (2008). *SOA Principle of Service Design.* Upper Saddle River, NJ: Prentice Hall PTR.

Erl, T. (2009). *SOA Design Patterns.* Upper Saddle River, NJ: Prentice Hall PTR.

Fowler, M. (1997). *Analysis Patterns: Reusable Object Models.* Reading, MA: Addison-Wesley.

Fowler, M. (1997). *Patterns of Enterprise Application Architecture.* Reading, MA: Addison-Wesley.

Gamma, E., Helm, R., Johnson, R., & Vlissides, L. (1995). *Design Patterns: Elements of Reusable Object-Oriented Software.* Reading, MA: Addison-Wesley.

Garland, J., & Anthony, R. (2003). *Large-Scale Software Architecture: A Practical Guide using UML.* West Sussex, UK: John Wiley & Son.

Hohpe, G., & Woolfe, B. (2004). *Enterprise Integration Patterns: Designing, Building, and Deploying Messaging Solutions.* Reading, MA: Addison-Wesley.

Hunt, J. (2006). *Agile Software Construct.* London, UK: Springer.

Larman, C. (2003). *Agile and Iterative Development: A Manager's Guide.* Reading, MA: Addison-Wesley.

McGovern, J., Ambler, S. W., Stevens, M. E., Linn, J., Sharan, V., & Jo, E. K. (2003). *A Practical Guide To Enterprise Architecture.* Upper Saddle River, NJ: Prentice Hall PTR.

Mellor, S. J., Scott, K., Uhl, A., & Weise, D. (2004). *MDA Distilled: Principles of Model-Driven Architecture.* Reading, MA: Addison-Wesley.

Reengineering Center. (1995). *Perspectives on Legacy System Reengineering.* Software Engineering Institute, Carnegie Mellon University.

Roshen, W. (2009). *SOA-Based Enterprise Integration.* New York, NY: McGraw-Hill.

SDLC. (2013). Software Development Life Cycle. *SDLC.* Retrieved December 11, 2014, from http://www.sdlc.ws/

Systems Reengineering Patterns. (2000). Systems Reengineering Patterns. *Heriot-Watt University.* Retrieved July 26, 2010, from http://www.reengineering.ed.ac.uk/

KEY TERMS AND DEFINITIONS

Agile Software Architecture: A software architecture that lays out blue prints of the organization and structure of software components as well as well defined mechanism on how components can be tested and integrated into the system that would sustain the agile approach through out the software development life cycle.

Agile Software Development Process: An evolutionary and iterative approach to software development with focuses on adaptation to changes.

COBOL: The programming language designed for commercial business data processing used for applications that often form the backbone of the IT structure in many corporations since 1960.

Domain Specific Language DSL: Extension of UML with additional properties according to the stereotypes assigned to modeling elements to capture semantics required for COBOL code generation.

Enterprise Service Bus (ESB): A software architecture model used for designing and implementing the interaction and communication between mutually interacting software applications in service oriented architecture (SOA).

Intelligent Agent: An autonomous entity which acts upon the circumstances and direct its activities towards achieving goals.

Legacy Integration: The integration and Web extension of existing (legacy) systems, especially mission-critical mainframe systems, in order to leverage existing IT assets.

Mainframe: Mainframe computer systems like IBM z/OS.

Model Driven Software Development (MDSD): A model centric rather than a code centric approach to software development with code generated from models.

Re-Engineering Legacy Enterprise IT System: Integrating legacy enterprise IT system that is difficult to maintain and enhance into a new architecture which allows modification and evolution to meet new and constantly changing business requirements.

Service Oriented Architecture (SOA): A technical software architecture that allows client applications to request services from service provider type applications in a host system.

Software Component: A software unit of functionality that manages a single abstraction.

Software Crisis: A term used in the early days when software projects were notoriously behind schedule and over budget and maintenance costs were exploding.

Software Development Life Cycle (SDLC): The process, methods or a set of methodologies applied to create or alter software projects.

Waterfall Model: A sequential design, used in software development processes, in which progress is seen as flowing steadily downwards (like a waterfall) through the phases of Conception, Initiation, Analysis, Design, Construction, Testing, Deployment and Maintenance.

Chapter 5
Rapid Agile Transformation at a Large IT Organization

Pan-Wei Ng
Ivar Jacobson International, Singapore

ABSTRACT

This chapter describes the agile transformation of an IT organization in China with about 4000 people including contractors. In the span of one year, 47 teams and 1700 engineers moved from traditional to agile way of working. There was a 44% reduction in development lead-time, 5% reduction in production defects and 22% reduction in production incidents. This agile transformation occurred at two levels. At the organization level, adoption speed was crucial, as we wanted to reach critical mass in rapid time with limited coaching resources. This was very much an entrepreneur startup problem, where customers in our case are teams and members in the IT organization. At the team level, a practice architecture provided a roadmap for continuous improvement. A theory-based-software-engineering approach facilitated deeper learning. Beyond the usual factors for leading successful change, this transformation exemplified the use of a startup mentality, social networks, practice architecture, simulation, gamification, and more importantly integrating theory and practice.

1. INTRODUCTION

Today, agile development has "crossed the chasm" and became mainstream (Maurer & Melnik, 2007). Many organizations have adopted agile development (Vijayasarathy & Turk, 2008). However, failures to agile adoption are not uncommon and the ride towards agility can be bumpy (McAvoy & Butler, 2009). Regardless, the industry is now seeking new frontiers towards agile development. For example, teams are extending agile principles to IT operations in the form of DevOps (Spinellis, 2012), and to novel product development in the form of Lean Startup(Ries, 2011). Still, there are others who want to be successful not only in small development, but also in large development, such as using Large Scale Scrum (LeSS)(Larman & Vodde, 2013), Scaled Agile Framework (SAFe) (Leffingwell, 2010)and Disciplined Agile Delivery (DAD)(Ambler & Lines, 2012). Many authors and organizations have shared their experiences in large-scale agile development. Babinet and Ramanathan shared their experiences

DOI: 10.4018/978-1-4666-9858-1.ch005

with dependency management in salesforce.com(Babinet & Ramanathan, 2008). Read and Briggs shared their experiences with large-scale agile design(Read & Briggs, 2012). Paasivaara and Lassenius shared experiences with scaling Scrum to large distributed development, with specific emphasis on the product owner role(Paasivaara & Lassenius, 2011). Fitzgerald et. al studied scaling agile methods to regulated environments in an industry setting(Fitzgerald, Stol, O'Sullivan, & O'Brien, 2013). However, there is little literature discuss how to effectively, systematically and rapidly enable a large organization to transform to an agile development, which is the emphasis of this chapter.

In this chapter, we highlight the enabling approaches that helped an IT organization of 4000 people including contractors transform from a traditional way of working into an agile one that is responsive to business needs. The author was the lead coach and advisor to this transformation. Our work with this IT organization occurred at two levels, organization and team.

At the organization level, it is really a change management process. A number of works exist on leading such changes including Kotter's 8 step process for leading change(Kotter, 1995), Prochaska's stages of change, (Prochaska et al., 1994) Lewin's three steps to organization change (Lewin, 1989) and Gleicher's formula for change(Dannemiller & Jacobs, 1992). However, our experience is that an organization was not a monolithic entity, but a complex network of social entities, where each entity can influence another. An agile transformation endeavor is then about systematically propagating change (i.e. the message and spirit of agility) across the organization to different entities (i.e. teams), often across organizational silos. Even though the IT organization in our case study had a top-down culture, a top-down directive would not work in the long run, but instead would kill the spirit of agility and innovation. Thus, agile transformation is about seeking out teams who would embark on the agile transformation journey with us and help us spread the message. This in effect is very much like a startup company. Blank (Blank, 2013)stated that a startup is a company designed for rapid search to find a scalable and repeatable business model. In the same way, we are rapidly searching for a way to scale the agile transformation across the organization to all teams. This involves not only organization changes such as removing silos, but also community activities to spread various teams' successes.

At the team level, it is about how interested teams could become agile. The challenge here is about introducing the right set of practices to achieve quick wins given their context, their current limited lack of understanding of agile methods and their limited resource. These practices can be familiar ones like Scrum(Schwaber, 1997), continuous integration(Duvall, Matyas, & Glover, 2007), automated testing(Gamma & Beck, 2006), agile requirements(Leffingwell, 2010), etc. or something novel that emerged when engaging the teams in their daily work. Regardless, practices have to be contextualized and supported by sound theoretical and empirical basis. Our previous work on Theory Based Software Engineering (TBSE) (Jacobson, Ng, McMahon, Spence, & Lidman, 2013) plays an important role in linking context, practice and theory within a practice framework. This practice framework is crucial because it evolved into the organization's knowledge of how to conduct software development in the future.

The goal of this chapter is to present our experiences, the lessons learnt and the strategy that emerged as we engaged with the leaders and teams of the IT organization. We organize this chapter as follows. Section 2 describes the agile transformation case study and the events that occurred as well as the results. Section 3 describes our approach and strategy at the organization level, which involved many aspects of change management such as executive support, changing internal processes, establishing communities, rewards, etc. We adopt and agile approach to agile transformation and created a minimum viable "product" to get quick wins and traction. Section 4 describes our approach and strategy at the team level. Central to our approach here was the use of TBSE to rapidly capture practices with supporting theories to evolve a practice architecture, a knowledge-base per se. to harvest and spread the use of agile practices across different teams in the IT organization. Section 5 discusses the lessons learnt and evaluates the generality our approach. Finally Section 6 concludes our findings and future work.

2. THE AGILE TRANSFORMATION JOURNEY

Our case study involved a large IT organization of 4000 people, which served the in-house needs of its 140,000 strong parent company, which we will henceforth call Company X. The IT organization develops products for internal use. Product development teams ranged from 5 to 200 people depending on the size and complexity of the products. There were many integration points between these products. Some were developed in-house, some evolved from off-the-shelf packaged software. There were web-based products, as well as mobile products. External contractors performed most of the actual development work. Contractor cohorts had a relatively high turnover rate, in extreme cases ranging about 30% per year. Project managers were relatively young but hardworking.

Company X was rapidly expanding into new markets and enlarging their product offerings. Naturally, their supporting IT systems were complex and development schedules were tight. Business users were not satisfied with the IT products. They were not easy to use. For example, some user-interface forms have had many inputs and were not responsive. Enhancements and changes took a long time to be delivered. Even though the IT organization delivered releases every 3 months, the development lead-time from requirements agreement with business users to delivery took about 5 months.

The adoption of agile methods is a kind of management innovation. Accordingly, we can attempt to understand the nature of the IT organization's agile transformation journey through the innovation diffusion curve (P.-W. Ng, 2014) as shown see Figure 1.

In reality, the IT organization did progress through the phases in the innovation diffusion curve, which we describe below.

Phase 0: *Pre-Agile Exploration.* The IT organization executives were seeking a way to overcome their challenges and saw the benefits of agile development. However, not everyone was on board at the beginning. Several product teams explored using agile development such as using Scrum at a small scale on their own. Since the organization has a whole was still operating under legacy waterfall processes, team level improvements could not propagate beyond their limited realm and there was little positive impact.

Phase 1: *Early Agile Adoption.* Gradually, the IT organization executives recognized that they had to change their software development approach and decided to embark on agile transformation at

Figure 1. Agile adoption innovation curve

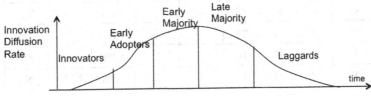

the organizational level. An agile working group was established to identify legacy processes and governance procedures that had to be changed, the new practices to be introduced, the coaching needed and the success measures. Several pilot product teams were chosen. After five months of introducing agile practices with the help of internal and external coaches, these pilot teams achieved the following results (see Table 1).

Table 1 is divided into 5 main columns, namely, product name, team size, development cycle-time (in months), production defect improvement rate, and whether the team started to invest in automated testing. For example, team A had 10 internal staff, 67 external contractors, thus a total of 77 persons in the development team. Before adopting agile practices, its development cycle time was 3 months. After adopting agile practices, it improved to a 1 month cycle time representing a 67% improvement. Its product defect rates saw a 94% improvement compared to the same period in the previous year. This comparison adjusted for seasonal fluctuations. This team also started to invest in automated testing.

Almost all products achieved a faster development cycle time. The exception was product B, which did not release any software at all during the 5-month agile adoption window. Most products achieved better quality with dramatic improvement in production defect rates. The exception was product E, which saw poorer quality. Product F being recently developed did not have data from the previous year for comparison.

Phase 2: *Early Majority.* The successes gave executives the boldness to spread the use of agile practices. Many product teams were eager to participate in the transformation as well. After another 6 months encouraging results were reported:

- 47 product teams and a total of 1700 persons adopted agile practices.
- 75% of the product teams gained the ability to delivery releases on a monthly basis (from a previous delivery cycle of about 3 months)
- End-to-end requirements realization from idea to delivery time was shortened by 44%. Product teams improved their response to business requirements better and faster
- Production defect density and production incident were reduced by 5.2% and 22.73% respectively. This implied that we reduced lead-time and cycle-times significantly with no loss of quality, but increased quality.

Table 1. Pilot product team achievements

Product	Team Size			Cycle Time (month)			Defect Imp.	Auto Test
	Int	Ext	Total	Before	After	Imp		
A	10	67	77	3	1	67%	94%	Yes
B	11	30	41	4	4	NA	NA	NA
C	5	44	49	4	1	75%	53%	Yes
D	16	72	88	5	1	80%	54%	Yes
E	4	10	14	2	1	50%	-54%	Yes
F	16	58	74	4	2	50%	N.A.	No

○   Of the 47 product teams that adopted agile practices, we received more than 10 letters of recommendation from their respective business departments.

The IT organization executives were satisfied with the results. There were other intangible benefits such as improved collaboration within teams (especially between business analysts, developers and testers), business and IT started to collaborate better, legacy processes were updated to reflect the new agile way of working.

3. ORGANIZATION TRANSFORMATION AS A STARTUP

Similar to any change initiative in this IT organization, an agile working group (AWG) was established to lead the agile transformation. The author worked as an advisor and architect within the AWG and also as an external coach to various departments and product teams. AWG's initial concerns were as follows:

- What would their new operating model look like?
- How should they introduce changes to the teams?
- What teams should they introduce agile methods to first?

The AWG operated in a manner similar to typical change leadership approaches such as the agile office described in(Rogers, 2010). However, as initial successes were assured, their operating mode morphed to that of a startup, with a focus on finding a repeatable and scalable model to influence this transformation. While there was some level of executive support, the AWG had autonomy in strategizing the transformation. The AWG did not use a not a top-down, command and control approach, but exercised influence and attempting to make the changes contagious(Power, 2011).

3.1 Kick Starting the Transformation

Gleicher's formula for change (Dannemiller & Jacobs, 1992) states that for change to happen: D x V x S > R, where:

D: dissatisfaction with current situation.
V: Vision for change.
S: Initial first steps understood.
R: resistance to change.

The dissatisfaction to change was clear in the IT organizations. Their business customers were complaining about their software. Lead-times were long and protracted. The vision, i.e. the new operating model, was gradually made clear to them through the emerging practice architecture which we will describe in Section 3.2. There were product teams who had resistance and concerns with challenges like the lack of time and resources, how to work with smaller batches and shorter time scales, and so on. The strategy was to work on the path of least resistance, to get successful teams to help spread the message. Product teams joined the agile transformation on a purely voluntary basis. As a result, there were some that dropped of, but majority stayed. Due to the scale of the transformation, there were sufficient good messages to spread around. The AWG actively sought our barriers to working in an agile way and systematically influence participants to make necessary changes.

3.2 Emerging a Practice Architecture

One of the most important jobs of the AWG was to understand and explain how agile principles and practices could fit together and be adapted to different development scenarios and contexts such as small-scale development (10 people), large-scale development (200+ people), involving multiple business units, legacy migration, COTS packages, in-house development, enhancements, business process re-engineering, new development, and so on. Moreover, product teams had different levels of maturity. Some had automated testing in place and were already delivering high quality software, while others had rather poor quality. As a result, they had different needs for and different paths towards a better way of working. Thus, mass customization of development processes was a necessity(Berger, 2013).

Moreover, it had been reported that being able to regularly reflect and continuously improve is a challenge in many organizations(Mathiassen & Sandberg, 2014). Product teams in this IT organization had the same challenge too. Early adopters who adopted Scrum just stopped at Scrum. The AWG had to provide a roadmap to motivate then to continually improve.

For the above reasons, the AWG drafted a practice architecture description (PAD) that evolved throughout the transformation journey. Just as software architecture description (SAD) is presented through multiple views(Babb, Hoda, & Norbjerg, 2014), this practice architecture description had multiple views and different levels of abstraction. One of the most important views that emerged is the execution view that shows how different roles collaborate to deliver software (see Figure 2).

The execution view shows small teams with product owners and Scrum masters scale to form larger teams with "super product owners" and "Super-Scrum masters". This Super-Scrum teams receives feature requests from business representatives through a product development flow (P. B. Kruchten, 1995). Moving towards the front-end on left-hand-side of Figure 2, feature requests originates from validated ideas based on lean startup(Reinertsen, 2009), design thinking (Maurya, 2012) and Cynefin's sensemaking approach (Brown, 2009). Moving towards the back-end processes on the right-hand-side, working software is continuously integrated and tested into a pre-production environment and then continuously deployed to the production. Feedback from users goes back to the requirements processes in a DevOps manner (Kurtz & Snowden, 2003).

In addition to the execution view, the emerging PAD (see Figure 3) has views.

At the top of Figure 3, the financial budgeting and performance management view addresses concerns at the enterprise level. This level applies concepts from beyond budgeting (Bogsnes, 2008; Kim, Behr, & Spafford, 2014).

At the layer below, the process customization view addresses concerns regarding how practices are integrated and customized for classes of product teams. This mostly involves how roles and work products are mapped to specific product team structures.

On the left, the practice architecture view lists the available practices that product teams can consider for continuous improvement. This includes dependency relationships between practices.

On the right, the impacted entities view facilitates discussion on the impact to a product team's current organization, and their focal point of process improvement.

Figure 2. AWG practice architecture (execution view)

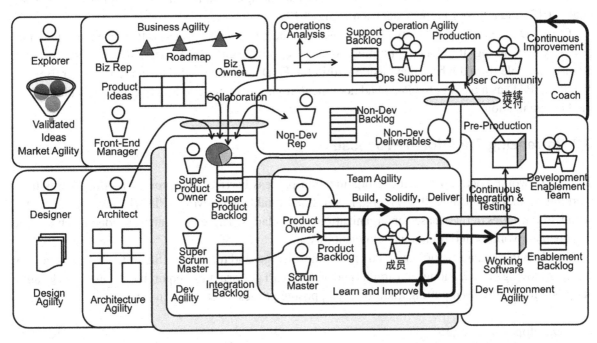

Figure 3. AWG practice architecture

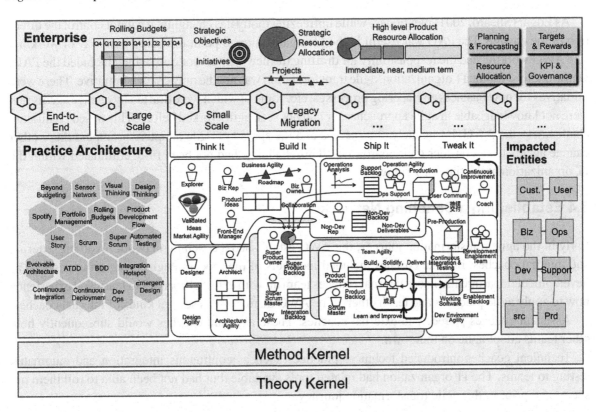

At the bottom, the PAD highlights that practices are designed on top of a method kernel (Jacobson et al., 2013) and a theory kernel (Jacobson et al., 2013).

The PAD as used in the IT organization was useful for several purposes. It explained a potential new way or working. It helped pinpointing areas of improvement. Developers and leaders in product teams were able to find where they reside within the PAD and saw what they could do better. Beyond providing PAD as a picture, the PAD had documentation, guidelines and training materials tailored for the IT organization.

3.3 Unfreezing Traditional Processes

The AWG worked actively to remove organization process barriers that prevent product teams from working in an agile manner. The IT organization had established CMMI/IPD (Hope & Fraser, 2013) with KPI measures defined based on organizational boundaries. These KPIs such as reducing churn-rate had coerced workers into traditional silo mentality.

Kurt Lewin's change theory involved unfreezing, change, and refreezing (Sheard, 2001). Unfreezing meant removing organizational constraints and archaic KPI performance requirements on would be agile adopters. It also involved putting traditionally opposing parties together, such as:

- Developers and testers.
- Developers and operations.
- Developers and business representatives.

As Edgar (Sheard, 2001) mentioned, while unfreezing motivates changing, it cannot control the direction of the change. The PAD was useful in the IT organization to point towards a new way of working. The AWG working had the responsibility for drafting the new way of working, which included the PAD. Unfortunately, for the IT organization, agile transformation was not the only change initiative. There were initiatives for new business engineering processes, etc. some of which were drafted by change agents that were not knowledgeable in agile approaches, or had not seen agile worked before. This posed significant challenge to the AWG. Fortunately, the success and the spread of agile adopters prompted these other change agents to re-consider their approaches. This challenge had not been fully eliminated within the IT organization at the time of writing.

3.4 Establishing a Coaching Network

Early in the agile transformation journey, the AWG established a coaching network involving external and internal coaches. Internal coaches included members of the process-engineering group, as well as development departments. These internal coaches team up with external coaches to learn and experience how to apply agile practices and teach others. The AWG distinguishes several kinds of internal coaches:

Assistant coaches paired with external coaches. These assistant coaches would subsequently help other teams adopt agile on their own.

Technical coaches introduced technical practices such as continuous integration and automated testing to teams. The IT organization had related tools available, but had not been able to roll them out successful prior to this agile transformation journey.

Agile custodians were project managers/leaders in product teams that volunteered to adopt agile and ensure that agile practices continued after coaches departed.

Assistant coaches came largely from the process-engineering group and had very little development experience. It was almost impossible to find potential coaches who excel at both management and technical aspects, and thus the AWG segregated assistant coaches from technical coaches.

Teaming between internal assistant coaches and external coaches yielded many advantages. External coaches brought in the know-how to agile practices, whereas assistant coaches could explain changes to organization processes that were taking place. This greatly facilitated unfreezing mindsets.

3.5 Transformation Gamification

The IT organization had a reward policy and system in place for change initiatives. Managers had the authority to submit requests for rewards for good performance. Developers in the IT organization were relatively young and many were in the early 30s and late 20s. This provided conducive environments for gamification (Radoff, 2011; Schein, 1996).

Points were awarded for reaching specific targets.

Badges were given for adopting practices (from the practice architecture described in Section 3.2) within acceptable criteria

Leadership boards were used during progress meetings.

During progress meetings, product teams, specifically custodians would present their current state of agile adoption and what they were going to do next to department heads and department-level AWGs.

3.6 Community Networks

The AWG held regular community activities. This included:

- General sharing about what agile is about,
- Sharing about specific agile practices such as requirements management, automated testing,
- Publicizing success stories.

The IT organization had an internal social network platform (SNP) that hosted success story reports, presentation and training materials, internal blogs on applying agile practices. In addition, the AWG had budget to send staffs to attend agile conferences to broaden their horizons. These attendees had the responsibility to share what they have learnt to others. Internal coaches had the responsibility to share what they experience and learnt as well.

4. TEAM TRANSFORMATION THROUGH PRACTICAL THEORY BUILDING

Coaching teams, each comprising an external coach and an internal assistant coach facilitated agile adoption at the team level (teams ranged from 10 to 200+ persons). A technical coach sometimes joined coaching teams when internal tools were used. Due to the high volume of product teams adopting agile practices and the comparatively low number of coaching teams, facilitation had to be very focused. Most coaching teams worked with product teams in three phases, namely, getting to know the product team, kick starting the product teams into agile practices, and letting product teams self-direct their next step towards improvement.

4.1 Theory Based Software Engineering

The AWG was keen to harvest success stories and highlights to share with would be agile adopters and senior management. AWG also wanted to gather lessons learnt, to understand what worked, what didn't, what could work better and factors affecting success.

Coaching teams used a theory-based software-engineering (TBSE) approach (Jacobson et al., 2013) as depicted by Figure 4. Coaching teams worked together with the product agile custodian to understand current context, pain points and objectives of agile adoption before choosing appropriate practices from the practice architecture description (PAD).

Theories such as queuing theory, Little's Law, Conway's Law, etc. explained why practices work (Werbach & Hunter, 2012). Observations from introducing the practices validated and tuned the theories, as well as provided for enriching practices and their corresponding practice descriptions. Teams were encouraged to seek explanations and alternate explanations as to why practices produced the desired effects. This, we hoped to encourage deep learning.

4.2 Kick Starting

With an understanding of product team's context, coaching teams kick started the teams into an agile way of working. This usually took about a day and involved the following:

- An introduction to agile and lean principles, such as work-in-process limits, and backlog prioritization.
- An overview of practices in the practice architecture description.
- A whole team training and simulation on Scrum and Super-Scrum (Dybå & Dingsøyr, 2008; Ng, 2013) using the product team's requirements.

Figure 4. Theory based software engineering

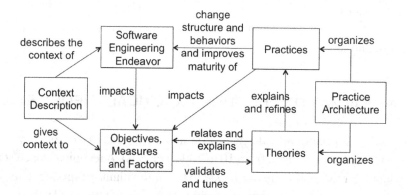

Prior to the kick-start event, coaching teams clarified team roles and responsibilities under new way of working. Product teams were responsible for consolidating requirements to be delivered for the next iteration or release. This preparation time took between one to three weeks.

During the kick-start event, product custodians learnt how to conduct iteration planning and complying with work-in-process limits.

Within two weeks of the kick-start event, the product teams had to do a product demo to the coaching team based on what they completed. Some teams would complete most of their requirements (either in the form of user stories or some other format), while others completed very little. The idea was not to get teams to complete all requirements, but to get the teams into a habit of iterating and the feel of a regular heartbeat and constant retrospective and learning.

There was a growing trend that the preparation times became shorter as internal coaches started to realize that long agile adoption preparation time was an old-styled "get-it-right-first-time" syndrome rather than continual learning and adapting. Moreover, there was no evidence that a longer preparation time ensured product teams would achieve iteration objectives 100% first time.

During the demo, product agile custodians learned from the coaching teams how to conduct demos and retrospectives. It was also during this time that team members determined how to tune and improve their practices or learn new ones. This was by reflecting at the factors that affect their behavior and seeking ways to adjust the factors through the TBSE approach. As such, team members reflected on both their theory and their practice at the same time.

4.3 Collecting Highlights and Lessons Learnt

Coaching teams were given the responsibility by the AWG to collect highlights of working in an agile manner. At the beginning of the adoption journey, teams applying Scrum and Super-Scrum (i.e. Scrum involving beyond 50 persons) practices were rather refreshing to the AWG and executives. But agile is not just Scrum and executives get tired of hearing the same practices. The value of external coaches laid in seeking novel practice areas and attacking complexity.

The AWG worked out a simple calculation to determine what product teams did could be deemed a highlight, i.e. a highlight index, which was a product of three parameters:

- Context complexity (depending on size of the team, the complexity of the product, number of external integration).
- Practice novelty (depending on whether the practice had been tried elsewhere in the IT organization).
- Contribution value (depending on the amount of guidance and content the product team could add to the practice architecture).

There were no explicit scales defined for these parameters, but the comparisons were performed on a relative manner. The highlight index gave an indication whether what product teams did was news worthy. This provided yet another kind of point system for coaching teams to gamify the agile transformation itself. The drive was to find novel practices, exemplify their usage and share such practices within the community. Examples of novelty included:

- Applying Super-Scrum on a large scale first in a 100 person team, to a 150 person team on different sites, and later to a 200 person team;

- Involving business representatives in small scale and later to large scale;
- Applying product development flow in the IT organization's social network development and later to their partner relationship system;
- Applying a human sensor network (based on the Cynefin's framework (Brown, 2009; Kurtz & Snowden, 2003)) to gather narratives about the agile adoption from different groups;
- Applying behavior driven development (BDD) to their search engine and later to their enterprise service bus (ESB).

Coaching teams were prized for reaching out to novel practices, and as a result spanned new practice areas in the practice architecture. Product teams on the other hand were prized for reducing development lead-times, and improving quality, which at the same time validated the practice architecture in the IT organization.

5. DISCUSSION AND EVALUATION

As highlighted by Dyba (P. Ng, 2014) and the Software Process Improvement (SPI) manifesto (Dybå, 2005) agile transformation must focus on business objectives and involve and engage stakeholders at all levels. Our agile transformation journey did indeed confirm and validate these factors. Executives in this IT organization did indeed have a real business need and stakeholders at all levels were open to discussion. When seemingly disagreements occurred, it was found that stakeholders were seeking to understand. Therefore, in a way, this agile transformation journey was a replication of earlier studies on success criteria for effective organizational change.

The real question is what truly highlights the contribution of this agile adoption, and what makes it special as compared to other agile adoption journeys of similar scale. We believe the answers can be found in two areas, namely the technical aspects and the human social aspects

5.1 Integrating Theory and Practice

As Kurt Lewin said so eloquently, "There is nothing so practical as sound theory" (Beck, 2000). In the IT organization's agile adoption journey, the integration of theory and practice manifested itself in the form of the AWG practice architecture (see Section 3.2) and the TBSE approach (see Section 4.1).

The AWG practice architecture depicted in Figure 3 is definitely not the first attempt in assembling practices into a unified framework. Before agile became mainstream, the Rational Unified Process (RUP) (Pries-Heje & Johansen, 2010)was one of the more prominent process frameworks. RUP then faced competition from extreme programming (XP) (P. Kruchten, 2004) and Scrum (Schwaber, 1997) as many felt that RUP was heavyweight. However, since both XP and Scrum were targeted at small teams, they did not get much attention from more traditional and larger organizations. Frameworks like LeSS (Larman & Vodde, 2013), SAFe (Leffingwell, 2010) and DAD (Ambler & Lines, 2012) attempted to address the challenges about scaling agile and are receiving much attention. At the surface, LeSS, SAFe and DAD look remarkably different, they have much in common, and as they evolve, they learn from one another and are based on similar themes such as lean thinking, fast feedback loops, being lightweight.

It has been found that more than 70% of organizations that adopted agile approach do not just adopt prescribed methods as is, but mixed them with other agile approaches and even traditional approaches [1] . For example, Ericsson combined elements of SAFe and LeSS in their continuous planning and development approach (West, Grant, Gerush, & D'silva, 2010).

The AWG practice architecture borrowed and adapted practices from SAFe, LeSS, DAD and even specific instances like Ericsson to suit the IT organization's product development context. For example, we incorporated the early phase manager used in Ericsson to manage the requirements input flow. We incorporated whole team release from SAFe, but our planning cycles was generally one month with weekly sprints instead of the 3 months planning cycle and 2-week sprints prescribed in SAFe. Planning meetings usually took half a day instead of 2 full-days prescribed by SAFe. There was a 150-person product team who had multi-site iteration-planning meetings every two weeks. Thus, without any prompting by the coaching team, it operated in a manner more similar to LeSS than SAFe.

In addition, the AWG practice architecture description had several useful qualities.

- **Affinity:** One of SAFe's novelties is its "big picture", i.e. the entire framework in a single picture similar to Figure 3. Such a picture is useful to explain how the agile operating model works. The AWG practice architecture took this idea to the IT organization's context. Members of the IT organization could generally find their role or what they need to do when introduced to Figure 3. This made it easier to explain how members can contribute to working an agile manner.
- **Improvement Roadmap:** As mentioned earlier, reports have shown that many organizations did not invest sufficiently in retrospectives and learning and therefore did not improve much. The AWG practice architecture, specifically the list of practices on the right, was that it showed product teams potential areas of improvement. Each practice, represented as a hexagon, was a unit of improvement with associated guidelines and parameters, which team could contextualize and consume.
- **Theoretical Basis:** Each practice in the AWG practice architecture had a description explaining why the practice works, when it should be applied, they expected benefits and effort to apply the practice. This again helped teams consume practices and contribute to the experiences behind the practices.

5.2 Practice-Based Simulation and Gamification

From the very onset of the agile adoption journey, the AWG placed emphasis on the human-social aspects of the transformation, and in particular the use of simulation and gamification.

Figure 5 presets a graph that depicts the relationships between improvement targets (e.g. reducing lead-time), practices (e.g. product development flow, and Super-Scrum), simulation and gamification approaches.

Simulations kick-started product teams in applying practices like Scrum, Super-Scrum, product development flow, etc. Coaching teams were encouraged to devise new simulations (including role-playing and games) to illustrate how practices work. The use of simulation was a key reason why product teams could transit from a traditional approach to an agile iterative approach. In a particular case, a 200-person product team was taught Scrum and Super-Scrum in batches of 50, 50 and 100 persons over three days. This 200-person team started iterating and within a week, we had an integration demo. Whereas simulations kick started the process, demos got teams focused towards delivery.

Figure 5. Practice based simulation and gamification

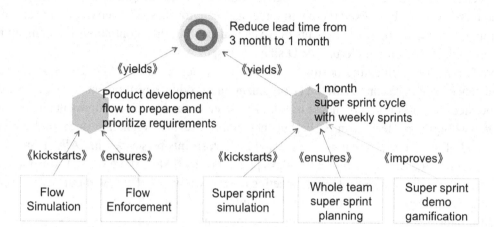

Demos frequently had gamification elements with points awarded to each 10-person sub-team for their work in each iteration. For example, if a 10-person sub-team completed all their agreed user stories to their product owner's satisfaction, they would score 10 points. This motivates team members to achieve sprint objectives.

Figure 5 is just one of the many diagrams illustrating the dependencies, between process improvement targets, practices, simulation, gamification and process improvement actions. AWG's practice architecture had many such diagrams for different kinds of process improvement targets such as reducing defect rates, etc. The key was to make thought processes visible and motivate team members to think deeply how they could improve.

6. CONCLUSION

The agile manifesto (Lewin, 1951) began with a declaration that "We are uncovering better ways of developing software by doing it and helping others do it." Perhaps this opening statement is the heart of what being agile is all about. Being agile is not just about valuing individuals and interactions over processes and tools, working software over comprehensive documentation, customer collaboration over contract negotiation, and responding to change over following a plan.

Agility requires the willingness and openness to experiment and improve on top of a practical and theoretical basis. The IT organization's agile transformation journey was an example demonstrating how this could be achieved. Within a span of one year, we reached 47 teams and 1700 engineers. There was a 44% reduction in development lead-time, 5% reduction in production defects and 22% reduction in production incidents. Such remarkable success could be lauded, but one have to go beyond such successes or even failures to understand what makes or breaks such journeys.

Kruchten (Heikkilä, Paasivaara, Lassenius, & Engblom, 2013) highlighted that successful agile adoption depended on context. Chow and Cao (Kruchten, 2007) found 36 factors affecting the success of agile adoption. Although empirical studies (Chow & Cao, 2008) (Endres & Rombach, 2003)on agile methods are plentiful today and easily accessible by practitioners, there is still little work on the applicability of practices and factors affecting their introduction. In particular, the IT organization's concern was whether the success it had could be replicated, sustained, or even improved, with pitfalls avoided. Fortunately, this IT organization had already a good start by integrating theory and practice as discussed in Section 5. Nevertheless, much still needs to be done as this IT organization embarks on its second year into the agile transformation journey.

REFERENCES

Ambler, S. W., & Lines, M. (2012). *Disciplined agile delivery: A practitioner's guide to agile software delivery in the enterprise.* IBM Press.

Babb, J., Hoda, R., & Norbjerg, J. (2014). Embedding reflection and learning into agile software development. *IEEE Software, 31*(4), 51–57. doi:10.1109/MS.2014.54

Babinet, E., & Ramanathan, R. (2008). *Dependency management in a large agile environment.* Paper presented at the Agile 2008 Conference. doi:10.1109/Agile.2008.58

Beck, K. (2000). *Extreme programming explained: embrace change.* Addison-Wesley Professional.

Berger, J. (2013). *Contagious: Why things catch on.* Simon and Schuster.

Blank, S. (2013). *The four steps to the epiphany.* K&S Ranch.

Bogsnes, B. (2008). *Implementing beyond budgeting: unlocking the performance potential.* John Wiley & Sons.

Brown, T. (2009). *Change by design: how design thinking transforms organizations and inspires innovation.* New York: HarperBusiness.

Chow, T., & Cao, D.-B. (2008). A survey study of critical success factors in agile software projects. *Journal of Systems and Software, 81*(6), 961–971. doi:10.1016/j.jss.2007.08.020

Dannemiller, K. D., & Jacobs, R. W. (1992). Changing the way organizations change: A revolution of common sense. *The Journal of Applied Behavioral Science, 28*(4), 480–498. doi:10.1177/0021886392284003

Duvall, P. M., Matyas, S., & Glover, A. (2007). *Continuous integration: improving software quality and reducing risk.* Pearson Education.

Dybå, T. (2005). An empirical investigation of the key factors for success in software process improvement. *Software Engineering. IEEE Transactions on, 31*(5), 410–424.

Dybå, T., & Dingsøyr, T. (2008). Empirical studies of agile software development: A systematic review. *Information and Software Technology, 50*(9), 833–859. doi:10.1016/j.infsof.2008.01.006

Endres, A., & Rombach, H. D. (2003). *A handbook of software and systems engineering: Empirical observations, laws, and theories.* Pearson Education.

Fitzgerald, B., Stol, K.-J., O'Sullivan, R., & O'Brien, D. (2013). Scaling agile methods to regulated environments: an industry case study. In *Proceedings of the 2013 International Conference on Software Engineering.* doi:10.1109/ICSE.2013.6606635

Gamma, E., & Beck, K. (2006). *JUnit*. Academic Press.

Heikkilä, V. T., Paasivaara, M., Lassenius, C., & Engblom, C. (2013). *Continuous release planning in a large-scale scrum development organization at Ericsson*. Springer. doi:10.1007/978-3-642-38314-4_14

Hope, J., & Fraser, R. (2013). *Beyond budgeting: how managers can break free from the annual performance trap*. Harvard Business Press.

Jacobson, I., Ng, P.-W., McMahon, P. E., Spence, I., & Lidman, S. (2013). *The essence of software Engineering: applying the SEMAT kernel*. Addison-Wesley.

Kim, G., Behr, K., & Spafford, G. (2014). *The phoenix project: A novel about IT, DevOps, and helping your business win*. IT Revolution.

Kotter, J. P. (1995). Leading change: Why transformation efforts fail. *Harvard Business Review, 73*(2), 59–67.

Kruchten, P. (2004). *The rational unified process: an introduction*. Addison-Wesley Professional.

Kruchten, P. (2007). Voyage in the agile memeplex. *Queue, 5*(5), 1. doi:10.1145/1281881.1281893

Kruchten, P. B. (1995). The 4+ 1 view model of architecture. *Software, IEEE, 12*(6), 42–50. doi:10.1109/52.469759

Kurtz, C. F., & Snowden, D. J. (2003). The new dynamics of strategy: Sense-making in a complex and complicated world. *IBM Systems Journal, 42*(3), 462–483. doi:10.1147/sj.423.0462

Larman, C., & Vodde, B. (2013). Scaling Agile Development. *Crosstalk*, 9.

Leffingwell, D. (2010). *Agile software requirements: lean requirements practices for teams, programs, and the enterprise*. Addison-Wesley Professional.

Lewin, K. (1951). Field theory in social science: selected theoretical papers (D. Cartwright, Ed.). Academic Press.

Lewin, K. (1989). *Changing as three steps: unfreezing, moving, and freezing of group standards. In Organizational Development. Theory, Practice, and Research* (3rd ed.; p. 87). Irwin.

Mathiassen, L., & Sandberg, A. B. (2014). Process Mass Customization in a Global Software Firm. *Software, IEEE, 31*(6), 62–69. doi:10.1109/MS.2014.21

Maurer, F., & Melnik, G. (2007). *Agile methods: Crossing the chasm*. Paper presented at the Companion to the proceedings of the 29th International Conference on Software Engineering.

Maurya, A. (2012). *Running lean: iterate from plan A to a plan that works*. O'Reilly Media, Inc.

McAvoy, J., & Butler, T. (2009). *A failure to learn in a software development team: the unsuccessful introduction of an agile method. In Information Systems Development* (pp. 1–13). Springer.

Ng, P. (2014). Software Process Improvement and Gaming using Essence: An Industrial Experience. *Journal of Industrial and Intelligent Information, 2*(1), 45–50. doi:10.12720/jiii.2.1.45-50

Ng, P.-W. (2013). Making Software Engineering Education Structured, Relevant and Engaging through Gaming and Simulation. *Journal of Communication and Computer, 10*, 1365–1373.

Ng, P.-W. (2014). Theory based software engineering with the SEMAT kernel: preliminary investigation and experiences. In *Proceedings of the 3rd SEMAT Workshop on General Theories of Software Engineering*. doi:10.1145/2593752.2593756

Paasivaara, M., & Lassenius, C. (2011). *Scaling scrum in a large distributed project*. Paper presented at the Empirical Software Engineering and Measurement (ESEM), 2011 International Symposium on. doi:10.1109/ESEM.2011.49

Power, K. (2011). *The Agile Office: Experience Report from Cisco's Unified Communications Business Unit*. Paper presented at the Agile Conference (AGILE). doi:10.1109/AGILE.2011.7

Pries-Heje, J., & Johansen, J. (2010). *Spi manifesto*. European System & Software Process Improvement and Innovation.

Prochaska, J. O., Velicer, W. F., Rossi, J. S., Goldstein, M. G., Marcus, B. H., Rakowski, W., & Rosenbloom, D. et al. (1994). Stages of change and decisional balance for 12 problem behaviors. *Health Psychology, 13*(1), 39–46. doi:10.1037/0278-6133.13.1.39 PMID:8168470

Radoff, J. (2011). *Game on: energize your business with social media games*. John Wiley & Sons.

Read, A., & Briggs, R. O. (2012). *The many lives of an agile story: Design processes, design products, and understandings in a large-scale agile development project*. Paper presented at the System Science (HICSS), 2012 45th Hawaii International Conference on. doi:10.1109/HICSS.2012.684

Reinertsen, D. G. (2009). *The principles of product development flow: second generation lean product development* (Vol. 62). Celeritas Redondo Beach.

Ries, E. (2011). *The lean startup: How today's entrepreneurs use continuous innovation to create radically successful businesses*. Crown Business.

Rogers, E. M. (2010). *Diffusion of innovations*. Simon and Schuster.

Schein, E. H. (1996). Kurt Lewin's change theory in the field and in the classroom: Notes toward a model of managed learning. *Systems Practice, 9*(1), 27–47. doi:10.1007/BF02173417

Schwaber, K. (1997). *Scrum development process. In Business Object Design and Implementation* (pp. 117–134). Springer. doi:10.1007/978-1-4471-0947-1_11

Sheard, S. (2001). Evolution of the frameworks quagmire. *Computer, 34*(7), 96–98. doi:10.1109/2.933516

Spinellis, D. (2012). Don't Install Software by Hand. *Software, IEEE, 29*(4), 86–87. doi:10.1109/MS.2012.85

Vijayasarathy, L., & Turk, D. (2008). Agile software development: A survey of early adopters. *Journal of Information Technology Management, 19*(2), 1–8.

Werbach, K., & Hunter, D. (2012). *For the win: How game thinking can revolutionize your business*. Wharton Digital Press.

West, D., & Grant, T., Gerush, M., & D'silva, D. (2010). Agile development: Mainstream adoption has changed agility. *Forrester Research, 2*, 41.

KEY TERMS AND DEFINITIONS

Agile Software Architecture: A software architecture that lays out blue prints of the organization and structure of software components as well as well defined mechanism on how components can be tested and integrated into the system that would sustain the agile approach through out the software development life cycle.

Agile Software Development: Agile software development is a group of software development methods in which requirements and solutions evolve through collaboration between self-organizing, cross-functional teams. It promotes adaptive planning, evolutionary development, early delivery, continuous improvement, and encourages rapid and flexible response to change.

Feature Driven Development: Feature Driven Development (FDD) is an agile method that focuses on delivering working software in a timely manner by using simple, client focused and practical software process. This method works well without tailoring to both small (< 8 team size) and large teams (> 30 team size).

Scrum: Scrum is one of the popular agile methodologies which aims to address the challenges of projects involving complex scope of work using a simple process dependent on a small team who are motivated, collaborative and highly focused on producing working software every 2-4 weeks.

Waterfall Model: A sequential design, used in software development processes, in which progress is seen as flowing steadily downwards (like a waterfall) through the phases of Conception, Initiation, Analysis, Design, Construction, Testing, Deployment, and Maintenance.

ENDNOTE

[1]   http://agilemanifesto.org/

Chapter 6

A Transformation Approach for Scaling and Sustaining Agility at an Enterprise Level:
A Culture–Led Agile Transformation Approach

Ahmed Sidky
ICAgile, USA

ABSTRACT

The sustainability of agile transformations is deeply linked to how the organization "transforms" to agile. Sustainable, effective agile transformations affect all the elements of culture such as, leadership style, leadership values, work structures, reward systems, processes, and of course the work habits of people. How to affect that culture shift is the key question we will present in this chapter. The author will present two different common transformation approaches (organizational-led and process-led) and then describe a hybrid version called culture-led transformation that is designed to change critical organizational and personal habits to improve and sustain organizational agility.

1. INTRODUCTION

Many leaders feel increasingly overwhelmed by the pace of change and are being constantly challenged to understand the causes of major disruptions in the marketplace and in their organizations. The rate of change will only increase as their organizations and their marketplaces become more networked and technology continues to advance. The ability of an organization, as a whole, to respond in a healthy and disciplined manner to these constant changes and disruptions is what we refer to as Organizational Agility (or Enterprise-level Agile).

The purpose of this chapter is to introduce a transformation approach for achieving sustainable organizational agility. In this chapter we present the organization ecosystem, which plays a key role in the culture of an organization and subsequently in its agility. Next we explore a couple of common agile

DOI: 10.4018/978-1-4666-9858-1.ch006

transformation approaches while highlighting sustainability challenges with both. Next we present the Culture-led Transformation Approach, which focuses on changing organizational habits in staged approach leading to sustainable changes. Lastly, we will present how to design an Agile transformational roadmap for the Culture-led Approach. As we conclude we will briefly discuss how Culture-led Transformation Approach relates to the Agile Adoption Framework (Sidky, Arthur, J. D., & Bohner, 2007).

2. ORGANIZATIONAL AGILITY

We define Organizational Agility as a culture (a) based on the values and principles of Agile, (b) supported by the organizational ecosystem (which we define as an organization's leadership, strategy, structure, processes and people) and (c) manifested through personal and organizational habits (how work really gets done in the organization).

The first part of this definition is the notion of a culture based on the values and principles of Agile. When the word Agile is mentioned, many people immediately think of Scrum, eXtreme Programming or some other Agile methodology in the IT space. Agile, itself, is not a process, framework or any particular methodology; it is a mindset, a culture, a way of thinking. This mindset is all about learning and discovery. Agile is about a culture of continuous learning. The idea, therefore, is to frame Agile as the mindset, values and principles behind various methodologies, rather than as the practices associated with any methodology.

Understanding Agile as a mindset is foundational to discussing the transformational effort needed to achieve organizational agility. When organizations view Agile as just another process (even if it is viewed as an efficient process that enables a team to embrace change) then the transformation journey is simply about adopting a new process. But when agile is correctly viewed as a set of cultural habits, then the agile transformation now entails the change of the entire organizational culture.

2.1. Important Question: Agile Teams or Organizational Agility

The analogy for achieving organizational agility is that of creating strawberry jam. Think of one team doing agile as a single strawberry – where it is sweet and it has benefits, just like an agile team. However we can all agree that a single strawberry (one agile team) is obviously not strawberry jam (where jam represents organizational agility), however it is a clear ingredient of the jam.

The confusion and challenge arises when we want to "scale" agile. When an organizations sees success with the one strawberry (one agile team) it develops a desire "scale agile" by starting-up more agile teams in the hope of achieving organizational agility. That is like adding more strawberries to a bowl and hoping that the result will be strawberry jam. The reality is that by starting more agile teams, you end up with agile teams within a non-agile organization. This is very different from bringing strawberries and going through a transformational process to change the strawberries to jam.

As depicted in Figure 1, there is a chasm between team-level agile (a bunch of strawberries) and enterprise-level agile or organizational agility (the jam). The chasm exists because usually team-level agile is achieved by a change of process and roles, and perhaps in some cases the "culture" and behaviors of the team members, but that is very different from changing the organizational culture. For organizational agility to happen, and be sustainable, it must entail a transformation of culture.

Figure 1. Creating strawberry jam: An analogy for Scaling Agile Teams

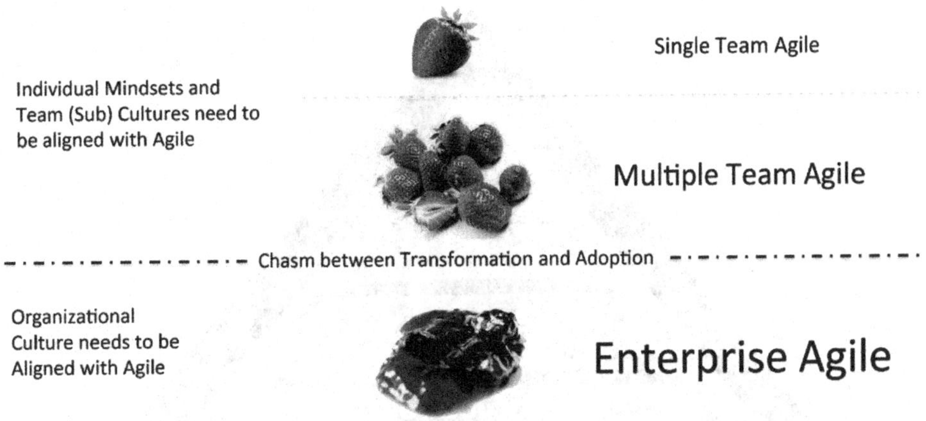

Single Team Agile

Individual Mindsets and
Team (Sub) Cultures need to
be aligned with Agile

Multiple Team Agile

– · – · – · – · – · – Chasm between Transformation and Adoption – · – · – · – · – · – ·

Organizational
Culture needs to be
Aligned with Agile

Enterprise Agile

One of the first discussions that need to happen when an organization wants to "transition to Agile" or "Scale Agile" is to decide whether the goal is to establish multiple agile teams (just a bunch of strawberries) or organizational agility (creating strawberry jam). One might argue that establishing multiple agile teams is a necessary step towards achieving organizational agility. While that is true to some degree, the scaling approach for agile, or in other words the transformation approach, will greatly depend on what you want as the end result; a change of culture or a change of process. Table 1 highlights briefly the difference between the approaches utilized for process changes verses cultural transformations.

The approach discussed in this chapter will serve those who desire to start a transformation that wants to truly change the culture and establish organizational agility. That brings up an important question, how can we transform culture? For the sake of simplicity we view culture as result of the organization's ecosystem – its Leadership, People, Strategy, Processes, and Structures – and we will discuss this in the next section.

3. THE ORGANIZATIONAL ECOSYSTEM

Figure 2 illustrates the relationship between culture and the elements of the organizational ecosystem (Leadership, People, Strategy, Processes, and Structures). The culture of an organization is represented as

Table 1. Difference between process changes and cultural transformations

Process Change / Incremental Change	Organizational and Culture Transformation
Focus on Process and Technology	Focus on People
Cascading Decisions	Shared Vision
Training	Educating
Communication	Buy-in
Compliance	Commitment

Figure 2. The elements of the organizational ecosystem and its relation to culture

the red "bungee-cord" or "rubber-band" that is shaped as a result of all the elements of the ecosystem and at same time culture creates a "container" that holds all these elements in alignment with each other. Next we will explore each of the elements of the organizational ecosystem to see how they impact the culture.

3.1. Leadership

When we refer to leadership, we are interested in various elements of leadership, starting with the overall style of leadership. Is it collaborative, or command-and-control, or something else like consensus-driven? We are also looking at the values that leadership holds. What are the things that leadership truly aspires towards every day in practice, not what is published in some brochure as the "values?" Do leaders really aspire towards transparency, creativity, sustainability, or do they aspire towards perfection, compliance and protection? Do they value effort or do they only value getting it right the first time? What are their habits when it comes to dealing with challenges or constraints? How do leaders react naturally (and automatically) when problems start to surface? Do they automatically coach and mentor or direct and command? All these elements of leadership play a critical role in shaping the culture of an organization.

3.2. Strategy

The second element we believe is important is the strategy of the organization. With strategy we are looking at how (not what) an organization sets it goals and how they achieve alignment to work together towards meeting those goals. What are their measures of success and do they ultimately drive behaviors that achieve those goals? What do people get rewarded for; do they get rewarded for successes only, or also for learning? What is the decision making process in the organization? Are decisions made to be inclusive of all stakeholders, or are only specific stakeholders allowed to be part of decision making? Again all of these strategic-level elements have a substantial impact on the organization's culture and also are greatly influenced by the culture.

3.3. Structure

Once the values of leadership become apparent, along with the manifestation of those values in terms of how the strategy is laid out, another element that shapes the culture of an organization is the organizational structures that exist. How are people organized to achieve the strategies that are laid out? Are they structured into isolated silos or overlapping teams? Are people working in silos encouraged to compete or collaborate with each other? Are teams only concerned with their own objectives or are they really concerned with the success of the entire organization? Is the organization keen on building networks or hierarchies? How are roles and responsibilities determined in the organization; task-based, outcome-based, or seniority-based? Are people given large spans of control to promote empowerment or narrow spans of control to ensure control? All of these elements related to how the organization is structured shape (and are shaped by) the culture of the organization.

3.4. Process

The next element that shapes the culture is the established business processes of the organization. A business process is a collection of related, structured activities or tasks that are performed by one or more roles to produce a specific service or product (ultimately serve a particular goal that is in line with the strategy). Within processes we are interested in the policies and procedures (written or implicit) that govern the operation of the organization. We look at the operational processes that constitute the core business and create the primary value stream. This element includes the processes that define how requirements are gathered, how design is created and reviewed, how software is developed, testing, and deployed. How are things procured and purchased when needed? How are customers engaged and how often? We are also looking at the supporting processes, like account management, technical support, and even reimbursement processes. Are they built on an assumption of trust or mistrust and abuse? The way processes are designed and implemented and governed shape (and are shaped) by the culture of the organization.

3.5. People

The remaining item in the organizational ecosystem is perhaps the most foundational, and that is the people themselves. People have beliefs, values, norms and habits that are all influenced by the culture of the organization and ultimately contribute to the culture of the organization as well. What do people believe their impact and contribution is to the company? Do they feel like assembly-line workers that are told what to do? If so, then sayings like "Just tell me what I need to do." will be heard frequently, and will not be odd. Does the culture fear failure and therefore doesn't attempt new creative and innovative approaches? Do people value collaboration or competition? That value will have an impact of how people approach success in the organization.

Even beyond the values and beliefs people hold, there are habits that people have developed over the years that kick-in automatically when they want to succeed and get things done. Those habits are manifested in terms of how work really gets done in the organization. The power and danger of these habits is that habits are what people do "automatically" usually without much thought. People fall back on habits and do what they have tried before and succeeded "automatically" to get work done in the company. In other words, it is what they do to succeed WITHOUT thinking because it has proven to work time and time again.

For example, some people may have a habit of circumventing the process when they want to get things done. Why? Because they have done it repeatedly, or they have seen others do it, and it has worked, so it becomes an organizational habit to circumvent processes. Even people that are just joining the organization will look at what other people do to succeed and they start to develop those habits. Habits become an integral part of the "culture" of how things get done. Other organizations may have habits of collaboration. People have developed an organizational habit that makes them automatically and without thinking reach out to others and work with them (even across organizational boundaries) because they have seen that work before. An effective agile transformation aims to change these "default" ways people work; essentially changing the personal and organizational habits, and changing the way people think about work and their norms.

4. SCALING AGILE TO REACH ORGANIZATIONAL AGILITY

The sum total of all the five elements presented in the previous section (Leadership, Strategy, Structure, Process and People) creates the culture of the organization and the culture keeps these five elements in alignment and harmony.

4.1. Importance of Maintaining Cultural Alignment at All Times

Research conducted by Jim Collins and Jerry Porras (in their book Built to Last: Successful Habits of Visionary Companies) (Collins, 2004) shows that the key distinguishing factor for high performing organization (see Figure 3) is the existence of a strong aligned culture. An aligned culture is where all elements of the organization work in concert together.

For example, if the leadership style is command-and-control and that is aligned with the strategy and measures of success, then the structures are designed to promote command and control. Additionally, the policies, procedures and processes are all in alignment with promoting and supporting the command and control culture. It is therefore not surprising that the people in the organization believe that command and control culture is best for the organization. At that point, when all the elements are in harmony together, then we have an aligned culture.

Whether the culture is command and control or collaborative does not matter as much as whether all the elements in the organization are aligned and consistent with the culture. A strained or unaligned culture occurs when one or more elements are not in harmony with the others.

When we look at a large sample of organizations trying to adopt agile, we see that due to their understanding of agile as a process, the change efforts focus on changing the process element of the organization (as depicted in Figure 4). As teams adopt agile they introduce more collaborative processes and practices (for instance, daily stand-ups, group estimation, collaborative planning, and team rooms).

Figure 3. Research by Jim Collins & Jerry Porras around alignment of culture and performance

Collins & Porras studied:
- 18 "visionary" vs. comparisons

Key distinguishing factor:
- presence of a **Strong, Integrated** and **Consistent Culture**

Most critical differentiating factor:
- **Alignment** – where all elements of the organization work in concert

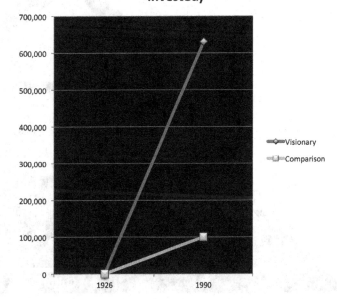

However by only changing the "process" element of the diagram they have thrown the organizational culture into a state of misalignment and unsustainability. The misalignment comes from the fact that now the processes are pushing towards a collaborative culture but the remaining elements of the culture are not in sync. For example, it is common to see that leaders' values and habits have not changed to be more collaborative, nor have the reward systems changed to encourage the new collaborative processes. The misalignment then leads to lack of sustainability of the change because the culture will eventually "push back" on the processes element and try to align it with the rest of the elements making-up the culture.

If you change one or even two elements but keep the rest the same, the same results can be expected. For example, Scrum teams change the process element to introduce collaborative practices and also change the roles and responsibilities of a typical team by introducing two roles; the ScrumMaster and Product Owner. However, those changes may still be at odds with the rest of the organization if none of the other elements change. You can see this misalignment manifested in behaviors such as teams constantly complaining that they can't get "buy-in" from leadership to dedicate people to certain roles and even the people in those roles may have habits and beliefs that don't enable them to be effective in their role, and don't help them facilitate collaboration between the team.

Another example. Many agile adoption efforts change process elements and introduce new processes and practices that encourage learning and discovery (e.g. early feedback and retrospectives) but again, are the rest of the organizational elements in alignment? Do the people value learning and discovery or do they see learning as indicator for the lack of competency. Does leadership encourage learning and reward it, or is there a culture of "get it right the first time" and learning is viewed as a lack of proper planning? Is learning and discovery included as part of goals, strategies and rewards?

Figure 4. Depicting an unaligned culture as a result of change efforts focused only on process

These are the real challenges that confront agile adoption and transformation efforts that only (or primarily) focus on changing one or two of organizational ecosystem elements without truly focusing on changing the entire culture.

The other interesting phenomenon is that once the change agent or sponsor exerting the pressure to change the process element (depicted by the arrow in Figure 4) goes away, the culture (represented in the bungee cord or rubber band around the triangle) pushes the process element back into alignment with the rest of the organization and all that investment in "change" turns out to be not sustainable.

For transformations to be successful they must be sustainable and live on to become the new culture of the organization. For that to happen successfully the culture as a whole needs to transform by evolving and changing all of the elements of the ecosystem together as part of a shared journey.

4.2. Common Transformational Approaches

In the this section we will illustrate two common transform approaches – approach #1: process-led and approach #2: organization-led. While these are very common transformational approaches, they both cause the organizational culture to be misaligned during the transformation, thereby putting the transformation effort at risk, and more importantly usually resulting in an unsustainable agile transformation.

As we present these two approaches, the diagram we use will show the different stages of the transformation from the current state (represented by the blue triangle) to the end state (represented by the green triangle). The color red will be used to show how the culture becomes misaligned. After presenting the two common approaches for transformation, we will present a third approach (culture-led) that transforms the culture in a manner that keeps the alignment of culture intact (not red) as much as possible during the transformation.

Approach 1: Process-Led Transformations

The term agile was coined and made popular through the software industry and, unfortunately, many people have boiled agile down to a set of practices and processes for developing software. Some have extended it beyond the software world and even then limited it to a management process or methodology. Therefore naturally the agile transformation will start with changing the process element of an organization.

Figure 5 shows that once you change the process element to support agility, and no other elements change (as in Stage 1 of Figure 5), the organization's culture becomes misaligned. As soon as the change agent stops "pushing" the change goes away because the culture (the red bungee cord around the triangle) will push the Process element back into alignment with the structures, strategy, leadership style, and the people's beliefs.

However the change agent may persist and push harder, thereby changing some of the peoples' beliefs as well as some aspects of the structure and strategy (as in Stage 2 of Figure 5). It will take a lot of effort to keep pushing the change forward (as shown in Stages 3 and 4 of Figure 5) until gradually the remaining elements of the organization transform.

While this approach is not impossible, it is risky because throughout the entire transformation the organizational elements are not in alignment (the triangle is red) and the culture will keep trying to "push

Figure 5. Process-led Agile Transformation Approach

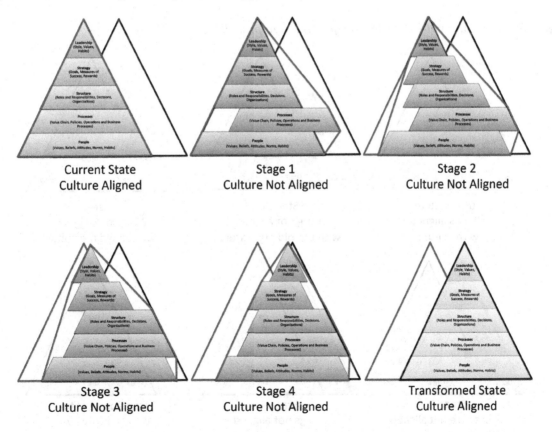

back" all the changing elements to their original state of equilibrium. Organizations need to have strong change champions and lots of patience and perseverance to achieve sustainable organizational agility through this approach. I personally have not see this approach succeed in organizations.

Approach 2: Organization-Led Transformations

Another view for organizational transformation is what we call the organization-led transformation. In this approach we look at the entire organization as a bunch of smaller nested organizations as indicated in Figure 6.

Since agile started in the software industry, we usually see the IT organization as the only part of the organization that adopts the new way of thinking (as depicted in Stage 1 of Figure 6). This is assuming that they (the IT organization) embark upon a proper transformation, which includes moving all the elements of its triangle (leadership, strategy, structure, process and people). However, when we look at the big picture, which is the agility of the entire organization or enterprise, the question arises, how sustainable can the IT organization be with a culture that is not in alignment with the rest of the enterprise? Can they sustain the cultural tension between them and rest of the entities in the enterprise (represented in the red bungee cord) that are trying to pull them back)? As much as we tend to believe that parts of organizations operate in silos and can act as separate entities, the reality is for the enterprise as a whole to be high performing, its entire culture needs to be aligned.

Figure 6. Organizational-led Agile Transformation Approach

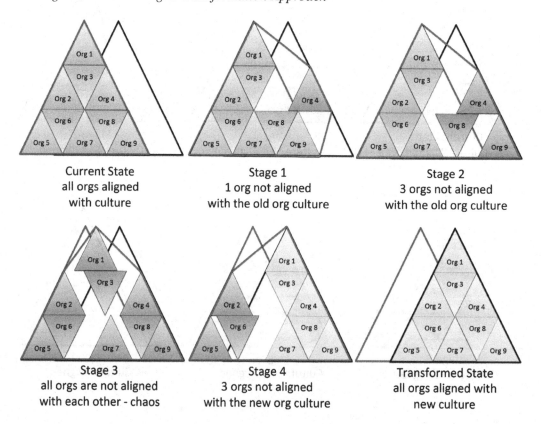

Sometimes the organization (whether IT or some other part component) pioneering the transformation is successful enough (and influential enough) that it becomes a beacon attracting other parts of the organization to transform (as depicted in Stage 2 of Figure 6). While it may promote transformations to happen across other parts of the organization, all those entities are still subject to the "pressure" of conforming to the rest of the organization. The overall organization will remain misaligned until it reaches a critical mass, such that enough entities in the organization start to transform to the new way of working and that becomes the new dominant culture (as depicted in Stage 4 of Figure 6).

5. CULTURE-LED TRANSFORMATION

After looking at the two common approaches to transformation (Process-led and Organizational-led), it becomes apparent that sustainable transformations may need to find a different approach to increase the probability of success for the transformation. This is how we combined the best of both approaches in what we are labeling "Culture-led transformation."

Before we proceed it is important to note that both the process-led approach or the organizational-led approach are common approaches to transformation, even for organizations that know that the journey to agile is more than just process change or just changing one of its business units. The reason they pick a process-led approach or an organizational-led approach is that the organization is worried about changing too much too quickly – they are worried about the high risk of change and its impact on its performance. So they decide to change just the process aspect of the organization, or decide to change one sub-component within the larger organization or enterprise.

In a culture-led transformation we assume that the organization understands the reality of the transformation being about mindset and culture, and that they realize that to reap all of the benefits of organizational agility, the transformation needs to go beyond one part of the organization (usually IT) and span the entire organization. At the same time, the organization wants to reduce the risk of the transformation and minimize the impact on day-to-day operations. It is based on that mindset (reducing risk while striving for complete transformation) that we present the culture-led approach.

In culture-led transformation the organization designs a values-based roadmap that aims at transforming the entire organization, together, in small increments (we will show how to design such a roadmap in 6 of this chapter). These increments focus on instilling specific agile behaviors, values and habits across the entire organization. The key is that these small increments of change span all the elements of the organizational ecosystem (its leadership, strategy, structure, process and people). In Figure 7 you can see how all the elements of the organizational ecosystem are changing together in small increments.

For example, think of a case where we are focusing the transform on one thing – embracing the agile value of collaboration and effective communication. We will not think about iterations or WIP limits. We will not think about Test-Driven Development or Continuous Delivery for now. We will simply try to create a new organizational culture that embraces and manifests higher levels of communication and collaboration. In this case, the roadmap for change will highlight the changes that need to happen to each element in the organizational ecosystem to promote and support this new habit and culture.

As seen in Stage 1 in the previous diagram, the entire "triangle" moves (transforms) together. You create a shared vision for the entire organization. You create a common journey. The transformation is not for some people and not others. You are enforcing an important concept; this affects all of us, and we are all in this together. Contrast this approach with what we commonly observe in organizations

Figure 7. Culture-led transformation

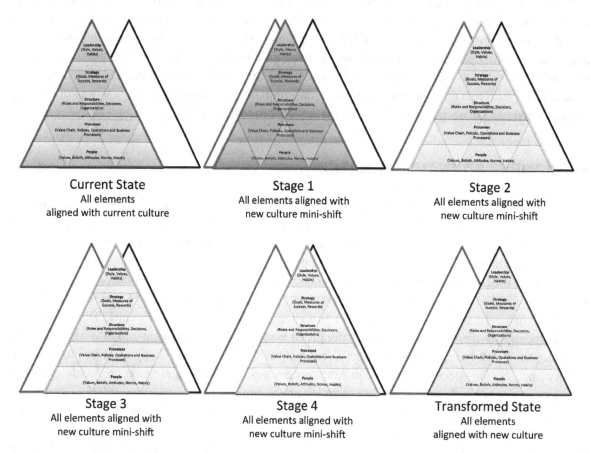

transforming to agile. They change the process to be more collaborative but the rewards system still promotes individual heroics. How sustainable it that? How long will it take before teams go back to their old habits – which are supported and enforced by the rest of the organizational elements?

The remaining sections in the chapter will show you how to create an agile transformation roadmap to achieve a culture-led transformation.

5.1. Important Considerations for the Culture-Led Transformation Approach

While the culture-led transformation approach described above has it obvious merits there are things that people need to be aware of to avoid some of its pitfalls.

Example Teams/Organizations

A key element of the Culture-led transformation is to establish what we call "Examples." Examples can be teams, projects or organizations, but the key is that they go "all the way". They show the organization what the end result could look like. They are the motivation for the organization to keep going through the long transformation journey.

Because transformation journeys are long in duration, organizations try to "accelerate" them to see instant (or very quick) results. While we support the idea of quick wins and showing success early, we also want to emphasize that sustainable organizational transformation is not something that can be achieved overnight (because we are changing mindsets, habits and culture of the organization to make sure its sustainable). Therefore to balance between the need for quick wins that motivate us and show us the end result in a tangible way we can relate to and to give the organization the time and space it needs to truly transform, we see it as necessary to have Examples during what can seem like a rather slow organization transformation journey of the rest of the organization.

As you can see when comparing Figure 8 and Figure 6, a key difference between these Examples (Figure 8) and what we saw in the organizational-led transformation (Figure 6) approach is that Examples exist while the rest of the organization is also transforming. Everyone is changing but the Examples are modeling what the change will look like. We are also using the Examples to experiment and learn what will work and not in our organization.

It is important to keep in mind that Examples are not pilot projects or organizations that will start the journey first while the rest of the organization is "waiting" to see if they will work. It is also important to choose these Examples wisely so that they provide motivation and visibility to the end result across the entire enterprise, not just one part of the organization.

Figure 8. Culture-led transformation with example organizations

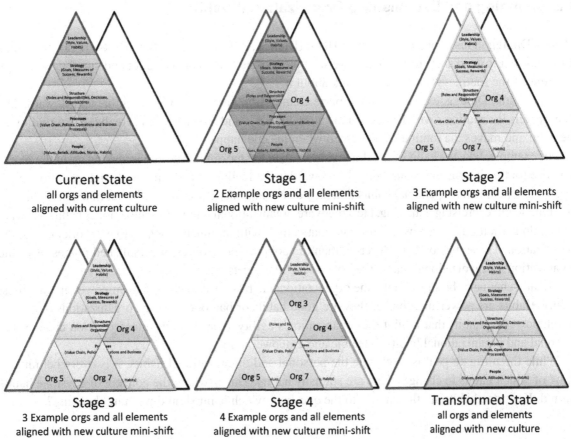

Executive Support

As you can see, the Culture-led approach requires a high degree of executive buy-in and commitment since they (the leadership element of the triangle) are involved in the transformation and they need to enable change that will span the entire organization.

While we recognize that getting executive support may be a constraint, our experience has been that is something that cannot be skipped or watered-down. If an organization wants sustainable organizational transformation, they need to recognize that they are changing all the elements of the organization and impacting the culture and mindset, and that is not something that can be done (from our experience) without a high degree of executive support. Without that degree of executive support teams can adopt agile on a team level, but that team or sub-system exists within a broader organization that has a different culture and that will continue to "pull them back" to the old culture and current way of doing things (the organizational habits).

We are not saying this to demotivate or discourage people from adopting agile on a team or sub-organizational level, we just want people to have realistic expectations. Team-level agile can be achieved with and without a high level of executive support, and while it may be hard to sustain, it is not impossible. However, the journey for sustainable organizational agility and the transformation needed for that, based on our experience, cannot be achieved without a very high degree of ownership from the executives of the company.

5.2. Changing and Establishing Organizational Habits

Charles Duhigg in his book, The Power of Habit (Duhigg, 2012), suggests that habits are not conscious decisions, but instead are routines. Once we start the routine, we go on autopilot and simply go through the steps of the routine–we don't even think about it.

In his book, Duhigg, explains that the basic elements of a habit are: Cue, Routine and Reward. The Cue triggers the routine – which is executed automatically – and then a reward is realized that reinforces the habit and makes the routine trigger again when the cue happens again.

For example, take the habit of brushing your teeth in the morning. The cue is waking up in the morning. The routine is brushing your teeth. The reward is the feeling of a clean mouth and fresh breath.

Just like people have personal habits that they do as "automatic routines" without much thought (e.g. brushing teeth, exercising, smoking, etc.) there are organizational habits. Organizational habits are what people do in their day-to-day work life "automatically" (without much thought) to get work done in the organization. These may be very different than the policies, procedures or established processes of the organization – organizational habits are how work "really gets done" in the organization.

For any change to be sustainable, the organizational habits need to change to empower and manifest agility. Habits are powerful, whether they are good habits or bad ones. Today, organizations may have dis-empowering habits that inhibit the organization's agility. A successful transformation changes the personal and organizational habits to enable and empower agility.

While the ultimate goal is to change the personal and organizational habits, it is overwhelming to think of which habits to change; there are so many habits. This is where the concept of keystone habits started. Keystone habits are the answer to the question, which habit should we start changing?

Keystone habits are habits that have the power to start a chain reaction changing other habits across the organization. Keystone habits start a process that, over time, transforms everything.

For example, a non-keystone habit is turning the water off while you brush your teeth. While this is a great habit, there is little probability that this habit will change the rest of your life. On the other hand, Regular physical activity, is a keystone habit, because for many people it starts other habits like eating healthy, proper sleeping and so on. The key to a keystone habit is that it commonly has ripple effect beyond the original habit. The healthy eating and proper sleeping are not part of the original goal (the exercise); instead, these healthy changes are part of a chain reaction that happens when you incorporate the keystone habit.

6. CREATING AN AGILE TRANSFORMATION ROADMAP BASED ON KEYSTONE HABITS

To summarize thus far, culture-led agile transformation focuses on changing all the elements of the organizational ecosystem at the same time (Leadership, Strategy, Structure, Process and People) but in small manageable stages. Each of these stages will focus on introducing a keystone habit into the organization.

The design of the stages needed for the transformation is what we label as The Agile Transformation Roadmap. This roadmap helps provide the organization with the bigger picture of the Agile transformation. The way we design a Transformation Roadmap is by creating a 2 dimensional table. One dimension will be the elements of the organizational ecosystem (Leadership, Strategy, Structure, Process and People) and the other dimension will be the stages of the transformation. For each stage in our transformation, we will identify a Keystone habit for the organization to focus on (see Figure 9).

To fill out each row in the roadmap, the following questions need to be answered.

- What does Leadership need to know, or do to enable, support and promote this keystone habit?
- What needs to change for our Strategies to enable, support and promote this keystone habit?
- What needs to change for our Structure to enable, support and promote this keystone habit?
- What needs to change for our Processes to enable, support and promote this keystone habit?
- What do People in the organization need to know, or do to enable, support and promote this keystone habit?

Figure 9. Empty framework for an Agile Transformation Roadmap

	Leadership	Strategy	Structure	Process	People
Stage n: Keystone Habit #n					
Stage 4: Keystone Habit #4					
Stage 3: Keystone Habit #3					
Stage 2: Keystone Habit #2					
Stage 1: Keystone Habit #1					

Every organization needs to consider what changes need to happen within every element of the organization to promote the new culture and turn it into an organizational culture that causes people to do something automatically because it has proven to help them succeed at work. It is when people in the organization do not view these changes as "the new process" or the "flavor of the month" To keep going with this example, what needs to change about processes to promote communication and collaboration? What policies, and activities need to be changed or introduced to guarantee more communication and collaboration and engrain that habit into the culture? What needs to change with regard to peoples' beliefs, values and personal habits to support the new behavior of communication and collaboration? All these questions need to be answered by the organization to successfully shift the organization to the next step towards organizational agility.

6.1. Suggested Stages and Keystone Habits for Agile Transformation Roadmap

A lot of agile experience, change management and organizational context is put into the design of the agile transformational roadmap and deciding what practices need to be introduced in each stage of the transformation to establish new organizational habits. From our experience and research we suggest that the first 4 Keystone Habits to be introduced are:

Stage 1: Establish a habit of *communicating and collaborating.*
Stage 2: Establish a habit of working and *delivering in circular – evolutionary slices* to realize early value.
Stage 3: Establish a habit of *integrating all efforts* – integrated work streams, integrated work team.
Stage 4: Establish a habit of *gathering feedback from multiple levels* – truly open to change and learning.

It has been our experience that these stages, done in this sequence, have yielded good results, however, during your agile transformation, these stages may be modified depending on what is deemed best fit for the organization. Figure 10 illustrates what an empty Agile Transformation Roadmap would look like populated with the 4 stages and keystone habits we recommend.

6.2. Transforming Leadership and People

It is critical for the organization to realize that sustainable culture-led transformations cannot be outsourced or bought from a consulting or coaching company. While agile consulting and coaching companies can assist with the design of the transformation approach and roadmap, the major change has to come from within.

As illustrated in Figure 11, sustainable cultural transformation relies on transforming both the human elements (leadership and people) as well as the non-human elements (strategy, structure and process) of the organization. It is quite unfortunate that most (but not all) of the transformation efforts I have seen in the Agile industry have focused on transforming the non-human elements, even though I think most people would agree that true sustainable change happens when the human elements transform. Transforming the human elements is done through learning, education, coaching and mentoring.

Figure 10. Agile Transformation Roadmap with 4 recommended stages and keystone habits

	Leadership What does Leadership need to know, or do to enable, support and promote this keystone habit?	**Strategy** What needs to change for our Strategies to enable, support and promote this keystone habit?	**Structure** What needs to change for our Structure to enable, support and promote this keystone habit?	**Process** What needs to change for our Processes to enable, support and promote this keystone habit?	**People** What do People need to know, or do to enable, support and promote this keystone habit?
Keystone Habit #n					
Keystone Habit: Adaptation Establish a habit of gathering feedback from multiple levels – truly open to change and learning					
Keystone Habit: Integration Establish a habit of integrating all efforts – integrated work streams, integrated work team					
Keystone Habit: Evolution Establish a habit of working and delivering in circular – evolutionary slices to realize early value					
Keystone Habit: Collaboration Establish a habit of communicating and collaborating					

6.3. Sustainable Transformation through Learning and Education

Education is a critical component in a sustainable agile transformation. Sustainable agile is realized when people have truly change the way they think – and this requires education. If we truly understand that we need to change the mindset of everyone in the organization, including its leaders, then we need a combination of education and coaching and mentoring to successfully equip people with the knowledge and skills they need to develop and execute the agile habits we talked about earlier. If we think of agile as a process, not a mindset, then we default to training instead of education.

There is a clear difference between education and training - education is about the changing of the way people think about their day-to-day work – how to govern an agile project, while keeping flexibility, how to build code while reducing the cost of change, to undertake analysis by focusing on vertical slices of business value.

Training is about the mechanics of how practices are done, such as a template for writing a user story. Education will focus on changing the thought process to focus on value and enable the educated to think and decide what works for them and for their team.

Lots of agile teams have gone through Scrum training, or even better, Agile training. While we believe there is value in these trainings, what we are illustrating here is way beyond that. Most of these training

Figure 11. Distinguishing between the human and non-human elements of an Agile Transformation

Human Elements:
The keys for sustainably transforming the leadership and people elements:

- A common education journey (not training) to change how people work and illustrate how to live the Agile Mindset in their job
- Leadership Coaching (how to inspire performance not mandate it)
- Mentoring and Coaching on an individual and team level.

Non-Human Elements:
The keys for sustainably transforming the strategy, structure and process elements:

- Designing and Implementing a multi-stage roadmap to agility that changes all three of these element in synergy and harmony
- A combination of consulting, mentoring, organizational coaching, business process re-engineering and organizational change management to roll-out the changes across the organization

sessions discuss the practices and ceremonies of the practices, like how to do release planning, how to write user stories or how to facilitate a daily stand-up. While this training is needed, this is not education. Education goes beyond the practices and into the day-to-day, minute-by-minute thought process of people. Education will help people BE agile not just DO agile. Education illuminates their hearts and minds and helps them realize how an agilist acts and thinks in-between and beyond the daily meetings and work-sessions. It changes their beliefs, values and habits. That is truly when agility becomes sustainable – when it is embodied in the DNA of the people running the organization (at both leadership and staff levels) (see Figure 12).

The International Consortium for Agile (ICAgile) has gathered experts from around the world to define a learning and educational roadmap for various disciplines needed by organizations aspiring for sustainable organizational agility. ICAgile has published a set of learning objectives that creates a clear learning roadmap for what people need to learn within each discipline (such as Development, Testing, Leadership, and Coaching) to become knowledgeable and capable to work in a way that enables, promotes and manifests the organizational agility towards which the organization is transforming.

6.4. Transforming Strategy, Structure, and Process

In the previous section we highlighted an important missing element, in most transformations, is the learning and education component. The journey for the leadership and individual contributors (people) is mostly an educational journey. People need to understand why they are doing the routine of the habit and what they are getting out of it.

Figure 12. Agile Transformation Roadmap emphasizing the roles of learning and education

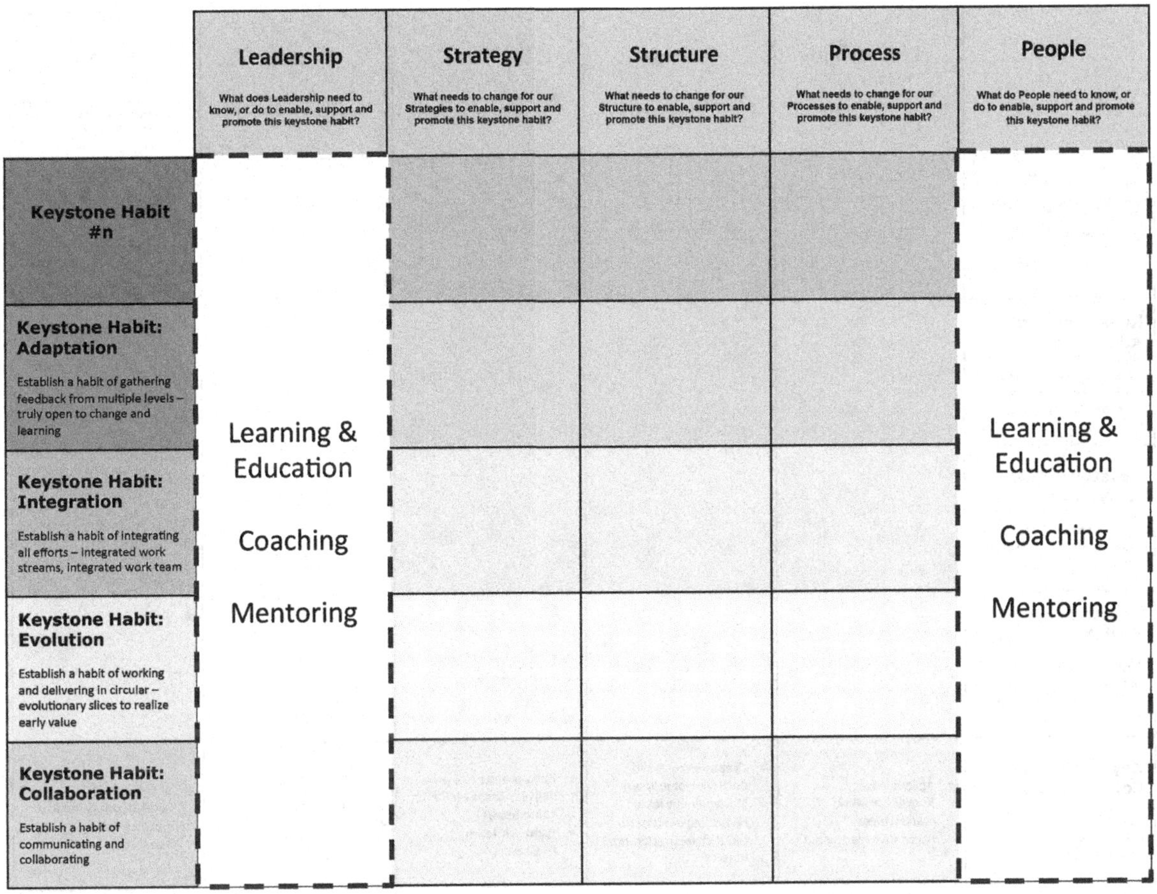

	Leadership	Strategy	Structure	Process	People
	What does Leadership need to know, or do to enable, support and promote this keystone habit?	What needs to change for our Strategies to enable, support and promote this keystone habit?	What needs to change for our Structure to enable, support and promote this keystone habit?	What needs to change for our Processes to enable, support and promote this keystone habit?	What do People need to know, or do to enable, support and promote this keystone habit?
Keystone Habit #n					
Keystone Habit: Adaptation Establish a habit of gathering feedback from multiple levels – truly open to change and learning	Learning & Education Coaching Mentoring				Learning & Education Coaching Mentoring
Keystone Habit: Integration Establish a habit of integrating all efforts – integrated work streams, integrated work team					
Keystone Habit: Evolution Establish a habit of working and delivering in circular – evolutionary slices to realize early value					
Keystone Habit: Collaboration Establish a habit of communicating and collaborating					

As for the strategy, structure, and process components of the roadmap these elements will need to change to support the Keystone habits. This is where a lot of the agile practices can come in and also this the place that can accommodate scaling models like the Scaled Agile Framework and Disciplined Agile Delivery.

Consider this example. Suppose we are going to introduce the keystone habit of "Enhancing Communication and Collaboration." The entire organization will embark on a journey to change the ecosystem (leadership, strategy, structure, processes and people) to establish the habit and realize the benefits associated with that keystone habit.

To support these changes the leadership will go through a learning program and possibly also some coaching and mentoring to learn what the Agile mindset is about as well as how to manage Knowledge Workers and how collaboration is not "touchy feel stuff" but truly the engine of an innovative, knowledge work, organization. Similarly the people need learn also what the Agile mindset is and why they should value collaboration (even if it takes longer). People need to belief that collaboration will yield better results and that it is worth the investment. This is how these new strategies, structures and processes can be supported. Then by having all the 5 elements of the organization promote collaboration it will become a habit in the organization. Figure 13 shows an example of how the roadmap may look like when starting with collaboration as the first Keystone habit.

Figure 13. Agile Transformation Roadmap with first stage populated with Agile Practices

	Leadership	Strategy	Structure	Process	People
	What does Leadership need to know, or do to enable, support and promote this keystone habit?	What needs to change for our Strategies to enable, support and promote this keystone habit?	What needs to change for our Structure to enable, support and promote this keystone habit?	What needs to change for our Processes to enable, support and promote this keystone habit?	What do People need to know, or do to enable, support and promote this keystone habit?
Keystone Habit #n					
Keystone Habit: Adaptation Establish a habit of gathering feedback from multiple levels – truly open to change and learning					
Keystone Habit: Integration Establish a habit of integrating all efforts – integrated work streams, integrated work team					
Keystone Habit: Evolution Establish a habit of working and delivering in circular – evolutionary slices to realize early value					
Keystone Habit: Collaboration Establish a habit of communicating and collaborating	❖ Agile mindset ❖ Knowledge work management ❖ Facilitative leadership	❖ Create a cross-silo portfolio value team ❖ Management level rewarding system for team collaboration not heroics	❖ Each project has a delivery team and a value teams ❖ Establish team facilitators	❖ Chartering ❖ Information radiators ❖ Collaboration tools ❖ 15 minute daily touch points ❖ Retrospectives	❖ ICAgile's Agile Fundamentals (which includes the agile mindset)

6.5. Things to Keep in Mind about Your Roadmap

Since each organization is unique, each organization should have a different roadmap. The key to making sure that your roadmap is correct is to frequently inspect and adapt it. Just like in knowledge work you won't know if you got it right till you do it, similarly, your first roadmap probably won't be completely right and it is also probably the best starting point you have. The most important thing is to inspect and adapt and discuss what changes need to happen to the roadmap as execution begins. Don't try to take a "checklist mentality" or "linear approach" to agile transformation – that would be pretty ironic.

Here are a couple of important things to key in mind:

1.   It's going to be a fairly long journey. The strategy, structure and processes of companies are established (and deeply rooted) elements in an organization. Sudden change to them may work in some cases, but in most cases it doesn't. So just as the educational journey for leadership is multi-stage and probably multi-year, the transformational roadmap for the strategy, structure and process also will probably be multi-stage and multi-year – it actually should go hand-in-hand with the educational component of the roadmap.

2. The transformational journey should span the entire organization. The entire organization is engaged in a common journey to reach a shared vision. By having one part of the organization change and not the other we are creating misalignment again within the overall culture. Due to the size of the change it is very tempting to "try it out" in a "small contained group" within the organization first to see if the new changes work first. Our advice in this situation is to make smaller changes – if needed - but keep everyone in the organization engaged – not just one "pilot" group.

7. MEASUREMENTS

The final component that needs to be addressed in a culture-led transformation is measurement. One of the main reasons we promote a culture-led transformation is that we want to ensure that the culture doesn't get misaligned and strained during the transformation.

The measurement system is primarily established to:

- Validate quantitatively the progress of the transformation.
- Validate quantitatively the impact of the transformation.
- Validate quantitatively the alignment of the culture.

7.1. Progress of the Transformation

Any agile transformation, especially multi-year transformations like the one discussed in this chapter, need to show, via quantitative evidence, that the transformation people are investing time, energy, money, and other resources in is progressing. The team needs to define what progress means and establish a measurement system to show evidence of progress. While the impact of the transformation (as described in the next section) is really the more important measure from our perspective, measuring progress is still important, because for the impact to be substantial, it will take time, and if progress is not being tracked, funding for the transformation may get cut before the impact can be realized.

7.2. Impact of the Transformation

While measuring progress is important to justify the investment put into the transformation, the true measure of the transformation is its impact. Measures need to be defined upfront for what the anticipated impact from the transformation will be, and then measurement systems (how to measure) need to be established from day one to show the impact of the transformation – even if it is small. The challenge here is that defining the measurements and establishing a system to measure them is not easy, and so many transformation efforts skip doing it and just start the transformation. The power of starting the measurement of impact from day one is that first of all it forces the organization to think about what impact they expect the transformation to have, and more importantly how to measure that impact. Measures of impact provide a sense of accomplishment for the team and the organization along their journey, while at the same time they illustrate what the return on investment realized from the journey has been.

7.3. Alignment of the Culture

The last piece of the measurement system needs to be a mechanism to monitor the mindset and culture that are changing across the organization. Basically, the organization needs to be aware when the "triangle" is not moving together and when one element is causing the culture to be misaligned or strained. Today most organization don't "measure" this but rather experience its symptoms every day of the transformation.

When organizations start to measure impediments associated with the transformation like the lack of buy-in and lack of commitment to initiatives, what they are really doing is subtly measuring the strain on the culture (the rubber band) and its alignment. If the elements of the organization (leadership, strategy, structure, processes and people) are all aligned, why would there be lack of buy-in or lack of commitment? Lack of buy-in and commitment is an indicator that something is not yet aligned.

For example, if there is a complaint about buy-in, that could indicate that management is trying to do something and people are not aligned or vice versa. If "management" is not bought-in to something the team is doing then that is an indication that the elements of the "triangle" are not moving together. The lack of buy-in could be because the staff had started on the education journey but not the leadership, or vice versa.

The point is that when there is misalignment in the culture, all sorts of challenges appear during the journey. The organization should identify how they will measure the alignment of culture during the transformation and put in place the measurement system to gather that quantitative data. That way, the organization will be aware (and address issues) that come up once the culture gets out of alignment. The team should develop a hypersensitivity to the alignment of culture, because it is the key to protecting the company from a drop in performance during the transformation.

8. THE AGILE ADOPTION FRAMEWORK

After presenting the Culture-led Agile Transformation approach in the chapter, it is important to link it to the Agile Adoption Framework (Sidky, 2008; Sidky, Arthur, J. D., & Bohner, 2007). Since 2007 (A. A. Sidky, J. D., 2007), the framework has been applied at a number of organizations around the world. Due to confidentiality restrictions only some of that work has been published (Ahmed, 2009). The experiences acquired over those years have given the author important insights to enhance the Agile Adoption Framework.

The Culture-led Agile Transformation approach presented in the chapter and the Agile Adoption Framework share the same essence – they both present a staged agile transformation approach that is methodology agnostic and based on behaviors and values. They both share the same understanding that an organization must customize the practices they adopt based on their organizational readiness and the realities of their environment. One of the main components in Agile Adoption Framework was the Sidky Agile Measurement Index (SAMI). SAMI consists of 5 levels that provided organizations with guidance on the steps to focus on to become more agile. The same values explained in Stages 1-4 on the SAMI have become the basis for the 4 keystones habits highlighted in Culture-led Agile Transformation.

What has evolved since the Agile Adoption Framework is the idea of selecting a target agile level for a project and then reconciling it with the organization's readiness. I have found that idea to be hindering. Projects and teams should evolve practices constantly as their environment changes. What is more important to me now is to focus on educating people in the organization and on teams to the essence of the Agile mindset and a deep understanding of the practices so that they are really empowered to BE agile not just execute on a predetermined set of Agile practices.

We still believe conducting an organizational readiness assessment for Agile is important and plays a critical part in the design of the Agile Transformation Roadmap highlighted in Section 6 of this chapter.

9. CONCLUSION

Organizational agility is not an end state, but rather a continuous journey. The key to sustainable agility is to ensure that the organizational culture is aligned throughout the journey; thereby ensuring that the culture of the organization is not fighting back against the changes the organization is experiencing.

The journey to transform an organization and increase it agility is not a quick one. Transformations need time to be properly absorbed by the organization and by its people. In this chapter we present the keys to sustainable organizational agility. The keys are centered on the concept of Culture-led transformation where the goal is to transform all the elements that shape the culture (leadership, strategy, structure, process and people) together in a common journey so that the culture remains aligned through the transformation period.

The key to transforming the leadership and people aspect of the organization is to engage them in a common educational journey. The key to the strategy, structure, and process components is to establish a roadmap that spreads the transformation over a period of time suitable for the organization while highlighting key value-based milestones along the way. The last key to the transformation is to establish a strong measurement system that focuses on measuring the progress and impact of the transformation, and just as importantly, the alignment of the culture throughout the transformation.

By focusing on these three keys, we have seen organizations change the way they think and embody a culture that is aligned with the new way of thinking, thereby changing the organization itself, along with the habits of the people in the organization. Once the habits are changed, the new way of working becomes the normal way of working and that is how sustainable agility is achieved in organizations.

REFERENCES

Ahmed, E., & Sidky, A. (2009). 25 percent Ahead of Schedule and just at "Step 2" of the SAMI. In *Proceedings of the 2009 Agile Conference*. IEEE Computer Society. doi:10.1109/AGILE.2009.63

Collins, J., & Porras, J. (2004). *Built to Last: Successful Habits of Visionary Companies*. HarperBusiness. doi: 10.1002/hrdq.1092

Duhigg, C. (2012). The Power of Habit: Why We Do What We Do in Life and Business, Random House. *Journal of Child and Family Studies, 22*(4), 582–584. doi:10.1007/s10826-012-9645-6

Sidky, A., & Arthur, J. D. (2007). *A Structured Approach to Adopting Agile Practices: The Agile Adoption Framework*. (Ph. D. Dissertation). Virginia Tech. doi: 10.2481/dsj.6.S70

Sidky, A., & Arthur, J. D. (2008). *Value-Driven Agile Adoption: Improving An Organization's Software Development Approach*. Paper presented at the New Trends in Software Methodologies, Tools and Techniques.

Sidky, A. S., Arthur, J. D., & Bohner, S. (2007). A Disciplined Approach to Adopting Agile Practices: The Agile Adoption Framework. *Journal of Innovations in Systems and Software Engineering, 3*. doi:10.1007/978-1-84628-821-0

KEY TERMS AND DEFINITIONS

Agile Software Development: Agile software development is a group of software development methods in which requirements and solutions evolve through collaboration between self-organizing, cross-functional teams. It promotes adaptive planning, evolutionary development, early delivery, continuous improvement, and encourages rapid and flexible response to change.

Extreme Programming: Extreme Programming (XP) is an agile methodology that specifically emphasizes the use of agile technical practices (e.g. Test Driven Development) for the success of an agile project. Practical experience shows that XP complements Scrum well and both the methods work well together.

Feature Driven Development: Feature Driven Development (FDD) is an agile method that focuses on delivering working software in a timely manner by using simple, client focused and practical software process. This method works well without tailoring to both small (< 8 team size) and large teams (> 30 team size).

Refactoring: Refactoring aims to have a cleaner "code" by restructuring the code without changing its external behaviour. The idea is to improve the design of the code with the intention of making it easy to use.

Scrum: Scrum is one of the popular agile methodologies which aims to address the challenges of projects involving complex scope of work using a simple process dependent on a small team who are motivated, collaborative and highly focused on producing working software every 2-4 weeks.

Chapter 7
Design of a Framework to Implement Agility at Organizational Level

Jagadeesh Balakrishnan
National University of Singapore, Singapore

ABSTRACT

While many existing Agile product development methodologies like SCRUM, Extreme Programming (XP), Dynamic Systems Development Method (DSDM), Feature Driven Development (FDD) etc. cover aspects related to developing & delivering a product solution, they are not meant to provide an end to end framework for an organization to transition / embrace and adopt agile way of software development. For an organization's agile journey to be successful we should consider several organizational elements like how to do a business case for agile, how to build agile leadership qualities for staff at all levels (especially Managers), how to setup & govern an agile organization, how to assess an agile organization etc.

1. INTRODUCTION

Agile methods have gained a lot of prominence in the industry as a development method of choice. While many existing Agile product development methodologies like SCRUM, Extreme Programming (XP), Dynamic Systems Development Method (DSDM), Feature Driven Development (FDD) etc. (Dingsøyr et al., 2012) cover aspects related to developing and delivering a product solution, they are not meant to provide an end to end framework for an organization to transition / embrace and adopt agile way of software development.

For an organization's agile journey to be successful we should consider several organizational elements like how to do a business case for agile, how to build agile leadership qualities for staff at all levels (especially Managers), how to setup and govern an agile organization, how to assess an agile organization etc. Further the design of the agile framework should combine different agile methodologies SCRUM, DSDM, XP etc. (Qumer and Henderson-Sellers, 2008) and build a matrix of methodologies that could be applied to a specific project need. By building such an agile framework, organizations would benefit by referring to a holistic framework to manage their organizational agile initiatives.

DOI: 10.4018/978-1-4666-9858-1.ch007

2. WATERFALL VS. AGILE DELIVERY

Before looking at a framework design for Agile, let us try to organize some of the basic differences between waterfall and agile delivery from a people, process and customer perspective. This comparison is in no way intended to highlight that agile is better than a waterfall approach. The focus rather is on trying to appreciate the fundamental differences between the two approaches. There might be many situations where both approaches have an intersection point (e.g. Plans versus Goals. Both waterfall and agile approaches have plans and goals but waterfall prefers having a detailed plan approach while agile favors a more goal driven execution approach) (Chan & Thong, 2009) (see Tables 1, 2, and 3).

2.1. People Perspective

Underlying Agile Principle: "People are trusted to do the right things, at the right time, and in the right way".

Table 1.

Waterfall Focus	Agile Focus
Hierarchy – Focus on command and control approach	Synergy – Focus on cooperation of various people involved in the project
Seniority – Decisions are taken by the senior most resource	Competence – Decisions are taken by the most competent team member for that task
Directed – Workers wait for instructions and are directed on what to do and how to do.	Autonomous –Workers are encouraged to choose what they want to work on and how they want to execute work.
Managers – Focus is on managing work	Facilitation – Focus is on facilitation instead of management
Appraisal – Workers are evaluated by senior authority for performance and given feedback	Reflection – Team reflects collectively on improvements and takes the next step towards success together

Table 2.

Waterfall Focus	Agile Focus
Plans – Focus is on planning the work and working the plan!	Tactics – Focus is on following a solution oriented approach. What works for a given situation is given priority over planned arrangements if needed.
Linear – Detailed step by step instructions to execute all parts of work.	Iterative – Work solution emerges iteratively.
Rule based – Everything that is done in a project is based on a set of agreed rules	Goal based – Everything that is done is based on the goals of the system or project.
Scheduled – Detailed scheduled for all activities are drawn out	Time boxed – Specific activities are identified and are strictly time boxed
Quality Assured – A separate QA team reviews work all the time.	Peer Reviewed – Work is continually peer reviewed
Task based – Tasks drive allocation of work to team members	Role based – Roles drive selection of tasks by team members

Table 3.

Waterfall Focus	Agile Focus
Requirements – Focus is on satisfying well written requirements	Needs – Focus is on meeting the changing needs of the customer
Content – Focus is on written content in the form of requirements document	Context – Focus is on context and requirements can change dynamically if the context changes.
Deliverables – Focus is on completing agreed deliverables	Value – Focused is always on delivering value to the customer
Critical path – Work is centered around critical path for the activities	Priority List – Work is always centered around the list of priorities for the current iteration
Baselined – Requirements and plans are baselined and put under change control.	Evolving – Requirements and plans are allowed to evolve dynamically (adapt to change than control change)

2.2. Process Perspective

Underlying Agile Principle: "In an Agile project, quality is not tested in, it is designed in".

2.3. Customer Perspective

Underlying Agile Principle: "Things that do not deliver value to the customer probably need not exist".

It is clear from the above differences that Agile focuses more than waterfall development on aspects like people empowerment, embracing change and delivering value.

3. AGILE ADOPTION TREND

The IT industry is replete with examples of many short term trends emerge and die very soon. Some protagonists do argue that Agile is also a buzz word and will have a limited lifespan. However, agile adoption is widespread as evidenced by latest Gartner hype cycles (2013, 2014) (Cohn, 2005) and adoption levels of agile are increasing day by day consistently. A few samples of top organizations adopting agile are given below (DeMarco & Boehm, 2002).

A brief industry scan would show the deep adoption of agility in many organizations.

- The Accenture Agile Delivery Capability is a process that has been tailored to meet the needs of defense organizations (Accenture, 2009). This is a customer focused process that uses a disciplined and rigorous process as well as flexibility.
- At Cisco, the software engineers are using agile development principles into practice, and also work closely with the customers to produce software that meets the needs of the customers ().
- The Collaboration and Communications Group (CCG) at Cisco stated the use of agile methodologies in the company, although other teams have also adopted these techniques (Cisco Systems, 2011). Cisco had used the waterfall method for a very long time, but it ended up adopting this method in 2008 (Cisco Systems, 2011).
- Dell also implemented the Dell Agile Working Solution Blueprint which helped in the end to end delivery with other befits related to cost cutting, productivity enhancements' and improved performance (Dell Corporation, 2008)

- Barry Boehm identified Agile as the important trend in 2000's in his work (Boehm, 2006).
- Gartner has put Agile Development Methodology near the end of "Trough of Disillusionment" (Fenn & Linden, 2005). This Hype cycle shows that Agile is starting the journey in the "Slope of Enlightenment" right now. This means that stable adoption of Agile is predicted widely across the industry in the next 5 – 10 years.

The above industry data hints that organizations increasingly adopt agile methods to develop projects. While there are several agile models that address how an agile project needs to be executed, a unified framework that can be applied at the organizational level does not exist. So, it is critical to define an agile framework that addresses the organizational agile needs.

4. ORGANIZATIONAL AGILE FRAMEWORK

There are many agile methodologies currently existing in the industry. According to the IT Knowledge portal http://www.itinfo.am, some of the important agile methodologies are given below.

- Scrum (www.scrumalliance.org)
- Feature Driven Development (FDD) (http://en.wikipedia.org/wiki/Feature-driven_development)
- Dynamic Systems Development Method (DSDM) (http://www.dsdm.org)
- Agile Unified Process (AUP) (http://www.ambysoft.com/scottAmbler.html)
- Lean IT Methodology (Source: Wikipedia)
- Extreme Programming (XP) (Source: Wikipedia)
- Crystal family of standards (Source: Wikipedia)
- Evolutionary Development Model (EVO) (Source: Wikipedia)

An initial study and analysis of the agile models given above reveal that they contribute towards running a project the agile way and do not directly scale up to an organizational level to meet the needs of any project that is run the agile way. This "scaling" needed at organizational level underlines the purpose behind creating a separate organizational agile framework.

4.1. Building Organizational Agile Framework: Where to Start?

To build an organizational agile framework, every organization should first start by interpreting the four agile manifesto values and 12 agile principles to *its own business context*. While the agile principles look straightforward, its applicability to each organization will vary considerably as illustrated in the example below (see Table 4).

Let us consider the principle, "responding to change over following a plan". If an organization aims to follow this value as it is without interpreting it to the specific context of its own projects then the organization is tossing itself for a colossal failure in implementing this Agile Value. Some of the pertinent Questions to ask while interpreting an agile principle are given below:

- Should our project welcome changes 100% and not follow the plan at all? The answer is mostly NO.

Table 4. Consider the 4 agile manifesto values

- Individuals and interactions over processes and tools
- Working software over comprehensive documentation
- Customer collaboration over contract negotiation
- Responding to change over following a plan

- Should we follow the plan 100% and not entertain changes? This is a sure NO - NO.

It is obvious that there will never be straightforward silver bullet answers on how diligently a project follows an Agile Value. However, even a simple group discussion / meeting involving important organizational stakeholders on interpreting these agile values / principles to organizational context and deciding "How much agility is good enough?" will go a long way in helping the organization steer its agile journey in a proper direction.

4.2. Agile Ecosystem versus Methodology Approach: The Amazon Rain Forest Example

Jim High smith advocates an "Ecosystem point of view" as opposed to the "methodology point of view" while handling organizational agility (Highsmith, 2002). A simple example to illustrate the importance of ecosystem view is given below.

Let us consider the Amazon Rain forests. Wikipedia shows that the Amazon rain forest is home to about 2.5 million insect species, tens of thousands of plants, and some 2,000 birds and mammals. To date, at least 40,000 plant species, 2,200 fishes, 1,294 birds, 427 mammals, 428 amphibians, and 378 reptiles have been scientifically classified in the region.

Now, let us imagine that a "so called" Agile Coach is requested to take a cross section of mammals from the 427 different varieties of mammals. The superficial Agile Coach interprets a fundamental agile principle on "speed of delivery" as "deliver as fast as possible" and creates a rule "All mammals should run at a speed of at least 25 km / hour" because agility means better speed. We have to be at least running at the speed of 25 km / hour to satisfy our minimum agility goals.

What would ensue are chaos, failure and destruction because a single "Agile" expectation is set for all mammals. It is obvious that different mammals have different speeds and agility levels. A common agility expectation for every mammal is not only impractical but also senseless.

Now, imagine the case of an Agile Coach working in an IT organization. If this coach expects all projects (regardless of technology, customer segment, market needs) to produce working software every day or week, then will the projects be able to do so? Digital projects by its very nature are evolving and might hugely benefit by very frequent working software. A Banking product might have regulations, audits and also have a low risk appetite. Frequency of release of a banking product might be once every quarter while a mobile application might be looking at a release every week.

What is highlighted here is that we should not relegate agile projects to the status of a fixed process culture where every project is expected to deliver at a fixed speed or frequency. An ecosystem based approach where conscious acknowledgement that different projects have different delivery needs should be taken (Cohn, 2005).

Interpretation of agile principles and taking an ecosystem view are two fundamental pillars on which a practical agile journey of every organization rests.

5. DESIGN OF ORGANIZATIONAL AGILE FRAMEWORK

The next step after interpreting the agile values is to build an organizational framework design that guides projects the agile way inside the organization.

There are several analytical tools and frameworks that could possibly be used to examine software development methods. However, the key advantage of 4-DAT (4 Dimensional Analysis Tool) is that it evaluates methods from the perspectives of agility, software process and lifecycle phases as well as how the methods do in practice (Qumer & Henderson-Sellers, 2006).

4-DAT specifically provides a mechanism to measure agility (degree of agility) of any method quantitatively at a specific level in a process and using specific practices. 4-DAT will help to examine agile methods from four perspectives given below:

- Method scope
- Agility characterization (based on the key attributes introduced for this case)
- Characterization of agile values (based on those proposed in the Agile Manifesto)
- Software process characterization

A detailed treatment of the different perspectives presented above can be referenced from "An evaluation of the degree of agility in six agile methods and its applicability for method engineering by (Qumer and Henderson-Sellers, 2008).

Note – Our focus for this chapter is to use the 4-DAT approach to compare a few popular agile frameworks like Scrum, FDD and DSDM in a structured manner and identify the additional elements necessary to help implement these frameworks at Organizational level. The gaps identified in individual frameworks against the parameters evaluated would help to create an action item list that could be used to build a unified organizational agile framework which is the central purpose of this chapter.

5.1. Possible Challenges in Scaling Existing Agile Frameworks to Organizational Level

There are several types of challenges in scaling agile frameworks at organizational level like customer related, requirements related, team related and model related challenges (Adkins, 2010). Addressing customer related challenges are top priority because customer involvement is one of the fundamental principles of agile. Addressing Requirements challenges will also be a key factor because the ability to adapt to changing requirements is a central agile principle. Agile is ultimately about empowered and motivated teams and the doers of work are the "agile teams", so the challenges the team faces will decide the success or failure of the agile initiative. Finally, the model specific challenges have to be carefully addressed at organizational level to ensure the model is adapted to the organizational needs and not looked at from an " as is" silver bullet point of view.

Challenge 1: Customer-Related Challenges

Customer's insufficient knowledge of the requirements due to the complexity and size of the system poses significant challenges ((Cao and Ramesh, 2008). These challenges are even more pronounced when customers are not available or not willing to commit to the project (Fitzgerald et al., 2006).

Challenge 2: Requirements Related Challenges

Frequently changing requirements poses a challenge to the team that is developing the software. Also the expectation that business will coordinate with developers closely is practically difficult to achieve.

Challenge 3: Team Related Challenges

When the teams are distributed, face to face interaction is difficult. Further when the team size grows, the ability to do face to face interaction decreases drastically.

Challenge 4: Model Challenges

The study elements for studying model specific challenges like team size, leadership approach, reward mechanism, engineering approach etc. are compared for the three selected models in the section below (see Table 5).

5.2. Addressing Challenges in Agile Frameworks

The summary of findings identified is in turn used as feeders to define design building blocks for an organizational agile framework below (see Table 6).

5.3. Organizational Agile Framework Design

The organizational agile framework that is defined below covers the designs blocks that are identified in the above section (see Figure 1).

5.3.1 Agile Models + Model Selection Criteria

This block provides the flexibility to choose different agile models (SCRUM, FDD, and DSDM) depending on specific project or client requirements (see Table 7).

5.3.2 Agile Rewards and Recognition System

- Many companies are shifting to Agile Software development. However, the companies continue to use their existing performance evaluation methods.
- Most companies are clueless on how to do appraisals in an agile environment. This creates a "chasm".

Table 5.

Study Element	Scrum	FDD	DSDM	Summary of Findings
1. Team Size	• Single team size to be less than 8 -10. • Multiple teams of 8 -10 members possible using Scrum of Scrum approach.	No limit for team size. Scalable from small to large teams	Minimum 2 and Maximum 6 (But multiple small teams can work)	If the development team size increases beyond 8 Scrum has to be broken down in to multiple scrum teams. - FDD does not have any restriction on team size. DSDM advocates team size of 2-6 per team. In the practical software development teams in industry a single team with 25 team members are common. So, this is an area which needs further consideration in framework definition.
2. Leadership Approach	Scrum advocated Adaptive leadership approach	Does not explicitly talk about any preferred leadership approach	DSDM advocates flexible approach to leadership	All the 3 models directly or indirectly advocate having adaptive leadership approach for projects but do not specify how leaders should function at an organizational / project level.
3. Reward Mechanism	All 3 models do not deal with any ideas on how agile teams should be rewarded.			No mention on how teams should be rewarded in an agile projects in any of the models.
4. Maturity Assessment	No specific indicators identified for measuring higher or lower maturity in terms of agile practices prescribed by the model.			No mention on maturity assessment of agile projects in any of the models.
5. Engineering practices for Agile	Scrum does not cover any agile engineering techniques like Test Driven development, Refactoring etc.	FDD advocates strong testing, peer review and an object oriented approach to development	No specific engineering practices prescribed.	None of the 3 models focus on engineering practices specifically.
6. Metrics	Scrum speaks of "velocity" and burn down charts. However none of the 3 models deal with the significant metrics that are needed to successfully manage agile projects.			No mention on agile metrics in any of the models.
7. Customer Satisfaction	Adapting to changing customer needs is a fundamental philosophy for all the three models. However, there is no specific technique or mechanism suggested on how customer satisfaction should be looked at for an agile project.			No mention on measuring customer satisfaction in any of the models.
8. Tailoring Criteria for agile methods	All the three models are flexible and can be adapted. However, specific guidelines or practices on how to tailor the models to a specific project situation is not available.			No mention on tailoring criteria in any of the agile models.
9. Overall Governance	FDD covers a detailed project monitoring strategy. However, none of the three models provide a guidance on how an agile project should be governed.			No mention on Overall Governance of an agile project in any of the models.

- An Agile appraisal system is not a top down supervisor evaluation. In an Agile appraisal system, the focus is given to the following parameters
  - Peer Review: Each team member rates himself and others in the team objectively
  - Team rating: A portion of weightage is given for overall team instead of individual heroism

Table 6.

Design Building Block Identified	List of Gaps Addressed in the Design Building Block
10. Agile Models + Model selection criteria	• Team Size • Customer related challenges • Requirements related challenges • Team related challenges • Tailoring criteria for agile models
11. Agile Rewards and Recognition System	• Reward Mechanism
12. Business Culture	• Business Agility • Business Culture
13. Adaptive Agile Leadership	• Leadership Approach • Physical Environment
14. Agile Customer Satisfaction (ACS)	• Customer satisfaction survey (End user, Product Owner, stakeholders)
15. Governance	• Organization structure • Cost, Standards • Metrics • Keeping the process cost effective
16. Development Pool	• Developer pool, Team size (indirect)
17. Engineering Took Kit	• Engineering Practices for Agile • Configuration Control Process
18. Maturity Model	• 4-DAT Maturity Assessment • Process Management Processes

Figure 1. Organizational Agile Framework Design(Qumer and Henderson-Sellers, 2008)

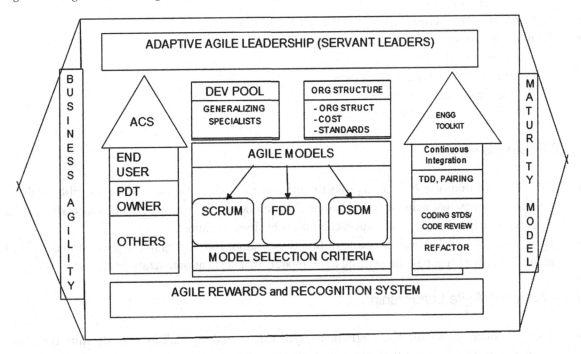

Table 7.

Model	Selection Criteria
SCRUM	• Team size of 6-8. • To achieve scalability, there can be multiple scrum teams of 6-8 team members operating under the Scrum of Scrum mode • Collocated • Customer closely interacting with project • Frequent iterations (2 weeks -1 month) • Requirements complex (neither very clear nor totally blurred)
FDD	• Use when large, distributed agile teams are a need for the project • Team size can be of any order • Requirements should be breakable in to features • Favors object oriented approach to development
DSDM	• Use whenever feasibility and business study are necessary to ascertain whether the project has to be undertaken • Should be able to create prototypes for the system during early stages of the project • Minimum team size of 2 and maximum 6. • To achieve scalability, there can be multiple team groups of 2-6 members within the same project
Combination mode	• Models could be combined depending on the project type. For example, DSDM phase feasibility study could be added to the SCRUM model (see paper framework designs in appendix for a few sample combination ideas)

- ○ Product produced
- ○ Overall adherence to agile process
- ○ Leadership qualities
- ○ Customer rating
- Agile appraisals generally follow a 360 degree approach
- Caution should be taken to avoid measuring following items in agile appraisals:
  - ○ Individual velocity
  - ○ Sum of all task hours for a person
  - ○ Number of tasks/person
  - ○ Accuracy of task estimates

5.3.3 Business Agility

- Most organizations use Agile as a project management strategy. On the contrary, Agility is also a business strategy that helps survive changing market demands. Salesforce.com successfully used Agile as a business strategy and succeeded in its business ventures.
- Business Agility is beyond the scope of this dissertation. Hence it is not addressed in detail but identified only as a gap in the existing agile models that scale at organizational level.

5.3.4 Adaptive Agile Leadership:

- There are many leadership challenges in an Agile Environment – traditional leadership styles may not work. Without using titles, power or influence, the leader has to get work done from team members
- Agile Leaders are leaders who possess the following characteristics:

    i.   Flexible
    ii.   Responsive to change
    iii. Willing to learn new ways
    iv. Willing to adopt new ways
    v.   Lead effectively to survive successfully in the modern, complex, ever changing business environment

- Agile Leadership is the art of being flexible under the influence of rapidly changing internal / external circumstances
- The ability to change or be changed is a crucial skill for Agile leaders

One of the popular leadership approaches for agile is the Servant Leadership Approach. The servant-leader is servant first. It begins with the natural feeling that one wants to serve, to serve first. Then conscious choice brings one to aspire to lead (Greenleaf, 1977).

5.3.5 Agile Customer Satisfaction (ACS)

Compared to traditional waterfall projects where customer satisfaction is measured at the end of the project, the agile customer satisfaction is more dynamic and it involves getting direct feedback from many stakeholders involved in the project.

A good agile customer measurement should have the following characteristics:

- "Barely sufficient"
- Easy to collect and/or coalesce (<5 minutes)
- Affirm the Agile principles
- Focused around delivering customer value
- Should not cause any "metrics dysfunction"

Feedbacks should be measured at various levels in an agile project as given below

- Direct end user
- Product Owner
- Relevant stakeholders involved in the project

5.3.6 Agile Organization Structure

Agile organization structure is different from traditional structure because there is no pyramidal structure in Agile Enterprise. Pyramids inevitably create decision-making bottlenecks as information gets passed up the chain of command. Agile organization structure is inspired by nature – Set of birds, swarm of bees, and an army of ants.

Agile organization work best in a network like structure where coordination is promoted over control. Senior management of an organization should make sure people are well trained, and then should trust these trained people to act without having to ask permission first.

5.3.7 Agile Metrics

Metrics collection should be less at an agile project level but it could be considered as a major activity at the governance level. It is advisable for the organization to decide what metrics should be collected at team level, project level and program level.

Good agile metrics are generally easy to collect and don't become an impediment to the team's work, measures business outcomes over activity (e.g. value delivered vs. number of tasks completed), looks at trends, not just a single point in time, encourages whole team results over individual results.

5.3.8 Development Pool

At an organization level, a process is necessary to recruit agile developers who are generalizing specialists and supply them to various projects. The development pool should also be maintained in an agile fashion with very less "bench" and very high active project experience for the developer pool. Trainings on motivation, team building, collaboration, agile values, user experience design etc. should be imparted to the developers along with the specific technology trainings. Developers who complete an agile project can return to the developer pool and get reassigned to another agile project. As much as possible, the selection of projects in which the developer works should be on a self-inspired, voluntary basis.

5.3.9 Engineering Tool Kit

- Agile models do not prescribe any specific engineering techniques to be followed directly during project development.
- It is essential to have an expandable engineering toolkit that can be referred by an agile project.
- Some of the mandatory agile engineering practices are Continuous Integration, Refactoring, Test Driven Development, Code Review and Pair Programming.
- overlooked in the initial development phase, improving both the overall quality

This organizational framework design covers only a minimal set of engineering practices.

It should be borne in mind that there could be several other agile engineering techniques that could be applied depending on the project context and client requirements.

6. SUMMARY

Having an organizational agile framework would help any organization succeed in its agile journey in a structured manner. The agile projects would also be comforted by the fact that there is organizational level "thinking" and guidance and support on how to execute the agile project. The organizational agile framework described in this chapter also has the following advantages.

- *Flexibility:* The design framework created is flexible. New agile models could be added inside this framework design without any impact to existing design blocks. This way, the organization adopting this framework has the flexibility to add /modify an agile model which is defined as part of the framework

- *Expanding Team Sizes:* The model defined can be applied for various team sizes. The project team has to pick an agile framework that is suitable for its project and use the framework.
- **Scalability:** This model is totally scalable. New engineering techniques and new agile models could be added to this framework easily
- *Recommendations:* The aim of designing this organizational agile framework is not to apply it "as such" without tailoring to various organizations. It is recommended that any organization using this framework "tailors" the model to suit its specific organization context before applying the model.

7. ADDITIONAL ELEMENTS FOR ORGANIZATIONAL AGILE FRAMEWORK

- *Agile Maturity Model:* There is very little work done in the area of agile maturity models. Any future work in the related area could focus on building an agile maturity model to assess agile project maturity
- *Testing the model:* The analysis of the results of applying this model to projects could serve as a feedback loop to improve this organizational agile design further.

REFERENCES

Adkins, L. (2010). *Coaching agile teams: a companion for ScrumMasters, agile coaches, and project managers in transition.* Addison-Wesley Professional.

Boehm, B. (2006). A view of 20th and 21st century software engineering. In *Proceedings of the 28th international conference on Software engineering.*

Cao, L., & Ramesh, B. (2008). Agile requirements engineering practices: An empirical study. *Software, IEEE, 25*(1), 60–67. doi:10.1109/MS.2008.1

Chan, F. K., & Thong, J. Y. (2009). Acceptance of agile methodologies: A critical review and conceptual framework. *Decision Support Systems, 46*(4), 803–814. doi:10.1016/j.dss.2008.11.009

Cohn, M. (2005). *Agile estimating and planning.* Pearson Education.

DeMarco, T., & Boehm, B. (2002). The agile methods fray. *Computer, 35*(6), 90–92. doi:10.1109/MC.2002.1009175

Dingsøyr, T., Nerur, S., Balijepally, V., & Moe, N. B. (2012). A decade of agile methodologies: Towards explaining agile software development. *Journal of Systems and Software, 85*(6), 1213–1221. doi:10.1016/j.jss.2012.02.033

Fenn, J. & Linden, A. (2005). *Gartner's Hype Cycle Special Report for 2005.* Gartner.

Fitzgerald, B., Hartnett, G., & Conboy, K. (2006). Customising agile methods to software practices at Intel Shannon. *European Journal of Information Systems, 15*(2), 200–213. doi:10.1057/palgrave.ejis.3000605

Greenleaf, R. K. (1977). *Servant leadership.* New York: Paulist Press.

Highsmith, J. A. (2002). *Agile software development ecosystems 13*. Addison-Wesley Professional.

Kettunen, P., & Laanti, M. (2008). Combining agile software projects and large-scale organizational agility. *Software Process Improvement and Practice*, *13*(2), 183–193. doi:10.1002/spip.354

Qumer, A., & Henderson-Sellers, B. (2006). Measuring agility and adoptability of agile methods: a 4-dimensional analytical tool. In *Procs. IADIS International Conference Applied Computing 2006*, (pp. 503-507). IADIS.

Qumer, A., & Henderson-Sellers, B. (2008). A framework to support the evaluation, adoption and improvement of agile methods in practice. *Journal of Systems and Software*, *81*(11), 1899–1919. doi:10.1016/j.jss.2007.12.806

KEY TERMS AND DEFINITIONS

4-Dat: 4-DAT (4 Dimensional Analysis Tool) is an analysis tool that helps to measure agile methods from the perspectives of agility, software process followed and method application in practice.

Continuous Integration: Continuous integration is a prescribed software engineering practice which advocates merging the developer working copies with a central, shared mainline several times a day.

Dynamic Systems Development Method: Dynamic Systems Development Method (DSDM) is an agile project delivery framework that combines the best practices of development and business to yield a seamless delivery mechanism for both simple and complex projects (Kettunen and Laanti, 2008).

Extreme Programming: Extreme Programming (XP) is an agile methodology that specifically emphasizes the use of agile technical practices (e.g. Test Driven Development) for the success of an agile project. Practical experience shows that XP complements Scrum well and both the methods work well together.

Feature Driven Development: Feature Driven Development (FDD) is an agile method that focuses on delivering working software in a timely manner by using simple, client focused and practical software process. This method works well without tailoring to both small (< 8 team size) and large teams (> 30 team size).

Refactoring: Refactoring aims to have a cleaner "code" by restructuring the code without changing its external behaviour. The idea is to improve the design of the code with the intention of making it easy to use.

Scrum: Scrum is one of the popular agile methodologies which aims to address the challenges of projects involving complex scope of work using a simple process dependent on a small team who are motivated, collaborative and highly focused on producing working software every 2-4 weeks.

TDD: Test Driven Development (TDD) is a development process which advocates the writing of automated test case that defines a new function, then producing the minimum amount of code to pass that test.

Chapter 8
A Survey of Agile Transition Models

Imran Ghani
Universiti Teknologi Malaysia, Malaysia

Naghmeh Niknejad
Universiti Teknologi Malaysia, Malaysia

Dayang Abang Jawawi
Universiti Teknologi Malaysia, Malaysia

Murad Khan
Universiti Teknologi Malaysia, Malaysia

Seung Ryul Jeong
Kookmin University, South Korea

ABSTRACT

Nowadays, since business environment is highly dynamic, software necessities are continuously being improved in order to meet the needs of modern industrialized world. Therefore, IT organizations seek for a quick way of software delivery and for adapting to the necessary technological changes. From this ideal viewpoint, traditional plan-driven developments lag behind to overcome these conflicts. The purpose of this chapter is to present the existing models and frameworks which guide organizations to adopt agile methods. This may help organizations to follow professionals' suggestions during their migration from traditional systems to agile development.

1 INTRODUCTION

Since the purpose of organizations are improving return on investment (ROI) and controlling the risk of projects failure effectively, Agile software development has become as the most debated solution in the last decade and many companies are transforming from traditional development to Agile developments methods like SCRUM(Druckman, 2011).

For the first time, the word agile was utilized incorporation with software process in 1998 (Aoyama, 1998).The ability of sensing and rapidly responding to business scenarios in order to remain creative and aggressive in an unsteady and quickly changing business environment is agility(Highsmith, 2002). The agile attitude for developing is the agility of development teams, development process and their environment (Boehm & Turner, 2004). This approach integrates shared ideals of various stakeholders

DOI: 10.4018/978-1-4666-9858-1.ch008

and a philosophy of regular providing the customers with product features in short time-frames (Moniruzzaman & Hossain, 2013; Southwell, 2002). This frequent and regular feature delivery is achieved by team based attitude (Coram & Bohner, 2005).

Beck et al. (Beck et al., 2001) expressed that customers are unable to define their requirements exactly due to the rapid change in the world of technology and companies which are used the new technologies in their products. Therefore, agile approaches are intended to cover the changing needs in software technology environment. In 2001(Ambler, 2002), a group of 17 software consultants with different backgrounds created the Agile Software Development Alliance to define a manifesto for agile software development principles. Agile methods stressed on the unexpectedness challenges in practice based on the communication among people and their innovation instead of processes. The main purpose of agile methods is to improve and increase the responses time to requirements, environmental changes and achieve the deadlines (Rao, Naidu, & Chakka, 2011). Beck et al. (Beck et al., 2001) expresses agile software development manifesto as the following:

1. Individuals and interactions over processes and tools
2. Working software over comprehensive documentation.
3. Customer collaboration over contract negotiation.
4. Responding to change over following a plan.

Agile software development methods illustrate a series of processes that have been produced by experts (Ågerfalk, Fitzgerald, & In, 2006).Dynamic Systems Development Method (DSDM) (Stapleton, 2003) is recognized as the first method for agile development by Larman and Basili(Larman & Basili, 2003). Other best known methods are Extreme Programming (XP) (Beck, 2000), Scrum (Takeuchi & Nonaka, 1986), Crystal Methodologies Family (Cockburn, 2006), Agile Modeling (Ambler, 2002), Feature-Driven Development (FDD) (Anderson, 2004), and Adaptive Software Development (Highsmith, 2013).

Agile methods focus on producing the software early and avoiding to waste time in costly plans and delivering a valuable result to the customer in a limited time as soon as possible. To achieve this goal documentation has a lower priority during developing an agile project and it has to be provided while the project has finished and delivered to the customer (Van Vliet, 2007). Highsmith and Cockburn (Highsmith & Cockburn, 2001) declared that agile methods emphasis on the integrity of working code and the efficiency of people which are working together with courtesy. The authors believed that during project development, people would exchange their ideas by discussing face to face more quickly than by reading or writing documents.

According to Forrester report in 2006, almost 17% of companies adopted agile methods and more than 50% of the participated companies were involved to adopt them (Schwaber, Laganza, & D'Silva, 2007). The percentage of this statistic increased in 2009 in a study that showed 76% of participated companies initiated at least one or two agile projects (Ambler, 2009a). Today, many major companies have implemented agile in whole or some parts of their projects, namely: Yahoo!, Microsoft, AOL, Shopzilla, CNBC, Google, Siemens and Rockstar (Smith & Sidky, 2009). Scott Ambler conducted a survey during 13 February till 24 March 2014(Ambler, 2014). In his research the challenges faced by organizations and the state of agile adoption in organizations were examined. Figure 1 shows the adoption of agile programs success rates in organizations. However, there are some failures (5%) in agile adoption but there are more successes in organizations.

Figure 1. Success rates of organizations agile adoption programs (Ambler, 2014)

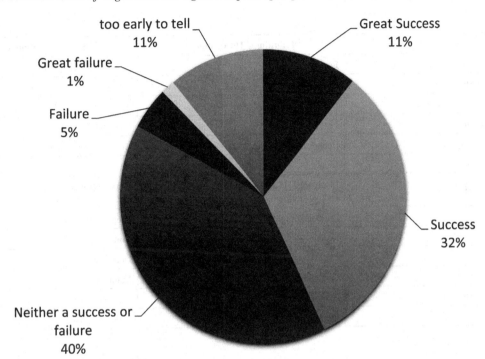

Practically, a small number of organizations are capable of adopting agile development methods directly and successfully within a short period of time while a complete transition may often take a few several years (2 -3 years). Moreover, it may not be appropriate for organizations to be completely agile in every aspects of development. Perhaps it is better to keep famous and reliable components of a more traditional method inside an entire agile project (Qumer & Henderson-Sellers, 2008). In this chapter, almost all frameworks, models, roadmaps and guidelines have been collected to assist managers and agile experts to choose a proper way to transfer from traditional methodology to agile development confidently and more successfully. In addition, the differences between traditional development and agile development are also discussed.

2 Traditional Development vs. Agile Development

Agile Software Development Methods (ASDM) has many various differences with Traditional Software Development Methods (TSDM). According to Boehm (Boehm, 2002), there are nine discriminant elements between agile and traditional methodologies. Due to his study, the main purpose of ASDM is based on high rapid value in contrast with TSDM which is based on high assurance.

Moreover, organizations have found that agile project teams in contrast with traditional one provide higher quality, have greater level of success rates, deliver a greater degree of return on investment (ROI), enjoy higher level of stakeholder satisfaction, and provide system to market earlier(Brock & Puckle Hobbs, 2010).It is not reasonable to conclude based on the average of agile successfulness that all agile projects are successful or all organizations have obtained the possible benefits of agile in an equal manner. Table 1 summarized some differences between traditional and agile development.

Table 1. Differences between traditional development and agile development (Awad, 2005; Nerur, Mahapatra, & Mangalaraj, 2005)

	Traditional Development	Agile Development
Fundamental Assumption	Predictive	High quality adaptive
Management Style	Autocratic	Decentralized
Knowledge Management	Explicit	Tacit
Communication	Formal	Informal
Perspective to change	Change sustainability	Change adaptability
Documentation	Heavy	Low
Development Model	Mechanistic (bureaucratic with high formalization	Organic (flexible and participative encouraging cooperative social action)
Emphasis	Process-Oriented	People-Oriented
Cycles	Limited	Numerous
Domain	Predictable	Unpredictable, Exploratory
Upfront Planning	Comprehensive	Minimal
Return on Investment	End of Project	Early in Project
Team Size	Large	Small/Creative

3 RESEARCH REVIEW

This section depicts the research method utilized in this review chapter. The aim of this work is to find out models, frameworks, roadmaps, and guidelines for transitioning and adopting agile from traditional software developments to agile software development from previous studies and to classify them for future works. To extract models suggested by previous researchers, this study conducted a vast search on electronics database as listed in Table 2. The corresponding research questions in this chapter are:

Q1: How companies can transfer from traditional methods to agile methodologies?
Q2: Which models and frameworks could be used for transitioning to agile software development?

Table 2. Search on electronic database

Source	URL
ACM Digital Library	http://dl.acm.org
IEEE Xplore	http://ieeexplore.ieee.org
ScienceDirect	http://www.springerlink.com
Springer	http://www.springerlink.com
Google Scholar	http://scholar.google.com

4 AGILE TRANSITION MODELS, FRAMEWORKS

The most important issue in organizations is the way of doing the transition while a traditional model is the core of a company and all employees have the proficiency in that. It is certain that in the beginning steps, all things would seem to be complicated for everybody but agile can be performed successfully with proper and strong support of top management teams and agile coaches. In this section, almost all models and frameworks, considered as guides for organizations to transit from a traditional method to an agile method, are reviewed.

4.1 Agile Scaling Model

A contextual model is defined by Ambler (Ambler, 2009b) to describe a roadmap for adopting agile strategies more efficiently and meeting the unique challenges that encountered by system delivery teams. As is clearly shown in Figure 2, Agile Scaling Model is divided into three categories.

The First category optimized for small teams that improving fairly simple systems. It consists of core agile methods that are self-organizing, have a value-driven system development lifecycle, and refer to a part of the development lifecycle. The second group covers the whole software development lifecycle from the beginning of the project till transforming the system into the marketplace or production environment. The last division concentrates on well-ordered agile delivery where more than one scaling

Figure 2. Agile scaling model (Ambler, 2009b)

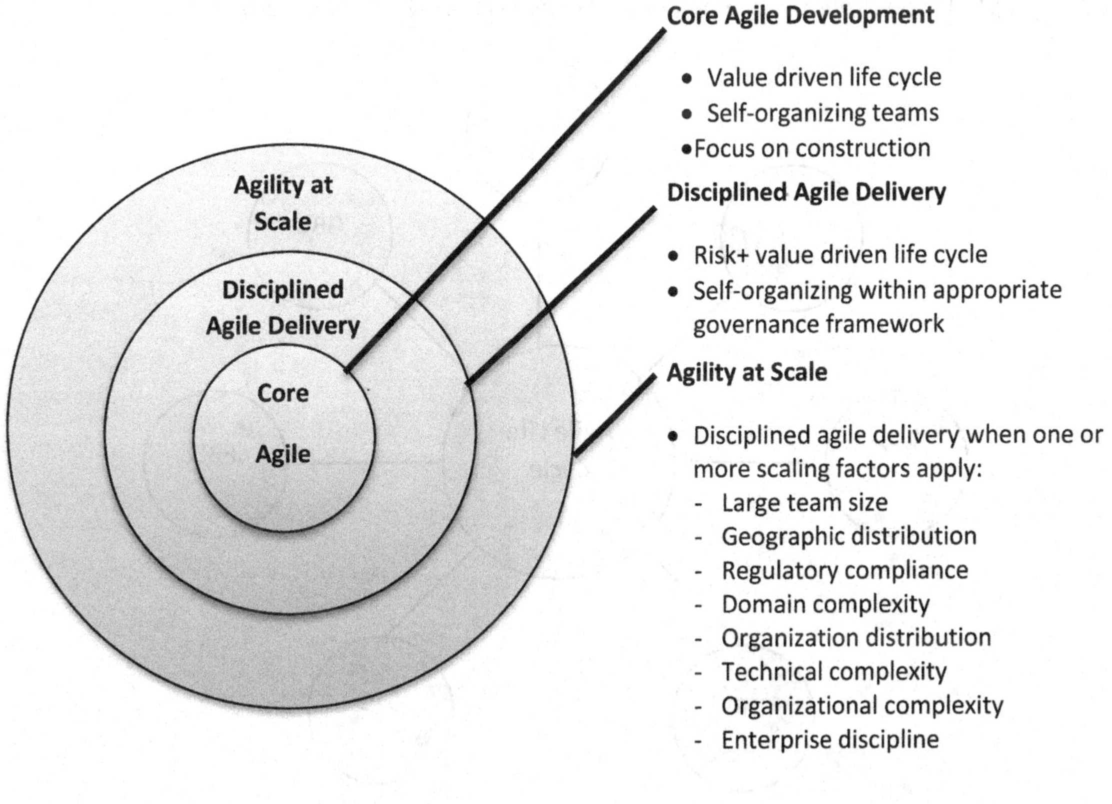
Core Agile Development
• Value driven life cycle
• Self-organizing teams
•Focus on construction
Disciplined Agile Delivery
• Risk+ value driven life cycle
• Self-organizing within appropriate governance framework
Agility at Scale
• Disciplined agile delivery when one or more scaling factors apply:
- Large team size
- Geographic distribution
- Regulatory compliance
- Domain complexity
- Organization distribution
- Technical complexity
- Organizational complexity
- Enterprise discipline
Agility at Scale
Disciplined Agile Delivery
Core
Agile

factors are feasible. Ambler (Ambler, 2009b) mentioned eight factors as scaling factors, namely: team size, regulatory compliance, geographical distribution, technical complexity, organizational complexity, enterprise discipline (like enterprise architecture, and governance), and organizational distribution.

4.2 A Mapping Model for Transform Traditional Method to Agile Method

Popli and Chauhan (Popli & Chauhan, 2013) proposed an agile model based on common life cycle method that is appropriate for various types of teams. They illustrated a mapping function to move from traditional method to agile method. Figure 3 presents the agile model proposed by Popli and Chauhan.

This model includes seven main components which are the basic components of an agile culture:

TFR: Team Formation by good Recruitment policy.
GBC: Goal Building Cycle with quality analyst, business analyst and customer.
EBE: Effort and Budget Estimation.
CTC: Coding and Testing activities with Communication.
DRF: Demonstrations in Review with Feedback.
REC: Risk Evaluation and Correction.
SFP: Satisfaction For all Parties.

Figure 4 shows the mapping function that take place in the current organization when transformation decision has been taken by the management. Formula (2) indicated the mapping function MF. The role of

Figure 3. Agile Model Proposed by Popli and Chauhan (Popli & Chauhan, 2013)

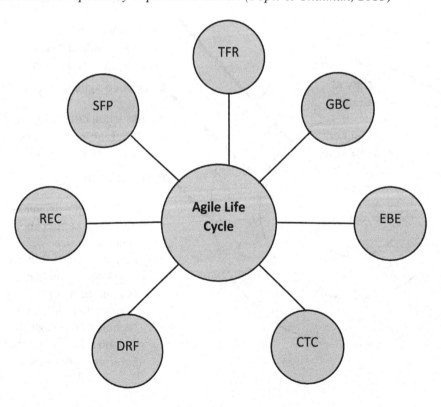

Figure 4. Mapping Function

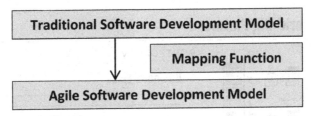

this formula is to direct the big team to small one (T), large function to small scenarios, lengthy iteration to a short one (I), lengthy response cycle to a quick response one, tardily delivery to a quick small one (D), lengthy meeting todiurnal small meeting (M), tardily testing to a test-driven one (TG), two monitors into a terminal to do pair programming (Moniruzzaman & Hossain), assessment in lines of code to story points (E), and last but not the least project director into no manager view (B), co-ordination efficiency (CE). As shown in Formula (1), CE depends on implicit and explicit factors.

CE=Implicit factors+ Explicit factors (1)
MF = (T, J, I, F, D, M, TG, MO, E, B, CE) (2)

4.3 Scaled Agile Framework

Leffingwell (Leffingwell, 2010) developed an agile adoption framework called Scaled Agile Framework (SAFe), which is an approved knowledge based framework to implement agile practices in organizations. This model serves as both the organizational and process model for agile requirements practices. As is clearly shown in Figure 5, the principal user interface of this framework is a graphical big picture that represents three level of scale, namely: Portfolio, Program, and Team.

At the team level, around seven team members of agile describe, make, and test the scenarios of user in sequences of interactions. At the next level, program level, the development of larger-scale system functionalities are completed through various teams in a synchronised Agile Release Train (ART) (Leffingwell, 2010). A long-lived team of an agile team is called ART which normally including50-125 members (Leffingwell, 2013).The portfolio level is describing a combination of investment themes are utilized to drive the investment preferences for the organization.The patternwill be utilized to guarantee that the work being implemented is the one required for the organization to convey its selected business approach (Leffingwell, 2010).Well, SAFe is not a simple, one-size fits all approach. However, SAFe is a framework that offers complicated solutions as it deals with complicated problems.

4.4 Agile Adoption Framework

Sidky et al. (Sidky, Arthur, & Bohner, 2007) presented an agile adoption framework (Figure 6) that includes two parts to assist and to direct organizations towards adopting agility. The first component is an agile measurement index to evaluate agile potential and the second component is a four stage process that uses the agile measurement index to specify how, and to what extent, agility can be expanded in an organization. This framework has no dependence on the agile methodologies; there are no limitations on utilizing Scrum, FDD or XP or any other agile methods along with this framework. In this framework,

Figure 5. Scaled Agile Framework (Leffingwell, 2010)

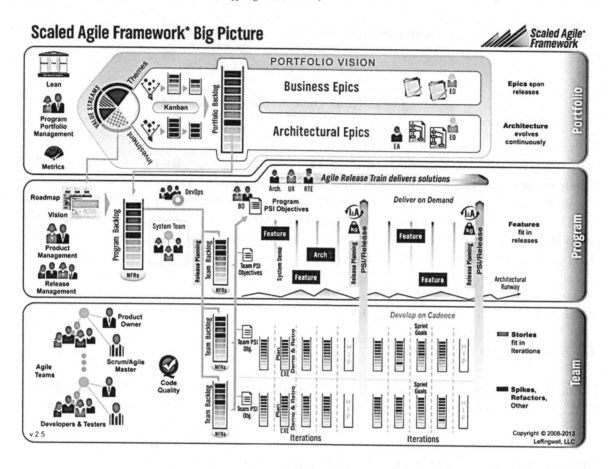

the coach utilizes the Sidky agile measurement index as a scale to assess the potential agility of a project or an enterprise. The four stage processes of the framework lead organizations to identify the best agile practices that fit with their environment and situation. The first stage identifies the terminating factors and discovers any limitation processes that prevent the success of agile adoption. The second stage uses the measurement index to specify the highest level of agility for each specific project. The third stage assesses the organizational readiness by using the measurement index. And the final stage specifies the last set of practices for agile adoption through adopting the target agile level from the second stage and the readiness of organization from the third stage.

However, the Agile Adoption Framework is only an essential element to adopt agility while an agile coach (who knows how to apply the framework) is also a crucial ingredient towards adopting agility.

4.5 Agile Adoption and Improvement Model

Qumer et al. (Qumer, Henderson-sellers, & Mcbride, 2007) presented a model to adopt, assess and improve agile software development process named Agile Adoption and Improvement Model (Figure 7). This model can be utilized as a road map for an agile adoption strategy to achieve the proper and worthy level of agile during a period of time. Agile Adoption and Improvement Model consist of three

Figure 6. Agile adoption framework overview (Sidky et al., 2007)

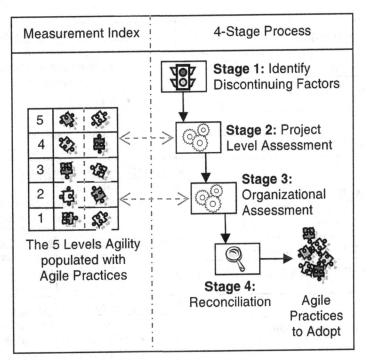

blocks and six agile steps. In addition, AAIM has an embedded agility measurement for quantitatively measuring the agility level. It is worth mentioning that each steps clearly describes the goals must be obtained to achieved a specific business [value via implementing an agile software development method. The following figure presents the Agile Adoption and Improvement Model.

4.6 Agile Software Solution Framework (ASSF)

Qumer and Henderson-Sellers (Qumer & Henderson-Sellers, 2008) have described a method to extend and customize the agile method into software development via an Agile Software Solution Framework (ASSF), concentrating on the Agile governance and Toolkit (Figure 8). Furthermore, these opinions have established practical application in the AAIM. The ASSF can be utilize to construct, adapt or customize situation-specific agile software processes based on each of the various contemporary concept perspectives by utilizing a circumstantial method engineering methodology, feedback, and a standard meta-model. It is noteworthy that ASSF consists of various numbers of models and processes, namely: an agile adoption and improvement model and process, an agility measurement model and process, agile software solution framework based on knowledge engineering and management process, an Agile Toolkit, and an agile workspace(Qumer & Henderson-Sellers, 2008).

4.7 ADAPT (Mike Cohn Model)

Mike Cohn introduces ADAPT model, a five-stage, sustainable approach for getting better at agile. The stages of ADAPT are as follow:

Figure 7. Agile adoption and improvement model (Qumer et al., 2007)

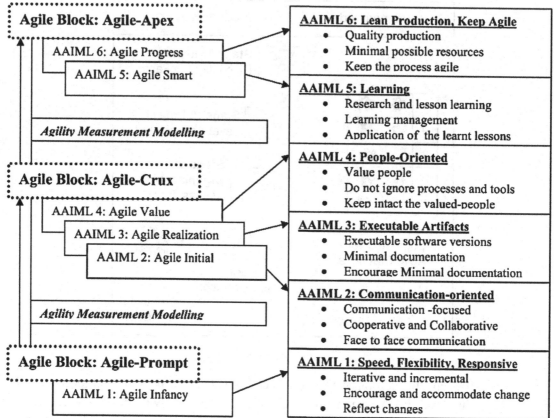

Figure 8. Agile software solution framework (Qumer & Henderson-Sellers, 2008)

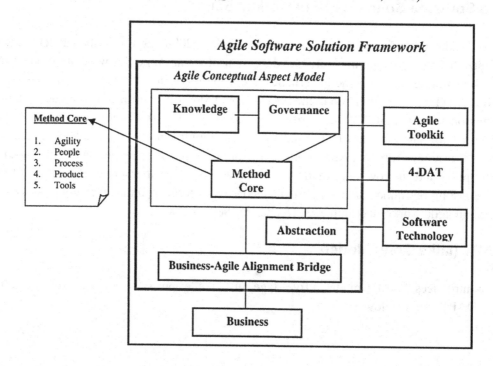

- Take away clear guidance for creating Awareness and realizing that the current approach does not work.
- Increasing Desire to change.
- Developing Ability to work in an agile manner.
- Promoting early successes to build momentum and get others to follow.
- Transferring the implications of being agile throughout the organization.

In addition, leave knowing how ADAPT can help an organization not only turn gradually into agile, but also make a sturdy base to go on the industry wide journey to achieve the proper organizational success rate (Cohn, 2010a).Moreover, ADAPT is derived from ADKAR (Awareness, Desire, Knowledge, Ability, and Reinforcement) change management model (Hiatt, 2006)and is appropriate for the scenarios of agile adoption anywhere the change endeavors required for migrating to an agile approach is comparatively low(Cohn, 2010b). Figure 9 presents the iteration toward agility based on Scrum method. As is clearly shown in this figure, Enterprise Transition Community (ETC) is a small group created to make a culture and environment for those people who are enthusiastic more for the success of the organization and also for the place where success directs to more enthusiasm from more people.

4.8 Cynefin Model

Cynefin as a sense-making framework was first established by Dave Snowden based on knowledge management and organizational strategy in 1999. Cynefin identifies the informal distinctions between the various types of systems and proposes new approaches to make a decision in complicated social environments. Some researchers believed that Cynefin is a useful model for agile adoption while others believed that it is more beneficial to use it as an analysis model to discover the type of environment, thus the best and the most suitable method can be chosen. Moreover, the Cynefin model defines five various

Figure 9. Iteration toward agility (Cohn, 2010b)

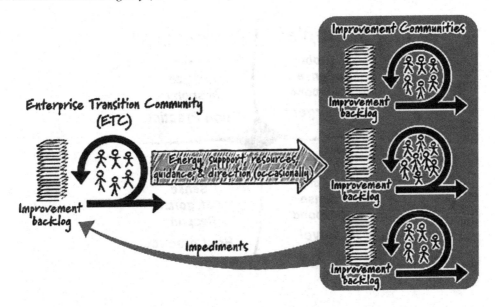

areas, namely: Simple, Complicated, Complex, Chaotic and Disorder. In addition, cause and effect are clearly related in a simple area, while in a Chaotic area there is no pattern and the connection between cause and effect are indirect and unclear. Figure 10 presents Cynefin framework.

4.9 Agile Culture Model

Michael Sahota (Sahota, 2012) has developed various practical models for working with organizations that are used agile and those that are tried to become agile. Sahota has represented that developing agile needs an alteration, which is more difficult than a simple adoption. Furthermore, Sahota introduced a model regarding to Schneider Culture Model (Schneider, 1994) that could be utilized to understand culture at the enterprise level. A culture model introduced the values and standards inside a group or company. It recognizes the significant matters about how people work with each other. The Schneider Culture Model described four clear and different cultures:

Collaboration culture is about working together
Control culture is about getting and keeping control
Competence culture is about being the best
Cultivation culture is about learning and growing with a sense of purpose

According to Culture Survey of Agile (Spayd, 2010) Sahota illustrated that the key elements of Agile Culture are Collaboration and Cultivation. The following diagram (Figure 11) represents results from the Agile Culture Survey consist of Scrum, XP and Lean-Kanban:

Moreover, Sahota explained the special cultures of Agile, Kanban, and Software Craftsmanship and provided a director to estimate how well a specific method adjusts with the culture of organization. Figure 12 shows the Agile Culture Model.

Figure 10. Cynefin framework (Snowden, 1999)

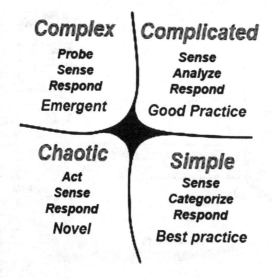

Figure 11. Agile culture survey (Spayd, 2010)

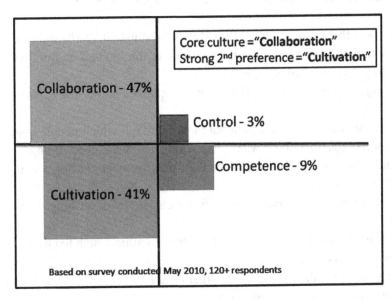

Figure 12. Agile culture model

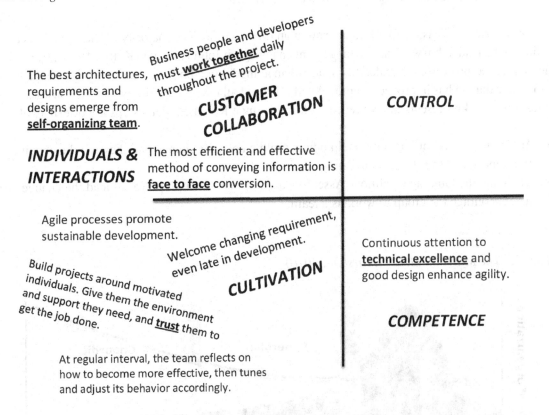

4.10 The Marshall Model of Organizational Evolution

Right shifting is a model that is presented by Bob Marshall (Marshall, 2010) and explains dynamic path for organizations at higher efficacy. It is worth mentioning that prevailing mindset characterizes this model. Marshall Model is presented at Figure 13.

The Marshall Model of Organizational Evolution is explained below and applies for many aims:

- To provide a vocabulary and shared rational model through which people associated in development can better talk together about what's happening, and what needs doing.
- Helping organizations see where they are on their improvement journey, and thereby better chose a suitable set of next steps.
- Reducing the risks associated with organizational change by describing the nature and scope of the challenge.
- Providing organizational change agents with a context within which to choose appropriate strategies, methods and tools.
- Helping reduce the time taken to overcome organizational homeostasis and thereby preserving the momentum of change at major decision points.

4.11 Kotter Model for Organizational Changes

A lot of theories are existed about transforming an organization. The majority of these theories are according to the leadership work and management change guru John P. Kotter (Kotter, 1996, 2013). Kotter who is a retired professor expanded his 8-step change model in a book named Leading Change back in 1996. After that he has improved the model and it is used all over the world by a lot of consulting companies. Figure 14 represents the Kotter Model. In continue Kotter Model's steps are briefly explained.

Step 1: Create a Sense of Urgency- Help others see the need for change and they will be convinced of the importance of acting immediately.

Step 2: Create the Guiding Coalition- Assemble a group with enough power to lead the change effort, and encourage the group to work as a team.

Figure 13. The Marshall Model (Marshall, 2010)

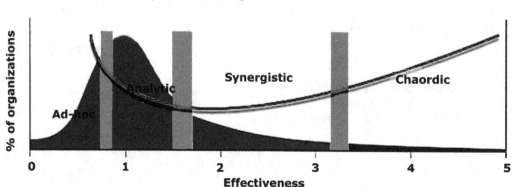

Figure 14. Kotter's 8- Step Change Model (Kotter, 1996, 2013)

Step 3: Create a vision for change- Create a vision to help direct the change effort, and develop strategies for achieving that vision.

Step 4: Communicate the Vision- Make sure as many as possible understand and accept the vision and the strategy.

Step 5: Remove obstacles-Remove obstacles, change systems or structures that seriously undermine the vision, and encourage risk-taking and nontraditional ideas, activities, and actions.

Step 6: Create Short-term Wins- Plan for achievements that can easily be made visible, follow-through with those achievements and recognize and reward employees who were involved.

Step 7: Consolidate improvement- Use increased credibility to change systems, structures, and policies that don't fit the vision, also hire, promote, and develop employees who can implement the vision, and finally reinvigorate the process with new projects, themes, and change agents.

Step 8: Anchor the Changes- Articulate the connections between the new behaviors and organizational success, and develop the means to ensure leadership development and succession.

4.12 CollabNet Agile Transformation Strategy

Angela Druckman who is a CollabNet's Certified Scrum Trainer presented a path for Agility that characterizes at a high level (Figure 15). It is a particular transition to Agile model in a white paper (Druckman, 2011) according to CollabNet knowledge working with organization around the world. CollabNet tools and services protect the path to Agility. As an extensive approach this strategic and tactic suggestion is designed to help the organization go down the path to Agility efficiently.

4.13 Force Field Analysis

Kurt Lewin created Force Field Analysis in 1946 (Lewin, 1946), that is an essential tool for analyzing the elements found in sophisticate problems (Figure 16). It builds problems in terms of elements or pressures that protect the status quo or restraining forces and the pressures that protect change in the wanted direction or driving forces. An element can be resources, people, tradition, attitudes, values, regulations, desires, needs and so forth. Force Field Analysis as a tool to manage change can help to recognize the factors that should be monitored and addressed if change is prosperous. The international expert Rachel Davies who participates in coaching teams of the efficacy application of Agile approaches utilized Force Field Analysis as a method to create an initiative Transition Backlog of job items protecting an agile transition that trainer and teams can work repeatedly.

Figure 15. CollabNet agile transformation strategy (Druckman, 2011)

Figure 16. Force field analysis (Lewin, 1946)

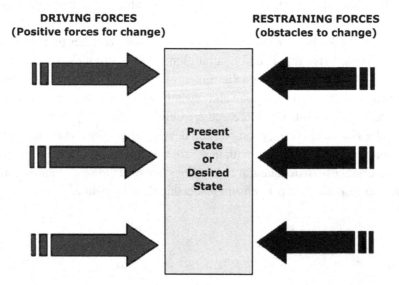

4.14 Fearless Change

Based on Rising and Manns (Rising & Manns, 2004)three elements one should consider when fostering change or innovation are the change agent, the organizational culture and the people who will participate in the change. All successful change agents have three things in common: a passionate belief in the idea they are advocating, a drive to see that idea be successful in the organization and some strategies to share the idea with others. The change agent is the most powerful and important element of change because without an individual who has a vision that things can be better, the whole process of change does not even begin. Every great social movement began with one person saying, "We can do this better and I have an idea on how to do it."

Culture is also an important consideration when introducing a new idea to an organization or a Team. If the culture of the organization supports new ideas and innovations, then the idea will spread more rapidly. If the organization is generally conservative to new ideas and innovations, or "too busy" to support new ideas, then one must set their expectations appropriately, have a great deal of patience and take a long view with respect to change. Change will happen, but will take much longer. The image (Figure 17) by MihaiIancu shows a variety of different patterns that can be applied to support the adoption of a new technology or idea.

Figure 17. Fearless Changes(Rising & Manns, 2004)

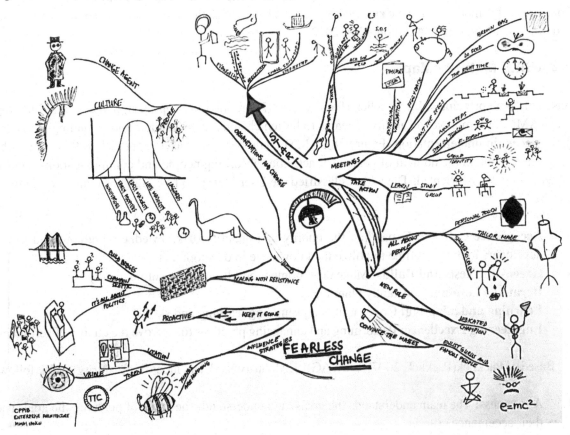

5 AGILE MATURITY MODELS

As it is considered before, the main purpose of this chapter is to presentthe existing models and frameworks to guide organizations to adopt agile methods. In this section, some agile maturity models are also briefly described to share with the readers.

5.1 Roadmap for Agile Success

Roadmap for Agile Success is the first agile maturity model for industries. It was introduced in 2012 by Corporate Executive Board (CEB) and then developed by Emergn. This model designed for organizations to help them to reach agile success. Roadmap is more than assessing Scrum that some benchmark models covered it. It is an extensive model that discuss about varieties areas to convey legible and practical measurement of the supplier's capabilities in agile. Roadmap for Agile Success evaluates your vendor's team composition and leadership, vision and mindset, stakeholder engagement, cultural acceptance and an extensive set of engineering topics (Adamopoulos, 2012).

Emergn has cooperated with CEB and Colabpro to expand Vendor Agile Maturity Index (VAMI). Vendor Agile Maturity Index evaluates the maturity of a vendor's agile in order to how they employ agile in client engagement. The clients put more pressure on their suppliers to apply agile and have a benchmark for how they use it effectively and it results in coming VAMI. VAMI lets both clients and vendors to work with each other and gain perception about the problems and the way to solve them. The final aim of this model is to make knowledge and create better relationships between vendors and clients and omit the ambiguities (Adamopoulos, 2012).

5.2 AGILE Maturity Map

Based on agile principles, Jay Packlick (Packlick, 2007) proposed an approach, named Agile Maturity Map (AMM), to improve the ability of teams to hasten change, increase their understanding, and raise their success in implementation (Figure 18). AMM could be viewed as an approach to think about the adoption of agile in the domain of goals over activities absorbing people and communication-oriented rather than process-oriented. The author classified the User Stories to five high level purposes name as AGILE:

- **Acceptance Criteria:** Expanding the quality and quantity of knowledge communicated to the developers in the right time to utilize the knowledge in development.
- **Green-Bar Tests and Builds:** Make development builds and tests automatically.
- **Iterative Planning:** Constantly planning.
- **Learning and adapting:** Concentrate on promoting learning and skills
- **Engineering Excellence:** Performing and enhancing practices to improve the quality of softwares.

Based on Packlick(Packlick, 2007) study, AGILE Maturity Model includes five maturity level as follow:

1. **Awareness:** The team understands the goals, and understands the value of pursuing the goals and their acceptance criteria.
2. **Transformation:** The team indicates responsibilities towards obtaining the goals.

Figure 18. AGILE Maturity Model (Packlick, 2007)

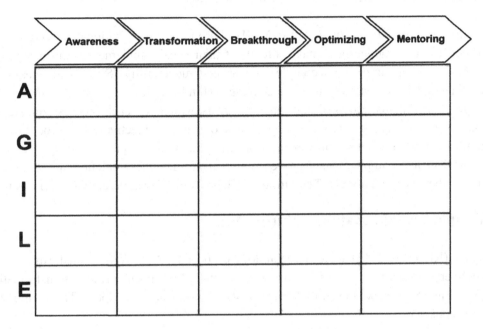

3.   **Breakthrough:** The team now regularly utilizes agile practices that meet the goals.
4.   **Optimizing:** Enhancements are made continuously in the goal area.
5.   **Mentoring:** The team training and mentoring other teams in the goal area.

5.3 Agile Maturity Model

According to Scott Ambler (Ambler, 2010), the most important goal of a maturity model is to prepare a direction for a company to assist enhancing an aspect of its business. Therefore, a marketing maturity model should provide clear instruction to improve organizations approach to marketing. The Author has described the Agile Maturity Model (AMM) which has five-level model and develops guidance to enhance the efficiency of agile software development in organizations.

Level 1- The Rhetorical step: At this stage, agile professionals accept that developers have the ability to cope with tomorrow's problems tomorrow.
Level 2- The Certified step: The aim of this stage is to ride on the coattails of endorsement programs execute through non-agile groups.
Level 3- The Plausible step: Organizations initiate to concentrate on agile approaches that may actually feasible inside the organizational context where they discover themselves.
Level 4- The Respectable step: The members of agile teams accept a complete delivery lifecycle and modify their strategy to deal with the special requests of the situation where they discover themselves.
Level 5- The Measured step: By this approach organization collect evidence from documented and unified tools to deliver organization with correct information in real time, allowing organization to guide the project according to real practical information.

5.4 Agile Capability Maturity Model Integration

The Capability Maturity Model Integrated (CMMI) is proposed to institutionalize an aggregation of predefined conveyance practices and make sure about their steady implementation for increasing the possibility that a team or company can complete the projects successfully. "Successful" means completing projects on schedule and based on the defined budget(Humble & Russell, 2009). CMMI is contained a series of process domains, arranged into maturity levels. Moreover, each process domains includes various objectives. A company has to execute practices to meet the objectives of all process domains of a unique maturity level to assert its software development processes are at that maturity level. The documents of CMMI include sample practices for each objective. Since these practices are traditional plan-based software they usually have conflict with the agile software development values (Leusink, 2012).

5.5 Aditi Agile Transformation Maturity Model

Ravi Krishnan (Krishnan, 2013) at Aditi Technology proposed a Aditi Agile Transformation Maturity Model to deliver a guideline for different teams and functional groups involved in transformation journey to agility. Figure 19 shows the Aditi Agile Transformation Maturity Model. The prominent points of this model consist of:

- Agile project planning and management maturity model deliver a guideline for teams involving to transfer from a managed team services model to a self-managing and self-directed teams services model.
- Collaboration maturity model presents a framework for teams to initialize collaborating better in a progressive manner.
- Agile Requirements Engineering Maturity Model provides the product and business ownership teams with a migration strategy from the traditional Business Requirements Document depended on requirements management approach to an Agile approach.

Figure 19. Aditi Agile Transformation Maturity Model (Krishnan, 2013)

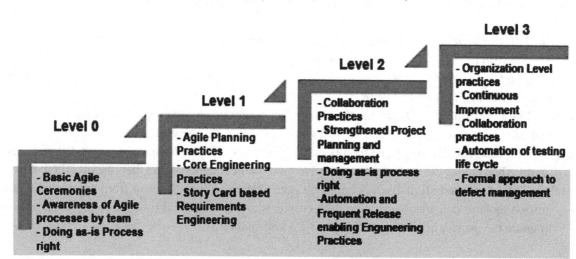

- Engineering Maturity Model delivers teams a model around adoption beginning with partly basic principles like refactoring to adopt more promoted practices.
- Metrics- Based on the level of the maturity of the Agile adoption, Aditi has come up with prescription around metrics the teams could adopt.
- Tooling- Aditi has come up with a well prescribed guideline for Agile teams in the adoption of tools across the lifecycle
- Organization readiness- An appropriate maturity model for transforming to agile enables organizations to implement a more stage wise approach and assists the various business units to increase at a sustainable step.

CONCLUSION

In spite of the Agile adoption and transformation success stories of individual organizations in the trade press, it is rather complicated to get an exact and representative depiction of Agile adoption. Organizations should know that adopting Agile will take a long time as a journey, normally 2-3 years to truly adopt agile. This study collected almost all models and frameworks proposed so far to guide organizations which agile model is the best for assisting them to transit from an old methodology to Agile Methods.

REFERENCES

Adamopoulos, A. (2012). *Roadmap for Agile Success*. Retrieved from http://www.emergn.com/insights/blogs/roadmap-for-agile-success/

Ågerfalk, J., Fitzgerald, B., & In, O. P. (2006). *Flexible and distributed software processes: old petunias in new bowls*. Paper presented at the Communications of the ACM.

Ambler, S. W. (2002). *Agile modeling. In Effective Practices for Extreme Programming and the Unified Process*. New York: Wiley & Sons.

Ambler, S. W. (2009a). *Ambysoft*. Retrieved 9 September, 2014, from http://www.ambysoft.com/surveys/stateOfITUnion200907.html

Ambler, S. W. (2009b). *The Agile Scaling Model (ASM)*. Adapting Agile Methods for Complex Environments.

Ambler, S. W. (2010). *The Agile Maturity Model (AMM)*. Retrieved from http://www.drdobbs.com/architecture-and-design/the-agile-maturity-model-amm/224201005

Ambler, S. W. (2014). *2014 Agile Adoption Mini-Survey*. AmbySoft.

Anderson, D. (2004). *Feature-Driven Development: towards a TOC, Lean and Six Sigma solution for software engineering, Theory of Constraints*. International Certification Organization, Microsoft.

Aoyama, M. (1998). Web-based Agile software development. *IEEE Software, 15*(6), 56–65. doi:10.1109/52.730844

Awad, M. A. (2005). *A comparison between agile and traditional software development methodologies*. University of Western Australia.

Beck, K. (2000). *Extreme programming explained: embrace change*. Addison-Wesley Professional.

Beck, K., Beedle, M., Van Bennekum, A., Cockburn, A., Cunningham, W., Fowler, M., & Jeffries, R. (2001). *Manifesto for agile software development*. Retrieved from http://agilemanifesto.org/

Boehm, B. (2002). Get ready for agile methods, with care. *Computer, 35*(1), 64–69. doi:10.1109/2.976920

Boehm, B., & Turner, R. (2004). *Balancing agility and discipline: Evaluating and integrating agile and plan-driven methods*. Paper presented at the Software Engineering. doi:10.1109/ICSE.2004.1317503

Brock, J., & Hobbs, P. E. (2010). *Agile Transformation – rethinking IT strategy in an uncertain world*. Retrieved from https://www-304.ibm.com/easyaccess/fileserve?contentid=208473

Cockburn, A. (2006). *Agile software development: the cooperative game*. Pearson Education.

Cohn, M. (2010a). *ADAPTing to Agile for Continued Success*. Paper presented at the Agile 2010.

Cohn, M. (2010b). *Succeeding with agile: software development using Scrum*. Pearson Education.

Coram, M., & Bohner, S. (2005). *The impact of agile methods on software project management*. Paper presented at the Engineering of Computer-Based Systems, 2005. ECBS'05. 12th IEEE International Conference and Workshops on the. doi:10.1109/ECBS.2005.68

Druckman, A. (2011). *Agile Transformation Strategy*. White Paper.

Eoyang, G. H. (2001). *Conditions for self-organizing in human systems*. The Union Institute.

Hiatt, J. M. (2006). *ADKAR: a model for change in business, government and our community*. Prosci Learning Center.

Highsmith, J. (2002). *Agile software development ecosystems*. Addison-Wesley Longman Publishing Co., Inc.

Highsmith, J. (2013). *Adaptive software development: a collaborative approach to managing complex systems*. Addison-Wesley.

Highsmith, J., & Cockburn, A. (2001). Agile software development: The business of innovation. *Computer, 34*(9), 120–127. doi:10.1109/2.947100

Humble, J., & Russell, R. (2009). *The agile maturity model applied to building and releasing software*. ThoughtWorks White Paper, Web Publishing. Retrieved from http://www.thoughtworks-studios.com/sites/default/files/resource/the_agile_maturity_model.pdf

Kotter, J. P. (1996). *Leading change*. Harvard Business Press.

Kotter, J. P. (2013). *Leading Change, With a New Preface by the Author*. Harvard Business Press.

Krishnan, R. (2013). *Aditi Agile Transformation Maturity Model*. Retrieved from http://confengine.com/agile-india-2014/proposal/236/agile-transformation-maturity-model#comments

Larman, C., & Basili, V. R. (2003). Iterative and incremental development: A brief history. *Computer*, *36*(6), 47–56. doi:10.1109/MC.2003.1204375

Leffingwell, D. (2010). *Agile software requirements: lean requirements practices for teams, programs, and the enterprise*. Addison-Wesley Professional.

Leffingwell, D. (2013). *SAFe Glossary*. Retrieved from http://scaledagileframework.com/glossary/

Leusink, B. (2012). *Agile software development process improvement in large organizations*. Academic Press.

Lewin, K. (1946). Force field analysis. In *The 1973 Annual Handbook for Group Facilitators*, (pp. 111-113). Academic Press.

Marshall, B. (2010). *The Marshall Model of Organisational Evolution (Dreyfus for the Organisation)*. Retrieved from http://fallingblossoms.com/opinion/content?id=1006

Moniruzzaman, A. B. M., & Hossain, S. A. (2013). *Comparative Study on Agile software development methodologies*. arXiv preprint arXiv:1307.3356

Nerur, S., Mahapatra, R. K., & Mangalaraj, G. (2005). Challenges of migrating to agile methodologies. *Communications of the ACM*, *48*(5), 72–78. doi:10.1145/1060710.1060712

Packlick, J. (2007). *The agile maturity map a goal oriented approach to agile improvement*. Paper presented at the Agile Conference (AGILE). doi:10.1109/AGILE.2007.55

Popli, R., & Chauhan, N. (2013). A mapping model for transforming traditional software development methods to agile methodology. *International Journal of Software Engineering & Applications*, *4*(4), 53–64. doi:10.5121/ijsea.2013.4405

Qumer, A., & Henderson-Sellers, B. (2008). A framework to support the evaluation, adoption and improvement of agile methods in practice. *Journal of Systems and Software*, *81*(11), 1899–1919. doi:10.1016/j.jss.2007.12.806

Qumer, A., Henderson-sellers, B., & Mcbride, T. (2007). Agile adoption and improvement model. In *Proceedings of European and Mediterranean Conference on Information Systems*.

Rao, K. N., Naidu, G. K., & Chakka, P. (2011). A study of the agile software development methods, applicability and implications in industry. *International Journal of Software Engineering and its Applications, 5*(2), 35-45.

Rising, L., & Manns, M. L. (2004). *Fearless change: patterns for introducing new ideas*. Pearson Education.

Sahota, M. (2012). An Agile Adoption and Transformation Survival Guide: Working with Organizational Culture. *InfoQ*. Retrieved from http://www.infoq.com/minibooks/agile-adoption-transformation

Schneider, W. E. (1994). *The reengineering alternative: A plan for making your current culture work*. Richard D Irwin.

Schwaber, C, Laganza, G, & D'Silva, D. (2007). *The truth about agile processes: frank answers to frequently asked questions*. Forrester Report.

Sidky, A., Arthur, J., & Bohner, S. (2007). A disciplined approach to adopting agile practices: The agile adoption framework. *Innovations in Systems and Software Engineering*, *3*(3), 203–216. doi:10.1007/s11334-007-0026-z

Smith, G., & Sidky, A. (2009). *Becoming agile: in an imperfect world*. Manning Publications.

Snowden, D. (1999). *Cynefin framework*. Retrieved from http://cognitive-edge.com/

Southwell, K. (2002). Agile process improvement. *TickIT International Journal*, 3-14.

Spayd, M. (2010). *Agile & Culture*. Retrieved from http://collectiveedgecoaching.com/2010/07/agile__culture/

Stapleton, J. (2003). *DSDM: Business focused development*. Pearson Education.

Takeuchi, H., & Nonaka, I. (1986). The new new product development game. *Harvard Business Review*, *64*(1), 137–146.

Van Vliet, H. (2007). *Software engineering: Principles and practice*. Wiley.

KEY TERMS AND DEFINITIONS

Agile Software Development: A software management and development approach that helps to create software quickly while addressing the issue of requirement change.

Scrum: This is an iterative, incremental software process, which is by far the most popular agile development process.

Waterfall Model: A sequential design, used in software development processes, in which progress is seen as flowing steadily downwards (like a waterfall) through the phases of Conception, Initiation, Analysis, Design, Construction, Testing, Deployment, and Maintenance.

XP: This methodology consists of a variety of practices. These practices are used by developers in creating the required software.

Chapter 9
Agile Assessment Methods and Approaches

Mina Ziaei Nafchi
Islamic Azad University – Boroujen, Iran

Taghi Javdani Gandomani
Islamic Azad University – Boroujen, Iran

ABSTRACT

Agile methods are widely used in software companies in recent years. Many software companies are replacing their traditional development methods with agile methods. Nonetheless, measuring agility that they have achieved has been a topic of debate. Software teams and companies need to know how agile they are or how much is the agility degree of their organization. Unlike traditional methods in software development, there is no standard or universal model (like CMM/CMMI) to measure maturity of agile teams and software companies. So far, only a few methods and tools have been proposed to measure the agility of software companies. The main aim of this chapter is introducing the structure and main features of the existing agile assessment methods and providing a brief discussion on drawbacks of these methods. This chapter tries to elucidate the actual position of agility measurement methods in measuring agility degree of companies who are trying to adapt to agile methods and practices.

INTRODUCTION

Agile methodologies emerged in software development due to prevent the inherent challenges of traditional methods and to offer some new values for developing working software. These values cover all the aspects of software development lifecycle including project management and development process. Migration from traditional to agile methods, which takes a huge time and effort, needs to be considered as an important issue because it can cause wasting time and money in software companies. So, those companies that are transforming to agile need to be aware about their situation in this transformation and make sure that they are in the right direction. Therefore, measuring the progress of agile transformation and adoption is considered as a helpful strategy.

DOI: 10.4018/978-1-4666-9858-1.ch009

Measuring the agility of companies that is known as agile assessment has been a topic of debate in the literature. There are some studies that suggested some approaches to assess the agility level of software companies. Different scopes and techniques have been proposed to assess agility degree such as fuzzy approaches, multi-level structures, and some comparative approaches. However, there is no popular and standard assessment model regarding this issue. The aim of this chapter is to conduct a review on the existing assessment models and techniques and to show the advantages and weaknesses of them.

The rest of this chapter is organized as follows: Section 2 briefly describes agile transformation process. Section 3 presents a brief description of the agility assessment models. Section 4 provides a discussion on each method and mainly explains weaknesses of these models. Finally, Section 5 concludes the discussion and addresses a potential future work.

AGILE TRANSFORMATION PROCESS

After creating Agile manifesto (Beck et al., 2001), many software companies and engineers have been interested in adopting agile methods in their development process. Most of them found agile methods as a helpful solution to cope with the inherent problems of traditional methods including heavy documentation, late release, customer dissatisfaction, difficulty in changing requirements, lack of transparency, and management bottlenecks (Cohen, Lindvall, & Costa, 2004). Indeed, they considered agile methods as a reaction to traditional methods (Boehm, 2002).

Although agile methods officially have been introduced in 2001, prevalence of them started after 2005, when some of the famous software companies started their transformation and reported their success stories (Chung & Drummond, 2009; Laanti, Salo, & Abrahamsson, 2011; Schatz & Abdelshafi, 2005). However, only a few of them changed their development style in all projects and teams.

An important issue is that transitioning to agile is not an easy and smooth project. Rather, it needs enough time and effort (Gandomani, Zulzalil, Ghani, & Sultan, 2013a, 2013b). There are many reports about introducing an agile method to a company in which the authors have explained the challenges, obstacles, hindrances, and problems they faced (Gandomani, Zulzalil, Ghani, Sultan, & Nafchi, 2013; Gandomani, Zulzalil, Ghani, Sultan, & Parizi, 2015). Based on these reports, most of the challenges are related to people and their role in agile methods (Conboy, Coyle, Wang, & Pikkarainen, 2011; Gandomani, Zulzalil, Abdul Ghani, Sultan, & Sharif, 2014). The rationale behind this is that, agile methods are totally different from traditional methods in terms of people and their roles in project management and software development (Cockburn & Highsmith, 2001). In this case, those who are adapted to traditional roles most often resist against new roles as agile methods expect (Gandomani, Zulzalil, Ghani, Sultan, et al., 2013; Nerur, Mahapatra, & Mangalaraj, 2005).

Beside people-related issues (Gandomani, Zulzalil, Abdul Ghani, et al., 2014), agile transformation is subject to other challenges including customer-related issues, tools and technology-related challenges, and so on (Gandomani, Zulzalil, Ghani, Sultan, et al., 2013; Gandomani, Zulzalil, & Nafchi, 2014; Nerur et al., 2005). Obviously, such a challenging process needs to be supported by appropriate enablers or facilitators (Gandomani, Zulzalil, Abd Ghani, Sultan, & Sharif, 2014).

Nonetheless, there are a few transformation models for moving to agile. However, none of them could not gain enough acceptance from industry and are subject to various challenges (Rohunen, Rodriguez,

Kuvaja, Krzanik, & Markkula, 2010). They mainly have tried to propose a multi-stage procedure for transitioning to agile by defining multi-level agility level. At the same time, reaching to a specific level of adoption can be considered as an indicator of progress in agile transformation process.

Agility assessment or measurement has been a concern in agile transformation and adoption. A few models and measurement method have been proposed for assessing agility degree in companies who are using agile methods. However, it seems that most of them are exposed many serious problems and challenges (S. Soundararajan, J. D. Arthur, & O. Balci, 2012).

With the aim of better understanding agility assessment methods and their structures, the next section describes the most important agility assessment models and tools in brief.

AGILE ASSESSMENT MODELS

As mentioned before, so far, a few agility assessment models and tools have been proposed. These models or tools intend to measure to what extent a software company has succeeded to adapt to agile methods in its software development process. However, some of these models have been introduced when researchers were looking for finding an agile transformation framework. The most important ones are as follows.

Sidky-Agile Measurement Index (SAMI)

Sidky et al. (Sidky, Arthur, & Bohner, 2007) proposed "Sidky agile measurement index" (SAMI) based on four components including agile levels, agile principles, agile practices and concepts, and several indicators. They categorized the practices in several levels in such way that related practices, those can lead to considerable improvement in process of agile adoption, be in same category. They also used principles of agile approach as a guide to ensure realizing agile values. Finally, they applied indicators for assessing the agility to assess the level of agility that companies have been adopted. According to these components, SAMI considers five levels of agility. These levels that came from the values of agile are collaborative, evolutionary, effective, adaptive, and encompassing.

To assess the agility level of a company, Sidky et al. (Sidky et al., 2007) applied goal-question-indicator-metric (GQIM) approach using principles as goals and indicated 300 indicators accompany with 40 practices. As they explained each indicator has been designed to measure a particular organizational characteristic necessary for the successful adoption of the agile practice to which the indicator is related (Sidky et al., 2007). Obviously, considering a huge number of indicators makes measurement so difficult and a time consuming process. Another negative point is that SAMI model is following CMMI approach in its origin, since CMMI considers multi-level maturity in software development. This point is totally different from what agile offers and is in contrast with agile approach (Esfahani, 2012; Gandomani & Nafchi, 2014)

4-D Framework

Qumer et al. (Qumer & Henderson-Sellers, 2008) proposed a four dimensional framework based on the features of flexibility, speed, leanness, learning and responsiveness to assess the agility of agile methods. They presented a specific definition of agile method based on these factors. These four dimensions are scope, features, agile values, and process. First dimension is about general scope such as project size, team size, development and coding style and so on. The second dimension is based on the definition of agile concepts and its features. The third is to check the existence of agile values in agile methods, and the last one considers the process of development in terms of engineering and management perspective. This assessment model has been introduced as the core of an agile adoption framework, called "Agile Adoption and Improvement Model" (AAIM) (Qumer & Henderson-Sellers, 2008). This framework, like SAMI, is following the CMMI approach which as mentioned previously, is not compatible with agile approach and is exposed to many criticisms (Esfahani, 2012; Gandomani & Nafchi, 2014).

OOP Framework

Soundararajan et al. (Shvetha Soundararajan, James D Arthur, & Osman Balci, 2012) proposed a framework to assess the "goodness" of agile methods under the name of OOP (objectives principles and practices). This framework assesses an agile method based on its adequacy, the capability of the organization to apply this method, and the effectiveness of the method in terms of meeting the expected outcomes. Based on agile manifesto and agile values they came with five objectives including objective of the agile philosophy, principles that supports the objectives, practices reflecting the principles, linkage among the principles, practices and objectives, and finally indicators to assess effectiveness of implementation of practices in a software company. OOP has mapped the addressed objectives with nine agile principles. Furthermore, OOP binds 27 agile practices to the principles. The researchers applied OOP on XP, FFD, and method A-a modified version of XP- and showed that XP is an agile method that most completely reflects that agile philosophy and is more adequate that FDD and method A.

Comparative Agility

A need to have a comparative approach which can compare the agility degree of companies seems to be necessary. The most well known approach for this goal is comparative agility (CA) proposed by Williams et al. (Williams, Rubin, & Cohn, 2010). CA is a tool to compare the agility level of individuals or organizations with other ones. The rationale behind this tool is that it may not be always necessary to know the agility degree of a software company, but it also a need to be aware about the position of the organization in comparison with other competitors. This tool that can be accessible through a website, consider seven dimensions to assess agility of a company. These dimensions are: Teamwork, Requirements, Planning, Technical Practices, Quality, Culture, and Knowledge Creating.

They defined some characteristics for each dimension and described them by 125 statements. Respondent (software companies) are required to response each statement according to their situation in form of Likert scale.

Although this method can be used directly to measure agility degree, it is helpful to assess agility level of a company compared to other software companies which voluntarily have declared their positions regarding to predefined dimensions.

Thoughtworks' Assessment Model

Thoughtworks as a leading company in Agile software development and consulting services developed an online survey to assess the agility degree of software companies who are employing agile methods in their projects (Thoughtworks, 2010). Software companies are assessed to check to what extent their teams are following agile best practices, to what extent they are enable to get to market fast, and finally, is their team set up to get software releases right the first time?

Software companies can get a report indicating their agility degree by filling out the proposed survey. This assessment tool comprises twenty questions about existence of agile practices in a company to indicate agility degree of the company.

Agile Maturity Model (AMM)

In another study (Patel & Ramachandran, 2009), a maturity model has been proposed to enhance and improve agile principles and objectives in software companies. This study proposed a five-level maturity level namely initial, explored, defined, improved, and sustained. The authors defined several key process areas (KPA) in each maturity level. This study also proposed a process of suitability assessment, adaptability assessment, and improvement framework to assess and improve agile best practices. The main criticism exposed to this model is what previously addressed for the other similar model. Forcing companies to adapt to specific practices is not consistent with agile approach.

Agility Assessment Model (AAM)

This model has been proposed to measurement of agility degree in software companies (Gandomani & Nafchi, 2014). The underpinning of this model is agile practices and their importance in agility. The model has been proposed based on the survey had been done in (Williams, 2012). The importance of each agile practice has been calculated based on the opinion of 326 respondents. In this model, 44 agile practices have been considered. This model simply measures the agility degree of a company based on the adopted agile practices in a company. This model has not the drawbacks of the previous explained model. In this model, there is no force to adapt to any agile practice. Software companies can freely adopt any agile practices they need. Obviously, adopting all agile practices brings highest agility degree.

Other Assessment Models / Tools

Beside the above famous model or tools to measure the agility degree of software companies, there are a few other checklists for assessing agility degree. For instance, Atlassian Jira includes an Agile Maturity Matrix which is used to assess how an organization is agile (Atlassian, 2013). Another one is Borland agile assessment that comprises 12 questions (Borland, 2009). Joe's Unofficial Scrum Checklist (Little, 2014) is also a check list to assess how a company has succeed to implement and adopt Scrum practices in its software development process. Moreover, there are some other checklists and guidance to help software companies to assess their progress in agile transformation that can indirectly be used for agile assessment.

DISCUSSION

Some of the aforementioned assessment methods have relied on agile practices and some others on agility levels they have defined. Generally, it seems that agility assessment is not a straightforward process.

Agile practices are those practices suggested by agile methods to achieve their specific goals. Each agile method has its own practice. For instance, stand-up meeting, retrospective, and sprint review are some of the Scrum practices and pair programming, refactoring, and unit testing are some of the XP practices. A detailed list of agile practices has been provided in other publications (Gandomani & Nafchi, 2014; Williams, 2012)

Among the addressed assessment models and tools, some of them are subject to serious challenges. Most of the challenges are about their compatibility with agile approach and their scopes, as follows.

SAMI model is an agile independent assessment model that defines five levels of agility. However, there are some drawbacks about it. First, there are some practices that companies are forced to adopt them to achieve related levels. These practices may not be compatible or necessary to the agile method the company has been adopted with (S. Soundararajan et al., 2012). Next, forcing companies to adapt to an agile method or some agile practices is not compatible with the flexibility promised by agile approach. So, using a set of pre defined practices is against the flexibility exists in the core of agility (Shvetha Soundararajan et al., 2012).

The above criticisms are also considered regarding to Agile maturity Model (AMM). It is completely contradictory with what agile approach promised.

Regarding 4-D framework, although the definition of agile and its key attributes are compatible with the reality of agile, this framework reduces the flexibility that is needed to be agile (Soundararajan et al., 2012). This is primarily because this model measures agility of a company by analyzing adoption of a set of practices. Like SAMI model, forcing companies to accept pre-defined sets of agile practices reduces the flexibility promised by agile. Furthermore, the defined agility level may not be "in-sync" with organizational objectives in a company (Soundararajan & Arthur, 2011). This framework mainly tries to localize agile rather than measuring agility degree of a company (Esfahani, 2012).

OOP framework is helpful for indicating goodness of each agile method comparing to other methods. But, it cannot be useful to measure progress of agile transformation because most often transitioning to agile does not mean adoption to a specific agile method. Indeed, most often software companies try to adapt to some agile practices rather than a whole particular agile method (Gandomani, Zulzalil, et al., 2013b).

Comparative agility method has not the problems that are seen in the SAMI and 4-D framework. This method considers agile practices as the core of the assessment model. However, this method only can indicate agile rate of a company comparing to the others who have used this method previously. Indeed, expectation of an agility degree from this method is wrong. It should be noted that a positive point about this method is the scope of agile practices that have been considered in this method.

Thoughtworks' model checks absence or presence of agile practices in a software company rather than assessing the degree to which those practices are used. This mainly because this model focuses on assessing the extent to which software company or team has been successful in agile transformation. However, this model covers only some of the agile practices and could be improved to cover a wider scope.

It seems that Agility assessment model is suitable in action. This is mainly because the importance (value) of each agile practice has been obtained from the opinion of many agile experts over the world. Also, this model covers almost all the most important agile practices.

Reviewing the above methods and tools reveal that agility assessment models is still a concern. While there is no standard model for assessing agility degree, most of the existing approaches suffer from some serious drawbacks. Obviously, each of them can be used only for the real purpose which has been considered when proposing that method. For instance, OOP is very good to assess goodness of any specific agile methods and CA is helpful to compare current agility degree of a company compared to its competitors.

The most important thing is that measuring agility is not easy, because it is a totally subjective. Nonetheless, employing Agile Assessment Model seems to be useful when a company or a team is continuously adapting to agile practices.

CONCLUSION AND FUTURE WORK

While prevalence of agile methods is increasing in software companies, there is still a gap to assess the agility degree of software companies. This review chapter showed that there are a few agility assessment methods to assess agility degree of software companies. However, they are subject to some serious challenges. In this chapter the most important assessment methods have been described and their positions in agility assessment have been explained. In general, there is no perfect assessment model which is both compatible to agile and comprehensive for assessing agility degree of software companies or teams who are adopting agile methods or practices. However, Agility Assessment Model can be considered as an appropriate model.

Considering the strengths and weaknesses of the current assessment model, a potential future work is providing a better assessment model which has not the drawbacks of the existing ones. Clearly, such a model is better to focus on the agile practices and their values in achieving agility in companies or teams. In this case, it can be an extension of Agility Assessment Model.

REFERENCES

Atlassian. (2013). *Agile maturity – How agile is your organization?* Retrieved Nov. 2013, from http://blogs.atlassian.com/2013/11/agile-maturity-how-agile-is-your-organization/

Beck, K., Beedle, M., van Bennekum, A., Cockburn, A., Cunningham, W., Fowler, M., . . . Sutherland, J. (2001). *Agile Manifesto*. Retrieved May 2014, from www.agilemanifesto.org

Boehm, B. (2002). Get ready for agile methods, with care. *Computer, 35*(1), 64–69. doi:10.1109/2.976920

Borland. (2009). *Borland agile assessment.* Retrieved Dec. 2013, from http://borland.typepad.com/agile_transformation/2009/03/borland-agile-assessment-2009.html

Chung, M. W., & Drummond, B. (2009). *Agile @ yahoo! from the trenches.* Paper presented at the Agile Conference (AGILE 2009), Chicago, IL. doi:10.1109/AGILE.2009.41

Cockburn, A., & Highsmith, J. (2001). Agile software development: The people factor. *Computer, 34*(11), 131–133. doi:10.1109/2.963450

Cohen, D., Lindvall, M., & Costa, P. (2004). An introduction to Agile methods. *Advances in Computers, 62*, 1-66. doi: 10.1016/S0065-2458(03)62001-2

Conboy, K., Coyle, S., Wang, X., & Pikkarainen, M. (2011). People over process: Key challenges in agile development. *IEEE Software, 28*(4), 48–57. doi:10.1109/MS.2010.132

Esfahani, H. C. (2012). *Transitioning to Agile: A Framework for Pre-Adoption Analysis using Empirical Knowledge and Strategic Modeling.* Canada: University of Toronto.

Gandomani, T. J., Zulzalil, H., Abdul Ghani, A. A., Sultan, A. B. M., & Sharif, K. Y. (2014). How human aspects impress Agile software development transition and adoption. *International Journal of Software Engineering and its Applications, 8*(1), 129-148. doi: 10.14257/ijseia.2014.8.1.12

Gandomani, T. J., & Nafchi, M. Z. (2014). Agility Assessment Model to Measure Agility Degree of Agile Software Companies. *Indian Journal of Science and Technology, 7*(7), 955–959.

Gandomani, T. J., Zulzalil, H., & Ghani, A. (2013). Obstacles to moving to agile software development; at a glance. *Journal of Computer Science, 9*(5), 620–625. doi:10.3844/jcssp.2013.620.625

Gandomani, T. J., Zulzalil, H., Abdul Ghani, A. A., Sultan, A. B. M., & Sharif, K. Y. (2014). Exploring Facilitators of Transition and Adoption to Agile Methods: a Grounded Theory Study. *Journal of Software.*

Gandomani, T. J., Zulzalil, H., Ghani, A. A. A., & Sultan, A. B. M. (2013a). Important considerations for agile software development methods governance. *Journal of Theoretical and Applied Information Technology, 55*(3), 345–351.

Gandomani, T. J., Zulzalil, H., Ghani, A. A. A., & Sultan, A. B. M. (2013b). Towards comprehensive and disciplined change management strategy in agile transformation process. *Research Journal of Applied Sciences. Engineering and Technology, 6*(13), 2345–2351.

Gandomani, T. J., Zulzalil, H., Ghani, A. A. A., & Sultan, A. B. M., & Parizi, R. M. (2015). The impact of inadequate and dysfunctional training on Agile transformation process: A Grounded Theory study. *Information and Software Technology, 57*, 295–309. doi:10.1016/j.infsof.2014.05.011

Gandomani, T. J., Zulzalil, H., & Nafchi, M. Z. (2014). *Agile Transformation: What is it about?* Paper presented at the 8th Malaysian Software Engineering Conference (MySEC), Langkawi, Malaysia.

Laanti, M., Salo, O., & Abrahamsson, P. (2011). Agile methods rapidly replacing traditional methods at Nokia: A survey of opinions on agile transformation. *Information and Software Technology, 53*(3), 276–290. doi:10.1016/j.infsof.2010.11.010

Little, J. (2014). *Joe's Unofficial Scrum Checklist.* Retrieved Dec. 2014, from http://agileconsortium. pbworks.com/w/file/66642311/Joe%E2%80%99s%20Unofficial%20Scrum%20CheckList%20V13.pdf

Nerur, S., Mahapatra, R., & Mangalaraj, G. (2005). Challenges of migrating to agile methodologies. *Communications of the ACM, 48*(5), 72–78. doi:10.1145/1060710.1060712

Patel, C., & Ramachandran, M. (2009). Agile Maturity Model (AMM): A Software Process Improvement framework for Agile Software Development Practices. *International Journal of Software Engineering, 2*(1), 3–28.

Qumer, A., & Henderson-Sellers, B. (2008). An evaluation of the degree of agility in six agile methods and its applicability for method engineering. *Information and Software Technology, 50*(4), 280–295. doi:10.1016/j.infsof.2007.02.002

Rohunen, A., Rodriguez, P., Kuvaja, P., Krzanik, L., & Markkula, J. (2010). *Approaches to agile adoption in large settings: a comparison of the results from a literature analysis and an industrial inventory.* Paper presented at the 11th international conference on Product-Focused Software Process Improvement, Limerick, Ireland. doi:10.1007/978-3-642-13792-1_8

Schatz, B., & Abdelshafi, I. (2005). Primavera gets Agile: A successful transition to Agile development. *IEEE Software, 22*(3), 36–42. doi:10.1109/MS.2005.74

Sidky, A., Arthur, J., & Bohner, S. (2007). A disciplined approach to adopting agile practices: the agile adoption framework. *Innovations in Systems and Software Engineering, 3*(3), 203-216.

Soundararajan, S., & Arthur, J. D. (2011). *A structured framework for assessing the "goodness" of agile methods.* Paper presented at the 18th IEEE International Conference and Workshops on Engineering of Computer-Based Systems, ECBS 2011, Las Vegas, NV.

Soundararajan, S., Arthur, J. D., & Balci, O. (2012). *A methodology for assessing agile software development methods.* Paper presented at the Agile Conference, Agile 2012, Dallas, TX. doi:10.1109/Agile.2012.24

Soundararajan, S., Arthur, J. D., & Balci, O. (2012). *A Methodology for Assessing Agile Software Development Methods.* Paper presented at the Agile Conference (AGILE). doi:10.1109/Agile.2012.24

Thoughtworks. (2010). *Agile assessments.* Retrieved June 2014, from http://www.agileassessments.com/

Williams, L. (2012). What agile teams think of agile principles. *Communications of the ACM, 55*(4), 71–76. doi:10.1145/2133806.2133823

Williams, L., Rubin, K., & Cohn, M. (2010). *Driving Process Improvement via Comparative Agility Assessment.* Paper presented at the Agile Conference (AGILE). doi:10.1109/AGILE.2010.12

KEY TERMS AND DEFINITIONS

Agile Software Architecture: A software architecture that lays out blue prints of the organization and structure of software components as well as well defined mechanism on how components can be tested and integrated into the system that would sustain the agile approach through out the software development life cycle.

Agile Software Development: A software management and development approach that helps to create software quickly while addressing the issue of requirement change.

Extreme Programming: Extreme Programming (XP) is an agile methodology that specifically emphasizes the use of agile technical practices (e.g. Test Driven Development) for the success of an agile project. Practical experience shows that XP complements Scrum well and both the methods work well together.

Scrum: Scrum is one of the popular agile methodologies which aims to address the challenges of projects involving complex scope of work using a simple process dependent on a small team who are motivated, collaborative and highly focused on producing working software every 2-4 weeks.

Chapter 10
Agile Software Development Challenges in Implementation and Adoption:
Focusing on Large and Distributed Settings – Past Experiences, Emergent Topics

Abbas Moshref Razavi
University of Malaya, Malaysia

Rodina Ahmad
University of Malaya, Malaysia

ABSTRACT

The first part of this chapter presents the results of a systematic literature review on Agile Software Development (ASD) challenges as are reported in implementation and adoption cases. The data only considers the concrete evidences of surfaced problems mainly according to work experience and case study articles. The results are analyzed so that types, nature and intensity of the problems are determined and, compared to each other, within three major classifications of "large organizations", "distributed settings" and "both large and distributed environments". The analysis reveals that, in ASD, common organizational and managerial issues have been replaced by communication and collaboration problems. The second part uses the results of the part one as a frame of analysis to render more interpretations e.g. signifying that non-agility preconceptions are the root of a majority of problematic projects. Besides, mediating between agile projects and traditional forms of management, and, economic governance are two major rival approaches that are emerging in response to these challenges.

DOI: 10.4018/978-1-4666-9858-1.ch010

INTRODUCTION

Today's organizations are forced to survive in a very competitive world. They need to be agile. In the realm of software development, Agile Software Development (ASD) is a natural response to such need for agility. However, ASD has initially been proposed for small, collocated teams with the possibility of face-to-face communication. Therefore, large organizations, whether they are developer in terms of large software firms and/or, consumer who uses the developed software solutions, usually have challenges to employ ASD due to their size and possibly geographical distribution.

Such challenges first and foremost appear to be related to the organizations' functional division of work (contrasting the work nature in agile teams) as well as their high volume of rules and regulations. Even if there are efforts to transform organizations into new, modern structures with agile processes, yet, their real complexities (that is mostly due to their size) still necessitate their large number of cumbersome rules. Moreover, organizations, usually still and very often, follow strategic plans which are inherently not agile. These plans are partly compulsory to conduct such organizations in long terms, though, partly may not be necessary and, are able to be shifted into more agile policy approaches and strategic planning (for instance, see Rodríguez, Partanen, Kuvaja, & Oivo, 2014; Parcell, & Holden, 2013). Nonetheless, in any event, there are resistances to agility whether because of the existing technical and knowledge barriers or organizational, social and cultural inertness.

Part I of this chapter examines and verifies the hypotheses of the previous paragraph in terms of whether such challenges do exist in adopting ASD, specifically in large organizations and/or distributed settings; and, if this is the case, what are their most frequent and prevailing ones. In Part II, through a thorough analysis, the current study attempts to understand the roots of these challenges and, consequently, provides predictions for a close future with this regard.

PART I: CLASSIFICATION OF CHALLENGES

Due to common acceptance of ASD and, as was previously mentioned, indispensability of large organizations to adopt ASD, this chapter intends to provide valuable information for adopters in terms of the challenges which would possibly be encountered in the course of implementation/adoption.

Therefore, the subsequent questions are attempted to be answered. First, what are the challenges of implementing or adopting ASD particularly for large and/or geographically distributed organizations/software development teams? Second, what have been the major types and categories of these challenges relating to managerial, cultural and technical aspect? Third, what are the main roots that the challenges have been emerged form? And, fourth, what is the prediction of new types of challenges in ASD adoption for a close future?

In this study, method implementation refers usually, not necessarily, to first-time-experience of an agile method for a specific project. On the other hand, method adoption normally signifies a long term report of transition to agile methods along with an essential organizational transformation in both managerial and cultural aspects. As such, this chapter strives to deal with both implementation and adoption based on the existing literature.

As was previously mentioned, here, the "large organization" scope of the study refers to large organizations that might be software firms (including very large ones e.g. Microsoft, Amazon, etc.) or large organizations who adopt ASD by their inner Software Development (SD) teams (e.g. BCI) or outsourcing to the other software firms.

By referring to "distributed settings", we have considered all the possibilities of distributed organizations and/or presence of off-shore (and near-shore; to clarify the concept see e.g. Vax, & Michaud, 2008; Zieris, & Salinger, 2013) teams, and likely, along with the concept of global software engineering. In this view, (spatial) distribution may happens in various forms, like in the cases of separated teams, separation between customer environment and development teams, out-sourced teams, global software engineering firms, and organizations which act as intermediators and brokers (between the client and developers).

Besides providing useful information about these challenges, this chapter proposes novel conceptualizations about how a traditional organization and/or its culture (i.e. even, in the cases like people with traditional culture in a newly renovated organization or, new, agile adopted work culture in an old-fashioned organization regarding its management and ways of planning) might be in conflict with adopting ASD.

Even though this study does not aim to provide a list of the applied solutions as well, yet, it is expected that knowing such challenges in advance would be helpful for the adopters.

METHOD

Data

This study relies on the data of an enormous set of implementation and adoption cases in large and distributed settings and their reported problems, challenges, barriers, risks, etc. The source papers were originally retrieved through various extensive systematic literature reviews that whose results have been/ will be published elsewhere; yet, here and for this chapter, they (i.e. the papers) merely serve as raw data. As such, all the data extractions and coding works and, the subsequent resolutions and interpretations, have been solely accomplished for the purpose of the current study. The source of the papers is limited to IEEE publication. This is because, the authors had previously found out that at least half of all the existing publications in the area of ASD, have been taken place in IEEE (MoshrefRazavi, & Ahmad, 2014) and additionally, a majority of these publications are in terms of work experiences or case studies of actual workplaces. As a result, it is estimated that this set of studied literature covers more than two third of all implementation and adoption cases of ASD upon a long period of 12 years (2003 and onward - the last access and updated result has been on December, 2014 from IEEE *Xplore* search engine).

Subsequently, from a large set of the found research papers (624 out of 2856 different items) which had been recognized to be relevant to managerial, cultural and organizational aspects of ASD, 205 papers are considered to be relevant to large and distributed settings. Eventually, in a fourth phase, 102 papers were selected for this study because of containing concrete evidences of problems and challenges surfaced during ASD implementation and adoption. These papers are mostly in the forms of work experience and case study, though, also include very few surveys and other types of research providing that they explicitly produce, classify and present lists of challenges based on their own data.

Therefore, the data from the case studies, qualitative researches and work experiences are treated as first-hand data which are directly related to, and report, the problems and challenges surfaced throughout the implementation processes of an agile method for a specific project, or, adoption of a given method for an inclusive organization and in a long run. By first-hand, we mean that the data is used as is (described) in simple words (and, if the description is too long, a conceptual label is applied to abstract it) disregarding other arguments and speculations of the correspondent authors. In other words, we collect data so as it is more relatable to, and generalizable regarding, the context of ASD as a whole, compared to that specific situation (of each given paper).

Based on the selection criteria, the selected papers (102) have been manually searched throughout the whole text for the statements of challenges and problems surfaced during their work practices. The search process usually examined work experience papers thoroughly whereas for the case studies, the focus has been on their "results" sections. For other types of research papers, including surveys, only the sections or tables columns under titles like problems, challenges, etc., have been sought.

Apart from work experiences and case studies, the data of surveys and other types of research are chosen only if, first, their raw collected data (i.e. the primary data of that survey, quantitative study, experiment, etc.) are about the problems and challenges in the given scope, and second, the authors systematically analyze, classify and report them under meaningful titles e.g. problems, challenges, risk, limitations, etc. Moreover, these kind of studies were selected for data extraction only if the authors provided extra information indicating that the problems and challenges are not mere conceptualization, classes or abstraction of the problems, but the factual, concrete, occurred problems in one or more implementation/adoption cases according to the respondents, interviewees and so on. By adopting this approach, we make sure that their reported data is of mere problems and, from valid and credible sources (e.g. developers, customers, etc.).

Methodical Discussion

The argument for this way of collecting data is that though the situational context and its conditions are of critical importance to understand the phenomenon and somehow to generalize it in the next step (by means of other appropriate methods which are not the case in the current study), yet, to theorize based on a large number of dispersed evidences, it is unavoidable to observe and recite the data in a relatively context-free form and, more in terms of universal facts (although here the word universal, as indicated in the previous subsection, is limited and, refers back, to the given context i.e. ASD implementation and adoption). Through this approach, the theorization is credited by means of a relatively high numbers of evidences in term of the extracted reported problems. Again, anyhow, to conclude based on a large set of evidences which are commonly accessible through literature, this approach is inevitable. Therefore, we attempt to produce a reference frame (within the ASD context) to assist new adopters. After all, any past experience would not be able to be used (whether theoretically or, even, practically) unless the experience can stand outside of its experienced setting so that could be used in a new one. And, since the intention here is to conclude on the basis of a large set of data, such a context in which these numerous explicit statements (of the surfaced problems) are meaningful and interpretable needs to be constructed. Another (alternative, expected) approach for generalization of such data, admittedly, is to build a comprehensive theory of all these proposed situational opinions and verify it by e.g. a quantitative method. Such approach also has its own limitations, which are the high number of authors' opinions (that might be, particularly in work experience cases, in the forms like guidelines, recommendations, suggestions, lessons learned, etc.) as well as the lack of effective ways to combine these amount of opinions, theoretically and in a convincing manner.

Nevertheless, in the second part of this chapter, we attempt to use the results of this first part as a foundation or an inclusive frame in which singular works could be interpreted. Thus, having such theoretical foundation may not integrate all the authors' opinions in a theoretical and unified way; however, it would make it possible to interpret notable opinions and postulations within this provided frame (i.e. the outcome of this, first, part of the chapter). In this sense, the alleged frame redefines the context (i.e. challenges in ASD implementation and adoption) and, provides means of understanding and analytical argument that will assist us to assess and position the works of single authors. The details are discussed in part II. It is added that, we believe that this way of work may develop a research methodology for studying literature in general, and, to utilize and interpret the results of systematic literature reviews particularly.

Meanwhile, to be more unbiased, to extract any evidence (i.e. surfaced problems), we have initially read the whole inclusive passage, along with noting the paper's structure and whose sections' titles at first. By following this approach, we have striven, as far as possible, not to have data in terms of the explicit, concrete phrases/sentences which contradict other contents of the same paper.

For dealing with surveys, this is important to consider the fact that their results are usually relative weighted lists of issues. Therefore, to include such data, it (i.e. the data) certainly needs more clarification by the same commensurate researchers in terms of providing additional, supportive information and context. Otherwise, as was previously discussed, their data might not be taken into account as reported, surfaced problems according to agile implementers/adopter. Obviously, those survey studies which did not seek for problems in ASD implementation and adoption were excluded here too.

Analysis

For the purposes of extracting, classifying and analyzing the data, a coding approach is used that roughly correspond to grounded theory method's coding techniques (Urquhart, 2013), although the whole study is not a grounded theory in terms of providing a theory based on the direct comments of individuals to pinpoint processes and actions of human behavior. Conversely, we argue that the main theme of the analysis approach, here, is "comparative analysis" as is the focal point in GT (Glaser & Strauss, 1967). Therefore, this study attempts to provide a useful classification of the reported problems and challenges by the following steps. Firstly, the phrases and sentences containing problems which concretely and certainly occurred in practice are chosen and listed along with some extra informative labels. These labels contain the types of reference to the problems e.g. problem, risk, challenge, barrier, impediment, etc. It also includes its origin as a general preconceived class (e.g. cultural, organizational, communication, planning, team formation, etc.) as well as a label that indicates a certain topic of ASD in which the problem occurred like time zone, cloud computing, tailoring the method, scrum master activities, metrics and so on. The second label (i.e. the class of the problem) is supposed to be well-known in the contexts of all papers, but the third one (i.e. ASD topic label) might be only the case in some papers. Both labels are supposed to assist later in classifying and presenting the reported problems.

The classification coding assists us to find out more about the data so that, not only produce a list of common challenges, but also provide a ground to find out relationships between these challenges and their possible roots e.g. whether those are because of complexity of organizational structure and processes, rules and regulations or cultural barriers.

The data is selected from the papers pertaining to large organizations and/or distributed settings. To provide a richer view on the results, the results are divided into three sets and classified separately. As such, readers have the chance to compare the frequencies and nature of the problems in three groups of large, distributed and large and distributed (both) respectively. From 103 papers which contain direct evidences about the surfaced problems and challenges, by using search keywords within the whole text (including "large", "distributed/remote/dispersed/offshore teams", "global software engineering"), 54 papers are considered to be related to ASD in large environments, 32 to distribute and 16 to both large and distributed.

Reported problems in each group, as was previously mentioned, coded in terms of a few words, phrases, a sentence or occasionally more so that each one independently represent a problem during agile implementation or adoption. As such, work experiences are usually able to provide a longer list of problems. Conversely, some long case studies may not provide exact reference to the surface problems in practice. In the next step, the problems are classified into basic categories, such as team challenges, cultural issues, organizational problems and process related limitations. In the third step, based on the data gathered, the initial categories are revised by merging and adding new ones as well as proposing subcategories in one or two more levels. By this way, not only a balanced map of problems is produced, but also the stresses (in terms of descriptions and frequencies) of problems in any particular areas become evident. This approach of analysis nearly complies with the guidelines of GTM in that the classes and categories are needed to be grounded in data and be compared constantly (Urquhart, 2013). Consequently, the results are not only a list, but aggregations of the found problems as well, which are able to show the emphases in different areas. Moreover, considering the aggregations of the problems' descriptions in various sources, the resulting knowledge is supposed to be relatively independent of the commensurate researchers' views.

PROPOSED CLASSIFICATIONS

Continuous comparison is an inseparable part of coding in GTM. As mentioned, we use the coding process generally based on those guidelines, however with this difference that it is used to analyze literature and by collecting explicit references to the surfaced problems. Shorter phrases or sentences were directly used as code (to refer to a certain set of problems) whereas the longer ones coded with meaningful labels. The codes are constantly compared and formed into new classes which are directly emerged from the data. To have a richer view on the data and, also have a better chance to pinpoint the surfaced problems, as indicated, three classifications are separately developed by associating the collected/coded problems to three groups of large, distributed or large and distributed (both). The first two groups i.e. large organizations/setting and distributed/off-shore development contain 54 papers, 216 coded phrases, and, 32 papers, 126 codes phrases respectively. A mind-map organizer software tool was used to flexibly group and organize the coded phrases. In both classifications, phrases which are directly related to large or distributed settings/factors, respectively, classified under one extra category (i.e. one particular class of "large scale" under the classification of "large organizations" for those problems that have directly referenced to large settings within their description, and, another class of "distributed problems" under the classification of "distributed settings" for the exact references to distributed/distance related problems). Finally, for papers with the subject of "large and distributed, both" (16 papers, 68 coded phrases), the classification is simpler due to the lower number of total coded phrases. Details of results are discussed in the following sections.

Analysis Ground and Method

As intended, the results show a list of surfaced problems as are reported in literature (particularly in case studies and work experiences) as well as problematic areas of implementation and adoption based on the extracted clusters of problems and challenges. This is due to the study's novel coding approach compared to usual systematic literature studies. Moreover, these clusters of problems or categories, which have been emerged by means of classification, are able to illustrate the problems in a higher level of abstraction (see abstracting and theorizing categories in Urquhart, 2013). Besides, contrasting to usual SLRs that are often able to pinpoint gaps of studies (e.g. Dybå & Dingsøyr, 2008; Hasnain, 2010; Kaisti et al., 2013; Xiaofeng, Lane, Conboy, & Pikkarainen, 2009), this study inherently may not induce that whether less reported problems in one certain area indicates less conducted studies, or, it is because of less problems. Even so, the latter proposition, i.e. having a less problematic area due to having less reported problems in that area, is still very probable.

As a result, the aggregated groups of problems may be regarded as varied stresses on problematic areas. In this way, besides striving to generalize certain, concrete problems that have been surfaced over the course of implementation/adoption, the primary emphasis is on grouping related problems. Note that, here the notion of related problems is very relative in the sense that they are more related to each other than others with respect to the classification intention and approach (i.e. continuous comparison), and, the number and types of found problems – that is why three sets of papers (i.e. large, distributed, large and distributed) have been noticeably occurred to be classified differently.

Concisely, the results are able to signify which areas are more stressful and problematic in the event of implementing/adopting agile methods if the setting is large or distributed.

Finally this method of analysis may assist to construct new concepts based the existing ones which is, in this case, nature and concept of problems in ASD implementation and adoption. The leverage is to construct concepts which are induced and formed based on a large set of the existing reported, concrete evidences. As a result, by this means of constructing abstract concepts, we may have valid theorized types of problems based on the real problems, instead of having preconceptions of problems and attempt to impose and justify them regarding any collected data set. However, it is evident that, this stage of theorization possibility is beyond the scope of this chapter. In other words, we do not intend to theorize and construct new classes of problems here, while it may be pursued in future.

Results

As was intended, the analysis results render a better insight on the context of ASD Implementation/ Adoption by providing organized lists of problems, which pinpoint the major challenging and stressful areas of implementation/adoption processes. Moreover, by means of a three-segmented classification of the problems organized in categories emerging through their relationships with each other and whose frequencies, this study provides a ground by which practitioners and scholars are assisted to understand how approaching towards large and/or distributed settings may trigger some sorts of problems and to what extent.

One extra benefit might be a preliminary analysis on how the factors of scale and (spatial) distribution in organizations may incorporate or contrast with each other and, as a result, possibly culminates the situation in terms of exacerbating the implementation/adoption challenges.

Anyhow, based on the aforementioned method of analysis in the previous subsection, the results are explained and concluded as follows.

"Large Organizations" Classification

As is expected, for large settings, there are clusters of problems on organizational and managerial aspects in general and, particularly in area of progress and planning and project management. In project management, specifically, there are serious problems that question how organizations may work with agile teams. In terms of project management, the question is how agile projects are managed and at the same time, aligned with traditional ways of (organizational) management.

Another case which is remarkably problematic and may easily related to the size of the organizations and their usually large and cumbersome set of rules and regulation is the (ASD) process itself. How to adopt agile methods in these large settings implies numerous details. Based on the data, we assert that the method itself is not that much problematic as the adaption to the details of regulated settings of large organizations. In other words, problems are more caused by the heavy efforts that are required to adapt AM to the existing, countless rules and regulations than the inherent difficulties of the methods themselves. Documentation is also much more under stress here (compared to the "distributed settings" classification) because of, again, the hefty set of rules and regulations and formal organizational approaches that cause the need for documents. These organizational regulations and formality also may be the initial root of problems associated with quality standards and assurance.

As was previously mentioned, the problems directly relative to large organizations (i.e. the problems which are explicitly associated to the relatively large size of the organizations/settings by the corresponding authors), are classified in a separate group (under "miscellaneous" category, see Figure 5). Considering the total number of the reported problems, there are relatively fewer problems explicitly attributed to the factor of size. It might be partly because of the ASD implementation/adoption problems commonalities between large and small/medium size settings. However, contrastingly, it also may be due to the fact that stakeholders are really "[in the jungle and] can't see the wood for the trees". Thus, the problems of "large organizations", specifically those are associated with the (ASD) process, documentation, quality assurance, cultural/organizational resistance and, aligning with strategic planning and progress control (see the following paragraphs), are more attributable to the (larger) size (of the organizational settings) than be in common with the cases pertaining to small and medium enterprises.

Cultural problems here are more about cultural/organizational resistance (contrasting "distributed settings" classification in which cultural problems are mostly formed around the cultural differences). Team problems are more of team management and progress control (associable to the formality of large organizations) rather than team communication (see distributed settings classification). Team organization and training (both, again, associable to the formality) are also noticeable in this classification. Cross-team relationships is also important here, not only because of usually high number of teams, but also due to the fact that, large organizations, deliberately or unconsciously, assume that agile teams are working within (sometimes, invisible) boundaries of functional units (e.g. departments) of an existing hierarchical management structure.

Team culture, personal conflicts and issues are of significance too (i.e. at least, as much as they are in "distributed settings" classification), however their nature here is more of political origin rather than being of inter-team issues (for example, competition and conflict between agile and non-agile software development teams as well as confrontation of agile teams with the traditional culture of the existing stakeholders, e.g. users, product owners or customers).

Although customers are source of many challenges in any event, comparing to the "distributed settings" classification, here their unavailability as well as the problems pertaining to long feedback loops are more frequently mentioned. These problems are attributable to the presence of a high number of customers (as is expected in large organizations) who are organized in several (mostly, formal) levels (see Figures 1-9).

Figure 1. Large Organizations

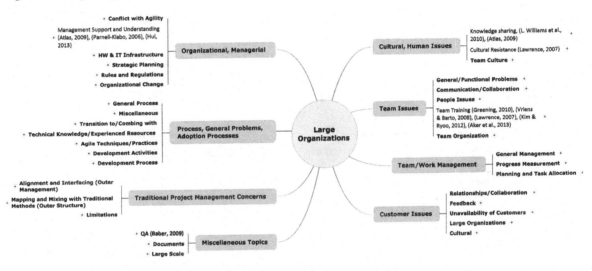

Figure 2. Large Organizations – Organizational and Managerial Challenges

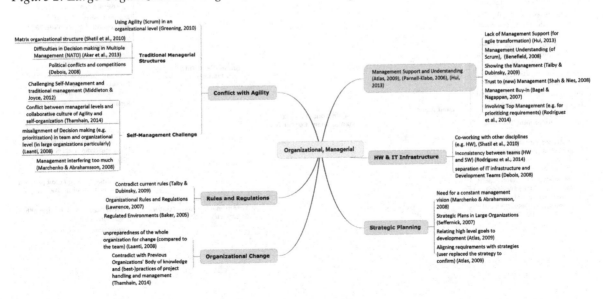

Figure 3. Large Organizations – Process, General Problems, Adoption Processes

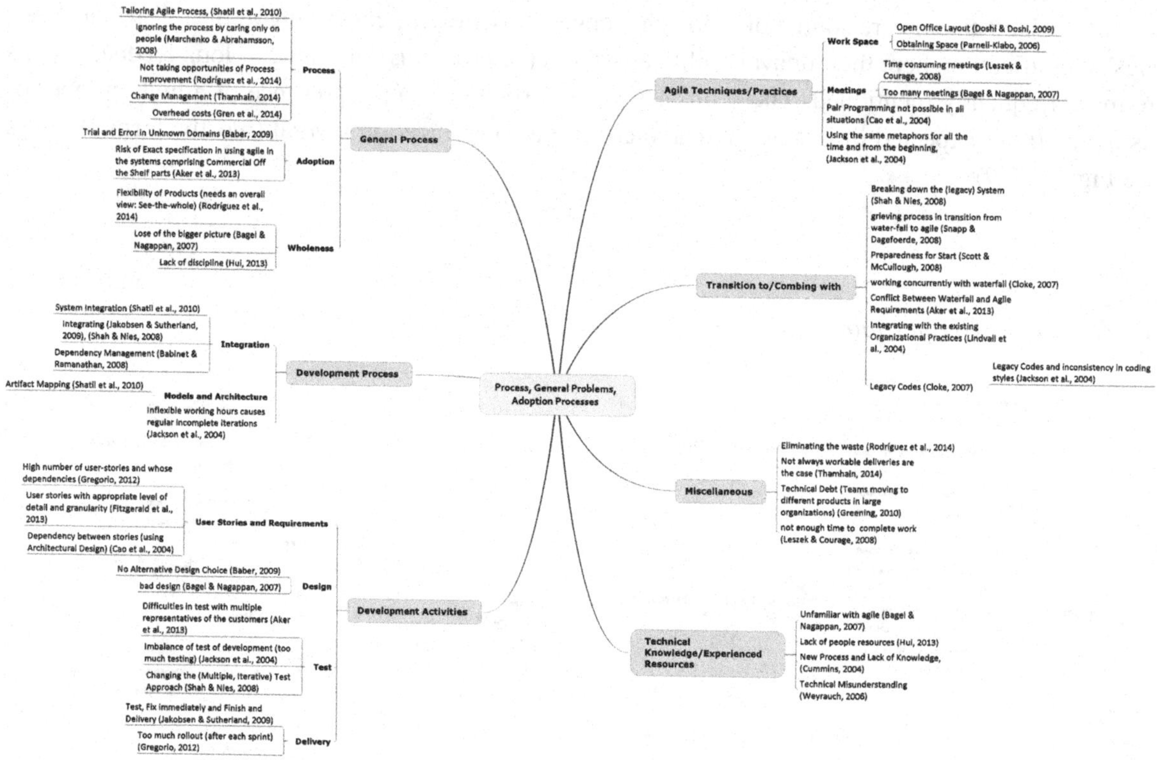

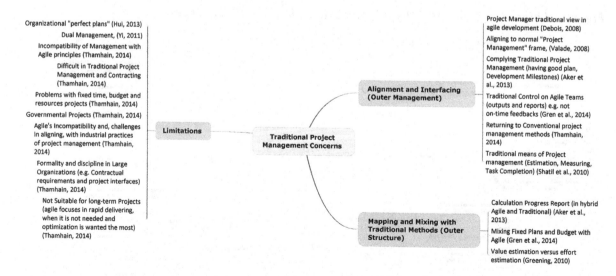

Figure 4. Large Organizations – Traditional Project Management Concerns

Figure 5. Large Organizations – Miscellaneous Topics

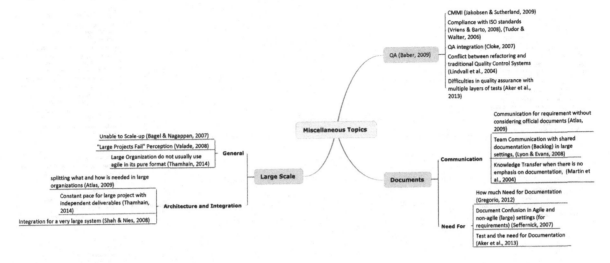

Figure 6. Large Organizations – Cultural, Human Issues

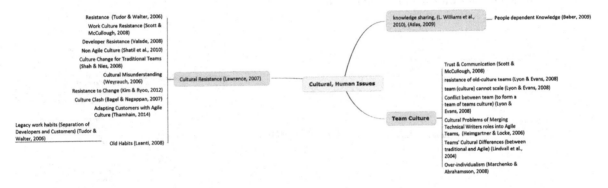

Figure 7. Large Organizations – Team Issues

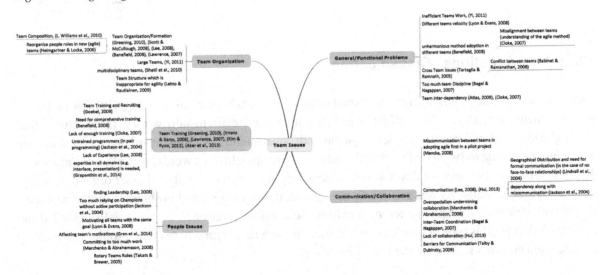

Figure 8. Large Organizations – Team/Work Management

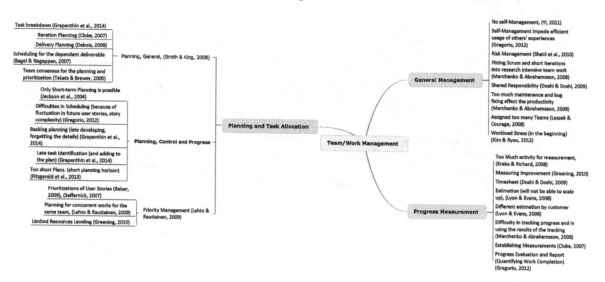

Figure 9. Large Organizations – Customer Issues

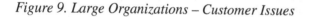

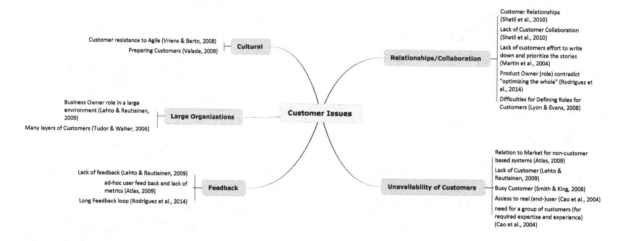

"Distributed Settings" Classification

In the second classification, namely "distributed settings" and offshore teams, there are very few problems with organizational nature. This is might be because distributed teams usually work in those settings that of a high culture of (agile) software development and, consequently, with less challenges of making top management understand what ASD or distributed development is. In other words, very often organizations do not approach to this ways of development unless they are somehow ready, whether organizationally, technically or culturally. As was previously mentioned, distributed-related problems (i.e. the problems that in their descriptions explicit references exist to the distributed settings) are separately classified and presented. Among this type of problems, differences in culture and time zones and, problems caused by distance and communication are the most prevailing.

Since the papers that are related to both large and distributed settings are considered for the third classification, here, the papers which contain references to being large (as for organizations or teams) are regarded to be inaccuracy in data (because these types of papers should only be appeared in the third classification). In fact, these cases are very few (only two, implicitly refer to largeness as a problem) indicating that the process of data collection have been reasonably precise and effective.

As was previously pointed, cultural problems in this classification are mostly rooted in differences between the teams distributed over the globe. However, the most salient problem in this category, which was not the case in large organizations, is trust. There are many references to trust as a problem within and across teams. Although this appears to be obvious in distributed settings; by making a comparison with "large organizations" classification, it also interestingly shows that the formality of large settings make "trust" not that much meaningful. Or, trust, or even seeking for trust, is a way of organizing (particularly, regarding self-organizing/managing nature of agile teams) thereby may replace - to some degrees - the formal ways of organization and management. This also suggests that to compose and construct large, organized structures for future firms, trust and means of self-management would possibly be a replacement of formality. Here, we are referring to the notion of self-management/organization (based on trust) in an abstract level that is (conceptually) higher than what is used in usual (agile) teams, and, as a means of synthesizing and weaving a relatively large body of work from smaller units. This topic is discussed in more details in the second part of this chapter.

Customer relationships problems mostly refer to inaccessibility to the customer due to the physical distance and differences in culture, which is not unexpected.

Team issues, by focusing on communication, are the main challenge in this classification. It seems that such problems are not only the case because of physical distances, but also due to the fact that a set of interconnected teams forms the main concept of work-body here contrasting to the traditional notion of organization in large settings. In other words, it appears that organizational problems here are replaced by teams' issues, because a set of teams factually replace the former concept of (formal) organization. As a result, instead of fitting the teams within a large frame i.e. organization, here, the work body constructed by autonomous, self-organized/managed teams. Therefore, this conclusion is drawn that for the projects which are primarily defined within the frame of an inclusive organization (including all the contractors, developers, executers, etc.) formality of that organization would potentially be the main theme of its problems (particularly, if the organization and its management is of traditional, hierarchical nature). On the other hand, if the project is initially more defined for a set of teams, the main challenges is communication, inside and cross teams.

As you may see, in this classification, among teams' issues, team management comes after team communication. Quality assurance is not that much problematic in these settings, perhaps because of less formality. Problems associated to documentation, as was mentioned in the previous subsection, are more of communication nature (e.g. using documents to communicate and relate geographically distributed teams) and not that much under stressed. This (i.e. less stress on documentation) is in compliance with agile principles even if geographical distribution puts forth challenges of stable and effective communication in the state of no-formal-documents.

Interestingly, aligning to traditional project management methods and approaches is not a significant problem here. It implies that the concept of distributed teams and settings is a step beyond traditional ways of managing (SD) activities.

Regarding process oriented problems, due to smaller size and less formality in distributed settings, problems are more practical and more communication related (e.g. sharing design, deployment). Moreover, there is an emphasis on collecting and communicating requirements across physical distances. One notable issue may be seen as the lack of overall control on the whole process of development. Issues like less thorough examination of code (in testing activities), late deployment, lack of systematic and ordered daily procedures of integration and deployment, inappropriate level of granularity in (software) requirements and, more saliently, deciding on architectural issues, all, may slightly imply drawbacks of such decentralized control on the whole development process. It can be argued that, though agile means of control and management are basically effective and successful, still when specifically considering the issues from a (SD) process point of view, facing few problems may be attributable to a need for enforcement of more strict (possibly, formal) controls. Adding to this, there are also several limitations which signifies that agile in its pure format and with the minimum formality may have its own problems (e.g. process fragility, lack of – guaranty – for process awareness, lack of common structure, excessively trial and error, too much overhead; see Figure 12 and Figure 15). Anyhow, this argument does not necessarily mean that such strictness will solve these problems and, will not bring about new ones (see Figures 10-15).

"Large and Distributed Environments" Classification

This classification, by definition, is an intersection between the two previous classifications. In practice, the reported, surfaced problems show some similarities as expected. However, as we argue in the following paragraphs, these similarities do not imply that this classification is nothing but a mere median of the previous two; and, depending on its various subclasses, may also show more inclination towards one of its two poles (i.e. large or distributed settings). As we discuss in details in Part II, this three-segmented classification and particularly this third one provide some clues and ground to show how new (agile) forms of organizational structure as well as new means of control and management may make larger scales of work bodies viable while being beyond of traditional organizations in terms of form and means of control. The stress here is more on the structure/form and how the work bodies are organized compared to the traditional means of control and management. Thus, in this sense, large and

Figure 10. Distributed Settings

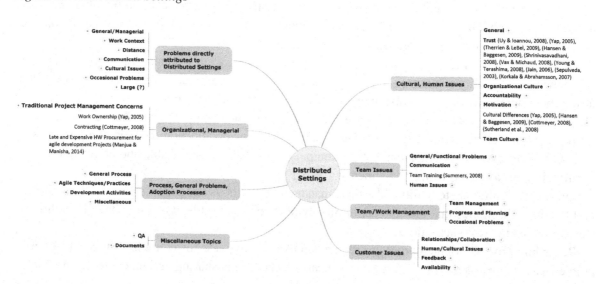

Figure 11. Distributed Settings – Miscellaneous Topics; Customer Issues

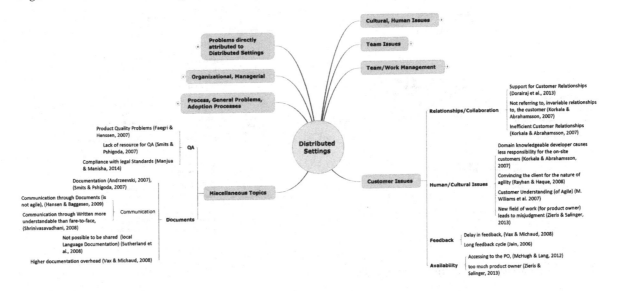

Figure 12. Distributed Settings – Problems directly attributed to Distributed Settings

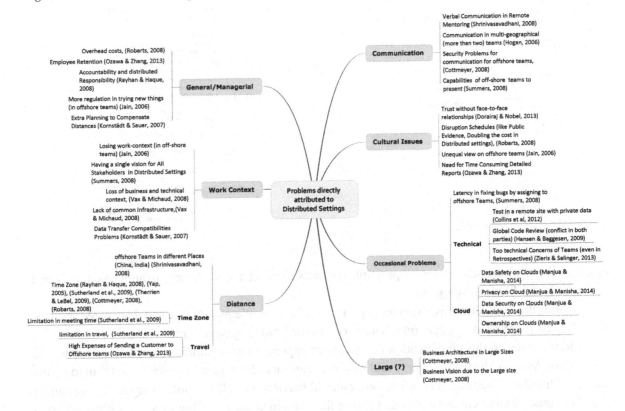

Figure 13. Distributed Settings – Cultural, Human Issues

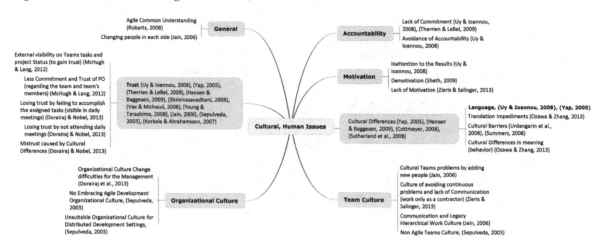

Figure 14. Distributed Settings – Team Issues

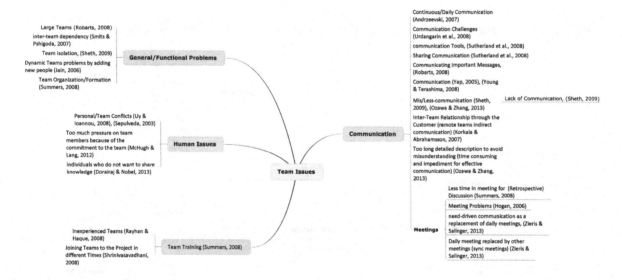

distributed environments may reveal principles for new (agile) large-scale organizations generally and, particularly, for SD firms/projects.

Anyhow, this subsection discusses the reported, surfaced problems in "large and distributed settings" regarding their emerged aggregation of categories in the following paragraphs.

Cultural issues in this classification are generally appears to be a summation of two previous classifications. As such, the list of cultural and human issues includes trust as a major issue (akin to similar ones of "distributed settings" classification), cultural barriers as well as political issues e.g. misunderstanding agile in large environments that shows the combined nature of both previous classifications; refer to (Murphy et al., 2013) for a detailed discussion.

However, the inclination towards each of two directions (i.e. large or distributed) shows interesting facts. For instance, in "large and distributed settings", though organizationally the environment is large,

Figure 15. Distributed Settings – Organizational/Managerial Challenges; Process, General Problems, Adoption Process; Team/Work Management

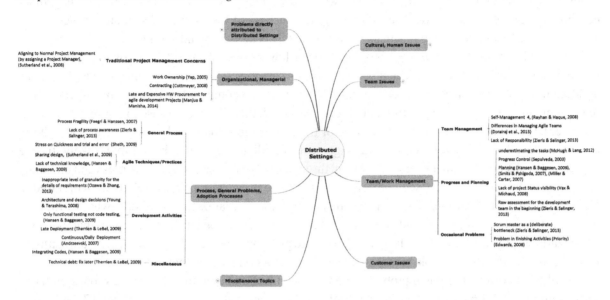

there are slightly less difficulties with organizational and managerial issues (5 out of 68 reported issues here compared to 5 out of 126 in "distributed settings"; whereas the number is 26 out of 216 in "large organizations" classification; see Figures 17, 15 and 2, respectively).

Noticeably, for classifying issues pertaining to "general, process related problems", we use the same emerged outline of the "large organization" classification for its second and third level of categorization; because it fits better and shows that, here, the process oriented problems are basically similar and (relatively) more detailed (compared to "distributed settings" classification).

Conversely, team issues are more inclined to the "distributed settings" classification. This, to some extents, strengthens our previous speculation that agile implementation/adoption in large organizations more emphasizes on process and managerial aspects merely because communication and team collaboration as means of control is not the case there as is in distributed settings. Therefore, this (i.e. the relative resemblance of "large and distributed environments" regarding teams issues to "distributed settings" rather than "large organizations") is not only because of the nature of work (i.e. geographical distribution) but also due to the fact that communication and team collaboration is a means of control, organization and management as such. It seems that this problem category (i.e. team issues) somehow replaces "organizational and managerial" category of "large organizations" classification. Overall, it means that large and distributed settings typically tend to be less traditional compared to large (and not distributed) organizations. As a result, it would be interesting to investigate that how large and distributed organizations may reconstruct and map their traditional, hierarchical structure of (SD) work and the means of command and control to agile ways of cooperation, communication, collaboration and coordination. Moreover, it might be conjectured that, for large organization, it should not be compulsory to be (geographically) distributed to move towards these non-traditional means of organization and control. Indeed, this appears to occur in large and distributed organizations first (according to our data) only because this type of organizations is more forced to abandon their traditional forms of existence for the sake of being able to deal with distributed, possibly offshore agile teams. This conjecture may result in a prediction that, large organizations will likely adopt new forms of control and management in a holistic, organizational level after witnessing the success of the existing distributed projects and, assuring that the commensurate practices were adequately established and stabled.

On the same basis, here, the emphasis is relatively low on the category of team/work management (i.e. there are relatively less aggregated problem in this category – Figure 17). It may be justified so as agile teams are more about communication and self-management compared to (formal) managerial issues (e.g. preplanning and progress control and report). As noted, this was not the case in the first classification (i.e. large organization) in which because of their prevailing traditional management and culture, emphases have been relatively more on management of agile teams (possibly and more likely, from a traditional project management perspective) e.g. through excessively stressing on progress and planning. It reinforces the previous proposed conjecture so that large organizations (as – relatively – opposed to "large and distributed settings") are more trapped in traditional organizational cultures whether they are aware of it or not. Contrastingly and arguably, this point should also be taken into account that, the large organizations' papers often refer to large and very large projects; whereas "large and distributed settings" classification's project cases, of themselves, usually are not comparably that much large.

Finally, the customers-related problems are more inclined and akin to large settings' ones, in terms of the number and complexity of customers' roles in large environments (see Figure 16, 17, and 18).

Figure 16. Large and Distributed Environments – Cultural, Human Issues; Team Issues; Problems directly attributed to Large Organizations and/or Distributed Settings

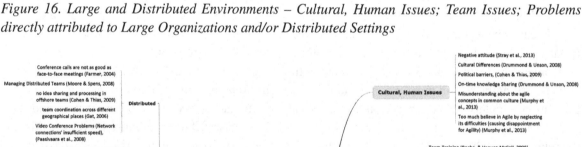

Figure 17. Large and Distributed Environments – Team/Work Management; Customer Issues; Organizational/Managerial Challenges

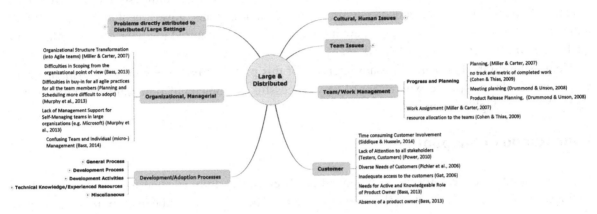

Figure 18. Large and Distributed Environments – Miscellaneous

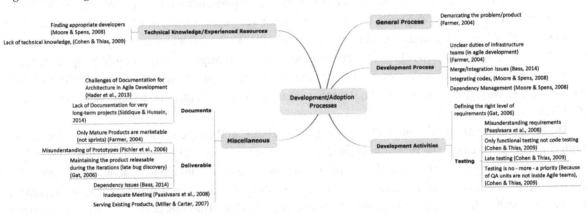

PART II: DISCUSSION ON PAST EXPRIENCES AND SPACULATIONS ON ASD TRENDES

This section attempts to illustrate the present status of agile development challenges in implementation and adoption on the basis of the existing experiences. We use the results of the previous part of this chapter as an interpreting frame so that by referring to salient literature (mostly the ones used as the initial data set for the first part), their authors' speculation will be analyzed. This section, and generally the current chapter, has a less emphasis on technical issues of ASD and, more focuses on its managerial, organizational and cultural aspects.

Thus, in this section we have a discussion on the authors' reflections of the emergent trends based on the overall studied texts rather than solely referring to the explicit and concrete reported problems. As a result, the expression of our understating of the given set of literature (and cross check with other sources, if applicable) turns to insights that would go beyond the quotes and frequencies of the surfaced problems (as illustrated in Part I). Anyhow, as previously implied, to organize our speculations and make them meaningful, we use the analyses and results of the previous part of this chapter as an interpreting frame.

Moreover, to provide a richer overview of the emerging trends in ASD, besides the aforementioned classifications, the given literature is also examined with respect to another dimension which is the areas of application of ASD e.g. embedded systems, regulated environments, governmental settings, (digital, real time) control systems as well as the environments which are required to apply ASD together with quality assurance systems and/or CMMI, etc.

Contrasting to the first part, the main intention of this part is to provide interesting insights about why there are sharp opposite experiences of very successful, yet, much failed implementation/adoption of ASD, both in high frequencies.

Wide Range of Adoption

First and foremost, agile software development has been successfully adapted for almost all kinds of settings, even in very highly disciplined environments. These include embedded systems (Berger & Rumpe, 2010; Shatil, Hazzan, & Dubinsky, 2010; Salo & Abrahamsson, 2008; Cunningham, 2005), governmental environments (Scott, Johnson & McCullough, 2008; Fruhling, McDonald, & Dunbar, 2008), industrial and regulated settings e.g. FDA regulated environments as are in (Weyrauch, K. 2006; Rasmussen, Hughes, Jenks, & Skach, 2009) and, even for very centralized, military environments with so many levels of direction and control (e.g. Aker et al., 2013) as well as controlling real-time systems (Ge, Paige, & McDermid, 2010). There are also experiences to align and adapt agile project management practices with traditional ones with fixed (partial) plans (Rong, Shao, & Zhang, 2010; Fruhling, McDonald, & Dunbar, 2008). Factually, it appears that ASD unavoidably run to any aspect of software development.

However, interestingly the numbers of (very) successful, and at the same time, failed projects are high. In successful cases, the main theme is like this. People openly welcome agile culture, not only in the scale of teams (from inside) but also across teams and organizational environments. In these stories, even complicated issues, like aligning ASD with the existing organizational structure and management, are handled straightforwardly. One more interesting point is that problems pertaining to incompatibilities between agile and non-agile methods/cultures do not surface at all, or if do, are timely addressed and resolved, often by means of innovative solutions. Such successful process of resolution usually is connected with a gradual gain of maturity in ASD and, through continuous teams' collaboration and cooperation. This straightforward resolution is regarded to be very interesting specifically when implementers/adopters come up with expectedly serious issues like cumbersome activities of project scoping, contracting and cost estimation, control and management, activity planning, progress evaluation and status reporting, which are very different between ASD and traditional, plan-based methods.

On the other hand, in problematic projects, all of these issues are often under full attention and stress. Particularly, alignment and cooperation with existing body of management and its culture is usually very problematic. This sharp contrast draws attention to how preparedness for agile development, whether technical, cultural or organizational, may prevent many problems in the course of implementation/adoption.

Through reading different stories, a source of challenge might be identified as follows. If an organization waits and expects agile teams align themselves with the existing pace of work, very likely everything in the implementation/adoption process would be jeopardized. Conversely, the organization's management needs to be flexible and ready to think agile and find ways to modify the existing rules and regulations. This proactivity should assist to prevent various problems from the beginning.

Another assertion is that in successful experiences, people involved are apparently more optimistic about the transition to agile and/or more feel the transition is inevitable. As such, successful cases might be consequent of a very competitive environment, so that it is not an option for the adopting organization to be ineffectual in this respect. For instance, organizations like Microsoft (Murphy et al., 2013), Yahoo! (Drummond & Unson, 2008; Cloke, 2007; Benefield, 2008), Amazon (Atlas, 2009), IBM (Cunningham, 2005), etc. do not have any other choice other than being successful in ASD and, inevitably, being proactive and flexible.

In the event of unsuccessful cases, large organizations are more likely to believe that their past experiences worth to be kept as far as possible (contrasting the ideas of Thamhain, 2014). This belief inherently causes more inertia towards ASD, which differs from traditional methods in various aspects, and, subsequently, puts forward difficult challenges of how to merge these past experiences and new agile practices while keeping their (both) advantages. As is mentioned in (Thamhain, 2014), there are a considerable amount of experience that is difficult to lose. This is whereas, taking variable environmental conditions into account, there is no final verdict about whether losing the old knowledge, how-tos and work practices in the course of transitioning to ASD is a must and/or useful or neither. Besides, obviously, having more agile organizations (i.e. presence of agility in organizational level along with agile culture of work, and, not only for SD e.g. as is described by Parcell, & Holden, 2013) definitely results in more chances to adopt agile successfully.

Additionally, from the eyes of implementers and adopters, their preconceptions and how they adhere to the traditional ways of development, whether they are used to it (as old habits) or forced to do it (due to the management, customers' requests or the existing rules and regulations), may show their future paths. In other words, the preoccupied minds of developers/adopters are regarded to be influential on future challenges in implementation/adoption. As a result, a forming conjecture is that transition to agile would be more viable if these preconceptions go away, yet, there is no certainty that if this (i.e. losing these old practices) is worthwhile, nor possible. Anyhow, by assuming the existence of such preconceptions (which is often the case), there is no more choice other than contemplating (to propose) reconciliation approaches and methods (i.e. reconciling between ASD and the existing rules, regulations and culture). After all, it is asserted that inasmuch as there is more dependency on old methods along with less familiarity with AM, there would surface more problems.

It is appear to be evident that there are two main approaches in resolving these aforementioned aligning/merging problems. One is an entire organizational transformation to agile, which is obviously not always possible. The other way is to find intermediating ways to control and govern agile teams from a (relatively) traditional body of management; see the discussion in (Thamhain, 2014) and, examples in (Siddique & Hussein, 2014): "introduction of a [management] layer at top", (Sutherland, Schoonheim, Rustenburg, & Rijk, 2008): "adding a project manager [role]", and, (Lyon & Evans, 2008): "Expressing [estimation data] in a Gantt chart view". These intermediating methods have been, more or less, effective; however, their overhead costs should be taken into account. Additionally, one neglected issue for this kind of intermediating/aligning solutions is that these ways possibly cause a latency for organizations to avoid or defer an inevitable, future transformation to agility (i.e. being agile in an organizational level, not only in SD). In practice, these aligning methods create a safe zone in that organizations may persist to not move towards agility.

EMERGING CHALLENGES

Organizations are forced to adopt ASD even if it contradicts their traditional, hierarchical views of themselves. It is expected that establishing agility in organizational level will be the future trend as well as challenge that, of itself, facilitates ASD implementation/adoption too.

In distributed settings more methods and tools are expected to be developed to handle remote communications and deal with face-to-face relationships (as is stressed by agile principles).

In large environments, it is required to propose and designate reliable methods for the sake of constructing larger bodies of work (e.g. in terms of organizational structures, departments, projects) by using (large) agile teams as building blocks. One associated challenge with this respect is that how organizations would be able to maintain their identity and integrity if their subunits are not connected and united through formal rules and means of command and control. This general (organizational) challenge is of special interest when the whole organization has to treat and interact with ASD teams in different aspects e.g. managing developers, collaborating with customers and dealing with management (support). As a result, for ASD projects, if not the organization as a whole, at least a larger part of that (compared to the ASD teams, themselves) is needed to be agile.

Another major trend, which put forward its own challenges, is how to discipline agile projects. This is specifically the case when we considering reconciling, aligning methods that supposed to intermediate a traditional body of management to its commensurate agile body of work i.e. ASD teams. To be fair, proposing (more) discipline for ASD may be partly due to the presence of a traditional culture in organizations, but also partly because it is sometimes argued that discipline is good for AM as such, either or both for the process or for the people who are involved in. Although, we are not in a position to judge such assertions, nonetheless, it is predicted that this prospect application of discipline in agile methods would be a source of new challenges in future. Imposition of more discipline, apart from its possible benefits e.g. more controllability, will perhaps also have negative impacts on performance and efficiency. It is reminded that, the extant ways of reconciliation and alignment, specifically for project management purposes and in large settings, have its own challenges now and, very likely in future too (refer to the previous section for the reference cases).

Finally, another source of challenge would be the approaches which attempt to govern agile project through (economic) measurement (Cantor & Royce, 2013; Brown, Ambler, & Royce, 2013; Bass, 2014). These approaches signifies that sort of control in that as long as the obtaining results (as is being measured) are in compliance with at-hand plans, objectives or criteria, then everything would be fine. These ways of governing agile projects implies the control from the inside of teams (as should be the case in self-organizing/managing teams) and, are in contrast with engineering governance (Ambler, & Royce, 2013) or, as we meant in the previous paragraph, governing by imposing (more) discipline that controls the process itself. Nevertheless, these methods are promising and, there are grounds to believe that they will reach to an acceptable level of reliability. Thus, without judging about their effectiveness and what they really want to and can measure, it is speculated that the mere application of such governing approaches is expected to have their own challenges, specifically considering the fact that these methods have not been matured yet.

CONCLUSION

ASD is a major breakthrough in software development. It has been successful and prevailing in all types of environments. Initially it worked in small, collocated teams with relatively loose settings in terms of rules and regulations. However, now, there are numerous reports stating that ASD has been successfully adopted in large (and very large) organizations, geographically distributed settings as well as highly regulated environments.

There are still numerous challenges. In the first part of this chapter, we have provided organized lists of problems to pinpoint stressful areas of ASD in the course of implementation/adoption. These problems are extracted from literature, mostly work experiences and case studies, providing that those (i.e. the problems) are based on exact and concrete evidences of difficulties, risks, challenges, etc. which surfaced throughout the course of implementation/adoption.

In the second part, a dichotomy has been depicted between very successful projects and very problematic ones. Our analysis shows that, in problematic cases, there are strong preconceptions about the necessities of maintaining existing (traditional) organizational structures and processes over the course of implementation/adoption of agile processes. Organizations usually hesitate to relinquish their existing body of knowledge and practices. Whether these necessities resulting from individuals' old habits, or mandatory organizational strategies, rules and regulations, it results in a cumbersome and complicated contention of how to align, merge or at least intermediate between these two traditions i.e. the existing organizational structures, processes and culture from one side, and, ASD (implementation/adoption) processes and agile culture from the other side. This contention, which has usually been neglected or not adequately addressed, is believed to be the origin of various types of issues in those problematic cases.

Thus, adopters need to be serious about any reconciliation/alignment if it is inevitable. They are also required to consider efforts to combine, balance and coordinate between these two traditions' managerial structures and practices. Additionally, there are always ambiguities about procedures and practices which have been used in the past (i.e. before introducing ASD) and, nonetheless, no exact agile counterparts or replacements for them may be found during the transition period. Sometimes, adopters simply do not know how to replace the existing practices even if they know the commensurate agile counterparts. Always, novelties and innovations are needed to deal with these reconciliation, alignment and intermediation issues.

However, the stress here is not on how to resolve these existing/possible inconsistencies and incompatibles between agile and non-agile methods; instead, it is recommended that for being agile better not to be non-agile as far as possible and from the beginning, mentally and practically, or, technically, organizationally and culturally.

Therefore, it is suggested to consider the agile development/implementation/adoption project as an initiation that unavoidably and eventually must be merged and absorbed into the existing organizational practices. Even better, organizations are advised to purposefully become agile (or at least, more agile) after accomplishing the project; something new that is expected to be the result of an inevitable (organizational) transformation. This perspective would be more vital, at the same time difficult though, where the scale of the organization is relatively large.

Meanwhile, this chapter provides a methodical ground to conduct research on existing literature and conclude from the results, particularly by forming a frame in which the position of any sole author/study is interpretable.

FUTURE RESEARCH DIRECTIONS

This chapter strengthens the stance that means of communication and collaboration (as is the case in self-organizing/managing teams) would be a replacement for the hierarchical means of command and control. Disregarding technical, intra-team and cultural aspects, it is suggested to contemplate this possibility (i.e. of the replacement) as new ways of designing and organizing bodies of work in large and even very large scales. Body of work here refers to both transient entities, like project, as well as permanent ones e.g. organizational units and, even the whole organization, depending on the case and the level of abstraction and application. This postulation comes from the evidences that show, first, the communication and collaboration issues, as is the case in agile projects, replace the organizational problems to a large degree. And, second, the organizations that adopt agility in higher levels and more extensive areas, have generally been more successful to manage and accomplish their agile projects.

As such, it is expected that this perspective inspires and renders new abstract (agile) ways of organizing work-bodies suitable for large scale settings. Such prospect ways not only may be used to analyze and find possible flaws in an existing agile project/organization, and, assist organizations who are transitioning to AM, but also may provide a ground to better understand traditional organizations with regard to the issues like organizational behaviors and workarounds. The argument is if any work-body functions effectively, that is because it is somehow agile; specifically in those cases which, officially, we expect dysfunction. For instance, consider the presence of a workaround case (see Ferneley & Sobreperez, 2006, for the clarification of the concept i.e. workaround) where not only it does not lead to malfunction, conversely, even (often) yields a better performance. In such settings, through analyzing it in a hypothetical agile frame, a shadow agile pace of works may be revealed inside that traditional setting. As a result, this approach may resolve possible existing conflicts or improve the performance in such settings.

Methodically speaking, it is recommended to systematically analyze aggregated clusters of data, as are obtained in the way that this study did, in relation to each other and situationally. By this means, any cluster may expose a distinct phenomenon within the context under study. Nevertheless, the exact approach and the expected emerging phenomena verily depends on the data, how it is collected and for what purpose.

REFERENCES

Aker, S., Audin, C., Lindy, E., Marcelli, L., Massart, J. P., & Okur, Y. (2013). Lessons Learned and Challenges of Developing the NATO Air Command and Control Information Services. In *Proceedings of International Systems Conference (SysCon 2013)*. Orlando, FL: IEEE. doi:10.1109/SysCon.2013.6549974

Andrzeevski, S. (2007). Experiencing Report 'Offshore XP for PDA development'. In *Proceedings of Agile Conference (Agile 2007)*. Washington, DC: IEEE

Atlas, A. (2009). Accidental Adoption: The Story of Scrum at Amazon.com. In *Proceedings of Agile Conference (AGILE '09)*. Chicago, IL: IEEE. doi:10.1109/AGILE.2009.10

Babar, M. A. (2009). An Exploratory Study of Architectural Practices and Challenges in Using Agile Software Development Approaches. In *Proceedings of Software Architecture, 2009 & European Conference on Software Architecture (WICSA/ECSA 2009). Joint Working IEEE/IFIP*. Cambridge: IEEE.

Babinet, E., & Ramanathan, R. (2008). Dependency Management in a Large Agile Environment. *In Proceedings of Agile 2008 Conference (AGILE '08)*. Toronto, ON: IEEE. doi:10.1109/Agile.2008.58

Baker, S. W. (2005). Formalizing Agility: An Agile Organization's Journey toward CMMI Accreditation. In *Proceedings of the Agile Development Conference (ADC'05)*. Denver, CO: IEEE. doi:10.1109/ADC.2005.27

Bass, J. M. (2013). Agile Method Tailoring in Distributed Enterprises: Product Owner Teams. In *Proceedings of 8th International Conference on Global Software Engineering (ICGSE 2013)*. Bari: IEEE. doi:10.1109/ICGSE.2013.27

Bass, J. M. (2014). Scrum Master Activities: Process Tailoring in Large Enterprise Projects. In *Proceedings of 9th International Conference on Global Software Engineering (ICGSE 2014)*. Shanghai: IEEE. doi:10.1109/ICGSE.2014.24

Begel, A., & Nagappan, N. (2007). Usage and Perceptions of Agile Software Development in an Industrial Context: An Exploratory Study. In *Proceedings of First International Symposium on Empirical Software Engineering and Measurement (ESEM 2007)*. Madrid: IEEE. doi:10.1109/ESEM.2007.12

Benefield, G. (2008). Rolling out Agile in a Large Enterprise. In *Proceedings of the 41st Hawaii International Conference on System Sciences*. Waikoloa, HI: IEEE. doi:10.1109/HICSS.2008.382

Berger, B., & Rumpe, B. (2010). Supporting Agile Change Management by Scenario-BasedRegression Simulation. *IEEE Transactions on Intelligent Transportation Systems*, *11*(2), 504–509. doi:10.1109/TITS.2010.2044571

Brown, A. W., Ambler, S., & Royce, W. (2013). Agility at scale: Economic governance, measured improvement, and disciplined delivery. In *Proceedings 35th International Conference of Software Engineering (ICSE)*, San Francisco, CA: IEEE. doi:10.1109/ICSE.2013.6606636

Cantor, M., & Royce, W. (2013). Economic Governance of Software Delivery. *IEEE Software*, *31*(1), 54–61. doi:10.1109/MS.2013.102

Cao, L., Mohan, K., Xu, P., & Balasubramaniam, R. (2004). How Extreme does Extreme Programming Have to be? Adapting XP Practices to Large-scale Projects. In *Proceedings of the 37th Hawaii International Conference on System Sciences*, Waikoloa, HI: IEEE.

Cloke, G. (2007). GET YOUR AGILE FREAK ON! Agile Adoption at Yahoo! Music. In *Proceedings of Agile Conference (Agile 2007)*, Washington, DC: IEEE. doi:10.1109/AGILE.2007.30

Cohen, B., & Thias, M. (2009). The Failure of the Off-shore Experiment: A Case for Collocated Agile Teams. *In Proceedings of Agile 2009 Conference*. Chicago, IL: IEEE. doi:10.1109/AGILE.2009.8

Collins, E., Macedo, G., Maia, N., & Dias-Neto, A. (2012). An Industrial Experience on the Application of Distributed Testing in an Agile Software Development Environment. In *Proceedings of Seventh International Conference on Global Software Engineering*. Porto Alegre: IEEE. doi:10.1109/ICGSE.2012.40

Cottmeyer, M. (2008). The Good and Bad of Agile Offshore Development. *In Proceedings of Agile 2008 Conference (AGILE '08)*. Toronto, ON: IEEE. doi:10.1109/Agile.2008.18

Cummins, D. (2004). Using Competition to Build a Stronger Team. In *Proceedings of Agile Development Conference*, Salt Lake City, Utah: IEEE doi:10.1109/ADEVC.2004.25

Cunningham, J. (2005). Costs of Compliance: Agile in an Inelastic Organization. In *Proceedings of the Agile Development Conference (ADC'05)*. 202-211. Denver, Colorado: IEEE. doi:10.1109/ADC.2005.18

Greening, D. R. (2010). Scaling Scrum to the Executive Level. In *Proceedings of the 43rd Hawaii International Conference on System Sciences*. Honolulu, HI: IEEE.

Debois, P. (2008). Agile infrastructure and operations: how infra-gile are you? In *Proceedings of Agile Conference (AGILE '08)*. Toronto, ON: IEEE. doi:10.1109/Agile.2008.42

Dorairaj, S., & Noble, J. (2013). Agile Software Development with Distributed Teams: Agility, Distribution and Trust. In *Proceedings of 35th International Conference on Software Engineering (ICSE)*. San Francisco, CA: IEEE. doi:10.1109/AGILE.2013.7

Dorairaj, S., Noble, J., & Allan, G. (2013). Agile Software Development with Distributed Teams: Senior Management Support. In *Proceedings of 8th International Conference on Global Software Engineering (ICGSE 2013)*. Bari: IEEE. doi:10.1109/ICGSE.2013.33

Doshi, C., & Doshi, D. (2009). A Peek into an Agile Infected Culture. *In Proceedings of Agile 2009 Conference*. Chicago, IL: IEEE. doi:10.1109/AGILE.2009.65

Drummond, B., & Unson, J. F. (2008). Yahoo! Distributed Agile: Notes from the World Over. In *Proceedings of Agile 2008 Conference (AGILE '08)*. Toronto, ON: IEEE.

Dybå, T., & Dingsøyr, T. (2008). Strength of evidence in systematic reviews in software engineering. In *Proceedings of the Second ACM-IEEE international symposium on Empirical software engineering and measurement (ESEM '08)*, Kaiserslautern, Germany: ACM. doi:10.1145/1414004.1414034

Edwards, M. (2008). Overhauling a Failed Project Using Out of the Box Scrum. In *Proceedings of Agile 2008 Conference*. Toronto: IEEE. doi:10.1109/Agile.2008.35

Faegri, T. E., & Hanssen, G. K. (2007). Collaboration, Process Control, and Fragility in Evolutionary Product Development. *IEEE Software*, *24*(3), 96–104. doi:10.1109/MS.2007.68

Farmer, M. (2004). DecisionSpace Infrastructure: Agile Development in a Large, Distributed Team. In *Proceedings of the Agile Development Conference (ADC'04)*. Salt Lake City, Utah: IEEE. doi:10.1109/ADEVC.2004.11

Ferneley, E., & Sobreperez, P. (2006). Resist, comply or workaround? An examination of different facets of user engagement with information systems. *European Journal of Information Systems*, *15*(4), 345–356. doi:10.1057/palgrave.ejis.3000629

Fitzgerald, B., Stol, K. j., O'Sullivan, R., & O'Brien, D. (2013). Scaling Agile Methods to Regulated Environments: An Industry Case Study. In *Proceedings of 35th International Conference on Software Engineering (ICSE)*. San Francisco, CA: IEEE. doi:10.1109/ICSE.2013.6606635

Fruhling, A., McDonald, P., & Dunbar, C. (2008). A Case Study: Introducing eXtreme Programming in a US Government System Development Project. In *Proceedings of the 41st Hawaii International Conference on System Sciences*. Waikoloa, HI: IEEE. doi:10.1109/HICSS.2008.4

Gat, I. (2006). How BMC is Scaling Agile Development. In *Proceedings of Agile Conference (AGILE'06)*. Minneapolis, MN: IEEE.

Ge, X., Paige, R., & McDermid, J. (2010). An Iterative Approach for Development of Safety-Critical-Software and Safety Arguments. In *Agile Conference (AGILE 2010)*. Orlando, FL: IEEE. doi:10.1109/AGILE.2010.10

Glaser, B., & Strauss, A. (1967). *The Discovery of Grounded Theory, Strategies for Qualitative Research*. London: Weidenfeld and Nicolson.

Goebel, C. J. (2009). How Being Agile Changed Our Human Resources Policies. In *Proceedings of Agile 2009 Conference*. Chicago, IL: IEEE. doi:10.1109/AGILE.2009.49

Grapenthin, S., Book, M., Poggel, S., & Gruhn, V. (2014). Facilitating Task Breakdown in Sprint Planning Meeting 2 with an Interaction Room: An Experience Report. In *Proceeding of 40th Euromicro Conference Series on Software Engineering and Advanced Applications (SEAA 2014)*. Verona: IEEE. doi:10.1109/SEAA.2014.71

Gregorio, D. D. (2012). How the Business Analyst Supports and Encourages Collaboration on Agile Projects. In *Proceedings of International System Conference (SysCon 2012)*. Vancouver, BC: IEEE. doi:10.1109/SysCon.2012.6189437

Gren, L., Torkar, R., & Feldt, R. (2014). Work Motivational Challenges Regarding the Interface BetweenAgile Teams and a Non-Agile Surrounding Organization: A case study. In *Proceedings of Agile Conference (AGILE 2014)*. Kissimmee, FL: IEEE. doi:10.1109/AGILE.2014.13

Hadar, I., Sherman, S., Hadar, E., & Harrison, J. J. (2013). Less is More: Architecture Documentation for Agile Development. In *Proceedings of 6th International Workshop on Cooperative and Human Aspects of Software Engineering (CHASE)*. San Francisco, CA: IEEE. doi:10.1109/CHASE.2013.6614746

Hansen, M. T., & Baggesen, H. (2009). From CMMI and isolation to Scrum, Agile, Lean and collaboration. *In Proceedings of Agile 2009 Conference*. Chicago, IL: IEEE. doi:10.1109/AGILE.2009.18

Hasnain, E. (2010). An overview of published agile studies: a systematic literature review. In *Proceedings of the National Software Engineering Conference (NSEC '10)*. Rawalpindi, Pakistan: ACM. doi:10.1145/1890810.1890813

Heimgartner, S., & Locke, M. (2006). A Tale of Two Writing Teams. In *Proceedings of Agile Conference (AGILE'06)*. Minneapolis, MN: IEEE.

Hogan, B. (2006). Lessons Learned from an eXtremely Distributed Project. In *Proceedings of Agile Conference (AGILE'06)*. Minneapolis, MN: IEEE. doi:10.1109/AGILE.2006.37

Hui, A. (2013). Lean Change: Enabling Agile Transformation through Lean Startup, Kanban, and Kotter: An Experience Report. In *Proceedings of Agile Conference (AGILE 2013)*, Nashville, TN: IEEE. doi:10.1109/AGILE.2013.22

Jackson, A., Tsang, S. L., Gray, A., Driver, C., & Clarke, S. (2004). Behind the Rules: XP Experiences. In *Proceedings of the Agile Development Conference (ADC'04)*. Salt Lake City, UT: IEEE. doi:10.1109/ADEVC.2004.9

Jain, N. (2006). Offshore Agile Maintenance. In *Proceedings of Agile Conference (AGILE'06)*. Minneapolis, MN: IEEE.

Jakobsen, C. R., & Sutherland, J. (2009). Scrum and CMMI – Going from Good to Great Are you ready-ready to be done-done? In *Proceedings of Agile 2009 Conference*. Chicago, IL: IEEE. doi:10.1109/AGILE.2009.31

Kaisti, M., Rantala, V., Mujunen, T., Hyrynsalmi, S., Könnölä, K., Mäkilä, T., & Lehtonen, T. (2013). Agile methods for embedded systems development - a literature review and a mapping study. *EURASIP Journal on Embedded Systems, 2013*(15).

Kalliney, M. (2009). Transitioning from Agile Development to Enterprise Product Management Agility. In *Proceedings of Agile 2009 Conference*. Chicago, IL: IEEE. doi:10.1109/AGILE.2009.64

Kim, E., & Ryoo, S. (2012). Agile Adoption Story from NHN. In *Proceedings of 36th International Conference on Computer Software and Applications*. Izmir: IEEE.

Korkala, M., & Abrahamsson, P. (2007). Communication in Distributed Agile Development: A Case Study. In *Proceedings of 33rd EUROMICRO Conference on Software Engineering and Advanced Applications (SEAA 2007)*. Lubeck: IEEE. doi:10.1109/EUROMICRO.2007.23

Kornstädt, A., & Sauer, J. (2007). Tackling Offshore Communication Challenges with Agile Architecture-Centric Development. In *Proceedings of the Working IEEE/IFIP Conference on Software Architecture (WICSA'07)*. Mumbai: IEEE. doi:10.1109/WICSA.2007.39

Krebs, W., Kroll, P., & Richard, E. (2008). Growing and Sustaining an Offshore Scrum Engagement, In *Proceedings of Agile 2008 Conference*. Toronto: IEEE.

Laanti, M. (2008). Implementing Program Model with Agile Principles in a Large Software Development Organization. *In Proceedings of 32nd Annual IEEE International Computer Software and Applications Conference (COMPSAC 2008)*. Turku: IEEE. doi:10.1109/COMPSAC.2008.116

Lawrence, R. (2007). XP and Junior Developers: 7 Mistakes (and how to avoid them). In *Proceedings of Agile Conference (Agile 2007)*, Washington, DC: IEEE. doi:10.1109/AGILE.2007.67

Lee, E. C. (2008). Forming to Performing: Transitioning Large-Scale Project Into Agile. In *Proceedings of Agile 2008 Conference (AGILE '08)*. Toronto, ON: IEEE. doi:10.1109/Agile.2008.75

Lehto, I., & Rautiainen, K. (2009). Software Development Governance Challenges of a Middle-Sized Company in Agile Transition. In *Proceedings of ICSE Workshop on Software Development Governance (SDG '09)*. Vancouver, BC: IEEE. doi:10.1109/SDG.2009.5071335

Leszek, A., & Courage, C. (2008). The Doctor is "In" – Using the Office Hours Concept to Make Limited Resources Most Effective. In *Proceedings of Agile 2008 Conference (AGILE '08)*. Toronto, ON: IEEE. doi:10.1109/Agile.2008.46

Lindvall, M., Muthig, D., Dagnino, A., Wallin, C., Stupperich, M., Kiefer, D., & Kähkönen, T. et al. (2004). Agile Software Development in Large Organizations. *Computer, 37*(12), 26–34. doi:10.1109/MC.2004.231

Lyon, R., & Evans, M. (2008). Scaling Up - pushing Scrum out of its Comfort Zone. *In Proceedings of Agile 2008 Conference (AGILE '08).* Toronto, ON: IEEE. doi:10.1109/Agile.2008.19

Manuja, M., Manisha. (2014). Moving Agile based projects on Cloud. In *Proceedings of International Advance Computing Conference (IACC).* Gurgaon: IEEE.

Marchenko, A., & Abrahamsson, P. (2008). Scrum in a Multiproject Environment: An Ethnographically-Inspired Case Study on the Adoption Challenges. In *Proceedings of Agile 2008 Conference (AGILE '08).* Toronto, ON: IEEE. doi:10.1109/Agile.2008.77

Martin, A., Biddle, R., & Noble, J. (2004). The XP Customer Role in Practice: Three Studies. In *Proceedings of the Agile Development Conference (ADC'04).* Salt Lake City, UT: IEEE. doi:10.1109/ADEVC.2004.23

McHugh, O., Conboy, K., & Lang, M. (2012). Agile Practices: The Impact on Trust in Software Project Teams. *IEEE Software, 29*(3), 71–76. doi:10.1109/MS.2011.118

Mencke, R. (2008). Product Manager's Guide to Surviving the Big Bang Approach to Agile Transitions. *In Proceedings of Agile 2008 Conference (AGILE '08).* Toronto, ON: IEEE. doi:10.1109/Agile.2008.65

Middleton, P., & Joyce, D. (2012). Lean Software Management: BBC Worldwide Case Study. *IEEE Transactions on Engineering Management, 59*(1), 20–32. doi:10.1109/TEM.2010.2081675

Miller, A., & Carter, E. (2007). Agility and the Inconceivably Large. In *Proceedings of Agile Conference (Agile 2007),* Washington, DC: IEEE.

Moore, E., & Spens, J. (2008). Scaling Agile: Finding your Agile Tribe. In *Proceedings of Agile 2008 Conference (AGILE '08).* Toronto, ON: IEEE. doi:10.1109/Agile.2008.43

Moshref Razavi, A., & Ahmad, R. (2014). Agile development in large and distributed environments: A systematic literature review on organizational, managerial and cultural aspects. In *8th Malaysian Software Engineering Conference (MySEC),* Langkawi, Malaysia: IEEE.

Murphy, B., Bird, C., Zimmermann, T., Williams, L., Nagappan, N., & Begel, A. (2013). Have Agile Techniques been the Silver Bullet for Software Development at Microsoft? In *Proceedings of International Symposium on Empirical Software Engineering and Measurement (ESEM 2013).* Baltimore, MD: ACM/IEEE. doi:10.1109/ESEM.2013.21

Ozawa, H., & Zhang, L. (2013). Adapting Agile Methodology to Overcome Social Differences in Project Members. In *Proceedings of Agile Conference (AGILE 2013).* Nashville, TN: IEEE. doi:10.1109/AGILE.2013.13

Paasivaara, M., Durasiewicz, S., & Lassenius, C. (2008). Distributed Agile Development: Using Scrum in a Large Project. In *Proceedings of International Conference on Global Software Engineering (ICGSE 2008),* Bangalore: IEEE. doi:10.1109/ICGSE.2008.38

Parcell, J., & Holden, S. H. (2013). Agile Policy Development for Digital Government: An Exploratory Case Study. In *Proceedings of the 14th Annual International Conference on Digital Government Research*. Quebec City, Canada: ACM.

Parnell-Klabo, E. (2006). Introducing Lean Principles with Agile Practices at a Fortune 500 Company. In *Proceedings of Agile Conference (AGILE'06)*. Minneapolis, MN: IEEE. doi:10.1109/AGILE.2006.35

Pichler, M., Rumetshofer, H., & Wahler, W. (2006). Agile Requirements Engineering for a Social Insurance for Occupational Risks Organization: A Case Study. In *Proceedings of 14th International Requirements Engineering Conference (RE'06)*. Minneapolis/St. Paul, MN: IEEE. doi:10.1109/RE.2006.8

Power, K. (2010). Stakeholder Identification in Agile Software Product Development Organizations: A model for understanding who and what really counts. In *Proceedings of Agile Conference (AGILE 2010)*. Orlando, FL: IEEE. doi:10.1109/AGILE.2010.17

Rayhan, H., & Haque, N. (2008). Incremental Adoption of Scrum for Successful Delivery of an IT Project in a Remote Setup. In *Proceedings of Agile 2008 Conference*. Toronto: IEEE. doi:10.1109/Agile.2008.98

Robarts, J. M. (2008). Practical Considerations for Distributed Agile Projects. In *Proceedings of Agile 2008 Conference (AGILE '08)*. Toronto, ON: IEEE. doi:10.1109/Agile.2008.57

Roche, G., & Vaquez-McCall, B. (2009). The Amazing Team Race - A Team Based Agile Adoption. In *Proceedings of Agile 2009 Conference*. Chicago, IL: IEEE. doi:10.1109/AGILE.2009.67

Rodríguez, P., Partanen, J., Kuvaja, P., & Oivo, M. (2014). Combining Lean Thinking and Agile Methods for Software Development: A Case Study of a Finnish Provider of Wireless Embedded Systems. In *Proceedings of 47th Hawaii International Conference on System Science (HICSS)*. Waikoloa, HI: IEEE

Rasmussen, R., Hughes, T., Jenks, J., & Skach, J. (2009). Adopting Agile in an FDA Regulated Environment. In *Agile Conference (AGILE '09)*. Chicago, IL: IEEE. doi:10.1109/AGILE.2009.50

Rong, G., Shao, D., & Zhang, H. (2010). SCRUM-PSP: Embracing Process Agility and Discipline. In *Proceedings 17th Asia Pacific Software Engineering Conference (APSEC)*, Sydney, NSW: IEEE.

Salo, O., & Abrahamsson, P. (2008). Agile methods in European embedded software development organisations: A survey on the actual use and usefulness of Extreme Programming and Scrum. *Software, IET, 2*(1), 58–64. doi:10.1049/iet-sen:20070038

Scott, J., Johnson, R., & McCullough, M. (2008). Executing Agile in a Structured Organization: Government. In *Proceedings of Agile 2008 Conference (AGILE '08)*. Toronto, ON: IEEE. doi:10.1109/Agile.2008.40

Seffernick, T. R. (2007). Enabling Agile in a Large Organization Our Journey Down the Yellow Brick Road. In *Proceedings of Agile Conference (Agile 2007)*, Washington, DC: IEEE. doi:10.1109/AGILE.2007.23

Sepulveda, C. (2003). Agile Development and Remote Teams: Learning to Love the Phone. In *Proceedings of the Agile Development Conference (ADC'03)*. Salt Lake City, Utah: IEEE. doi:10.1109/ADC.2003.1231464

Shah, V., & Nies, A. (2008). Agile with Fragile Large Legacy Applications. In *Proceedings of Agile 2008 Conference (AGILE '08)*. Toronto, ON: IEEE. doi:10.1109/Agile.2008.86

Shatil, A., Hazzan, O., & Dubinsky, Y. (2010). Agility in a Large-Scale System Engineering Project: A Case-Study of an Advanced Communication System Project. In *Proceedings of International Conference on Software Science, Technology & Engineering*. Herzlia, Israel: IEEE. doi:10.1109/SwSTE.2010.18

Sheth, B. (2009). Scrum 911! Using Scrum to Overhaul a Support Organization. In *Proceedings of Agile 2009 Conference*. Chicago, IL: IEEE. doi:10.1109/AGILE.2009.23

Shrinivasavadhani, J. (2008). Remote Mentoring a Distributed Agile Team. In *Proceedings of Agile 2008 Conference (AGILE '08)*. Toronto, ON: IEEE. doi:10.1109/Agile.2008.89

Siddique, L., & Hussein, B. A. (2014). Practical insight about choice of methodology in large complex software projects in Norway. In *Proceedings of International Technology Management Conference (ITMC)*. Chicago, IL: IEEE. doi:10.1109/ITMC.2014.6918615

Smith, C., & King, P. (2008). Agile Project Experiences – The Story of Three Little Pigs. *In Proceedings of Agile 2008 Conference (AGILE '08)*. Toronto, ON: IEEE. doi:10.1109/Agile.2008.76

Smits, H., & Pshigoda, G. (2007). Implementing Scrum in a Distributed Software Development Organization. In *Proceedings of Agile Conference (Agile 2007)*, Washington, DC: IEEE. doi:10.1109/AGILE.2007.34

Snapp, M. B., & Dagefoerde, D. (2008). The Accidental Agilists: One Team's Journey from Waterfall to Agile. In *Proceedings of Agile 2008 Conference (AGILE '08)*. Toronto, ON: IEEE. doi:10.1109/Agile.2008.68

Stray, V. G., Lindsjørn, Y., & Sjøberg, D. I. K. (2013). Obstacles to Efficient Daily Meetings in Agile Development Projects: A Case Study. In *Proceedings of International Symposium on Empirical Software Engineering and Measurement (ESEM 2013)*. Baltimore, MD: ACM/IEEE. doi:10.1109/ESEM.2013.30

Summers, M. (2008). Insights into an Agile Adventure with Offshore Partners. In *Proceedings of Agile 2008 Conference (AGILE '08)*. Toronto, ON: IEEE. doi:10.1109/Agile.2008.37

Sutherland, J., Schoonheim, G., Kumar, N., Pandey, V., & Vishal, S. (2009). Fully Distributed Scrum: Linear Scalability of Production between San Francisco and India. *In Proceedings of Agile 2009 Conference*. Chicago, IL: IEEE. doi:10.1109/AGILE.2009.27

Sutherland, J., Schoonheim, G., Rustenburg, E., & Rijk, M. (2008). Fully Distributed Scrum: The Secret Sauce for Hyperproductive Offshored Development Teams. In *Proceedings of Agile 2008 Conference (AGILE '08)*. Toronto, ON: IEEE. doi:10.1109/Agile.2008.92

Takats, A., & Brewer, N. (2005). Improving Communication between Customers and Developers. In *Proceedings of the Agile Development Conference (ADC'05)*. Denver, CO: IEEE. doi:10.1109/ADC.2005.30

Talby, D., & Dubinsky, Y. (2009). Governance of an Agile Software Project. In *Proceedings of ICSE Workshop on Software Development Governance (SDG '09)*. Vancouver, BC: IEEE.

Tartaglia, C. M., & Ramnath, P. (2005). Using Open Spaces to Resolve Cross Team Issue. In *Proceedings of the Agile Development Conference (ADC'05)*. Denver, CO: IEEE. doi:10.1109/ADC.2005.49

Thamhain, H. J. (2014). Can We Manage Agile in Traditional Project Environments? In *Proceeding of Portland International Conference on Management of Engineering & Technology (PICMET)*. Kanazawa: IEEE.

Therrien, I., & LeBel, E. (2009). From Anarchy to Sustainable Development: Scrum in Less Than Ideal Conditions. In *Proceedings of Agile 2009 Conference*. Chicago, IL: IEEE. doi:10.1109/AGILE.2009.73

Tudor, D., & Walter, G. A. (2006). Using an Agile Approach in a Large, Traditional Organization. In *Proceedings of Agile Conference (AGILE'06)*. Minneapolis, MN: IEEE. doi:10.1109/AGILE.2006.60

Urquhart, C. (2013). *Grounded Theory for Qualitative Research, A Practical Guide*. London: Sage Publications.

Urdangarin, R., Fernandes, P., Avritzer, A., & Paulish, D. (2008). Experiences with Agile Practices in the Global Studio Project. In *Proceedings of International Conference on Global Software Engineering (ICGSE 2008)*. Bangalore: IEEE. doi:10.1109/ICGSE.2008.11

Uy, E., & Ioannou, N. (2008). Growing and Sustaining an Offshore Scrum Engagement. In *Proceedings of Agile Conference (AGILE '08)*. Toronto, ON: IEEE. doi:10.1109/Agile.2008.71

Valade, R. (2008). The Big Projects Always Fail: Taking an Enterprise Agile. In *Proceedings of Agile Conference (AGILE '08)*. Toronto, ON: IEEE. doi:10.1109/Agile.2008.63

Vax, M., & Michaud, S. (2008). Distributed Agile: Growing a Practice Together. In *Proceedings of Agile Conference (AGILE '08)*. Toronto, ON: IEEE.

Vriens, C., & Barto, R. (2008). 7 Years of Agile Management. In *Proceedings of Agile 2008 Conference (AGILE '08)*. Toronto, ON: IEEE. doi:10.1109/Agile.2008.97

Weyrauch, K. (2006). What Are We Arguing About? A Framework for Defining Agile in our Organization. In *Proceedings of Agile Conference (AGILE'06)*. Minneapolis, MN: IEEE. doi:10.1109/AGILE.2006.62

Williams, L., Rubin, K., & Cohn, M. (2010). Driving Process Improvement Via Comparative Agility Assessment. In *Proceedings of 2010 Agile Conference*. Orlando, Florida: IEEE. doi:10.1109/AGILE.2010.12

Williams, M., Packlick, J., Bellubbi, R., & Coburn, S. (2007). How We Made Onsite Customer Work - An Extreme Success Story. In *Proceedings of Agile Conference (Agile 2007)*, Washington, DC: IEEE. doi:10.1109/AGILE.2007.33

Xiaofeng, W., Lane, M., Conboy, K., Pikkarainen, M. (2009). Where agile research goes: starting from a 7-year retrospective (report on agile research workshop at XP2009). *SIGSOFT Software Engineering Notes Archive, 34*(5), 28-30.

Yap, M. (2005).Follow the Sun: Distributed Extreme Programming Development. In *Proceedings of the Agile Development Conference (ADC'05)*. Denver, CO: IEEE. doi:10.1109/ADC.2005.26

Yi, L. (2011). Manager as Scrum Master, In *Proceedings of Agile 2011 Conference*. Salt Lake City, UT: IEEE. doi:10.1109/AGILE.2011.8

Young, C., & Terashima, H. (2008). How Did We Adapt Agile Processes to Our Distributed Development? In *Proceedings of Agile 2008 Conference (AGILE '08)*. Toronto, ON: IEEE. doi:10.1109/Agile.2008.7

Zieris, F., & Salinger, S. (2013). Doing Scrum Rather Than Being Agile: A Case Study on Actual Nearshoring Practices. In *Proceedings of 8th International Conference on Global Software Engineering (ICGSE 2013)*. Bari: IEEE. doi:10.1109/ICGSE.2013.26

KEY TERMS AND DEFINITIONS

Agile Software Development: Agile software development is a group of software development methods in which requirements and solutions evolve through collaboration between self-organizing, cross-functional teams. It promotes adaptive planning, evolutionary development, early delivery, continuous improvement, and encourages rapid and flexible response to change.

Distributed Workforce: A distributed workforce is a workforce that reaches beyond the restrictions of a traditional office environment. A distributed workforce is disbursed geographically over a wide area – domestically or internationally. By installing key technologies, distributed companies enable employees located anywhere to access all of the company's resources and software such as applications, data and e-mail without working within the confines of a physical company-operated facility.

Scrum: This is an iterative, incremental software process, which is by far the most popular agile development process.

Software Component: A software unit of functionality that manages a single abstraction.

XP: This methodology consists of a variety of practices. These practices are used by developers in creating the required software.

Chapter 11
Usability Engineering in Agile Software Development Processes

Muhammad Aminu Umar
Ahmadu Bello University Zaria, Nigeria

Sahabi Ali Yusuf
Ahmadu Bello University Zaria, Nigeria

Sheidu Salami Tenuche
Ahmadu Bello University Zaria, Nigeria

Aminu Onimisi Abdulsalami
Ahmadu Bello University Zaria, Nigeria

Aliyu Muhammad Kufena
Ahmadu Bello University Zaria, Nigeria

ABSTRACT

As the popularity and acceptance of agile software development methodologies increases, the need to integrate usability engineering in the design and development processes is imperative. While, agile the focus is on technical and functional requirements not on end-user interaction, usability is usually only dealt with on the side. Combining this two in practice will go a long way in development of better product. Since the success and acceptance of software product depends not only on the technologies used but how well it integrates user-oriented methods. Therefore, this chapter puts together works on how usability engineering has been integrated with agile processes.

INTRODUCTION

Software plays a significant role in the lives of individuals and companies. Software engineering has been the major driving force for the conceptualization, design and development of software products. Several models for streamlining the development process have evolved and promoted over the years from the traditional waterfall model to more iterative and incremental development processes and recently to agile development methodology.

Agile software development process often refers to as "Agile" like any other process targets at final product from requirement engineering. This process has been promoted by software developers particularly the practitioners in the industry (Bhalerao, Puntambekar, & Ingle, 2009). Agile methods were established

DOI: 10.4018/978-1-4666-9858-1.ch011

to develop systems more quickly by spending the shortest possible time on analysis and design (Sohaib & Khan, 2010). More importantly agile methods are iterative, which mainly focus on teamwork, collaboration between customers and developer, while constant/frequent feedback from customers throughout the lifecycle of the software project and support early product delivery (Koskela, 2003).

Therefore, it will right to say that agile methodologies focuses more on the technical aspect of the development of the software product which did not focus on the system non-functional aspects such as usability. As more organizations adopt agile development practices, usability practitioners want to ensure that the resulting products are still design with users in mind (Sy, 2007). In Agilepractice, customer is considered as a business agent who understands the business value of end-user requirements.

Usability engineering is a science that studies how to understand and systematically address the usability demand of a customer (Lee & McCrickard, 2007). Usability engineering processes are important in that they focus on developing systems that are tailored for end users (Lee & McCrickard, 2007). On the other hand, software usability is defined as the capability of the software product to be understood, learned, operated, attractive to the user, and compliant to standards/guidelines, when used under specific conditions ("Software product evaluation—quality characteristics and guidelines for the user," 2001). Usability is considered as one of the most important quality factors in the design and development of an interactive software application (Fernandez, Insfran, & Abrahao, 2011). Hence, its processes focus on developing systems that are adapted for end-users (Sohaib & Khan, 2010).

Therefore, it's not enough to have a system with sound technical and functional output but a system that is design and develop with the end-user in mind (i.e. user-centered design concepts). Even though, it is reported that the use of agile methods can result in improved usability (McInerney & Maurer, 2005). This is due to the fact that the customer is involved throughout the development process. It should be noted however, that agile development processes involve a customer as a business representative who is responsible to specify the business value of user requirements, but this customer needs not necessarily tobe a real end-user (Hussain et al., 2008).

Consequently, this chapter discusses the place of usability engineering in the agile development processes put together from existing literatures on integrating agile methods and user-centered design approaches.

BACKGROUND

Agile Software Development

Agile software development is characterized by quick development of software product with limited time spent on analysis and design. This is to avoid failure caused as result of extended period of time during development. Agile methods are iterative, focus on teamwork, collaboration between customer and developer, feedback from customer throughout the lifecycle of the software project and support early product delivery (Sohaib & Khan, 2010). In ASD, design is considered to be a continuous process. This is done with the intention of best understanding user context and in the end deliver not only good product but also useable. As a result, the methods allowed for the delivery of high quality software sooner, and interaction concepts lent some degree of end-user understanding (Patton, 2002).

The benefits of agility among others include faster time to market, better responsiveness to changing customer requirements, and higher application quality, are undeniable to those who have mastered these practices. However, agile development in practice depends on many factors, including the particular skills of the development team, the particular project that it is being applied to, and the needs of the client (Eklund & Levingston, 2008). Therefore, in order to have a successful outcome in agile development, the clients need to be onside and committed. This is in line with the four key values of agile software development which constitute the agile manifesto, 2014.

1. Individuals and interactions over processes and tools
2. Working software over comprehensive documentation
3. Customer collaboration over contract negotiation
4. Responding to change over following a plan

Traditional software development approaches are not flexible and suitable in today's rapidly changing environment (Sohaib & Khan, 2010). In waterfall model for example, process activities are performed in a sequence of separate steps where preferably each step is finished before the next one begins. A main characteristic of this approach is that the software is detailed up-front. The requirements are defined, the design of e.g. the user interface is documented and passed on to development followed by implementation, integration and delivery. This up-front style results in the need for a lot of documentation since each project phase must be signed-off before proceeding to the next phase (Lee & McCrickard, 2007). An alternative to the sequential approach to software development is the iterative and incremental model. Iterative development is an approach to software development in which the project is composed of several iterations in sequence. Each iteration being a self-contained mini project composed of all work activities (requirements analysis, design, programming and test). The goal for iteration is to release an integrated, tested and partially completed but working system. Usually the partial system grows incrementally with new features iteration by iteration (Lee & McCrickard, 2007).

Agile methods do have practices that have quality assurance abilities, some of them are inside the development phase and some others can separated out as supporting practices (Sohaib & Khan, 2010).

Agile Methodologies and Life Cycle

Agile methodologies share many common practices like iterative and evolutionary development and delivery, adaptive planning and emphasis open face-to-face communication and people before documentation, processes and tools (Larman, 2003). They all embrace change by adapting to the situation rather than doing detailed predictive planning and locking down requirements.

Agile Methods have been adopted by many IT organizations and have generated many quality products of software industry (Bhalerao et al., 2009). These methods have gained higher edge on traditional software development by accommodating frequently changing requirements in high tight schedules (Bhalerao et al., 2009). Due to its iterative and evolutionary nature, the methods have promised higher customer satisfaction, low defect rates, higher usability and a solution to higher changing requirements. Agile teams include an on-site customer representative that works with the team daily to give feedback and define requirements for the software. This close collaboration allows the team to develop the software without needing a detailed written documentation up-front. Figure 1 shows a typical agile software development process.

Agile Methods include mainly; Extreme Programming (XP), Scrum, Feature Driven Development (FDD), Crystal methodology, Dynamic System Driven Development (DSDM), Adaptive Software De-

Figure 1. Agile Software Development. Source (Ntier Training, 2014)

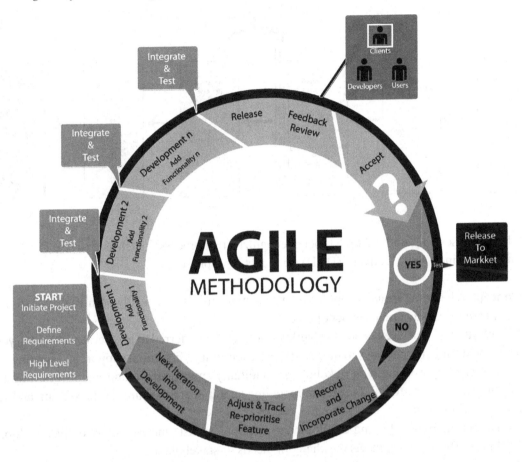

velopment (ASD), Open Source (OS), Agile Modeling (AM), and Pragmatic Programming (PP) . It has been observed that all aforementioned methods are based on agile manifesto and have their own software development life cycle for improving productivity and quality of software (Bhalerao et al., 2009).

Agile methodologies follow an iterative and incremental life-cycle. The process is composed of iterations, which can be described as self-contained mini project, and releases. The project is divided into multiple releases that each have their own scope and schedule. Each mini-release, with a subset of the features for the whole release, has its own requirements analysis, design, implementation, and quality assurance phases, and is called a working version (Sy, 2007). Each working version must be complete and stable, which makes it possible for the product release date to coincide with that of any working version.

All planning is done in collaboration by the whole team but it is the customer who decides what is included in the iteration based on the estimates of and the discussion with the developers (Lee & McCrickard, 2007). Iterations include work in all of the activities necessary for software development. The team works with requirements, design, code and test every day to keep their software ready to deploy at the end of any iteration (Bhalerao et al., 2009).

Agile Software Development Life Cycle is comprised of six phases: Concept, Inception, Construction, Transition, Production, and Retirement. (See Figure 2). Although many agile developers may balk

Figure 2. The Agile SDLC (Ambler, 2015)

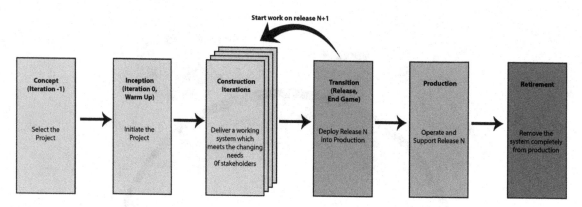

at the idea of phases, the fact is that it has been recognized that processes such as Extreme Programming (XP) and Disciplined Agile Delivery (DAD) do in fact have phases.

1. **Concept:** The initial idea/concept for the product or project is typically identified as part of your organizations product management process.
2. **Inception:** The first week or so of an agile project is often referred to as "Iteration 0" or "Cycle 0". The goal during this period is to initiate the project by gathering initial support and funding for the project; actively working with stakeholders to initially envision the requirements of the system at a high-level; starting to build the team; modeling an initial architecture for the system; and setting up the environment.
3. **Construction Phase:** During development iterations agilists incrementally deliver high-quality working software which meets the changing needs of stakeholders.
4. **Transition phase:** During the release iterations agile practitioners transition the system into production.
5. **Production:** The goal of this phase is to keep systems useful and productive after they have been deployed to the user community. The fundamental goal is to keep the system running and help users to use it.
6. **Retirement:** Eventually your solution may be removed from production, perhaps because it supports a line of business your organization has exited or because it has been replaced by a more effective solution.

On the surface, the agile SDLC of Figure 2 looks very much like a traditional SDLC, but when you dive deeper we will quickly discover that is not the case. Because the agile SDLC is highly collaborative, iterative, and incremental the roles which people take are much more robust than on traditional projects.

USABILITY ENGINEERING

Usability is generally regarded as ensuring that interactive products are easy to learn, effective to use, and enjoyable from the user's perspective. It involves optimizing the interactions people have with interactive products to enable them to carry out their activities at work, school, and in their everyday life. The main reason for applying usability techniques when developing a software system is to increase user efficiency and satisfaction and, consequently, productivity. More specifically, usability is broken down into the following goals:

- effective to use (effectiveness)
- efficient to use (efficiency)
- safe to use (safety)
- have good utility (utility)
- easy to learn (learnability)
- easy to remember how to use (memorability)

The Need for Usability

Usability engineering is a set of behavioral research methods and techniques that can be applied at every stage of the software development lifecycle, to improve the usability of the developed product by conducting usability studies that analyze users' needs or evaluate the product's usability. Usability engineering is a field that is concerned generally with human-computer interaction and specifically with making human-computer interfaces that have high usability or user friendliness. It provides structured methods for achieving efficiency and elegance in interface design. According to (Nielsen, 1992) Usability engineering deals with issues such should be user centered in order to develop an effective and efficient product. as system learnability, efficiency, memorability, errors and user satisfaction. Therefore, all designs

A key methodology for carrying out usability is called User-Centered Design (UCD). According to, UCD is an approach to designing ease of use into the total user experience with products and systems. It involves two fundamental elements; multidisciplinary teamwork and a set of specialized methods of acquiring user input and converting it into design. The following are the six core UCD principles, which correspond to the heart of UCD and provide as the structure for individual methods and procedures (Vredenberg, Isensee, & Righi, 2001). Set business goals, Understand users, Design the total customer experience, Evaluate designs, Assess competitiveness and Manage for users.

Scenario-Based Design (SBD) is one of the established usability engineering approach, a design-representation based process that uses scenarios-narratives describing users engaging in some task, in conjunction with design knowledge components called claims, which encapsulate the positive and negative effects of specific design features as a basis for creating interactive systems (Lee & McCrickard, 2007). SBD design practices allow usability engineers to design an interaction architecture that supports the users' tasks in an efficient and organized manner.

USABILITY ISSUES IN TRADITIONAL SOFTWARE PROCESS (WATERFALL MODEL)

The growing importance of computing systems in everyone's daily lives has made software development an inherently multidisciplinary endeavor (Norman, 2005; Olsen, 2005). This raises the question of how to develop systems in ways that can best leverage the perspectives, practices and knowledge bases of these different areas. Software engineers, who focus more on the design andImplementa6tion of software systems, and usability engineers who focus more on the interface design for end-users, are two areas of design that have not traditionally worked well together (Lee & McCrickard, 2007).

In this section we look at the traditional (Waterfall) software development lifecycle in relation to Usability engineering which is concerned with developing interfaces that people can use efficiently and effectively.

Waterfall Model

The waterfall development model originates in the manufacturing and construction industries; highly structured physical environments in which after-the-fact changes are prohibitively costly, if not impossible. Since no formal software development methodologies existed at the time, this hardware-oriented model was simply adapted for software development (Benington, 1983).This model is the earliest Software Development Life Cycle (SDLC) approach that was used for software development. The waterfall Model illustrates the software development process in a linear sequential flow; hence it is also referred to as a linear-sequential life cycle model. This means that any phase in the development process begins only if the previous phase is complete. In waterfall model phases do not overlap. Figure 3 shows the diagrammatic representation of different phases of waterfall model.

The general believe in any design process always goes with the slogan "Know Thy User" but in the waterfall model the slogan is "Know Thy Phases". The model follow the generic engineering paradigm of requirements, design, implement, verify and maintain. The model depend on building a detailed specification on which design is based. In other words, it is documentation driven, heavyweight and big design upfront.

Figure 3. Phases of Software Development. Source (Wikipedia, 2014)

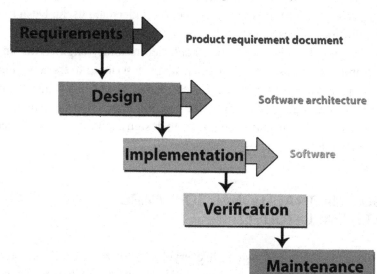

Advantages of Waterfall Model

- This model is easy and simple to understand.
- It is easy to manage due to the rigidity of the model-each phase has specific deliverables and a review process.
- In this model, phases are processed and completed one at a time. Phases do not overlap.
- Waterfall model works well for smaller projects where requirements are very well understood.

Disadvantage of Waterfall Model

- Once an application is in the testing stage, it is very difficult to go back and change something that was not well-thought out in the concept stage.
- No working software is produced until late during the life cycle.
- High amount of risk and uncertainty.
- Not a good model for complex and object oriented project.
- Not suitable for the projects where requirements are at a moderate to high risk of changing.

The Waterfall model is basically used for the project which is small and there are no uncertain requirements. At the end of each phase, a review takes place to determine if the project is on the right path and whether or not to continue or discard the project. In this model the testing starts only after the development is complete. In the waterfall model phases do not overlap (ISTQB, 2014). This is a serious constrain to the traditional development lifecycle as projects are generally large and requirements are subject to change which implies there is a high tendency of uncertainty in requirements analysis. For example, in internet and mobile technology, frequent changes in requirements, technology and staff have been observed (Bhalerao et al., 2009)Thus, software development process has become more cumbersome in such environment. Traditional Software Development Methods (TSDMs) are proven to be unsuccessful and software success rate of TSDMs is less than 40% in such environments (Cohn & Ford, 2003).

Also, very less customer action is involved during the development of the products. Once the product is ready, only then it can be demoed to the end users. Once the product is developed and if any failure occurs then the cost of fixing such issues are very high, because we need to update everywhere from document till the logic (ISTQB, 2014). It is either you discard the whole project and start all over or the client will have to compromise on the new features to be added to the requirement lists.

But the most important factor for the success of a software application is user acceptance (Hussain et al., 2008).An inherently usable and technically elegant application cannot be considered a success if it does not satisfy the end-users' needs. End-users are often left out of the development process.

USABILITY IN AGILE

Usability has been important factor in the design and development of a software product. Its processes focus on systems that are adapted for end user (Sohaib & Khan, 2010). Hence, its underlying practices and theories can give insights into user motivations, characteristics and work environments and draw on many different areas including psychology, sociology, physiology and human factors (Lee & McCrickard,

2007). Furthermore, usability measures the quality of users' experience when interacting with a product or system while, user-centered design is an approach for employing usability (Hussain et al., 2008).

Agile methods have been adopted by many IT organizations and have generated many quality products of software industry (Bhalerao et al., 2009). Similarly, usability evaluation have helped in the production of highly useable and user friendly product. Hence, agile practitioners have begun to explore ways of incorporating usability into agile methods (Lee & McCrickard, 2007). Agile been an iterative development methodology, it provides an opportunity for review of customer requirements towards producing the final product. Effort have been made to propose approaches of integrating agile methodologies and usability engineering vis-à-vis UCD (Ambler, 2008; da Silva, Martin, Maurer, & Silveira, 2011 ; Hussain et al., 2008; Sohaib & Khan, 2010). Usability engineering provides structured methods for achieving usability in the system development process.

Integrating usability engineering into agile software engineering will help reduce the risk of running into wrong design decisions by asking real end-users about their need and activities (Hussain et al., 2008). Considering the fact that both usability and agile focus on users, it makes it possible to integrate them. Both agile methods and usability practices follow cyclical development cycle, are human-centered and both emphasis team coordination and communication (Lee & McCrickard, 2007).

Interaction Design

Interaction Design is a methodology where the goal is to provide end-user with functions that are both desirable and useful. Following the fundamental tenets of user-centered design, the practice of interaction design is grounded in an understanding of real users, their goals, tasks, experiences, needs, and wants (Maier, 2015). Approaching design from a user-centered perspective, while endeavoring to balance users' needs with business goals and technological capabilities, interaction designers provide solutions to complex design challenges, and define new and evolving interactive products and services. In interaction design, interaction designers focus on what is desirable, while engineers focus on what they are capable of building, and business stakeholders focus on what is viable (Ambler, 2008).

Interaction designers otherwise known as user experience practitioners are very instrumental to the success of a software product. According to (Cooper, 2009) Interaction designers imagine the end-state so they can determine what actual business case the product will address and also establish a performance metric of the necessary trade-offs that development demands. They concern them- selves with is strategic vision and product conceptualization. Interaction designers are typically concerned with the interaction between users and computers, this is referred to as human-computer interaction. While the elements of usability engineering model according to Nielson (Nielsen, 1992) is early focus on users, user participation in the design, coordination of the different parts of the user interface, empirical user testing, and iterative revision of designs based on the test results. Agile methods also share some of this aims with usability. In practice, agile team also consists of an outsource usability practitioner or interaction designer who provides an independent analysis of designs and makes structured recommendations based on user responses and against best practice and usability standards (Eklund & Levingston, 2008). It has been suggested by Miller that interaction designers who are willing to understand and accept Agile development concepts are well-suited to take on the Agile customer role. Accordingly, (Cooper, 2009)concluded that interaction designers, at their strategic best, are superbly equipped to play the role of product owner effectively, efficiently, and collaboratively. Hence, they speak tech to the developers, speak business case to the managers, speak user personas to the marketers, and – being responsible craftsmen – are beholden only to the success of the project.

An interaction designer play a key role throughout the entire development process of any software. They perform the following activities as part of a project team (Maier, 2015):

1. **Form/inform a design strategy:** Although the boundaries here are fuzzy, it is certain that an interaction designer will need to know who he/she is designing for and what their goals are. A design strategy will help team members have a common understanding of what interactions need to take place to facilitate user goals.

2. **Identify and wireframe key interactions:** After the interaction designer has a good idea of the strategy motivating the design, he/she can begin to sketch the interfaces that will facilitate the necessary interactions. Some professionals will literally sketch these interactions on a note pad/dry-erase board while others will use software application (s) to aid them in the process; some will create these interfaces collaboratively while others will create them alone. It all depends on the interaction designer and their particular workflow.

3. **Prototype Interactions:** This depends on the project, the next logical step for an interaction designer might involve the creation of prototypes. There are a number of different ways in which a team might prototype an interaction, some of these include: XHTML/CSS prototypes and paper prototypes.

4. **Stay Current:** One of the hardest parts about being a practicing Interaction Designer is the speed of change in the industry. Every day, new designers are taking the medium in a different direction. Consequently, users are expecting these new kinds of interactions to appear on your website. The prudent interaction designer responds to this evolution by constantly exploring the web for new interactions, taking advantage of new technologies, and pushing the medium forward themselves.

Therefore, considering the fact that ASD practices favour high level of collaboration, UEX practitioners will conveniently fit into the team. Thereby, producing high-level and very broad modelling to address the majority of usability and user interface issues facing the team.

IMPACT OF USABILITY ON AGILE PROCESSES

As in other software development methodologies, usability has a great deal of impact on the final software product. Development processes from both areas such as XP and SBD share many of the same foundational concepts including iterative development and a focus on users and communication (Lee & McCrickard, 2007). However, according to these same authors, a joint approach is difficult because agile methods, which are incremental and iterative in nature, do not support any kind of comprehensive overview of the entire interface architecture which is an important part of making consistent and usable interfaces. Another major challenge of incorporating usability into agile development processes is the fact that development companies are having difficulty fitting external testing into projects and budgets rather they are more comfortable incorporating usability into normal development methods (Eklund & Levingston, 2008).

One of the problems of integrating these two methodologies is that traditionally they use different approaches on how resources are allocated in a project (da Silva et al., 2011). Agile methods strive to deliver small sets of software features to customers as quickly as possible in short iterations. On the other hand, UCD spend a considerable effort on research and analysis before development begins. While, (Ambler, 2008) believes that user experience addresses several issues that are critical to the success of agile software development teams.

Therefore, the need to fully integrate usability into agile development methodologies/processes cannot be overemphasized. In order to address this issue, authors, researchers and practitioners have proffered a number of solutions and suggestions. These ranges from; combination of usability and ASD process that begins with interface design and then continue with existing ASD processes (Constantine, 2001); employ a methodology where software development and usability engineering proceeds in parallel (Patton, 2002); invite usability analyst at the initial design and development stages to advice on principles and standards on current and best practices (Eklund & Levingston, 2008); the focus on integrating agile methods and UCD should be on design as well as on usability evaluation (da Silva et al., 2011).

The aforementioned suggestions are all geared toward achieving software products that are not only technically good but also highly useable. In order for ASD methods and usability engineering practices to work together effectively, the following are imperative (Lee & McCrickard, 2007):

- Developers design consistent and coherent interface architectures within an incremental agile development framework.
- Usability evaluations be streamlined so they better fit in accelerated development cycles while still providing useful results.
- Project members support communication and cooperation between designers, customers, users and other stakeholders who have different backgrounds and expertise. Even though, customer is involved throughout the project life cycle to provide inputs, usability practitioners want the final product should be usable. Traditionally, the project manager overseas the designer's work and is responsible for relationship with the client. In contrast, agile development has client closer working relationship with the designer, and the project manager overseas the process, less directly involved in design details (See Figure 4).

Figure 4. New team dynamics specified by Agile (Eklund & Levingston, 2008)

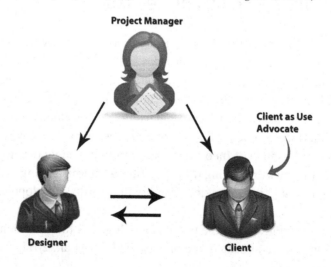

Therefore, it is not enough for agile development process to involve real end-user but also a usability expert; since, usability testing is not all about what users say and do, there is a significant component of expert analysis, particularly when it comes to making recommendations. The usability analyst will have undertaken many usability studies and be aware of best practice and well as guiding principles relating to consistency, feedback and other principles. Issues are identified and analyzed against a set of criteria, described in standard terminology such as navigation, page layout, aesthetic design and so forth. It is knowledge and understanding of these heuristics by the outsource usability analyst which highlights their value.

CONCLUSION

This chapter discussed usability engineering in agile software development processes. In order to take full advantage of the promises of agile methodologies, usability need to be taken seriously. As more organizations adopt agile as their standard methodology to produce software products that are technically sound, usability practitioners are concerned with the final product. Therefore, both communities need to work together to be able to achieve highly quality usable software.

As it is now, usability fits in well with ASD. However, gathering requirement from the actual end-user instead of the project customer/client will go a long way in improving the integration of the two. Therefore, usability and agile are well compatible and they can work together.

REFERENCES

Agile Manifesto. (2014, December 12). Retrieved from http://www.agilemanifesto.org

Ambler, S. W. (2008). Tailoring Usability into Agile Software Developement Projects. In E. Law, E. Hvannberg, & G. Cocklon (Eds.), Measuring Usability (pp. 75-95). London: Springer-Verlag.

Ambler, S. W. (2015, March 21). *Introduction to Agile Usability: User Experience (UX) Activities on Agile Development Projects*. Retrieved from Agile Modeling: http://agilemodeling.com/essays/agileUsability.htm

Benington, H. D. (1983). Production of Large Computer Programs. *IEEE Annals of the History of Computing, 5* (4), 350–361. doi:10.1109/MAHC.1983.10102

Bhalerao, S., & Ingle, M. (2007). Mapping SDLC phase with Various Agile Methods. *International conference on Advances in Computer Vision and information Technology,* (pp. 318-325). Aurangabad.

Bhalerao, S., Puntambekar, D., & Ingle, M. (2009). Generalizing Agile Software Development Life Cycle. *International Journal on Computer Science and Engineering, 1* (3), 222–226.

Cohn, M., & Ford, D. (2003). Introducing an Agile Process to an Organization. IEEE Computer Society, 74-78.

Constantine, L. L. (2001). Process Agility and Software Usability: Toward Lightweight Usage-Centered Design. *Information Age, 8* (2).

Cooper, A. (2009). *An Insurgency of Quality*. Retrieved March 11, 2015, from http://www.cooper.com/journal/insurgency-of-quality.pdf

da Silva, T., Martin, A., Maurer, F., & Silveira, M. (2011). User-centered design and Agile methods: a systematic review. *International Conference on Agile Methods in Software Development AGILE 2011*. doi:10.1109/AGILE.2011.24

Eklund, J., & Levingston, C. (2008). Usability in Agile development. *UX Research*, 1-7.

Exam Certification, I. S. T. Q. B. (2014, December 12). *What is waterfall model - advantages, disadvantages*. Retrieved from http://istqbexamcertification.com/what-is-waterfall-model-advantages-disadvantages-and-when-to-use-it/

Fernandez, A., Insfran, E., & Abrahao, S. (2011). Usability evaluation methods for the web: A systematic mapping study. *Information and Software Technology, 53* (8), 789–817. doi:10.1016/j.infsof.2011.02.007

Hussain, Z., Lechner, M., Milchrahm, H., Shahzad, S., Slany, W., Umgeher, M., & Wolkerstorfer, P. (2008). *Agile User-Centered Design Applied to a Mobile Multimedia Streaming Application* (A. Holzinger, Ed.). Berlin: Springer-Verlag. doi:10.1007/978-3-540-89350-9_22

ISO. IEC 9126. (2001). Software product evaluation—quality characteristics and guidelines for the user. Geneva: International Organization for Standardization.

Koskela, J. (2003). Software configuration management in agile methods. *ESPOO, 514*, 1–54.

Larman, C. (2003). *Agile and Iterative Development: A Manager's Guide*. Addison-Wesley.

Lee, J. C., & McCrickard, D. S. (2007). *Towards Extreme (ly) Usable Software: Exploring Tensions Between Usability and Agile Software Development*. IEEE Computer Society.

Maier, A. (2015, March 21). *Complete Beginner's Guide to Interaction Design*. Retrieved from UX Booth: http://www.uxbooth.com/articles/complete-beginners-guide-to-interaction-design/

McInerney, P., & Maurer, F. (2005). UCD in Agile Projects: Dream Team or Odd Couple? *Interaction, 12* (6), 19–23. doi:10.1145/1096554.1096556

Miller, L. (2006). *Interaction Designers and Agile Development: A Partnership*. UPA.

Nielson, J. (1992). Usability Engineering Life Cycle. *IEEE Computer, 25* (3), 12–22. doi:10.1109/2.121503

Nielson, J. (2012). *Introduction to Usability engineering*. RMIT University.

Norman, D. A. (2005). Do companies fail because their technology is unusable? *Interaction, 12* (4), 69. doi:10.1145/1070960.1070998

Ntier Training. (2014, December 10). *Agile Software Development*. Retrieved from http://www.ntier-customsolutions.com/training-courses/agile-software-development/

Olsen, G. (2005). The emperor has no lab coat. *Interaction, 9* (4), 13–17.

Patton, J. (2002). Hitting the target: adding interaction design to agile software development. *OOPSLA '02*.

Sohaib, O., & Khan, K. (2010). Integrating Usability Engineering and Agile Software Development: A Litereture Review. *International Conference On Computer Design And Appliations (ICCDA 2010)* (pp. V2-32). IEEE. doi:10.1109/ICCDA.2010.5540916

Sy, D. (2007). Adapting Usability Investigations for Agile User-centered Design. *Journal of Usability Studies, 2* (3), 112–132.

Vredenburg, K. S. I., & Righi. (2002). User-centered design: An integrated approach. Prentice Hall PTR.

Wikipedia. (2014). *Software Development Process*. Retrieved December 12, 2014, from http://en.wikipedia. org/wiki/Software_development_process

KEY TERMS AND DEFINITIONS

Agile: Software development approach that is characterize with quick development of software with minimal time spent on analysis and design.

Agile Methods: They are iterative procedures of software development that focus on timely delivery of software products.

Interaction Design: A methodology of providing end-users with desirable and useful functions.

Iterative Development: A strategy of breaking down the software development into smaller units, tested in a repeated cycles.

Usability: Ease of use of a software product.

Usability Engineering: The systematic study of the usability demand of software product user.

User-Centered Design: A methodology of carrying out usability.

Chapter 12
Fixed Priced Projects in Agile:
Fixed Projects in Agile Software Development Environments

Anuradha Chaminda Gajanayaka
Exilesoft (Pvt) Limited, Sri Lanka

ABSTRACT

Agile software development has established as a reliable alternative to waterfall software development model. Unfortunately the use of agile software development has been limited to time based contracts and not for time limited contracts. The main reason for this limitation is the "Agile manifesto" itself. The forth value of the manifesto states that agile believers find more value in "Responding to change over following a plan". This is the one of the main reasons why agile software development methods are not preferred for a fixed priced contract or time limited contract. The following case study provides an example on how the agile software development can be used for fixed priced software development contracts even when operating in offshore context. The agile software development concepts were used throughout to plan, execute, monitor, report, etc. for the project documented in this case study.

INTRODUCTION

Fixed Projects in Agile Software Development Environments

A fixed priced software development contract requires fixing all project parameters before the start of the project. There are three main project parameters referred as *triple constraints* (Zhang, 2008). They are (a) scope, (b) cost, and (c) schedule. There is a considerable upfront effort to fix the triple constraints and the outcome of this effort is the "project plan".

The main rational behind fixing the parameters upfront is to transfer the risk of scope/cost/schedule overruns to supplier. This approach has been criticized by many leading agile practitioners. (S. W. Ambler, 2003) argues that "Risk should be borne by the party best able to manage it" (p.158). There are many disagreements between how the agile thinkers want to run a project and what a fixed priced contracts demands.

DOI: 10.4018/978-1-4666-9858-1.ch012

The first major conflict can be found in the agile manifesto itself. The fourth value of the manifesto states agile believers fine more value in "Responding to change over following a plan". Further, the second principle of the manifesto states that agile believers *welcome changing requirements, even late in development. Agile processes harness change for the customer's competitive advantage.* This is in direct conflict of fixing triple constraints before the start of the project.

The second important conflict is that agile believers do not encourage big upfront planning effort to fix the project parameters. Agile thinkers believe this upfront effort is a waste. Mike Cohn (2011) explains how Scrum is not fighting the so called *cone of uncertainty* (p. 3). Agile followers believe in small planning step at the start and then iteratively improve the plan when the project moves forward. (Cohn, 2006) mentions: what is important is the "planning not the plan" (p. 9)

The result of these conflicts is creation of the common notion that agile software development is not suitable for fixed priced contracts. Fixed priced contracts are being managed using waterfall software development model(Schwaber, 2004) argues that scrum is not a silver bullet (Hoda, Noble, & Marshall, 2009). The downside of this has been fixed priced contracts do not get the benefits which agile software development offers.

It is not always possible for an agile software development organization to turn down all the fixed priced projects. Situations such as government contracts, tenders, etc. require fixing the triple constraints before the start of the project.

But certain sections of agile community are being in favor of using agile software development in fixed contracts. In one example, (Fowler, 2003) argues that is it is possible to use agile methods in fixed price contracts.

"There are two major challenges when applying agile methodologies in to a fixed price contract. One is how to fix the three parameters at the beginning and the second challenge is how to manage the fixed project while not violating agile values and principles. The second reason is how to manage the project once the parameters are fixed." (Fowler, 2003).

Any of these discussions has matured to result in a meaningful framework on how to apply agile software development in fixed priced contracts. This case study demonstrates how the project team managed to use agile software development concepts in a fixed priced contract. Team had to face many additional complexities than fixing triple constraints.

- The scope was to re-write a legacy system which was in production for number of years. The data migration & new system transition have to happen without affecting a single user
- Team had only seven working days to provide the project proposal
- Team and the client were geographically separated by 8000 kilometers and they didn't know each other before
- The time difference between the client and the supplier was 4.5 hours

The team involved in the project had 3 software developers, one project manager and one consultant architect. The consultant architect was able to locate himself at the client's site during the 7 days period where the proposal was made (Agile Methodology in Fixed Price projects. Global Advanced Research Journal of Engineering, 2013).

This was an offshore software development project using agile software development practices to manage & successfully deliver a fixed price contract.

PLANNING THE PROJECT

Difficulties in Planning

It was a special project for the organization in many different aspects. There were many unfamiliar factors for the team to face.

- The previous experiences of fixed priced development were not positive for the organization (D., Chiosi, Paltiel, Sax, & Walensky, 2011).
- There was only 7 working days available to submit the project proposal
- This was the first engagement with the client and parties were not known to each other

The team had to find a new approach for the project considering the above challenges. However the team was determined to carry out the project within the boundaries of agile manifesto. What they realized was that the known agile methodologies do not provide a good framework to manage such fixed priced projects (Lycett, 2001).

For example agile teams forecast the completion date is using backlog size and the velocity. Backlog size is estimated in story points using relative estimation technique. The velocity is how many story points the team can complete in a sprint. The velocity can only be found after completing few sprints. (Cohn, 2006). Therefore it is not possible to find a reliable project completion date at the beginning of the project. Also the project completion date gets affected by the fluctuations of velocity over the period of time. So these accepted agile practices do not give a meaningful way to plan, execute and monitor a fixed priced project.

Therefore the team decided to create their own tools and techniques for the project. Also they were to pick whatever the applicable practices from standard agile methodologies such as Scrum, XP, etc. They (Miyazaki & Suenaga, 2015) decided that four values and twelve principles of the agile software manifesto would act as the lodestar for the project.

Fixing the triple constraints

Team has to do the followings activities in the mentioned sequential order to provide a fixed price for the project.

1. Fix the scope
2. Fix the team size
3. Fix the effort
4. Derive the cost and schedule
5. Submit the project proposal

Team had to use the available seven days period carefully to submit the proposal. Team created two sub phases for the planning period. The first phase was reserved to domain study. The second phase was reserved to create the proposal for the project.

Domain Study

In the first phase, team planned to study the domain for three days. Client's product manager was available to interact with the team during the first phase. Team carried out an online workshop to explore the domain. Only four and half hours of overlapping time were available due to the time difference (Poppendieck, 2003).

Consultant architect, client's product manager and client's technical architect were connected from one end. Three developers and the project manager were connected from the other end. All the video conferencing and screen sharing were done through Skype. The below mentioned activities were carried out during the online workshop (Stropek, 2014).

Defining the product vision

The first activity of the online workshop was to define the "Vision of the product". Two groups were created with a mix of onsite members and offshore members. The offshore members had very little knowledge and the whole product knowledge was with the onsite team. The consultant architect was the facilitator (Strydom, 2006).

The product vision activity turned to be a Q&A session which all the questions came from offshore members and the onsite member had to provide the answer. The following format was used to define the product vision.

- For (target customer)
- Who (statement of the need or opportunity)
- The (product name) is a (product category)
- That (key benefit, compelling reason to buy)
- Unlike (primary competitive alternative)
- Our product (statement of primary differentiation) (Poppendieck, 2003)

Two groups created two separate product visions and thereafter they consolidated their findings to create single vision for the product. The created vision was not perfect but there were two objectives of this exercise.

First objective was to create a placeholder phrase which can be used to cross check the software which team will create later in the project. The most important purpose was to break the ice between the members and to facilitate effective collaboration as the members were not known before. The main pillar of agile software development is the "individuals and interactions" (van Cauwenberghe, 2015).

Product stakeholder behavior analysis

The next activity was to analyze the behavior of the product stakeholders. The following table was used to analyze the behavior of the product stakeholders (see Table 1).

Team again divided in to two groups and performed the analysis independently. It again turned out to be a Q&A session as where the domain knowledge flows from onsite members to offshore members (Yaju, Kataoka, Eto, Horiuchi, & Mori, 2013).

Table 1. Stakeholder analysis example for a warehouse management system

Stakeholder	Main Feature(s) Being Used	Purpose of Using the System	Number of Users	Usage Medium
Warehouse clerk	Issue goods, receive goods	To issue and receive goods from the warehouse	50+	Personal computer connected to WWW
Procurement manager	Stock replenishment report	Identify what stocks to replenishment	1	Laptop/Tablet connected to WWW
Warehouse controller	Stock summary report	Keep a track of stock movement	3	Laptop connected to WWW

After the consolidation of the individual working, team ended up with having a better idea about the product stakeholders. Number of product stakeholders identified were more than ten.

Product Usage Flow

The major exercise of the domain workshop was the creation of the *product usage flow*. Product usage flow is a high-level description of product stakeholders' action in to the system. The usage flow format was adopted from *usage scenario* from Agile Modeling (S. W. Ambler, 2002).

Team had to engage in multiple discussions to understand each stakeholder's actions in the system. The product manager conducted detail demonstrations of the existing product. Team also had the access to existing test system where they gathered first-hand knowledge on the existing system (Zeng, Rainforth, & Cook, 2015).

Team enforced a self-limitation to number of points in the usage flow not to exceed 30 points. The main reason for this was not to lose in the minor product details and discussion as the usage flow still acted as a high-level description of the product.

But it was utmost important for the team to understand the details of the product as they were to forecast the project parameters. The details were to come from the product backlog and it was the next activity which the team took upon (Zhang, 2008).

Defining the Backlog

It was decided early in to planning that the team would use the product backlog at the estimation basis. Therefore team had to write the product backlog carefully. They engaged in multiple round of refinement to come up with the final backlog.

The starting point for the backlog was the usage flow. Each point in the usage flow acted as a "theme" for the backlog in scrum terminology (Cohn, 2006). Team discussed each point of the product usage flow in detail and defined the associated requirements, conditions, constraints, etc. Team had to engage additional discussions with onsite members as well as to go through the test system again & again. Team created the associated stories for each theme based on the understanding they gained through these additional activities. This was a typical user story creation workshop adapted from scrum methodology.

After working on this for two days, team was able to come up with a backlog around one hundred and fifty user stories. Team believed that the current backlog had enough clarity for the initial estimate.

They concluded that they have reached the point of diminishing return of accuracy of the requirements compared to the effort they have to put in.

Note: Team moved away from the popular user story template of, As a … I want to … So that …

Team used a free flowing pattern for the user stories such as "Create warehouse", "Issue Good receiving notes", etc. The main reason for this is that the "As a …" format forces to focus on too much detail than required at this stage.

CREATING THE PROJECT PROPOSAL

The second phase of the planning activity to create the project proposal as team now had good understanding in to the domain of the system.

Sizing the Backlog

The next step in the planning process was to come up with the effort estimate. Team did not use the story point estimate technique as they are not able to derive a reliable velocity since the project is not started yet. The second major drawback of the relative estimation technique is that all the stories have to be scanned to find the correct relative size of a story. For example to estimate the 20th story, one need to compare it against all the 19 stories which were estimated earlier (Cohn, 2006). Getting this consistency across one hundred and fifty stories would require lot of effort and time which team did not have at this moment.

Team decided to re-arrange the user stories in a way such that each story would take one week for a developer to complete. This is typically known as *equal sizing*. The main advantage of this is that team does not require the velocity in order to come up with the completion date.

The backlog at this point of time had stories with difference sizes. Therefore team broke the larger stories and combine the smaller stories to make them equal. The larger stories were broken adding a pre-fix to the story. For example, the initial data migration story was broken as "Experimental" data migration, "Basic" data migration, "Final" data migration, etc. The smaller stories were combined together by using the word "management". For example, "user list", "user create", "user edit" stories were combined to single story named "user management" story.

The "one week" developer effort was an important calibrator as it was natural for a developer to forecast what he can complete within a week. The range of one week was not too short to be stuck in dependencies as well as not too long to go in to fuzzy zone of estimation.

Team realized that they have to count the effort on certain non-functional tasks such as setting up project & deployment environments, etc. to make the final estimate more reliable. Also they had to define some common functionality such as "Email service", "Document attachment service", etc. which they labeled as project infrastructure stories. Some of those tasks required effort of more than one week. They broke down those tasks further to create one week stores. For example, team ended up with stories such as "Experimental" deployment, "Basic" deployment, etc.

The next step was how to plan for testing & milestone preparation. Again team created stories worth of one week such as "Brower testing – Google Chrome + Safari", "Milestone 1 – preparation", etc. Milestone preparation stories were used to cover effort of releasing, demo preparation, etc.

After the backlog was completed then team had to simple count of number of stories in order arrive at the effort in man weeks.

Note: The theory behind the equal sizing estimates is the probability theory of *Law of large number (LLN)*. This law states that "the average of the results obtained from a large number of trials should be close to the expected value, and will tend to become closer as more trials are performed." The expected value of each story is one week and as there were around one hundred and twenty stories in the backlog, the average results would close to the expected value. (This will not be available with story point estimates as each story size differ from each other)

Defining Milestones

Team decided to set down some milestones in backlog to make the planning more visible. These milestones are to be probable releases if customer is satisfied with the working software at that point. Team used the first principle in agile manifesto in order to derive the milestone. The first principle states "our highest priority is to satisfy the customer through early and continuous delivery of valuable software".

Team created meaningful milestones focusing on delivering most valuable features first. Some of these features would not be possible to use in isolation at the beginning but it provided ample time for customer to give feedback. Therefore most valuable features are harden most when the first release is in production.

The first milestone was "Basic demo of the core functionality of the system". The second milestone was "Advanced demo of the core functionality". The third milestone was the "Basic version of the system". Team defined 7 such milestones.

Then team identified the stories that required to go in to each milestone block. While doing this team had to re-design some of the existing stories so that they would fit in to the milestone. Team used Google spreadsheet to do this activity.

Through this team adhered to first principle of agile manifesto and planned to deliver valuable software to the customer early as possible.

Arriving at the Schedule

The schedule was a simple summary of milestones as team had the milestone embedded into the backlog. Team had three developers and therefore they would be able to burn three stories each week. Therefore if first milestone had 15 stories, team would be able to deliver it by end of 5th week. By doing this team marked what stories would be delivered in 1st week, 2nd week, etc. Therefore they knew what week the each story would be delivered. The following table illustrate how the schedule plan was made (see table 2).

Team continued using the Google spreadsheet which gave them enough flexibility with the formulas.

Here the team kept the schedule planning simple as they were expecting changes to the plan during the project execution. Team was planning to adhere to the last value of the agile manifesto "Responding to change over following a plan".

Project Proposal

Creating the project proposal was a simple activity now as team created all the required documents by now. What was required was to compile their working documents in to one single proposal and fine tune the work they already completed.

Table 2. Project schedule and milestone plan

#	Week #	Milestone	Story	Status	Notes
1	Week 1	Milestone 1	Story zxc	Planned	
2	Week 1	Milestone 1	Story vbn	Planned	
3	Week 1	Milestone 1	Story mlk	Planned	
4	Week 2	Milestone 1	Story jhg	Planned	
5	Week 2	Milestone 1	Story fds	Planned	
6	Week 2	Milestone 1	Story aqw	Planned	
7	Week 3	Milestone 1	Story ert	Planned	
…	…	…	…	…	
15	Week 5	Milestone 1	Completion of milestone	Planned	
…	…	…	…	…	

The project proposal had a summary of the scope, schedule, cost and a description about how the project estimation was done. The backlog, technical diagrams and the contract were the major appendices for the project proposal.

Conclusion of the Project Planning

After the submission of the project proposal, the team completed the initial stage for the project. It was then up for customer decide the whether they would like to go ahead with the project or not.

Team was confident that they gave a realistic proposal with the approach they adopted to plan this fixed price project. They were happy that they went beyond the traditional planning of a typical fixed priced project and used agile values and principles for the planning process. They were further confident that they will be able to execute and manage the project by adhering to the values and principle of agile manifesto.

What is remarkable is that the team was able to come up with a confident proposal in seven days with all the challenges and limitations they had to face.

Development Start

Team got the positive news of customer accepting the proposal after few weeks from the proposal submission. The team was ready to start on development as soon as the contract was signed.

Team had very little to plan further as most of the planning happened at the proposal submission. The main thing they had to do additionally was to agree on the times for meetings such as iteration planning, demos, daily sync up, etc.

The project started with a quick round up meeting and the first iteration planning meeting. Everybody agreed to go along with iterations with two weeks of calendar time.

Execution, Monitoring and Control

The monitoring of the project was very simple as the expected velocity was clear from the day one. The iteration was two weeks long and with three developers, the expected velocity was six stories per iteration. Team broke an iteration in to two equal parts thus giving them a target of three stories per week. So the simple target for each developer was to complete a single story for a week.

The sizing of one story per week gave just the right amount of time for a developer to be creative when implementing the story. This was due to the fact that developers were not focusing on small daily tasks but border one week stories. (Team was focusing on the story not the sub-tasks of the story. Team created the sub-tasks only when really necessary). This allowed them to be innovative and adaptive to deliver things which would be valuable to customer rather than just following a pre-defined script. This was one of the major innovative achievements which team was able to be creative and adoptive but still achieving the initially defined fixed targets.

While the team progressed over the time, team gained valuable knowledge in to the project and the product. Team realized their estimation errors when they got more and more knowledge. Therefore team knew what were the stories they under-estimated and what were over-estimated after few initial iterations.

Team used this knowledge to their advantage rather than to their dis-advantage. Team balanced the two weeks of the iteration with over-estimated stories and under-estimated stories. This was by taking 3 stories which were under estimated and 3 stories which were overestimated for one iteration. So team kept the velocity in control.

One disadvantage this balancing was that team had to re-shuffle the initial project schedule & the milestone plan. This was due to the fact that team was picking stories from here and there to balance the iteration. But they ensured that the defined milestones are not disturbed by re-shuffling the stories within a milestone.

Note: It was important to keep the milestone intact to keep a check on the uncontrollable scope creep. There was a risk of adding more and more new things in to the plan as team re-shuffled the stories. The milestones clearly marked the boundaries of the available space to change.

But the plan was further changed over the period of time based on two major factors.

1. Team Adhered to the Time Boxing Not to the Scope

What happened here is that team always used one week to complete the story, irrespective whether they were able to complete the defined functionality in less time (the definitions were not strict either as team didn't have any requirement specifications). Team was developing the basic versions of the features at the initial period. So at the initial period, team had enough additional functionality of the same feature to continue development for the week even though defined work is completed before week ended.

(The main focus on these kind of situations was to balance this kind of over-estimated story with an under-estimated story for the iterations as mentioned above. But it was not always possible to achieve as team had to adhere to the milestones.)

The result of this was that team had already implemented some of the stories that were in the bottom of the backlog. For example, if there were four stories were planned for a feature, by the time team completed 3rd story, there were not much left to do with the 4th story and it was not required.

2. Changes

As in any software development project, certain changes were introduced during the development process. The main sources for changes were

1. Missed functionality at the planning
2. Improvements
3. Wrongly implemented functionality
4. Additional features that was added to existing system after the planning point
5. Bugs

The final result of these factors was that the initial plan got outdated after certain period of the time in to the development. The team proposed the "re-planning" to customer and he accepted it. This is adhering to the fourth value of agile manifesto "Responding to change over following a plan".

Re-Planning

Team conducted a re-planning effort at the middle of the project as the initial plan got outdated. Customer agreed to accept the new plan within the initially defined cost & schedule. The factors that were to consider in re-planning were;

*   There were around fifteen stories which were not needed as team covered the features of those stories from already completed stories
*   There were around five stories which became obsolete as those features were not required any longer
*   Altogether there were twenty stories which were not required at the point of re-planning
*   There were around twenty five new stories which was required to be factored in to as changes
*   So the net impact to the plan in terms of schedule, cost and effort was that five additional stories has to be completed to finish off the project
*   As an additional point, the team was having an average velocity of nearly seven stories per iteration (target was six stories).
*   Once this was factored in to the picture, the forecasted completion date was in the range of what was planned originally even with additional stories.

After the re-planned was completed, the team came up with the new plan and reminder of the project was executed based on the new plan. This was again re-iterated the agile value of "Responding to change over following a plan".

Quality Assurance

It was critical to ensure that team produce valuable working software from the day one. Therefore team had to ensure that no defects were accumulated at the end. Team engaged in many activities to ensure this.

One of the major factors was to use the continuous delivery from the start. Team used a cloud deployment environment called *apphabour* to set up automated deployment at the initial stage. This was due to the reason that customer couldn't provide the proper deployment environment at the start. Team pushed the working software at each commit and customer and stakeholders provided the immediate feedback. This early feedback ensured that team has less defects as well as cost of fixing a defect was less.

Another important aspect for the development was to use *SonarQube* as a code analysis tool in collaboration with continuous integration. Team was able to control the code quality through SonarQube. Each developer spent first fifteen minutes of every morning to improve and keep an eye on the code quality through SonarQube in additional to normal routines. This ensured no technical debt was accumulated at the end of the project.

Team had to rely on themselves on manual testing as they did not have an external tester available for them. Team used *Kanban* board to keep a track on the daily tasks. Instead of traditional three column Kanban board (To do, in progress and done), they created an additional "Test" column. Team had a routine where once a story is completed by a developer, he moved it to "Test" column. Separate developer picked the story from the teat column and perform manual testing on the story. If the testing developer is satisfied he moved to "Done" column. Otherwise the stories went back to the "in progress" column to fix the identified bugs. Through this the team was able to keep a good hold of the functional quality.

Reporting

The project reporting was performed at the each iteration. The main matrix was the forecasted project completion date. This was arrived at the following simple equation (see Figure 1).

Consider the following example;

- Project started on 2014 May 12th and reporting date is 2015 November 28th
- By the reporting date, there are fifty six stories to complete and team had an average velocity of 6.1 stories per sprint so far.
- The Figure 2 explains how the equation is used in this situation.

Further team visualize the completion of the backlog through "Feature completion harness". It is a combined bar chart which shows the status of each feature. Feature is a collection of stories which has a direct reference to the line in the usage flow (see Figure 3).

Team used horizontal bars to represent the features (collection of user stories) and different colors in the bar to represent the status of individual stories. The last bar shown in the example has four different colors in the bar. Blue shows stories which are in the "Completed" status. The dark green shows the stories that are in "Done" status. The black color represent the stories in "Removed" status and red color represent the stories that are in "To do" status. In this project, the statuses "Completed" and "Done" represent stories which have been finished and accepted. The "Removed" status means those stories are no longer required to be developed and "To Do" status means those stories are to be developed. The last status is "In Progress" which represents the stories which are currently under development at the point of report generation.

The usage of color codes gave the reader an instant overview of the current status of development. If everything is green in a bar, it means that feature is completed. In vice versa, everything is brown, it means everything has to be started of that feature.

Figure 1. Report equation

$$Forecasted\ completion\ date := \frac{Stories\ to\ be\ completed}{Average\ velocity} \times 14\ days\ + Current\ date$$

Figure 2. Example on how to apply report equation

$$Forecasted\ completion\ date := \frac{Stories\ to\ be\ completed}{Average\ velocity} \times 14\ days\ + Current\ date$$

$$Forecasted\ completion\ date := \frac{56}{6.1} \times 14\ days\ + 2014.11.28$$

$$Forecasted\ completion\ date := 129\ days\ + 2014.11.28$$

$$Forecasted\ completion\ date := \mathbf{2015\ April\ 06}$$

Figure 3. Report example

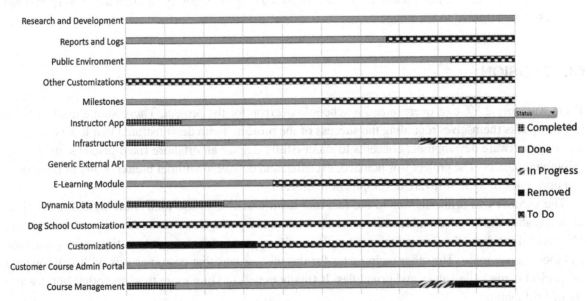

Team engaged further in the standard scrum practices such as iteration planning, daily scrum, iteration demos, retro, etc. as these practices are independent on billing model. These were again acted as reporting points.

Risk Management

The risk management for a software project is inevitable, irrespective of the process being used. The agile software development provides a different view how the risks should be managed. The CMMI©, ISO, etc. requires to manage risk as a separate activity whereas agile software development experts advise to manage risks within the stories.

In any case, it was critical to manage the risks for the project on real time to achieve the initially set targets of the scope, cost and schedule. Even a slight delay somewhere can accumulate further and expand in to uncontrollable level. Therefore it was very important to have monitor the progress strictly and take necessary corrections spontaneously. The following mechanisms were put in place to ensure that risks are identified and addressed without delays.

1. Weekly reporting and progress points so the maximum waste is minimized
2. Monthly sync up meetings with customer and team so that each other discuss and forecast where things can go wrong and address them
3. The size of the project provided some cushion to play around. In one situation the existing system's data dump got delayed for a considerable time resulting the stories for data migration got delayed. Still the team was able to find other work to complete and take data migration stories in a point where they don't have to alter the new data structures.
4. Focus on quality from the beginning. Team used a combination of TDD, UI automation, rotational testing, pair programming, etc. to ensure that team did not accumulate bugs at the end. Also through Sonar team ensured that code quality is at its best thus high readability and maintainability ensured less time required to fix a bug.

CONCLUSION

There was only 2.5% cost overrun & 7% schedule overrun for the project. These single digit overrun figures speaks themselves regarding the success of the project. Team demonstrated that it is possible to use agile software development concepts to successfully deliver an offshore fixed priced software development project. The project was planned, executed and delivered without breaking any of the values and principles of agile software development manifesto.

The success was primarily due to the fact that team was able to use their thinking & creativity to discover, alter and invent certain practices within the boundary of agile software development manifesto. This indeed validates the first value of the agile manifesto *"Individual and interactions over processed and tools"* once more. The other main factor for the success was that customer was willing to operate the project using agile values and principles. It finally benefitted him more than any other but it was a significant factor.

Agile methods provide one additional advantage for a fixed priced project. Agile methods focus on getting rapid feedback whereas in waterfall model feedback is only possible at the end. This provides an opportunity for correction at every two weeks' time. It keeps the project in check and the maximum waste is limited to two weeks. This makes the cost and schedule to be kept in check continuously.

The highlights of this case study were;

- Online workshop & product usage flow
- Equal sizing estimation technique
- Milestone based delivery schedule
- Re-planning
- Code quality analysis and continuous delivery

With these highlights, team created a framework within agile software development which can be used to successfully deliver fixed priced software development project. Further team demonstrated how this framework can be used.

REFERENCES

Agile Methodology in Fixed Price projects. Global Advanced Research Journal of Engineering, Technology and Innovation. (2013). *Systemic Foresight Methodology, 2*, 243-249.

Ambler, S. (2002). Agile modeling: effective practices for extreme programming and the unified process. Academic Press.

Ambler, S. W. (2003). Usage Scenarios. *An Agile Introduction, 2753*, 208.

Cohn, M. (2006). The Purpose of Planning. Journal of Planning Education and Research, 25(4), 446–448. doi:10.1177/0739456x0602500412

Fowler, M. (2003). Bliki: FixedPrice. *Geochemistry, Geophysics, Geosystems, 4*(11). doi: 10.1029/2003gc000608

Hoda, R., Noble, J., & Marshall, S. (2009). *Negotiating contracts for agile projects: A practical perspective. In Agile Processes in Software Engineering and Extreme Programming* (pp. 186–191). Springer. doi:10.1007/978-3-642-01853-4_25

Lycett, M. (2001). Understanding 'variation' in component-based development: Case findings from practice. *Information and Software Technology, 43*(3), 203–213. doi:10.1016/S0950-5849(00)00159-2

Michael, Chiosi, Paltiel, David, Sax, & Walensky. (2011). State of agile survey 2011. *Journal of General Internal Medicine, 26*(6), 661–667. doi: 10.1007/s11606-011-1637-5

Miyazaki, K., & Suenaga, H. (2015). *Extradiol Dioxygenases*. Metagenome.

Poppendieck, M., & Poppendieck, T. (2003). ixed-Price Contracts. In Lean software development: An agile toolkit. *Software Engineering Notes*, 28(6), 30. doi:10.1145/966221.966665

Schwaber, K. (2004). Fixed-rice, Fixed-Date Contracts. In Agile project management with Scrum. Academic Press.

Stropek, R. (2014). Molecular biology: RNA retrieved from intact tissue. *Nature, 505*(7483), 264. doi:10.1038/505264d

Strydom, R. (2006). Time is money - agile fixed price. Academic Press.

van Cauwenberghe, P. (2015). *Agile Fixed Price Projects part 1: "The Price Is Right".* Academic Press.

Yaju, Y., Kataoka, Y., Eto, H., Horiuchi, S., & Mori, R. (2013). Prophylactic interventions after delivery of placenta for reducing bleeding during the postnatal period. *Cochrane Database of Systematic Reviews, 11*, CD009328. doi:10.1002/14651858.CD009328.pub2 PMID:24277681

Zeng, P., Rainforth, W. M., & Cook, R. B. (2015). Characterisation of the oxide film on the taper interface from retrieved large diameter metal on polymer modular total hip replacements. *Tribology International, 89*, 86–96. doi:10.1016/j.triboint.2014.12.012

Zhang, J.-G. (2008). *What is project management.* Method Study of Software Project Schedule Estimation Guide.

KEY TERMS AND DEFINITIONS

Agile Software Development: Agile software development is a group of software development methods in which requirements and solutions evolve through collaboration between self-organizing, cross-functional teams. It promotes adaptive planning, evolutionary development, early delivery, continuous improvement, and encourages rapid and flexible response to change.

Offshoring: Offshoring is the relocation, by a company, of a business process from one country to another—typically an operational process, such as manufacturing, or supporting processes, such as accounting. Even state governments employ offshoring. More recently, offshoring has been associated primarily with the outsourcing of technical and administrative services supporting domestic and global operations from outside the home country ("offshore outsourcing"), by means of internal (captive) or external (outsourcing) delivery models.

Refactoring: Refactoring aims to have a cleaner "code" by restructuring the code without changing its external behaviour. The idea is to improve the design of the code with the intention of making it easy to use.

Scrum: This is an iterative, incremental software process, which is by far the most popular agile development process.

XP: This methodology consists of a variety of practices. These practices are used by developers in creating the required software.

Chapter 13

Behavior–Driven Development Using Specification by Example:
An Approach for Delivering the Right Software Built in Right Way

Praveen Ramachandra Menon
Independent Researcher, Singapore

ABSTRACT

This chapter highlights a crucial problem seen often in software development that is bridging the communication gap between business and technical language and that it can be addressed with "Behavior Driven Development" (BDD) methodology supplemented with "Specification By Example" approach of delivering the right software that matters. Effective communication has always been a challenge between clients, business stakeholders, project managers, developers, testers and business analysts because a "ubiquitous" language that every one can easily understand and use does not exist. Specification By Example serves as that ubiquitous language for all, helps build right software that matters through effective communication. Specifications are written in plain English language using the Gherkin syntax to describe various behaviors of software. BDD tools help write software specification using gherkin language and also create a living documentation that is automatically generated by programming language reflecting the current state of software at any given point of time.

INTRODUCTION

Behavior Driven Development (BDD) is an emerging practice in agile software development (North, 2006). BDD combines the general techniques and principles of Test Driven Development (TDD), Acceptance Test Driven Development (ATDD), Domain-Driven Design and object-oriented design. It provides software development and management teams an easy way to collaborate and create a shared understanding of system by building a domain vocabulary in English language that all the team members from various backgrounds can easily understand and use for communication with each other.

DOI: 10.4018/978-1-4666-9858-1.ch013

This chapter will highlight the key concepts involved from inception to completion, while building software using BDD technique in conjunction with specification by examples approach. The chapter will take the readers step by step through a real time example of building the vending machine software implemented in java. The chapter presents an immense opportunity to learn about agile practices involving BDD and TDD, which are some of the latest emerging trends. The whole BDD life cycle that also includes TDD implementation internally would be explained in detail using various diagrams and code snippets. This chapter starts with some background on history and evolution of the software development from early 1990s, definition and simplification of concept, author's hypothesis on BDD implementation, some controversies, myths, benefits and key challenges involved with BDD implementation and concludes with a real time example of building the software in a BDD way.

BDD when used in conjunction with specification by example approach helps reflect on some of the lean principles in software development by avoiding wasteful over-specification. BDD avoids spending time on details of requirements that keep on changing before even being developed. BDD gives an efficient way to perform end user perspective regression checks on the system and validates frequently whether actual behavior is as per specification with help of automated continuous code integration, build and deployment process. BDD provides most recent (almost instant) and reliable living documentation with minimal maintenance costs that truly reflects the current state of software being developed. When the specification is described with concrete examples, it becomes very easy to develop and test system and uncover ambiguities in behavior. Once this specification is automated it becomes an executable acceptance test. BDD practice can be easily fit into either short agile iterations or flow-based process, so that information on upcoming work is produced just in time (Adzic, 2009).

In BDD, ideally everyone in the team discusses and writes the specification with concrete examples. A team typically has developers, testers, business analysts etc. In agile teams at the least, product owner write the specification so that team will have clarity on what they need to develop. In BDD the acceptance tests focus on various behavior of system and will initially fail, as features are not yet implemented. As a sprint progress, the developers will implement the features just enough to make test cases merely pass. Different kinds of test code such as unit, integration and system or user acceptance tests are plugged in to automation framework that will internally pull down the inputs from specification. It validates expected output data from spec against the actual output obtained from system under test. Once the test cases pass, feature is marked complete. Later all the code are optimized and refactored for maintainability, efficiency and reusability.

This approach ensures higher product quality, setting clear expectations for all and the validation process becomes more efficient. This approach also leads to less rework as team collaboratively ensure a shared common understanding among all and thereby allowing better alignment of activities among different kinds of roles on a given project resulting into a flawless delivery.

BACKGROUND

In order to have a clear understanding on today's context of software development, it would be helpful to glance through the history and evolution of software development over past decades. From time to time the software development community has attempted to solve the classic problems emerged in industry.

History and Evolution of Software Development

Early 1990s

Two major influences, object-oriented programming replacing the procedural programming and the rise of Internet and dot-com boom shaped software development in 1990s. These emphasized speed to market and company growth as competitive business factors. Rapidly changing requirements demanded shorter product life cycles and hence were often incompatible with traditional methods of software development. Kent Beck introduced Extreme programming (XP) through his work on Chrysler Comprehensive Compensation System (C3) payroll project. XP generated significant interest among software communities in late 1990s.

Kent Beck (AS-22, 1968) discovered TDD in 1993. TDD cycle follows a simple mantra of "Red – Green – Refactor", which means first a developer writes an (initially failing) automated test case that represents an improvement or new functionality in software, then write enough code to pass these failing unit tests and finally refactor the code base arrived to acceptable standards. TDD is also very much related to test-first programming concepts of extreme programming that began around 1999 (Dinwiddie, 2011). TDD life cycle is illustrated in Figure 1.

Early 2000s

Now taking a closer look through evolution in software development for past fifteen years starting from early 2000s, agile took its birth when the agile manifesto was written in February 2001 by seventeen software developers at Utah in USA. Martin Fowler (McCall Smith, 2002) coined the name specification by example in 2002. Specification by example is an evolution of Customer Test practice of XP and Ubiquitous Language idea from domain-driven design. In 2003, TDD technique was rediscovered while it is related to test-first programming concepts from XP that began in 1999. Around the same time frame in 2003, Dan North coined the term BDD and claimed it to be different from TDD. Since then there has been lot of confusion around TDD and BDD concepts. This chapter makes a humble attempt in clarifying how BDD is certainly different from TDD, while the readers need to keep in mind that things are

Figure 1. Test driven development (TDD)

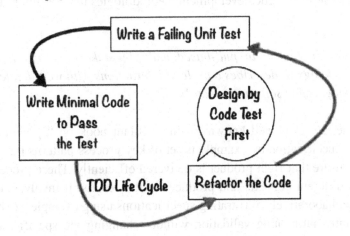

being still debated by the industrial gurus of both the practices on the constantly changing vocabularies and phraseologies from time to time.

On a higher level the TDD focuses on "how" software is developed while BDD focuses on "why" the software is developed. In other words TDD is more about "Is the product built right?" while BDD is more about "Building the right product".

Test Driven Development is more of a "Design" process rather than a "Testing" process itself. An advanced technique where automated unit tests are used to drive and design the software by enforcing loosely coupled and cohesive code base with decoupled dependencies. The unit tests get executed in seconds and provide an immediate feedback to developer and also provide a safety net to give confidence in making changes to working software without changing its core behavior. This advanced technique is of immense benefit in any type of software development (Unni, 2015).

BDD is more of Conversational building of software that matters to business rather than being automated acceptance tests verifying the product is built right. An approach for building a shared understanding on what software should do by specifying concrete examples. Work from outside –in to implement those behaviors using examples to validate what is being built. These examples are often automated as tests and become executable specification generating living documentation for the working and validated software. BDD originated by practitioners of XP who were looking for a way to involve all perspectives (Developer, QA, BA) in conversations about what software to build.

Dan North (North, 2006) is credited for developing the BDD technique in 2003. Dan soon realized a need to differentiate TDD implemented in different context or ecosystem. As per Dan, BDD is very much a TDD in an ecosystem or context where the entire team members are programmers including all the stakeholders, with a single subject matter expert embedded in the team. While in the context of broader audience that involves clients, testers, business analysts, programmers, project and program managers, and multiple subject matter experts covering multiple interrelated domains, the BDD becomes different and bigger thing than TDD. BDD then becomes a TDD++ as it serves as the communication language across all of the project stakeholders to create a single coherent vision and deliver the right software that matters.

In BDD, an outside-in approach is followed, which means from the User interface or scenarios to code development. So teams collectively create positive and negative scenarios for features to be developed. Scenarios with examples elaborate each feature and failing unit tests are written that pulls the data down from each of scenarios once the tests are hooked to features. Specification by example approach in BDD works best with short iterative or agile development methodologies like Scrum, Extreme Programming (XP) and Kanban.

BDD is a second-generation, outside-in, pull-based, multiple- stakeholder, multiple-scale, high- automation and agile methodology. It describes a cycle of interactions with well-defined outputs, resulting in the delivery of working, tested software. - Dan North

Gojki Adzic (Adzic, 2011) is well known for his brilliant book on *"Specification by example"*. According to him the Specification by example is set of key process patterns that facilitate change in software products to ensure that right product is delivered efficiently. These processes are patterns as they occur in several different contexts and produce similar results. It involves deriving scope from the goals, specifying collaboratively, illustrating specifications using examples, constantly refining the specifications, constantly automating validation without changing the specifications, validating the system frequently, and evolving the living documentation that reflects the true state of working software that matters (Dinwiddie, 2011). Living documentation is the ongoing updated working executable of software specification. When retrofitting executable specification into already existing suite of products, teams often have to make system and architecture more testable, which requires more senior people to plan and implement design changes.

MAIN FOCUS OF THE CHAPTER

This chapter mainly focuses on delivering the key concepts involved in BDD. Before getting started with example, it is required to understand the BDD loops – the inner and outer loop as shown in Figure 2.

The outer loop talks about building the right product that actually matters to customer. The inner loops talks about building the product in a right way using the TDD technique where tests drive the design and development of the product. Both the loops follow the cycle of red-green-refactor. The outer loop begins with first step "red", that is writing a failing acceptance test also known as scenarios for a feature. Then the second step "green" happens, that is creating just enough production code or features to pass those scenarios failing. Then finally comes the third step "refactor", which is refactoring the product requirements or features for maximizing the business vale to customers (McCall Smith, 2002). The inner loop (TDD) starts with first step "red" that is writing a failing unit test while the production code doesn't even exist. Then the second step "green" happens, that is creating just enough production code to make those failing unit tests pass. Then finally comes the third step "refactor", which is refactoring the code base for readability, optimization, efficiency, re-usability and maintainability.

Figure 2. BDD loops

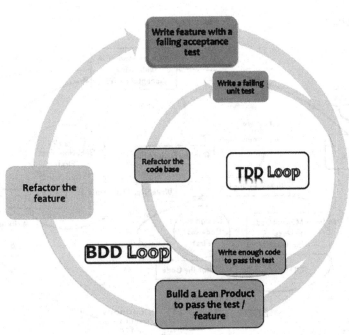

Author's Hypothesis on BDD Life Cycle

Theoretically, BDD can be done in two loops as described above but then there is a big assumption that each of team member already have cross-functional skills that includes but not limited to development, testing, automation skills to create entire regression suite of unit, integration, system or user acceptance tests, requirement analysis etc.

However, in reality it takes allot of practice, skills, enormous amount of effort and time to get every team member groomed to reach that state. Ideal path to follow would be a collaborative approach with continuous inspection, learning, adaptation and improvisation (Thomas, 2013). The author is suggesting a minor change in two-loop approach as described earlier for BDD (North, 2006). Suggested change is splitting the inner loop into two- one loop is TDD done by developers while second loop is ATDD or Behavior Driven Testing done by testers with automation skills. BDD life cycle now becomes three loop process – the outer Loop is the collaborative "value" delivery loop resulting in to Software that actually matters, one inner loop is TDD done by developers, other inner loop is about ATDD done by those with automation testing skills on the team. The BDD life cycle is shown in Figure 3.

The outer loop is a joined venture by three Amigos where in requirements are rigorously conversed and elicited bringing in the clarity and reducing wastage by eliminating the misunderstood or ambiguous requirements and rigorously running the software for continuous feedback there by learning, adapting and refining the product to maximize the business value and deliver the business goal. The inner loop is about TDD that is driven by developer who takes test first approach to arrive into a good design that makes the code base highly cohesive and loosely coupled and thereby making it extensible, flexible, testable and receptive to feedback. The other inner loop is about Automated End to End System Acceptance Testing driven by automation engineers that influences internally the TDD loop and outer loop and also reflect the true progress of feature being developed. The BDD mantra that team should follow while implementing BDD way of software development is displayed in Figure 4.

Figure 3. BDD life cycle

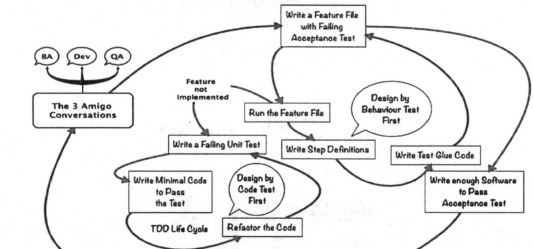

Figure 4. BDD mantra

BDD Mantra (also explained in Figure 2)

1. Create a feature file with failing scenario (feature file, non implemented step definition class) -Red

2. Create a failing unit test (TDD cycle starts) -Red

3. Write Minimum code to pass the unit test -Green

4. Refactor the code base – Yellow

5. Re-run the unit Test and see it pass -Green

6. Write the minimum Glue code to implement the Step definition class to pass the feature file -Green

7. Refactor the feature file, Step Definitions, Glue Code –Yellow

8. Re-run the feature file and see everything pass - Green

Issues, Controversies, Myths

Though BDD may look simple and obvious from a macroscopic level, there are some key challenges involved in this approach.

Key Challenges / Issues

1. **Team Collaboration:** The hardest part in software development is the collaboration missing between business and technology teams and BDD only provides a way to bridge this gap by introducing a ubiquitous language (gherkin syntax) but end of the day these teams still have to put in the manual effort for actually collaborating and having as many conversations as possible.

2. **Scenario Ownership:** Mostly the tendency is to have developers write the scenarios that would be noticeably different from client writing the same or different kinds of scenarios. And many teams still don't recognize the need of involving the end users or customers in writing the scenarios as they view this as the automated acceptance tests. These have to be viewed as the deliverable artifact to customers.

3. **Scenario Abstraction:** With a typical developer mindset the scenarios written would end up more fine-grained than the possible customer description with a level of abstraction missing. There is a tendency of ending up with a tight coupling between business and technical implementation for same reason. This particularly takes of the flexibility of implementation considerations while designing the application. Another challenge seen in writing these scenarios is to remain consistent with the language across all the tests.

4. **Scenario Maintenance:** While there have been several options to reduce redundancy in scenario writing using gherkin, the developer mindset mostly still consider gherkin's capabilities to reduce redundancy as limited to begin with. There is a strong urge to see DSL as a proper programming language. But in case of BDD as intent is to understand the behavior of product by customer, the

sophisticated usage of reusable capabilities within DSL adds bit of complexity that may actually hinder the understanding capability of customer. Another aspect is making changes to functionalities without re-factoring the acceptance tests due to fact that team members don't properly liaise given the time lines and small iterations.

5. **Cost effectiveness:** It is a given fact that automated acceptance tests are considered to be the most expensive in the pyramid of testing as compared to unit and integration level of testing and that they are most time consuming in terms of getting a feedback as well. Unit testing is believed to be the most immediate feedback loop due to the programmatic possibilities like mocking and dependency injection capabilities that enable tests to bypass the real time interaction of system that are very time consuming otherwise.

6. **Complexity Added:** There is a high need of a sophisticated complex Infrastructure to have such expensive automated acceptance tests or behavior end to end tests up and running all the time for a continuous feedback. While setting up these infrastructure is certainly feasible but will not be easy for an initial stage. There is also a complexity added by lots of moving pieces in this whole ecosystem that makes the test suites a bit of fragile to certain extent. So more technology would be needed to investigate to overcome those kinds of issues.

7. **Synergy Needed:** There has to be a lot of synergy between resources that write feature file and resources that actually implement those steps or keywords and challenge would be to keep them optimal, efficient and reusable as much as possible and this demands some cross functional training and synergy between teams for delivering efficiently. An agile mindset is needed for learning and adapting, so that BDD can truly evolve in its own pace.

Controversies

Some of the interesting controversies about BDD out there in market are as follows:

1. **BDD is nothing but TDD:** BDD is stolen from TDD conceptually with communication aspect added. TDD community has an argument that they do seem to test the behavior aspects and do not see any changes in both the mechanics.
2. **BDD is TDD++:** BDD is TDD done the right way and with some extra capabilities.
3. **BDD is same as Specification By Example:** BDD is all about writing specification using (Given –When –Then) Gherkin syntax and creating feature files with plenty of examples and writing almost every combination of them.
4. **BDD creates more harmony between Scrum and XP:** User story practices from scrum and test-driven development practices from XP, complement each other even better with help of BDD.
5. **BDD is BDD and nothing else:** As it supports not only unit design but also supports shared language understanding and design, the test design and more focused user experience design.

Myths vs. Reality

Some of the interesting myths about BDD out there in market as follows:

1. **Myth:** BDD is a Testing approach.
   Reality: BDD is more of a development focusing on behavior approach than testing.

2. **Myth:** BDD can be applied only for Web based or GUI applications.

    Reality: BDD is a development approach that can be taken for almost anything – web applications, middleware, windows API, web services, desktop applications etc.

3. **Myth:** Only Product Owners / BA should write feature files in isolation.

    Reality: BDD is an intensive collaboration of entire team members from the beginning till the end of entire product development life cycle.

4. **Myth:** BDD solves communication problem.

    Reality: No tool can fix any existing people or discipline issues. Deploying BDD and tools may facilitate more conversations in a focused manner but can't guarantee to eliminate the underlying issue that might have always existed such as lack of mindset or open communication within the team members. Each team member has to still put in personal effort to improve communication with each other.

5. **Myth:** Regression testing is the only long-term benefit from practicing BDD.

    Reality: Automated regression testing is just a by-product of the practice. Also less percentage of defects are found over a period of time in regression testing. BDD's real value is exploration of requirements ambiguity with concrete examples and getting everybody to same page using a common vocabulary for the domain. Also creating living documentation in a lean way that reflects the state of software and demonstrates progress of feature development (Unni, 2015).

Author has created a mind map for explaining BDD to readers summarizing various aspects involved in Figure 5.

Figure 5. BDD mind map

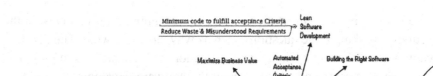
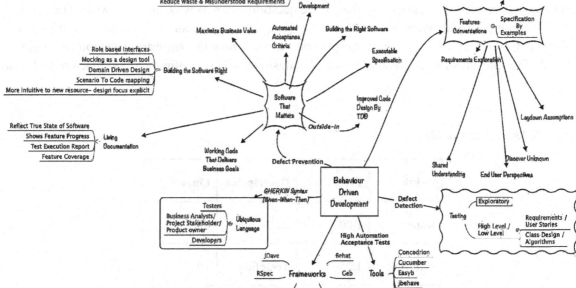

BDD EXAMPLE WALKTHROUGH

The Author has framed up some sample requirements for a commonly used product such as vending machine, which is encountered by almost everyone in a day-to-day life to keep it simple. Author will walk step by step in building the software for vending machine in a BDD approach using java as programming language, cucumber as gherkin tool, JUnit as unit test framework, spring framework, HSQLDB for in memory database, Maven as a build tool (Thomas, 2013).

Business Context

A client wants to develop software for vending machine they manufacture that focuses on selling variety of drinks. A drink has price, name and description associated with it as described in table listed in Figure 6.

Vending Machine Software Requirements

1. Customer should be able to purchase any valid drink present in the inventory.
2. Machine only accepts the exact price of drink as displayed from the user.
3. Machine should have the capability to monitor the drink stocks at any point of time.
4. Once a valid purchase happens, the stock count should be auto decremented for the appropriate drink.
5. Machine should have the capability to alert the customer in case of insufficient funds supplied by customer while buying a valid drink.
6. Machine should have the capability to alert the customer in case of an attempt made to purchase an invalid drink.

The three Amigos meet up and have plenty of conversations to clarify the ambiguities that exist in the requirements gathered by recursively asking three questions such as why, how and what. Then collaboratively coming up with features to implement by writing specification with concrete examples. The author intends to focus only on key concepts and illustrate how the software development could go using BDD approach with simple examples to demonstrate without getting into too much of technical

Figure 6. Stock details table

Drink	Price	Description	Quantity
water	1.00	Refreshing	20
softdrink	1.25	Tempting	10
juice	1.50	Healthy	15

details or other non-relevant stuff for instance about the language (java) specifics or the vending machine software features itself.

Technology Assumptions

Vending Machine Software is written in Java programming language and maven is used as the build tool. The BDD tool used in example is cucumber for writing the Gherkin syntax feature files.

Using Eclipse or any other IDE for java of choice create a java project "VendingMachine". Convert the project into a maven project to manage the dependencies. Project outline view should be as listed in Figure 7.

The project outline illustrates the maven dependencies managed for the project (Yadgar, Grumberg, & Schuster, 2009). The main dependencies as can be seen are JUnit, cucumber, spring framework, hsqldb and easy testing (fest-assert). With help of maven directory standard layout the Vending Machine project would have the project structure as listed out in Figure 8.

Figure 7. Project outline

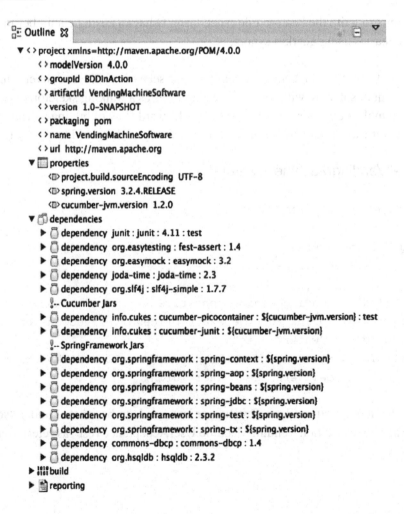

Figure 8. Project skeleton

Follow the BDD Mantra

Step 1: First step is to write the Feature File (specifying behavior) using cucumber tool capture all the required scenarios using gherkin syntax.

It is good practice to start with a happy case end-to-end scenario that can deliver a unit of potentially shippable increment of software with minimum capabilities as a walking skeleton of software being designed. In this example the author considers a straight forward flow of buying a drink say "water" from vending machine for exact price "$1" using a and the drink gets delivered to the customer.

Feature File –"VendingMachine. Feature"

```
Feature: Buying a drink from Vending Machine
In order to buy a drink
As a Vending Machine user
I want to pay the exact price listed

@BuyAnyValidDrinkFromVendingMachine @positive
Scenario: Buy a valid drink for the exact price displayed on vending machine
Given stock for drink "water" exist
When User puts in exact change for the price and selects the drink
Then Vending Machine delivers the "water" drink
```

In order to run the above feature file, a TestRunner.java needs to be created under "src/test-user/java" within the package "bddInAction.VendingMachine.UserAcceptanceTest" as referred in Table 1.

Table 1. Test Runner

```
package bddInAction.VendingMachine.UserAcceptanceTest;
import cucumber.api.CucumberOptions;
import cucumber.api.JUnit.Cucumber;
import org.JUnit.runner.RunWith;
@RunWith(Cucumber.class)
@CucumberOptions(
format = {"pretty", "html:target/cucumber-html-report", "json:target/cucumber-json-report.json"},
features ={"src/test-user/resources/bddInAction/VendingMachine/UserAcceptanceTest/"})
public class TestRunner {}
```

TestRunner.Java

Execute the test runner class using JUnit and console output window should display below:

```
Feature: Buying a drink from Vending Machine
In order to buy a drink
As a Vending Machine user
I want to pay the exact price listed

@BuyAnyValidDrinkFromVendingMachine
Scenario: Buy a valid drink for the exact price displayed on vending machine
_[90m# src/test-user/resources/bddInAction/VendingMachine/UserAcceptanceTest/
VendingMachineold.feature:8_[0m
        _[33mGiven _[0m_[33mstock for drink "water" exist_[0m
        _[33mWhen _[0m_[33mUser puts in exact change for the price and selects
the drink_[0m
        _[33mThen _[0m_[33mVending Machine delivers the "water" drink_[0m
        _[33mAnd _[0m_[33mthe stock for the drink must be auto decremented by
one_[0m

1 Scenarios (_[33m1 undefined_[0m)
4 Steps (_[33m4 undefined_[0m)
0m0.000s
```

You can implement missing steps with the snippets below:

```
@Given("^stock for drink \"(.*?)\" exist$")
public void stock_for_drink_exist(String arg1) throws Throwable {
    // Write code here that turns the phrase above into concrete actions
    throw new PendingException();
}

@When("^User puts in exact change for the price and selects the drink$")
public void user_puts_in_exact_change_for_the_price_and_selects_the_drink()
```

```
throws Throwable {
    // Write code here that turns the phrase above into concrete actions
    throw new PendingException();
}

@Then("^Vending Machine delivers the \"(.*?)\" drink$")
public void vending_Machine_delivers_the_drink(String drinkName) throws Throw-
able {
    // Write code here that turns the phrase above into concrete actions
    throw new PendingException();
}
```

Cucumber prints in console output all the missing steps that need to be implemented as shown above. Typically feature files can be run in multiple ways. The cucumber JUnit runner executes all the feature files present under the specified folder path. If a specific feature file needs to be executed then it can be explicitly called out as below:

```
features ={"src/test-user/resources/bddInAction/VendingMachine/UserAcceptance-
Test/VendingMachine.feature"},
```

Another way is to specify inside @CucumberOptions(), the scenario tags that need to be run along with the glue code to be used for the feature file as below:

```
tags = {"@BuyValidDrinkFromVendingMachine"},
glue = {"bddInAction.VendingMachine.UserAcceptanceTest.GlueCode"}
```

Execute the VendingMachine.feature using "TestRunner" class, run as a JUnit test and the console output will highlight the missing steps with code snippets to be implemented. The auto generated cucumber code snippets can be used right away in step definition file like a template.

```
format = {"pretty", "html:target/cucumber-html-report", "json:target/cucumber-
json-report.json"},
```

With above line of code in Test Runner class, cucumber will neatly captured pretty html page as displayed in the screenshot displayed in Figure 9. Cucumber also creates a json format report than can be potentially used for other reporting purpose under target folder.

Figure 9. Cucumber HTML Report

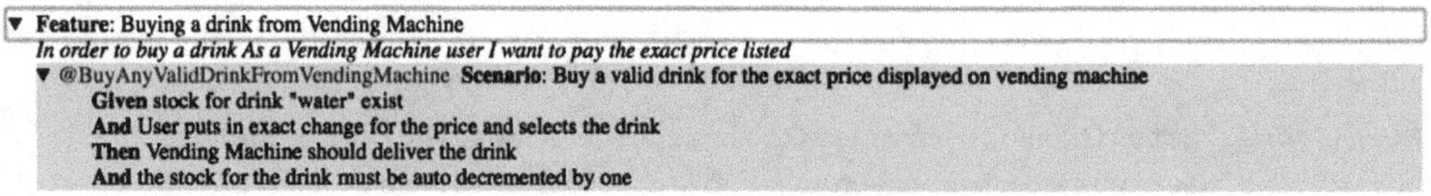

Table 2. VendingMachineSteps.Java

```
package bddInAction.VendingMachine.UserAcceptanceTest;
import cucumber.api.PendingException;
import cucumber.api.java.en.Given;
public class VendingMachineStepsOld {
@Given("^stock for \"(.*?)\" drink exist$")
public void stock_for_drink_exist(String arg1) throws Throwable {
// Write code here that turns the phrase above into concrete actions
throw new PendingException();
}
}
```

In html report, the yellow highlight over step indicates that the step is undefined, green highlight indicates that step passed when run, cyan color indicates the step got skipped while execution and red represents failure with error stack trace. Typically the feature files go yellow at start of the iteration and later on as the iteration progress it turns accordingly in to red or green based on failure or success. In this way the progress on features being worked on within the iteration by the team is constantly visible at any given snapshot of time. Missing steps highlighted in yellow need to be implemented in order to convert the specification to an executable specification. Create Step Definition class file "VendingMachineSteps" by copying the cucumber output from console for missing steps into this class as displayed in Table 2.

VendingMachineSteps.java

Re-run the test runner class and console would give a different output. Only mentioning the essence of output as below:

```
1 Scenarios (_[33m1 undefined_[0m)
4 Steps (_[33m1 pending_[0m, _[33m3 undefined_[0m)
0m0.081s

cucumber.api.PendingException: TODO: implement me at bddInAction.Vend-
ingMachine.UserAcceptanceTest.VendingMachineStepsOld.stock_for_drink_
exist(VendingMachineStepsOld.java:108)
```

Cucumber matches every step written in feature file with methods defined in step definition class using regular expressions. Cucumber has keywords like Given, When, Then and these are tagged on to the methods defined in step definition layer.

A closer look on the console output as mentioned below:

```
@Given("^stock for \"(.*?)\" drink exist$")
public void stock_for_drink_exist(String arg1) throws Throwable {}
```

In above code snippet the regular expression \"(.*?)\" would match the "water" that was specified as a parameter for the drink name in feature file and it is passed to the adjoining tagged method "stock_for_drink_exist()" as a string argument.

In the scenario, hypothetically speaking there has to be a class "VendingMachine" that would have methods like initializeStock(), checkStock(), buyDrink() at the minimum in order to implement the feature being discussed.

As per BDD mantra explained earlier, the first step is to write a failing acceptance test (scenarios in feature file). Then run the feature file using Test Runner class and result would be pending exception. At this point no further progress can be made until production code for feature is implemented.

Step 2: As per BDD mantra, developer begins the TDD loop by writing a failing unit test. Take simplest possible test such as validate the stock for drink "water" whether it matches the quantity (20) as per specification. Create the class for unit test case "VendingMachineTest" with code snippet as displayed in Table 3.

VendingMachineTest.Java

Running the "VendingMachineTest" as a JUnit test would produce a compilation error output as below:

```
java.lang.NoClassDefFoundError: VendingMachine
```

This is expected, as the class doesn't exist. Implement production code that resolves the compilation error by adding a new class "VendingMachine" with just enough code as displayed in Table 4.

VendingMachine.java

Re-run the unit test again "VendingMachineTest", test case should fail instead of getting compilation error. The console output should be:

```
org.JUnit.ComparisonFailure: expected:<[2]0> but was:<[]0>
```

The first milestone of TDD cycle is achieved as the failing unit test case was written first.

Step 3: As per BDD mantra, implement code just enough in an attempt to pass the failing unit test as displayed in Table 5.

Tip: While adding new piece of production code always follow principles like 'keep it simple and stupid' - KISS and follow the notion that 'you aren't going to need it' –YAGNI.

Table 3. VendingMachineTest.Java

```
public class VendingMachineTest{
VendingMachine vendingMachineUnderTest = new
VendingMachine();
@Test
public void checkThatWaterDrinkHasAStockOf20() throws
Exception{
int Quantity = vendingMachineUnderTest.
checkStock("water");
assertThat(Quantity).isEqualTo(20);
}
}
```

Table 4. Vending Machine –Create Skeleton class with stub method

```
public class VendingMachine{
public int checkStock(String string){
//Auto-generated method stub
return 0;
}
}
```

Table 5. Vending Machine –Implement Code

```
public class VendingMachine{
public int checkStock(String string){
return Integer.parseInt("20");
}
}
```

Table 6. Vending Machine Class – added initializeStock method

```
public class VendingMachine {
public boolean initializeStock() {
return true;}
public int checkStock(String drinkName) {
return Integer.parseInt("20");
}
}
```

Hardcode the return value for now with the specification value (20) for water drink. Re-run the unit test again and test case should pass.

Step 4: As per BDD mantra, code needs to be inspected for refactoring opportunities. In refactoring always look for code smells – duplicate code, methods too big, code never used, class complexity, separation of concerns, bad naming conventions etc. Looking at code snippet in Table 5, the parameter passed to "checkStock" method can be renamed from 'string' to a more appropriate name such as 'drinkName'. Thinking about requirements in bigger picture, before a vending machine can actually check for stock, it needs to initialize the settings. So "initiliazeStock" method needs to be implemented returning a boolean value. The refactored class is shown in Table 6.

Re-run the unit test "VendingMachineTest" to make sure nothing broke and test cases should pass. Continue adding more unit tests one by one for example checking the stock of other drinks like soft drink and juice as shown in Table 7.

Re-run the unit test again "VendingMachineTest" and test case should fail as the current code doesn't handle the logic for checking stock of multiple drinks. The console output should be:

```
org.JUnit.ComparisonFailure: expected:<[15]> but was:<[20]>
```

At this point again the TDD loop is repeated, write enough code to fix the failing unit test cases as shown in Table 8.

Table 7. Vending Machine Test - add two more tests

```
@Test
public void checkThatSoftDrinkHasAStockOf10() throws
Exception {
int stock = vendingMachine.checkStock("softdrink");
assertThat(stock).isEqualTo(10);
}
@Test
public void checkThatJuiceDrinkHasAStockOf15() throws
Exception {
int stock = vendingMachine.checkStock("juice");
assertThat(stock).isEqualTo(15);
}
```

Table 8. Vending machine class: Added logic to handle "checkStock" method for multiple drinks

```
public class VendingMachine {
public int checkStock(String drinkName {
if(drinkName.toLowerCase().contentEquals("water"))
return Integer.parseInt("20");
else if(drinkName.toLowerCase().contentEquals("softdrink"))
return Integer.parseInt("10");
else if(drinkName.toLowerCase().contentEquals("juice"))
return Integer.parseInt("15");
return 0;
}
}
```

Table 9. Vending machine refactored

```
public class VendingMachine{
private Map<String, AtomicInteger> stock = new HashMap<String, AtomicInteger>();
public VendingMachine(){}
public boolean initializeStock(){
stock.put("water", new AtomicInteger(20));
stock.put("softdrink", new AtomicInteger(10));
stock.put("juice", new AtomicInteger(15));
return true;
}
public int checkStock(String drinkName){
return stock.get(drinkName).intValue();
}
public void buyDrink(String drinkName){}
}
```

Re-run the unit test cases and they would all pass. After implementing code just enough to pass test cases, refactoring need to be performed. Currently a hard coded value is returned by method "check-Stock". The method "initiliazeStock" is returning true like a hardcoded value without doing much. Adding more test cases for validating the stock for other type of drinks would definitely fail on execution, as currently the method "checkStock" doesn't have the logic to handle different types of drink. Both methods can be refactored into something more meaningful as displayed in "VendingMachine.java" as displayed in Table 9.

So method "initializeStock" now loads all drinks to the specified quantities, then return value as true. Method "checkStock" returns the dynamic value associated with each drink. Re-run the unit test and console should give following output:

```
java.lang.NullPointerException at bddInAction.VendingMachine.VendingMachine.
checkStock(VendingMachine.java:25)
```

Null pointer is caused because the stock (Type as Map) within the "VendingMachine" class was never initialized. So constructor of the class needs to call the method "initializestock". Implement code change and re-run the unit test case, it would pass.

Continue to write another failing unit test to buy the drink "water" now that the vending machine has capability to initialize and check the stocks. Functionalities like "buy" and the "auto stock decrement" also needs to be implemented to mark it as a complete end-to-end successful transaction. Write failing test as displayed in Table 10.

The above code won't execute as "buyDrink" method doesn't exist in "VendingMachine" class yet. Go a head and generate stub method as shown in Table 11.

Table 10. Vending Machine Test – added test for buy method.

```
@Test
public void BuyAWaterDrinkSuccessfully(){
int stock = 20; //as per spec
vendingMachineUnderTest.buyDrink("water");
int quantity = vendingMachineUnderTest.checkStock("water");
assertThat(quantity).isEqualTo(stock -1);}
```

Table 11. Vending Machine Class – added stub buyDrink method

```
public void buyDrink(String string){
//TODO Auto-generated method stub
}
```

Now re-running the unit test cases will gives the below error:

```
org.JUnit.ComparisonFailure: expected:<[19]> but was:<[20]>
```

This is because the auto decrement capability is not yet added, so implement the code to handle this case as displayed in Table 12.

Step 5: As per BDD mantra, re-run all the unit tests. "BuyAWaterDrinkSuccessfully" and rest of the test cases would pass.

Everything looks good so far, but the behavior of the product associated with buy functionality is not yet entirely implemented. As per spec other pieces are still missing like validating the money paid by the user for the selected drink, alert the customer if insufficient or surplus payment is made, the actual delivery of the drink as part of a successful transaction.

Assume that requirements are not yet clear, from where the stock details should be retrieved. It could be in a database or possibly a rest call to fetch the price of the selected drink or some other approach. Thought process for a developer should be to come up with a good flexible design that can have implementation code independent of business requirement. Thus the requirement would never be tightly coupled with implementation details. Coding to interfaces from SOLID principles would be a good fit here.

Writing a "Drink Service" Interface may solve this problem and a concrete class at later point of time would implement the interface. Create "DrinkService" Interface as displayed in Table 13.

DrinkService.java

The interface defines a contract with two methods that need to be implemented for sure such as fetch price and initialize stock. The method "buyDrink" can be implemented for condition like insufficient fund purchase and more stuff can be done around the interface like creating a stub class for price data to be fetched for buy method until a real implementation of database or other alternative is achieved. Also the interface approach can immensely benefit the testing because it can be easily mocked or stubbed. This can be achieved by passing the interface reference object to the Vending Machine class constructor as argument. Finally after the changes, Vending Machine Class looks as displayed in Table 14.

Table 12. Vending Machine Class modified

```
public void buyDrink(String drinkName){
stock.get(drinkName).decrementAndGet();}
```

Table 13. Drink service interface

```
package bddInAction.VendingMachine;
import java.math.BigDecimal;
import java.util.List;
public interface DrinkService{
List<BigDecimal> fetchPrice(String name);
boolean initializeStock();
}
```

Table 14. Vending machine class modified

```
package bddInAction.VendingMachine;
import java.math.BigDecimal;
import java.util.HashMap;
import java.util.List;
import java.util.Map;
import java.util.concurrent.atomic.AtomicInteger
public class VendingMachine{
private final DrinkService drinkService;
private Map<String, AtomicInteger> stock = new HashMap<String, AtomicInteger>();
public VendingMachine(DrinkService drinkService){
this.drinkService = drinkService;
initializeStock();}
public boolean initializeStock(){
stock.put("water", new AtomicInteger(20));
stock.put("softdrink", new AtomicInteger(10));
stock.put("juice", new AtomicInteger(15));
return true;}
public int checkStock(String drinkName){
return stock.get(drinkName).intValue();}
public void buyDrink(BigDecimal decimal, String drinkName){
if(drinkName == "water" andand decimal.equals(drinkService.fetchPrice(drinkName).get(0)))
{
stock.get(drinkName).decrementAndGet();
}}
```

VendingMachine.java

Modifying the "buyDrink" method in vending machine class will now surely break the unit test case "BuyAWaterDrinkSuccessfully" that was written earlier as method signature has been altered. So the unit test case needs to be refactored as displayed in Table 15 in order to work.

Note the price value "0.50" is used being incorrect value as the intention is to write failing unit test for the "buy" method. But this unit test case won't run successfully, as it would give the compilation error for the constructor modification of vending machine class. So the way vending machine object is instantiated has to be refactored in the unit test case as well. Seems like now is the right time to create a stub that implements the interface Drink Service until a decision is made on how to implement the concrete class. Following is the code snippet for implementing the stub "DrinkServiceStub" class under "src/test-user/java" inside package "bddInAction.VendingMachine.UserAcceptanceTest.GlueCode" as displayed in Table 16.

Table 15. Vending machine test refactored

```
@Test
public void BuyAWaterDrinkSuccessfully(){
int stock = 20;
vendingMachineUnderTest.buyDrink(new
BigDecimal(0.50),"water");
int quantity = vendingMachineUnderTest.
checkStock("water");
assertThat(quantity).isEqualTo(stock -1);}
```

Table 16. Drink service stub

```
package bddInAction.VendingMachine.UserAcceptanceTest.
GlueCode;
import java.util.ArrayList;
import java.util.List;
import java.math.BigDecimal;
import bddInAction.VendingMachine.DrinkService;
public class DrinkServiceStub implements DrinkService{
@Override
public List<BigDecimal> fetchPrice(String name){
List<BigDecimal> drinks = new ArrayList<BigDecimal>();
drinks.add(new BigDecimal(1.0));
return drinks;}}
```

DrinkServiceStub.java

After re-running the unit test case console should display the below and mark test case failed:

```
org.JUnit.ComparisonFailure: expected:<[19]> but was:<[20]>
```

Note the value asserted in test case was "0.50" while as per requirement the price of Water drink is "1.0". So correct the expected value to be asserted is "1.0" in the test case and that would make it pass.

To implement the condition where user pays different than the exact price for the drink, write a failing unit test using the test data input as "1.50" or any amount greater than "1.0" which is the expected price of water. The system would again error out with above generic kind of error message which is misleading, instead system should specify that money paid by user is not matching to exact price or was higher or lower than expected price.

Condition for insufficient or surplus funds paid rather than the actual price listed also needs to be validated. Code for is as displayed in Table 17, in Vending Machine class for "buyDrink" method:

Re-run the unit test case for each of the price input data "0.50" and "1.50" separately and both tests would pass as now the code logic handles both the conditions.

Few more unit tests can be written as mentioned below to validate the requirements:

- "checkThatWaterDrinkHasAStockOf20" - checking whether the Stock for a drink was initialized correctly as per requirements which is 20 items.
- "checkWaterDrinkStockAfterOnePurchase" - checking whether the customer can do purchase of One drink use case end to end successfully.
- "checkWaterDrinkStockAfterThreePurchase" - checking whether the customer can perform multiple purchase of a drink successfully and the inventory of vending machine for that drink gets decremented accordingly.

Refer Appendix 1 for "VendingMachineTest file" that has the code snippet of entire unit test cases including the above-mentioned scenarios for more details.

Console window would show that all unit test cases pass as displayed in Figure 10.

"VendingMachine" class looks stable in functionality perspective for now, so focus should be shifted back on the BDD step definition that was paused in Step 2 in BDD life cycle as 'system under test' was

Table 17. Buy Drink Method Modified

```
public void buyDrink(BigDecimal decimal, String drinkName){
List<BigDecimal> drinks = drinkService.fetchPrice(drinkName);
if(decimal.subtract(new BigDecimal(drinks.get(0).doubleValue())).doubleValue() < 0){
throw new IllegalStateException("Transaction Failed: not enough funds");
}else if(decimal.subtract(new BigDecimal(drinks.get(0).doubleValue())).doubleValue() > 0){
throw new IllegalStateException("Transaction Failed: please put in exact amount");}
if(drinkName == "water" andand decimal.equals(drinkService.fetchPrice(drinkName).get(0)))
stock.get(drinkName).decrementAndGet();
}
```

Figure 10. Console output window for unit test execution

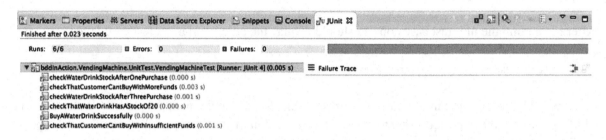

not implemented. At this point developer exits TDD loop and goes back to the outer loop as explained in BDD Loops Figure 4 earlier.

Step 6: As per BDD mantra, implement the Step definition & Glue code (code that hooks step definition to system under test) as displayed in Table 18. Start with first step definition – "Given stock for water drink exist".

VendingMachineSteps.java

Note that the new instance of "DrinkServiceStub" class is passed to constructor for instantiating the vending machine class. Run the feature file and user acceptance test cases would fail as shown in figure 11. Test case was asserted for "0" count for drink Water while the quantity initialized by vending machine is "20" as per requirement.

Change the assertion expected value as per the requirement (20) and re-run the test case and first step definition as shown below would pass.

Rest of step definitions would be still throwing pending exception. Implement the next failing step definition - as displayed in Table 19.

Test case is expected to fail because the price of water drink per spec is "1.00" and "IllegalStateException" error is expected as shown in Figure 12.

Fix the assertion expected value (1.00) as per requirement and re-run Test Runner, this time second step as would pass. Write the third failing step definition as displayed in Table 20.

Re-run the test runner to see the scenario fail at third step as shown in figure 13.

Table 18. Vending Machine Steps refactored

```
public class VendingMachineSteps {
@Given("^stock for \"(.*?)\" drink exist$")
public void stock_for_drink_exist(String drinkName) throws
Throwable {
VendingMachine vendingMachine = new
VendingMachine(new DrinkServiceStub());
boolean initialized = vendingMachine.initializeStock();
assertThat(initialized).isTrue();
int quantity = vendingMachine.checkStock(drinkName);
assertThat(quantity).isEqualTo(0);}
```

Table 19. Vending Machine second step added

```
@When("^User puts in exact change for the price and selects
the drink$")
public void user_puts_in_exact_change_for_the_price_of_
drink() throws Throwable {
VendingMachine vendingMachine = new
VendingMachine(new DrinkServiceStub());
vendingMachine.buyDrink(new BigDecimal(3.00), "water");
}
```

Figure 11. Feature execution HTML Report showing step 1 in VendingMachineSteps as a failing test

▼ **Feature**: Buying a drink from Vending Machine
In order to buy a drink As a Vending Machine user I want to pay the exact price listed
   ▼ @BuyAnyValidDrinkFromVendingMachine **Scenario**: Buy a valid drink for the exact price displayed on vending machine
     Given stock for drink "water" exist

```
org.junit.ComparisonFailure: expected:<[]0> but was:<[2]0>
        at sun.reflect.NativeConstructorAccessorImpl.newInstance0(Native Method)
        at sun.reflect.NativeConstructorAccessorImpl.newInstance(NativeConstructorAccessorImpl.java:39)
        at sun.reflect.DelegatingConstructorAccessorImpl.newInstance(DelegatingConstructorAccessorImpl.java:27)
        at java.lang.reflect.Constructor.newInstance(Constructor.java:513)
        at org.fest.assertions.ConstructorInvoker.newInstance(ConstructorInvoker.java:36)
        at org.fest.assertions.ComparisonFailureFactory.newComparisonFailure(ComparisonFailureFactory.java:60)
        at org.fest.assertions.ComparisonFailureFactory.comparisonFailure(ComparisonFailureFactory.java:46)
        at org.fest.assertions.Fail.comparisonFailed(Fail.java:83)
        at org.fest.assertions.Fail.failIfNotEqual(Fail.java:71)
        at org.fest.assertions.GenericAssert.isEqualTo(GenericAssert.java:217)
        at org.fest.assertions.IntAssert.isEqualTo(IntAssert.java:61)
        at bddInAction.VendingMachine.UserAcceptanceTest.VendingMachineStepsOld.stock_for_drink_exist(VendingMachineStepsO
        at *.Given stock for drink "water" exist(src/test-user/resources/bddInAction/VendingMachine/UserAcceptanceTest/Ve
```

   And User puts in exact change for the price and selects the drink
   Then Vending Machine should deliver the drink

Figure 12. Feature execution HTML Report showing step 2 in VendingMachineSteps as a failing test

▼ **Feature**: Buying a drink from Vending Machine
In order to buy a drink As a Vending Machine user I want to pay the exact price listed
   ▼ @BuyAnyValidDrinkFromVendingMachine **Scenario**: Buy a valid drink for the exact price displayed on vending machine
     Given stock for drink "water" exist
     And User puts in exact change for the price and selects the drink

```
java.lang.IllegalStateException: Transaction Failed: please put in exact amount
        at bddInAction.VendingMachine.VendingMachineImpl.buyDrink(VendingMachineImpl.java:65)
        at bddInAction.VendingMachine.UserAcceptanceTest.VendingMachineStepsOld.user_puts_in_exact_change_for_the_price(Ve
        at *.And User puts in exact change for the price and selects the drink(src/test-user/resources/bddInAction/Vending
```

   Then Vending Machine should deliver the drink

Table 20. Vending Machine third step added

```
@Then("^Vending Machine delivers the \"(.*?)\" drink$")
public void vending_Machine_delivers_the_drink(String drinkName) throws Throwable {
int stock = 20;
VendingMachine vendingMachine = new VendingMachine(new DrinkServiceStub());
assertTrue(vendingMachine.buyDrink(new BigDecimal(1.0), "water"));
int quantity = vendingMachine.checkStock(drinkName);
assertThat(quantity).isNotEqualTo(stock-1);
}
```

Figure 13. Feature execution HTML Report showing step 3 in VendingMachineSteps as a failing test

▼ **Feature**: Buying a drink from Vending Machine
In order to buy a drink As a Vending Machine user I want to pay the exact price listed
   ▼ @BuyAnyValidDrinkFromVendingMachine **Scenario**: Buy a valid drink for the exact price displayed on vending machine
     Given stock for drink "water" exist
     And User puts in exact change for the price and selects the drink
     Then Vending Machine should deliver the drink

```
java.lang.AssertionError: actual value:<19> should not be equal to:<19>
        at org.fest.assertions.Fail.failure(Fail.java:228)
        at org.fest.assertions.Fail.fail(Fail.java:218)
        at org.fest.assertions.Fail.failIfEqual(Fail.java:53)
        at org.fest.assertions.GenericAssert.isNotEqualTo(GenericAssert.java:228)
        at org.fest.assertions.IntAssert.isNotEqualTo(IntAssert.java:71)
        at bddInAction.VendingMachine.UserAcceptanceTest.VendingMachineStepsOld.vending_Machine_should_deliver_the_drink(V
        at *.Then Vending Machine should deliver the drink(src/test-user/resources/bddInAction/VendingMachine/UserAcceptan
```

Figure 14. Feature execution HTML Report showing all steps passed

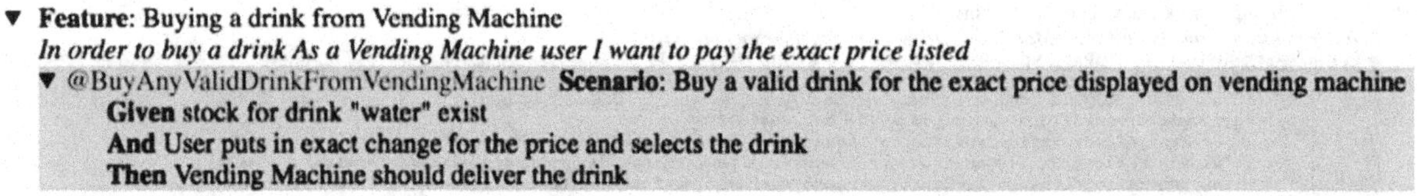

▼ **Feature**: Buying a drink from Vending Machine
 In order to buy a drink As a Vending Machine user I want to pay the exact price listed
  ▼ @BuyAnyValidDrinkFromVendingMachine **Scenario**: Buy a valid drink for the exact price displayed on vending machine
   Given stock for drink "water" exist
   And User puts in exact change for the price and selects the drink
   Then Vending Machine should deliver the drink

Fix the assert condition to "isEqualTo" as per requirement and re-run Test Runner again and this time all the steps pass as shown in figure 14.

Write the remaining step definitions in order to complete the other scenarios listed in feature file as displayed in Table 21.

Finally the entire user acceptance test cases pass as the step definition file was implemented with valid steps. As per BDD mantra the next step would be to refactoring.

Step 7: As per BDD mantra, begin with step definition layer "VendingMachineSteps" class refactoring for optimization to handle multiple drinks as current feature only works for one type of drink (water).

After re-factoring the step definition file would look as displayed in Table 22.

Re-run the Test Runner class and feature execution report would be green as shown in Figure 15.

The Console output should now look all green in the IDE and the entire scenario gets passed for all the drinks and conditions to be asserted per requirements. This is another mile stone completion of the BDD cycle. A snapshot of eclipse IDE and project after feature execution is captured in Figure 16.

Table 21. Vending Machine rest of step added

```
@When("^User puts in lesser amount than the price and selects the Drink$")
public void user_puts_in_lesser_amount_than_the_price_and_selects_the_Drink() throws Throwable {
try{
VendingMachine vendingMachine = new VendingMachine(new DrinkServiceStub());
purchased = vendingMachine.buyDrink(new BigDecimal(0.50), "water");
}catch(RuntimeException e){
errorMsg = e.getMessage().toString();
System.out.println("Transaction Failed: not enough funds for water");
}}
@Then("^Vending Machine should alert the user with exception insufficient funds$")
public void vending_Machine_should_alert_the_user_with_exception_insufficient_funds() throws Throwable {
assertEquals(errorMsg, "Transaction Failed: not enough funds");
}
```

```
@When("^User puts in greater amount than the price and selects the Drink$")
public void user_puts_in_greater_amount_than_the_price_and_selects_the_Drink() throws Throwable {
try{
VendingMachine vendingMachine = new VendingMachine(new DrinkServiceStub());
purchased = vendingMachine.buyDrink(new BigDecimal(1.50), "water");
}catch(RuntimeException e){
errorMsg = e.getMessage().toString();
System.out.println("Transaction Failed: please put in exact amount for water");
}}
@Then("^Vending Machine should alert the user with exception exact funds needed$")
public void vending_Machine_should_alert_the_user_with_exception_exact_funds_needed() throws Throwable {
assertEquals(errorMsg, "Transaction Failed: please put in exact amount");}}
```

Table 22. Vending Machine Step definition refactored

```java
public class VendingMachineSteps {
VendingMachine vendingMachine = new VendingMachine(new DrinkServiceStub());
boolean initialized = vendingMachine.initializeStock();
private int stock;
private int quantity;
private Drink drink;
private boolean purchased = false;
@Given("^stock for \"(.*?)\" drink exist$")
public void stock_for_drink_exist(String drinkName) throws Throwable {
assertThat(initialized).isTrue();
int quantity = vendingMachine.checkStock(drinkName);
switch (quantity) {
case 10:
assertThat(drinkName).isEqualTo("softdrink");
drink = Drink.softdrink;
break;
case 15:
assertThat(drinkName).isEqualTo("juice");
drink = Drink.juice;
break;
case 20:
assertThat(drinkName).isEqualTo("water");
drink = Drink.water;
break;
default:
System.out.println("No drinks available");
drink = Drink.unknown;
break;
}
}
```

```java
@When ("^User puts in exact change for the price of drink$")
public void User_puts_in_exact_change_for_the_price_of_drink() throws Throwable {
switch(drink) {
case water:
purchased = vendingMachine.buyDrink(new BigDecimal(1.00), "water");
break;
case softdrink:
purchased = vendingMachine.buyDrink(new BigDecimal(1.25), "softdrink");
break;
case juice:
purchased = vendingMachine.buyDrink(new BigDecimal(1.50), "juice");
break;
default:
System.out.println("Non supported Drink and cannot be purchased");
purchased = false;
break;
}
}
```

```java
@Then("^Vending Machine delivers the \"(.*?)\" drink$")
public void vending_Machine_delivers_the_drink(String drinkName) throws Throwable {
switch(drink) {
case water:
stock = 20;
quantity = vendingMachine.checkStock(drinkName);
assertThat(quantity).isEqualTo(stock -1);
assertTrue(purchased);
break;
case juice:
stock = 15;
quantity = vendingMachine.checkStock(drinkName);
assertThat(quantity).isEqualTo(stock -1);
assertTrue(purchased);
break;
case softdrink:
stock = 10;
quantity = vendingMachine.checkStock(drinkName);
assertThat(quantity).isEqualTo(stock -1);
assertTrue(purchased);
break;
default:
System.out.println("Non supported Drink and can not be delivered");
assertFalse(purchased);
break;}}}
```

Figure 15. Feature execution HTML Report for all scenarios with passing steps

▼ **Feature**: Buying a drink from Vending Machine
In order to buy a drink As a Vending Machine user I want to pay the exact price listed
 ▼ @BuyAnyValidDrinkFromVendingMachine **Scenario**: Buy a valid drink for the exact price displayed on vending machine
  Given stock for drink "water" exist
  And User puts in exact change for the price and selects the drink
  Then Vending Machine should deliver the drink
 ▼ @BuyAnInvalidDrinkFromVendingMachine **Scenario**: Buy an invalid drink from vending machine
  Given stock for drink "water" exist
  And User wants to buy an invalid Drink
  Then Vending Machine should alert the user with exception
 ▼ @BuyAValidDrinkForLessAmountThanPrice **Scenario**: Buy a valid drink for lesser amount than the expected price
  Given stock for drink "water" exist
  And User puts in lesser amount than the price and selects the Drink
  Then Vending Machine should alert the user with exception
 ▼ @BuyAValidDrinkForMoreAmountThanPrice **Scenario**: Buy a valid drink for more amount than the expected price
  Given stock for drink "water" exist
  And User puts in greater amount than the price and selects the Drink
  Then Vending Machine should alert the user with exception

After refactoring step definition layer, next would be to optimize the feature file treating it like a code and add more test data for the scenarios in feature file. This gives flexibility for business stakeholders to play with the stock inventory by changing the data input and there won't be any dependency as nowhere data is hardcoded inside the system. Feature file can be refactored as displayed in Table 23.

Figure 16. Eclipse IDE view with output console window

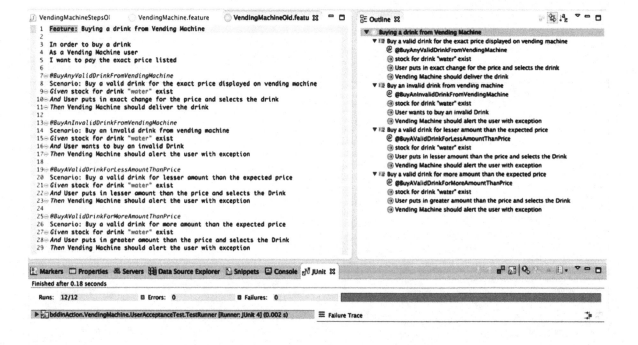

Table 23. Vending Machine feature file refactored

```
Feature: Buying a drink from Vending Machine
In order to buy a drink
As a Vending Machine user
I want to pay the exact price listed
Background:
Given stock for <Drink> exist
| Drink | Stock | Price |
| water | 20 | 1.0 |
| softdrink | 10 | 1.25 |
| juice | 15 | 1.50 |
@BuyAnyValidDrinkFromVendingMachine
Scenario: Buy any valid drink for the exact price displayed on vending machine
And User puts in exact change for the price and selects the drink
Then Vending Machine should deliver the requested drink
And the stock for the drink must be auto decremented
@BuyAValidDrinkForLessAmountThanPrice
Scenario: Buy a valid drink for lesser amount than the expected price
And User puts in "lesser amount" than the price and selects the <Drink>
|Drink | Stock | Price |
|water | 20 | 0.50 |
|softdrink | 10 | 1.00 |
|juice | 15 | 1.25 |
Then Vending Machine should alert the user with exception "insufficient funds"
@BuyAValidDrinkForMoreAmountThanPrice
Scenario: Buy a valid drink for more amount than the expected price
And User puts in "greater amount" than the price and selects the <Drink>
|Drink | Stock | Price |
|water | 20 | 1.25 |
|softdrink | 10 | 1.75 |
|juice | 15 | 2.25 |
Then Vending Machine should alert the user with exception "exact funds needed"
```

Step 8: As per BDD mantra, now re-run the feature file using "TestRunner" class and now everything should pass including unit and user acceptance test cases. This completes the final step of BDD mantra and also the outer loop of BDD life cycle. Please refer the Appendix 1 for final refactored step definition file "VendingMachineSteps".

The feature file executes for all the drink types in the vending machine. It not only details the specification with the concrete examples but also validates all the scenarios executed correctly in terms of expected initialized stock details, lesser or greater amount paid by user than actual price for drink, different error messages thrown by system.

Few things to be highlighted, which was done as part of feature file refactoring is:

1. Background: Cucumber provides this keyword so that common set of steps being repeated for all scenarios can be moved to Background section. These steps would be run before every scenario gets executed.

2. Same step definition can be shared among scenarios as exception messages are parameterized.

Then Vending Machine should alert the user with exception "insufficient funds"
Then Vending Machine should alert the user with exception "exact funds needed"

The exception message is passed as argument to the step definition layer methods so that corresponding glue code can be hooked and same step can be used for all the types of exception in the feature file.

3. Concept of Data Table in cucumber was used to load a bunch of data set for scenario verification purpose; in this case the expected stock details are defined in specification within a fixture table as <Drink>.

Running the BDD feature file again would give the below HTML report and all user acceptance tests now pass and are marked green as shown below in Figure 17.

To demonstrate how Integration Testing fits within the BDD cycle, consider the database implementation of vending machine stock details that was earlier achieved by "DrinkServiceStub" class. As discussed earlier in BDD mantra, write the failing integration test first – "DrinkServiceImplTest" as displayed in Table 24.

Figure 17. Feature execution HTML Report for refactored feature file with passing scenarios

▼ **Feature**: [New]Buying a drink from Vending Machine
In order to buy a drink As a Vending Machine user I want to pay the exact price listed
  ▼ **Background:**
      Given stock for <Drink> exist

Drink	Stock	Price
water	20	1.0
softdrink	10	1.25
juice	15	1.50

  ▼ @BuyAnyValidDrinkFromVendingMachine **Scenario**: Buy any valid drink for the exact price displayed on vending machine
      And User puts in exact change for the price and selects the drink
      Then Vending Machine should deliver the requested drink
      And the stock for the drink must be auto decremented
  ▶ **Background:**
  ▼ @BuyAnInvalidDrinkFromVendingMachine **Scenario**: Buy an invalid drink from vending machine
      And User wants to buy an invalid <Drink>

Drink	Stock	Price
vitamindrink	8	2.00

      Then Vending Machine should alert the user with exception "invalid drink"
  ▶ **Background:**
  ▼ @BuyAValidDrinkForLessAmountThanPrice **Scenario**: Buy a valid drink for lesser amount than the expected price
      And User puts in "lesser amount" than the price and selects the <Drink>

Drink	Stock	Price
water	20	0.50
softdrink	10	1.00
juice	15	1.25

      Then Vending Machine should alert the user with exception "insufficient funds"
  ▶ **Background:**
  ▼ @BuyAValidDrinkForMoreAmountThanPrice **Scenario**: Buy a valid drink for more amount than the expected price
      And User puts in "greater amount" than the price and selects the <Drink>

Drink	Stock	Price
water	20	1.25
softdrink	10	1.75
juice	15	2.25

      Then Vending Machine should alert the user with exception "exact funds needed"

Table 24. Drink Service Impl Test

```
@RunWith(SpringJUnit4ClassRunner.class)
@ContextConfiguration(locations = {"classpath:database-integration-context.xml"})
public class DrinkServiceImplTest{
@Autowired
private DataSource dataSource;
@Test
public void checkPriceOfDrinkWater()
{
DrinkService drinkService = new DrinkServiceImpl(dataSource);
List<BigDecimal> drinks = drinkService.fetchPrice("water");
BigDecimal price = drinks.get(0);
assertThat(price).isEqualTo(new BigDecimal(0.50));}}
```

DrinkServiceImplTest.java

This would give compilation error, as the "DrinkServiceImpl" class does not exist yet.

```
java.lang.NoClassDefFoundError: DrinkServiceImpl
```

Implement the code for class as displayed in Table 25.

DrinkServiceImpl.java

Run the Integration Test case as a JUnit test case and it would fail as below:

```
org.JUnit.ComparisonFailure: expected:<[0.5]> but was:<[1]>
```

That's great! Failing integration test milestone is achieved which is the first step of TDD. Now implement the "fetchPrice" method that actually interacts with a real database. For purpose of demo, project uses in memory HSQL DB with spring framework instead of traditional (on-disk) database systems.

Following configuration setup is needed for spinning up the Database. Create a "database-integration-context.xml" file under "src/test-integration/resources" folder with the xml content as displayed in Table 26.

Table 25. Drink Service Impl class

```
public class DrinkServiceImpl implements DrinkService{
private List<BigDecimal> price = new ArrayList<BigDecimal>();
public DrinkServiceImpl(DataSource dataSource){}
@Override
public List<BigDecimal> fetchPrice(String drinkName) {
price.add(new BigDecimal(1.0));
return price;}
@Override
public boolean initializeStock() {
return false;}}
```

Table 26. database-integration-context.xml file

```
<?xml version="1.0" encoding="UTF-8"?>
<beans xmlns="http://www.springframework.org/schema/beans"
xmlns:xsi="http://www.w3.org/2001/XMLSchema-instance"
xmlns:tx="http://www.springframework.org/schema/tx"
xsi:schemaLocation="http://www.springframework.org/schema/beans http://www.springframework.org/schema/beans/spring-beans-3.2.xsd
http://www.springframework.org/schema/tx http://www.springframework.org/schema/tx/spring-tx-3.2.xsd">
<bean name="dataSource" class="org.apache.commons.dbcp.BasicDataSource" destroy-method="close">
<property name="driverClassName" value="org.hsqldb.jdbcDriver"/>
<property name="url" value="jdbc:hsqldb:file://Users/praveen/Desktop/hsqldb-2.3.2/hsqldb/bin/vendingmachine;shutdown=true"/>
<property name="username" value="SA"/>
<property name="password" value=""/>
</bean>
<bean id="transactionManager" class="org.springframework.jdbc.datasource.DataSourceTransactionManager">
<property name="dataSource" ref="dataSource"/>
</bean>
<tx:annotation-driven transaction-manager="transactionManager"/>
</beans>
```

This confugres the hsqldb using spring framework. Information to run the server instance and create database, table and data needed are mentioned in Table 27.

Follow the configuration setup as per screenshot captured in Figure 18.

Table 27. hsqldb database manager swing command

```
Extract the hsqlDB ver 2.3.2 zip file to some path location …/VendingMachine/hsqldb-2.3.2/hsqldb/bin
##Run the dbmanager swing to create table and insert data##
cd …/hsqldb-2.3.2/hsqldb/lib
$ java -cp ../lib/hsqldb.jar org.hsqldb.util.DatabaseManagerSwing
```

Figure 18. hsqldb database manager swing interface

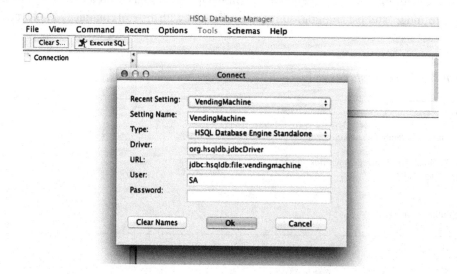

Table 28. SQL scripts to inject data for Stock

```
CREATE TABLE STOCK (
DRINK VARCHAR(10),
PRICE DECIMAL(6,2),
DESCRIPTION VARCHAR(50),
QTY INT);
INSERT INTO STOCK VALUES('water', 1.00, 'Refreshing', 20);
INSERT INTO STOCK VALUES('softdrink', 1.25, 'Tempting', 10);
INSERT INTO STOCK VALUES('juice', 1.50, 'Healthy', 15);
SELECT * FROM STOCK;
```

This would connect to database instance. Now run the SQL statements one by one as displayed below in Table 28.

Finally the stock details can be seen in database output window when running the SQL query as shown in Figure 19.

Modify the "DrinkServiceImpl" class to interact with database instance and replace the hardcoded price returned by "fetchPrice" method with inline query as displayed in Table 29.

DrinkServiceImpl.java

Now bring up the hsqldb server using below command from the lib directory where hsqldb is installed by using the commands displayed in Table 30.

Re-run the Integration Test case and the console window should get back the below error message as earlier:

```
org.JUnit.ComparisonFailure: expected:<[0.5]> but was:<[1]>
```

Figure 19. hsqldb- stock table query result view

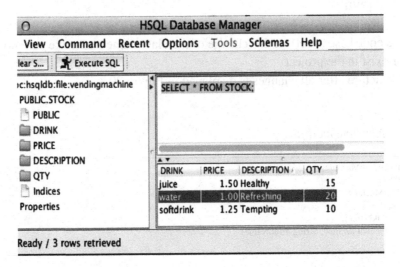

Table 29. Drink Service Impl modified

```
package bddInAction.VendingMachine;
import org.springframework.jdbc.core.JdbcTemplate;
import org.springframework.jdbc.core.SingleColumnRowMapper;
import javax.sql.DataSource;
import java.math.BigDecimal;
import java.util.List;
public class DrinkServiceImpl implements DrinkService{
private final JdbcTemplate jdbcTemplate;
public DrinkServiceImpl(DataSource dataSource){
this.jdbcTemplate = new JdbcTemplate(dataSource);}
@Override
public List<BigDecimal> fetchPrice(String drinkName) {
String query = "SELECT PRICE FROM STOCK WHERE DRINK = ?";
Object[] params = {drinkName};
return jdbcTemplate.query(query, params, new SingleColumnRowMapper<BigDecimal>());}
@Override
public boolean initializeStock() {
return false;}}
```

Table 30. hsqldb server start command

```
##Run standalone hsqldb server##
cd .../hsqldb-2.3.2/hsqldb/lib
$ java -cp hsqldb.jar org.hsqldb.server.Server --database.0 file:testdb --dbname.0 vendingmachine
```

Test case fails because price of water is asserted for wrong expected value "0.5" while it should be actually" 1.0" per requirement so making this minor change will pass the test case.

This finally completes the cycle of BDD. But the Vending Machine software can be still enhanced as needed. For instance another interface could be created for Vending Machine itself for future flexibility in change of implementation. So rename the existing the file "VendingMachine" to "VendingMachineImpl" and make it a concrete class implementation of new interface created as displayed in Table 31.

VendingMachine.java

Refactor the entire code base to reflect this change of the class name and make sure no unresolved type compilation error exist in the project.

Final project structure after all changes is displayed in Figure 20.

Table 31. Vending Machine modified

```
package bddInAction.VendingMachine;
import java.math.BigDecimal;
public interface VendingMachine{
boolean initializeStock();
int checkStock(String drinkName);
boolean buyDrink(BigDecimal decimal, String drinkName);
}
```

Figure 20. Final Project skeleton

FUTURE RESEARCH DIRECTIONS

The key take away from BDD software development approach is the collaborative conversations that go endlessly in loops (inner –TDD, outer –Behavior) which truly helps the software to evolve as a quality product confirming to all specified requirements and thereby ensuring customer satisfaction. Also the resultant product is always lean, built in the right way collaboratively by the team.

Mind mapping is a power technique to capture requirements and flows during the joined application development (JAD) technical sessions done by the entire team. Tests are as good as production code and should be treated similarly. They are like "fixed deposit" in bank and they more you deposit the more interest you earn on the same. Upfront investment is necessary to get lifelong dividends.

Identify the "right candidates" for each bucket of testing – Unit tests, Component tests, Integration tests, System / User acceptance tests. Always try to maximize the investment in Unit tests, as they are the most shortest feedback loop giving the maximum ROI (return on investment) for automation as they typically run in few milliseconds. Integration tests should be in a healthier proportion but lesser than unit tests as they are slow running tests. System tests should be strategically invested, as they are the longest feedback loop and most brittle in nature.

Taking the BDD to next level would be by achieving the true "cross-functional" capability within the team where every resource is eventually capable to articulate and refine requirements better, design solution better, test and develop the product better keep the building process lean. For example, in an ideal agile team, future state of BDD implementation could be like - Business takes care of writing feature files and checking them in to code base regularly for product backlog. Testing centric skilled resources begin with taking care of System and Integration tests and as time permits help the developers in writing unit tests, influencing the architecture and design to make it loosely coupled and more testable. Testers can also help developers build a robust, efficient and flexible design, adding more value in terms of quality engineering in every phase of software development life cycle (SDLC). Entire team can further concentrate on grooming their 'DevOps' (operational capabilities) skills that include – build script maintenance, continuous integration of code, automated build and deployment, execution of test suites, database management etc. DevOps integration targets product delivery, quality testing, feature development, and maintenance releases in order to improve reliability and security and provide faster development and deployment cycles. DevOps aids in software application release management for an organization by standardizing development environments. Events can be more easily tracked as well as resolving documented process control and granular reporting issues. This approach grants developers more control of the environment and also giving the infrastructure more application-centric understanding.

CONCLUSION

BDD life cycle has two inner loops within one outer loop that represents entire product development. One inner loop talks about designing the product by "behavior test first" approach often referred to as ATDD. Other inner loop talks about designing by "code test first" approach, often referred to as TDD. Both the loops run inside the bigger loop of product life cycle following a fail fast and learn fast approach. Entire team including business executes the outer loop, while technical team executes inner loop. The common aspect of all the three loops executed by the three Amigos in high collaboration is that they entirely follow the "TDD mantra" of "Red –Green –Refactor" on Requirements, Production Code and Test code.

BDD is actually the TDD with a shift of focus from code to the behavior and is more of a mindset rather than a set of tools. BDD also brings in a mindset of exploring the behavior of application by using scenario structure and having plenty of conversation around it between all the stakeholders. This helps in hashing out requirement ambiguity very early in game, focusing different aspects like feature injection, deliberate discover, real options, context questioning and outcome questioning thereby helping the teams to understand the risk in their projects and address them early on without a single test being written. It brings together the entire team with help of ubiquitous language and does take a lot in terms of patience, time and practice to reap the full benefits of this approach.

Finally, Specification by Example is just an approach used in conjunction with BDD that lays emphasis on having more specificity in requirements by giving concrete examples. This kind of specification facilitates lot of conversations among all the team members despite of their diverse background rather than just being automation approach in itself. Realistic examples help team to spot inconsistencies and functional gaps much faster than validating them through implementation in future.

REFERENCES

Adzic, G. (2009). *Bridging the Communication Gap- Specification By Example and Agile Acceptance Testing*. Academic Press.

Adzic, G. (2011). Specification by Example: How successful teams deliver the right software. *Childhood Education, 87*(4), 302–303. doi:10.1080/00094056.2011.10523198

AS-22 BNL. (1968). *Brookhaven National Laboratory*. BNL 50106 (AS-22). T. Brookhaven National Laboratory.

Dinwiddie, G. (2011). The three amigos. *StickyMinds Magazine*.

McCall Smith, A. (2002). The No. 1 Ladies' Detective Agency. New York: Anchor Books.

North, D. (2006). Introducing BDD. *Advances in Space Research, 37*(5), 958–962. doi:10.1016/j.asr.2005.12.009

Thomas, S. (2013). Specification by Example versus Behavior Driven Development. Academic Press.

Unni, E. J., & Farris, K. B. (2015). Development of a new scale to measure self-reported medication nonadherence. *Research in Social & Administrative Pharmacy, 11*(3), e133-143. doi: 10.1016/j.sapharm.2009.06.005

Yadgar, A., Grumberg, O., & Schuster, A. (2009). *Hybrid BDD and All-SAT Method for Model Checking*. Academic Press.

KEY TERMS AND DEFINITIONS

AGILE: Agile is a group of software development methods in which requirements and solutions evolve through collaboration between the self-organizing, cross-functional teams. It also promotes the adaptive planning, evolutionary development, early delivery, continuous improvement and encourages rapid and flexible response to change.

ATDD: Acceptance Test Driven Development is a practice in which the whole team collaboratively discusses acceptance criteria, with examples, and then distills them into a set of concrete acceptance tests before development begins. There are a variety of test automation frameworks that support defining the tests in advance of the implementation including FIT, Fitnesse and Robot Framework.

BDD: Behavior-driven development combines the general techniques and principles of TDD with ideas from the domain-driven design, object-oriented analysis and design to provide software development and management teams with a domain vocabulary using English language, shared tools and processes to collaborate on software development.

GHERKIN: Gherkin is the format for Cucumber Specifications. Technically speaking it is a small computer language with a well-defined syntax, but it's so simple that you don't have to know how to program in order to use it. It provides keywords like Feature, Scenario, Given, When, Then, And, But to write specification in readable English language.

KANBAN: Kanban is a new technique for managing a software development process in a highly efficient way. An example would be Toyota's "just-in-time" (JIT) production system. Although producing software is a creative activity and therefore different to mass-producing cars, the underlying mechanism for managing the production line can still be applied.

TDD: Test-driven development is a software development process that relies on the repetition of a very short development cycle: first the developer writes an (initially failing) automated test case that defines a desired improvement or new function, then produces the minimum amount of code to pass that test, and finally refactors the new code to acceptable standards.

XP: Extreme Programming is a software development methodology that is intended to improve software quality and responsiveness to changing customer requirements. As a type of agile software development, it advocates frequent "releases" in short development cycles, which is intended to improve productivity and introduce checkpoints at which new customer requirements can be adopted.

APPENDIX: USEFUL CODE SNIPPETS OF VENDING MACHINE SOFTWARE

Feature file written by all the three amigos covering entire scenarios they came up in discussion:

Feature File: "VendingMachine. Feature"

```
Feature: Buying a drink from Vending Machine
In order to buy a drink
As a Vending Machine user
I want to pay the exact price listed
@BuyAnyValidDrinkFromVendingMachine @positive
Scenario: Buy a valid drink for the exact price displayed on vending machine
Given stock for drink water exist
When User puts in exact change for the price and selects the drink
Then Vending Machine should deliver the requested drink
@BuyAValidDrinkForLessAmountThanPrice @negative
Scenario: Buy a valid drink for lesser amount than the expected price
Given stock for drink water exist
When User puts in lesser amount than the price and selects the Drink
Then Vending Machine should alert the user with exception insufficient funds
@BuyAValidDrinkForMoreAmountThanPrice @negative
Scenario: Buy a valid drink for more amount than the expected price
Given stock for drink water exist
When User puts in greater amount than the price and selects the Drink
Then Vending Machine should alert the user with exception exact funds needed
```

The final version of Unit Test Cases in "VendingMachineTest" file is displayed next.

VendingMachineTest.java

Vending Machine Test final version:

```
package bddInAction.VendingMachine.UnitTest;
import org.JUnit.Before;
import org.JUnit.Ignore;
import org.JUnit.Rule;
import org.JUnit.Test;
import org.JUnit.rules.ExpectedException;
import bddInAction.VendingMachine.DrinkService;
import bddInAction.VendingMachine.VendingMachine;
import bddInAction.VendingMachine.UserAcceptanceTest.GlueCode.DrinkServiceS-
tub;
```

```
import java.math.BigDecimal;
import static org.fest.assertions.Assertions.assertThat;

public class VendingMachineTest{
        private VendingMachine vendingMachineUnderTest;

@Rule
public ExpectedException expectedEx = ExpectedException.none();

@Before
public void setup(){
        vendingMachineUnderTest = new VendingMachine(new DrinkServiceStub());}

@Test
public void checkThatWaterDrinkHasAStockOf20() throws Exception{
        int Quantity = vendingMachineUnderTest.checkStock("water");
        assertThat(Quantity).isEqualTo(20);}

@Test
public void BuyAWaterDrinkSuccessfully(){
        int stock = 20;
        vendingMachineUnderTest.buy(new BigDecimal(1.00), "water");
        int quantity = vendingMachineUnderTest.checkStock("water");
        assertThat(quantity).isEqualTo(stock -1);}

@Test
public void checkWaterDrinkStockAfterOnePurchase(){
        vendingMachineUnderTest.buy(new BigDecimal(1.0), "water");
        int quantity = vendingMachineUnderTest.checkStock("water");
        assertThat(quantity).isEqualTo(19);}

@Test
public void checkWaterDrinkStockAfterThreePurchase(){
        int stock = 20;
        for(int i=1;i<4;i++){
        vendingMachineUnderTest.buy(new BigDecimal(1.0), "water");
        int quantity = vendingMachineUnderTest.checkStock("water");
        assertThat(quantity).isEqualTo(stock - i);}}

@Test
public void checkThatCustomerCantBuyWithInsufficientFunds(){
        expectedEx.expect(IllegalStateException.class);
        expectedEx.expectMessage("Transaction Failed: not enough funds");
```

```
        vendingMachineUnderTest.buy(new BigDecimal(0.50), "water");}

@Test
public void checkThatCustomerCantBuyWithMoreFunds(){
        expectedEx.expect(IllegalStateException.class);
        expectedEx.expectMessage("Transaction Failed: please put in exact
amount");
        vendingMachineUnderTest.buy(new BigDecimal(1.50), "water");}
}
```

The final refactored step definition file "VendingMachineSteps" is displayed next.

VendingMachineSteps.Java

Vending Machine step definition finally refactored

```
package bddInAction.VendingMachine.UserAcceptanceTest;

import static org.JUnit.Assert.*;
import static org.fest.assertions.Assertions.assertThat;
import java.math.BigDecimal;
import java.util.ArrayList;
import java.util.HashMap;
import java.util.Iterator;
import java.util.List;
import java.util.Map;
import static org.hamcrest.CoreMatchers.*;
import bddInAction.VendingMachine.Drink;
import bddInAction.VendingMachine.DrinkInventory;
import bddInAction.VendingMachine.VendingMachineImpl;
import bddInAction.VendingMachine.UserAcceptanceTest.GlueCode.DrinkServiceS-
tub;
import cucumber.api.DataTable;
import cucumber.api.java.en.Given;
import cucumber.api.java.en.Then;

public class VendingMachineSteps {
        VendingMachine vendingMachine = new VendingMachine(new DrinkServiceS-
tub());

        private int stock;
        private int quantity;
        Drink drink;
```

```
        String drinkName = null;
        private boolean purchased = false;

List<DrinkInventory> stocksSpecifiedBySpec = new ArrayList<DrinkInventory>();
Map<String, Integer> stockMap = new HashMap<String,Integer>();
Map<String, String> errorMap = new HashMap<String,String>();
List<String> waterComments = new ArrayList<String>();
List<String> softdrinkComments = new ArrayList<String>();
List<String> juiceComments = new ArrayList<String>();

@Given("^stock for <Drink> exist$")
public void stock_for_Drink_exist(DataTable cukeTable) throws Throwable{
        boolean initialized = vendingMachine.initializeStock();
        assertThat(initialized).isTrue();
        stocksSpecifiedBySpec = cukeTable.asList(DrinkInventory.class);

for(DrinkInventory drinkInventory: stocksSpecifiedBySpec){
                drinkName =drinkInventory.getDrink();
                int quantity = vendingMachine.checkStock(drinkName);
        switch (quantity) {
                case 10:
                        assertThat(drinkName).isEqualTo("softdrink");
                        drink = Drink.softdrink;
                        waterComments.add("User wants to buy softdrink!");
                        waterComments.add("Stock initialized for softdrink
");
                break;
                case 15:
                        assertThat(drinkName).isEqualTo("juice");
                        drink = Drink.juice;
                        waterComments.add("User wants to buy juice!");
                        waterComments.add("Stock initialized for juice");
                break;
                case 20:
                        assertThat(drinkName).isEqualTo("water");
                        drink = Drink.water;
                        waterComments.add("User wants to buy water!");
                        waterComments.add("Stock initialized for water");
                break;
                default:
                        System.out.println(" Drink not supported to be ini-
tialized");
                        drink = Drink.unknown;
```

```
                break;
                }
        }
}


@When("^User puts in exact change for the price and selects the drink$")
public void User_puts_in_exact_change_for_the_price_and_selects_the_drink()
throws Throwable {
for(DrinkInventory drinkInventory: stocksSpecifiedBySpec){
        BigDecimal price = drinkInventory.getPrice();
        String name = drinkInventory.getDrink();
        drink = Drink.valueOf(name);
        switch(drink) {
                case water:
                        new DrinkServiceStub();
                        purchased = vendingMachine.buyDrink(new BigDeci-
mal(1.00), drink);
                        waterComments.add("Accepted $ "+price.setScale(2)+"
for "+drink);
                break;
                case softdrink:
                        new DrinkServiceStub();
                        purchased = vendingMachine.buyDrink(new BigDeci-
mal(1.25), drink);
                        softdrinkComments.add("Accepted $ "+price.
setScale(2)+" for "+drink);
                break;
                case juice:
                        new DrinkServiceStub();
                        purchased = vendingMachine.buyDrink(new BigDeci-
mal(1.50), drink);
                        juiceComments.add("Accepted $ "+price.setScale(2)+"
for "+drink);
                break;
                default:
                        System.out.println(" Non supported Drink can't be
purchased");
                        purchased = false;
                break;
                }
        }
}
```

```
@Then("^Vending Machine should deliver the requested drink$")
public void vending_Machine_should_deliver_the_requested_drink() throws Throw-
able {

for(DrinkInventory drinkInventory: stocksSpecifiedBySpec){
        String name = drinkInventory.getDrink();
        drinkName = Drink.valueOf(name);
        switch(drinkName) {
                case water:
                        stock = 20;
                        quantity = vendingMachine.checkStock(drinkName);
                        assertThat(quantity).isEqualTo(stock -1);
                        stockMap.put(drinkName, (stock -1));
                        assertTrue(purchased);
                        waterComments.add(drinkName +" drink is delivered");
                        waterComments.add("");
                break;
                case juice:
                        stock = 15;
                        quantity = vendingMachine.checkStock(drinkName);
                        assertThat(quantity).isEqualTo(stock -1);
                        stockMap.put(drinkName, (stock -1));
                        assertTrue(purchased);
                        juiceComments.add(drinkName+" Drink is delivered");
                        juiceComments.add("");
                break;
                case softdrink:
                        stock = 10;
                        quantity = vendingMachine.checkStock(drinkName);
                        assertThat(quantity).isEqualTo(stock -1);
                        stockMap.put(drinkName, (stock -1));
                        assertTrue(purchased);
                        softdrinkComments.add(drinkName+" Drink is deliv-
ered");
                        softwaredrinkComments.add("");
                break;
                default:
                System.out.println("Non supported Drink and can not be deliv-
ered");
                        assertFalse(purchased);
                break;
                }
        }
```

```
        Iterator<String> water = waterComments.iterator();
        while(water.hasNext()) {
                Object element = water.next();
                System.out.println(element + " ");
                }
        Iterator<String> softdrink = softdrinkComments.iterator();
        while(softdrink.hasNext()) {
                Object element = softdrink.next();
                System.out.println(element + " ");
                }
        Iterator<String> juice = juiceComments.iterator();
        while(juiceComments.hasNext()) {
                Object element = juice.next();
                System.out.println(element + " ");
                }
        }


@Then("^the stock for the drink must be auto decremented$")
public void the_stock_for_the_drink_must_be_auto_decremented() throws Throw-
able {
        assertSame(Integer.valueOf(stockMap.get("water")),Integer.value-
Of(19));
assertSame(Integer.valueOf(stockMap.get("softdrink")),Integer.valueOf(9));
        assertSame(Integer.valueOf(stockMap.get("juice")),Integer.value-
Of(14));
}


@When("^User puts in \"(.*?)\" than the price and selects the <Drink>$")
public void user_puts_in_than_the_price_and_selects_the_Drink(String scenario,
DataTable specTable) throws Throwable {
        stocksSpecifiedBySpec = specTable.asList(DrinkInventory.class);
        Integer count = null;
        if(scenario.equalsIgnoreCase("lesser amount")){
                count = 0;
        }else if(scenario.equalsIgnoreCase("greater amount")){
                count = 1;
        }

switch(count){
        case 0:
                for(DrinkInventory drinkInventory: stocksSpecifiedBySpec){
                        String name = drinkInventory.getDrink();
                        drinkName = Drink.valueOf(name);
```

```
switch(drinkName) {
        case water:
        try{
                new DrinkServiceStub();
                purchased = vendingMachine.
buyDrink(stocksSpecifiedBySpec.get(0).getPrice(),drinkName);
                }catch(RuntimeException e){
                assertThat(e.getMessage().toString(),
is("Transaction Failed: not enough funds"));
                        errorMap.put(drinkName, e.getMessage());
                        System.out.println("Transaction Failed: not
enough funds for "+ drinkName);
}
        break;
        case softdrink:
        try{
                new DrinkServiceStub();
                purchased = vendingMachine.
buyDrink(stocksSpecifiedBySpec.get(1).getPrice(),drinkName);
                }catch(RuntimeException e){ assertThat(e.getMessage().
toString(), is("Transaction Failed: not enough funds"));
                        errorMap.put(drinkName, e.getMessage());
                        System.out.println("Transaction Failed: not
enough funds for "+ drinkName);
}
        break;
        case juice:
                try{
                        new DrinkServiceStub();
                        purchased = vendingMachine.
buyDrink(stocksSpecifiedBySpec.get(2).getPrice(), drinkName);
                        }catch(RuntimeException e){
                                assertThat(e.getMessage().toString(),
is("Transaction Failed: not enough funds"));
                                errorMap.put(drinkName, e.getMes-
sage());
                                System.out.println("Transaction
Failed: not enough funds for "+ drinkName);
}
        break;
        default:
                System.out.println(" Non supported Drink can't be
purchased");
```

```
                    purchased = false;
             break;}}

break;

case 1:
                              for(DrinkInventory drinkInventory: stocks-
SpecifiedBySpec){
                                   String name = drinkInventory.get-
Drink();

                                   drink = Drink.valueOf(name);
                                   switch(drink) {
                                        case water:
                                             try{
                                                  new Drink-
ServiceStub();
                                                  purchased =
vendingMachine.buyDrink(stocksSpecifiedBySpec.get(0).getPrice(),drink);
                                                  }
catch(RuntimeException e){
                                                            ass
ertThat(e.getMessage().toString(), is("Transaction Failed: please put in exact
amount")); errorMap.put("water", e.getMessage());
                                                            Sys-
tem.out.println("Transaction Failed: please put in exact amount for "+ drink);
}
                                        break;
                                        case softdrink:
                                             try{
                                                  new DrinkServiceS-
tub();
                                                  purchased = vending-
Machine.buyDrink(stocksSpecifiedBySpec.get(1).getPrice(),drink);
                                                  }
catch(RuntimeException e){
                                                       assertThat(
e.getMessage().toString(), is("Transaction Failed: please put in exact
amount"));
                                                       errorMap.
put(drink, e.getMessage());
System.out.println("Transaction Failed: please put in exact amount for "+
drink);
                                        }
```

```
                                        break;
                                        case juice:
                                                try{
                                                        new DrinkServiceS-
tub();

                                                        purchased = vending-
Machine.buyDrink(stocksSpecifiedBySpec.get(2).getPrice(),drink);
                                                }
catch(RuntimeException e){

                                                                assertThat(
e.getMessage().toString(), is("Transaction Failed: please put in exact
amount"));

                                                                errorMap.
put(drink, e.getMessage());

                                                                System.out.
println("Transaction Failed: please put in exact amount for "+ drink);
                                                }
                                        break;
                                        default:
                                                System.out.println("
Non supported Drink can't be purchased");

                                                purchased = false;
                                        break;
                                        }
                                }
                        break;
                        }
                }
        }
```

Chapter 14
The Agility of Agile Methodology for Teaching and Learning Activities

Deshinta Arrova Dewi Dewi
INTI International University, Malaysia

Mohana Muniandy
INTI International University, Malaysia

ABSTRACT

This paper presents the review of literatures that shows the contribution of the agile methodology towards teaching and learning environment at university level. Teaching and learning at university has since migrated from traditional learning to active learning methodology where students are expected to learn by doing rather than listening passively to lectures alone. The agile methodology naturally has promoted the active participation of team members during system development phases. Some literature have proposed ways of adopting agile into active learning to improve teaching and learning processes and have highlighted this method as a great success. We would like to highlight how efficient the agile concept is in tackling several situations in academic learning as shown by an interesting mapping of agile principles to the classroom environment. We also offer options for the agile evaluation framework to consider academic environment as a tool to obtain the agile performance feedback.

1. INTRODUCTION

Traditional teaching and learning have most often than not neglected the concept of active teaching and learning in academic environment. For decades, the academic community has been conducting researches and experiments in order to increase students' participation during their learning in the classroom (Cubric, 2013). Recent studies show the usage of technology, team discussion and sharing knowledge session have become favorite options to promote this active learning concept. Where the lecturer is the immediate source of the knowledge in the traditional learning, the active learning concept encourages lecturer to become the facilitator between the students and the knowledge itself. Active learning requires students

DOI: 10.4018/978-1-4666-9858-1.ch014

to be independent in getting the basic knowledge by searching the resources online or offline and doing discussion with classmates (Dillard., 2012; Hagan, 2012; Michael., 2007; Solomon., 2013). Lecturers provide clarification on what the students have learnt and emphasize more on providing higher level of thinking and challenges. The relationship of lecturer, knowledge and student is reflected in Figure 1.

The agile methodology has been introduced in the academic environment as a topic or subject for computer science students to learn about developing good software in a timely manner to satisfy client's requirement. The agile methodology underlines direct and frequent communication between client and developer through its incremental processes. The proposed solutions are evolved through communication and collaboration of organizations and teams. Therefore, the key success of agile methodology relies on communication among team members and the ability to adapt to rapid changes (A.H.W. Chun, 2004; D. Monett, 2013; J. C. Stewart, C. S. DeCusatis, K. Kidder, & and K.M. Anne, 2009) .

As teaching agile is part of the curriculum in many computing classes, some educational practitioners have started research on the efficient techniques to teach any subjects to students using agile methodology. By embracing a variety of tools and techniques, teaching using agile method has become an interesting topic of discussion among lecturers and instructors. Some lecturers and instructors have begun conducting experiments in teaching by adopting the agile concept itself.

2. RESEARCH QUESTIONS

The present research aims to collect previous works that have examined the use of agile methodology to improve the teaching and learning delivery. The following research questions (RQ) are raised therefore:

RQ1. What are the main goals of the previous researches?

Figure 1. Traditional Learning

Figure 2. Active Learning

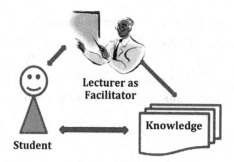

RQ2. What are suggested approaches and methods used?

RQ3. How the previous research is being conducted?

RQ4. What are case studies or datasets are used?

RQ5. Would it be possible to carry forward the previous research into a new method in teaching and learning?

3. AGILE PRINCIPLES AND CLASSROOM ENVIRONMENT

John C. Stewart is the main author of a paper (J. C. Stewart et al., 2009) that exposed his study regarding evaluating agile principle in active and cooperative learning environment. This is a big effort that may offer the agile evaluation framework in an actual classroom environment and may reflect the same concept of what is known as agile principle. Starting from extracted values available in the Agile Manifesto, the study proposes the new values of agile pedagogy that constitute modern teaching and learning methodology.

The values of the agile pedagogy extracted from the values of agile manifesto are:

1. Students over traditional processes and tools. (Agile manifesto value: Individuals and interactions over processes and tools).
2. Working project over comprehensive documentation (Agile manifesto value: Working software over comprehensive documentation)
3. Student and instructor collaboration over rigid course syllabi. (Agile manifesto value: customer collaboration over contract negotiation)
4. Responding to feedback rather than following a plan. (Agile manifesto value: Responding to change over following a plan).

There are 12 items of agile principles that is found to be well-suited and adoptable towards classroom environment. The mapping is shown below, in table 1.

This mapping has given the idea on the compatibility of agile manifesto in a pedagogy environment. From here, the study suggests framework of practices that promote teaching and learning to become more agile since it effectively focuses on student-centric approach. Besides that, the similarities of software development methodology and educational methodology are effortlessly seen in Table 1.

4. AGILE METHODOLOGY TOWARDS TEACHING AND LEARNING TECHNIQUES

Mario Vacca (D. Lembo & M. Vacca, 2012) from Italy proposed Extreme Programming instructional design that combines good practices formulated from project based learning and agile instructional design. This research design accommodates the inadequacy of current instructional design to face challenges of 21st century way of teaching and learning. Not only as an instructional design, but this research has also attempted the agile management and learning project. At this point, the agile and extreme programming principles are adapted to the instructional design context and the problem based

Table 1. Mapping of agile manifesto to pedagogical environment adopted from (J. C. Stewart et al., 2009)

Principles of the Agile Manifesto	Corollary to the Pedagogical Environment
Our highest priority is to satisfy the customer through early and continuous delivery of valuable software.	Our highest priority is to prepare the student to contribute to an organization through continuous delivery of course components that reflects competence.
Welcome changing requirements, even late in development. Agile processes harness change for the customer's competitive advantage.	The instructor and students welcome and adapt to changes even late in the semester. Agile pedagogical methods use problems and change as an opportunity to facilitate learning and better develop marketable skills in the students.
Deliver working software frequently, from a couple of weeks to a couple of months, with a preference to the shorter timescale.	Requiring working deliverables from the students over short time periods allowing for frequent feedback and guided problem solving and experimentation.
Business people and developers must work together daily throughout the project.	There is iterative interaction between the instructor and students (or student groups) throughout the course.
Build projects around motivated individuals. Give them the environment and support they need, and trust them to get the job done.	Trust that most students are motivated. Give them the environment and support necessary for them to be successful.
The most efficient and effective method of conveying information to and within a development team is face-to-face conversation.	To the extent possible, allow for direct face-to-face interaction with students or student groups.
Working software is the primary measure of progress.	Working deliverables (i.e. models, software, project deliverables, presentations, etc.) are the primary measure of student progress (not necessarily midterm & final exams that require rote learning and memorization).
Agile processes promote sustainable development. The sponsors, developers, and users should be able to maintain a constant pace indefinitely.	The cooperative learning environment where students actively seek guidance and tools to solve problems is the basis for teaching the skills needed for life-long learning.
Continuous attention to technical excellence and good design enhances agility.	Continuous attention to technical excellence and good design enhances learning.
Simplicity--the art of maximizing the amount of work not done--is essential.	While in education there is some value in exploring subjects in-depth just because there is student interest, however, understanding the problem and solving it simply and clearly is essential
The best architectures, requirements, and designs emerge from self-organizing teams.	Student groups and teams should self-organize, but all should participate equally in the effort of learning.
At regular intervals, the team reflects on how to become more effective, then tunes and adjusts its behavior accordingly.	At regular intervals, the students and instructor reflect and offer feedback on how to be more effective. All stakeholders then adjust accordingly with the goal of being more effective.

learning. The instructional design process is therefore viewed as constituted by roles (students, teachers and headmaster, parents, consultants, etc.) each of them performing some activities (lecturing, checking, solving problems, discussions, exercises, personal study, presentation production, etc.). The result was reported as successful in introducing new concepts such as collective instructional design, active transparency and active role of students and their parents.

Alvaro Soria (A. Soria, M. R. Campo, & G. Rodriguez, 2012)from Argentina proposed technique to improve the delivery of Software Engineering subject in university by using agile management. This study was intended to address the problem and bridge the gap between academic and professional context. The widespread of agile approaches such as Scrum and Agile Coaching are become teaching models able to cover the other model such as RUP (rational unified process). By using CMMI (Capability Maturity

Model Integration) as assessment reference, this evolutionary process accomplished high level of CMMI maturity for students in developing software.

Dagmar Monet (D. Monett, 2013) from Germany introduced agile project-based teaching and learning where the experiences were reportedly undertaken for 4 years. The project-based approach allows students to work with realistic project through which they learn agile concepts more efficiently by doing collaborative and self-organizing team.

John C. Stewart et al (J. C. Stewart et al., 2009) states that Jigsaw method can be likened to cooperative learning. Using Jigsaw method, students work in small groups that primarily do some acquisition and presentation of new materials, review or participate in informed debate. Stewart et al shows that Jigsaw has major correspondence with XP and Scrum in agile concept. Group members depend on their own collaboration to accomplish tasks. Stewart et al mentioned that the effective group members naturally assemble different strength and expertise, experience and knowledge, perspective and personalities. The role of lecturer has changed dramatically from source of knowledge to facilitator that discusses alternatives when groups are unhappy with their original plan, for example. Leading the class to summarize their discussion, making sure all group members participate and concluding the learning points are other roles of the lecturer.

Astonishingly, the agile concept has been adopted in e-learning environment as well. Michael Tesar is the main author and Stefani Sieber the co-author of (M. Tesar, 2010). Tesar and Sieber utilized agile e-learning environment to achieve high quality blended learning scenarios. The agile manifesto turns out to be a guideline for the agile e-learning scenario. The comparison of traditional project management, agile manifesto and the inferred principles for agile e-learning development is presented in Table 2.

On the other hand, the ATLM (The Agile Teaching and Learning Methodology) has been designed and used in the City University of Hong Kong (A.H.W. Chun, 2004). This paper explains the process architecture and objectives of the ATLM that emphasizes on agility, communication and learning processes. The e-learning platform and the technologies used provide great support on modern collaboration and knowledge sharing technologies. Some popular applications are introduced on the agile e-learning concept such as blogging, instant messaging, discussion forum, video conferencing, wiki and XML RSS.

Teaching cycle and learning cycle are the main concepts of ATLM that consists of iterative processes as shown below in Figure 3. Teaching cycle is about adjusting and monitoring lecture activities and tutorials, while the learning cycle is about sharing, practicing what has been learnt in assignments and independent studying. Adjusting and monitoring is actually the lecturers' effort to monitor students' progress and provide/obtain feedback as the main input for the next teaching cycle. The sharing, practices and independent study is students' effort to acquire knowledge, skill and enhance the learning experience. The ATLM is definitely student centric with the lecturer as facilitator.

Table 2. The agile e-learning development adopted by (M. Tesar, 2010)

Traditional Project Management (Agile Manifesto,2010)	Manifesto for Agile Software Development (Agile Manifesto, 2010)	Agile E-Learning Development
Process and Tools	Individuals and Interactions	Personalized Learning Processes
Comprehensive Documentation	Working Software	Usability of Learning Utilities
Contract Negotiation	Customer Collaboration	Learner Centered Design
Following a Plan	Responding to Change	Flexible Course Concept

Figure 3. Iterative Processes for ATLM adopted from (A.H.W. Chun, 2004)

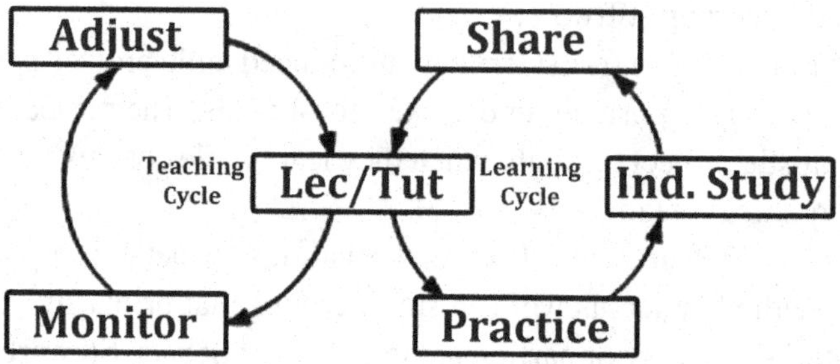

This paper has also stressed the teaching and learning best practices that consist of learning by sharing, teaching how to learn and using feedback to make necessary changes in ATLM when required. Feedback actually makes the ATLM more agile.

Table 3 depicts information about the overall literatures upon research questions 1,2 and 3. Majority they aim improvement for teaching excellent while (Hagan, 2012) provide insights about the current practice of the agile performance review and proposed solutions to achieve a better review.

Various approaches and methods have been employed for many types of learning and it promises successful results. Most previous works use mapping concept of agile methodology and learning activities to ensure the proposed framework is applicable. Literature (D. Lembo & M. Vacca, 2012) even

Table 3. The previous works towards the research questions 1-2-3

References	RQ1 Improve Teaching & Learning	RQ2 Approaches/ Methods RQ3 Data Sets or Case Studies
(J. C. Stewart et al., 2009)	√	Cooperative Learning with Jigsaw Methods for the Pace University students populations
(A.H.W. Chun, 2004)	√	E-learning as platform of implementing ATLM for computer science courses
(D. Lembo and M. Vacca, 2012)	√	New agile instructional design methodology by combining agile methodologies and some features of XP
(M. Tesar, 2010)	√	Using agile concept for blended learning scenario with the adoption of e-learning scenario
(A. Soria et al., 2012)	√	Teaching students effectively with the Scrum and agile coaching principles
(D. Monett, 2013)	√	Agile-based project in courses for the students in Berlin School of Economics and Law
(Cubric, 2013)	√	A new method for teaching agile project management and similar subjects in higher education.
(Solomon., 2013)	√	An innovative method of teaching agile by using agile principles
(Michael., 2007)	√	Agile approaches as alternative on learning
(Hagan, 2012)	Improving current performance review in a company	Reflections and new solution of doing things right for agile performance review.
(Dillard., 2012)	√	Flipped classroom with agile methodologies to promote problem solving in class.

came out with new systematic instructional design that is essential for teachers/lecturers to carry out their topic of the day.

The other research questions are addressed by literatures (J. C. Stewart et al., 2009) to (Cubric, 2013). The summary is presented in Table 4.

Our institution INTI International University has rolled out student centred learning in May 2010. Centre for Instructional and Technology Support (CITS) has conducted trainings to support lecturers in implementing student centred learning teaching strategies. Listed below are some of the strategies introduced to the lecturers.

1. Small Group Discussion
2. Problem-based Learning
3. Blended Learning
4. Cooperative Learning
5. Online Forum Discussion
6. Debate
7. Drama and Project
8. Field Trip
9. Role Playing
10. Peer Collaboration Learning
11. Reciprocal Peer Tutoring
12. Podcast
13. Lecture and Tutorial

The adoption of agile methodology by previous works proves to be in line with the strategies and justifies the flexibility of agile methodology to be adopted in the universities.

The mapping of literatures towards student centred learning strategies is shown in Table 5.

Table 4. The previous works towards present research questions

References	Addressing Research Questions
(J. C. Stewart et al., 2009)	RQ-1, RQ-2, RQ-3, RQ-4, RQ-5
(A.H.W. Chun, 2004)	RQ-1, RQ-2, RQ-3, RQ-4, RQ-5
(D. Lembo and M. Vacca, 2012)	RQ-1, RQ-2, RQ-3, RQ-4, RQ-5
(M. Tesar, 2010)	RQ-1, RQ-2, RQ-3, RQ-4, RQ-5
(A. Soria et al., 2012)	RQ-1, RQ-2, RQ-3, RQ-4, RQ-5
(D. Monett, 2013)	RQ-1, RQ-2, RQ-3, RQ-4, RQ-5
(Cubric, 2013)	RQ-1, RQ-2, RQ-3, RQ-4, RQ-5
(Solomon., 2013)	RQ-1, RQ-2, RQ-4, RQ-5
(Michael., 2007)	RQ-1, RQ-2, RQ-4, RQ-5
(Hagan, 2012)	RQ-1, RQ-2, RQ-4, RQ-5
(Dillard., 2012)	RQ-1, RQ-2, RQ-4, RQ-5

Table 5. The student centred strategies towards agile based teaching and learning

Student Centred Strategies	References
14. Small Group Discussion	(A. Soria et al., 2012; A.H.W. Chun, 2004; Cubric, 2013; D. Lembo and M. Vacca, 2012; D. Monett, 2013; Dillard., 2012; Hagan, 2012; Hagan., 2012; J. C. Stewart et al., 2009; M. Tesar, 2010; Michael., 2007; Solomon., 2013)
15. Problem-based Learning	(A. Soria et al., 2012; A.H.W. Chun, 2004; Cubric, 2013; D. Lembo and M. Vacca, 2012; D. Monett, 2013; J. C. Stewart et al., 2009; M. Tesar, 2010)
16. Blended Learning	(M. Tesar, 2010)
17. Cooperative Learning	(J. C. Stewart et al., 2009)
18. Online Forum Discussion	(A.H.W. Chun, 2004; M. Tesar, 2010)
19. Debate	-
20. Drama and Project	-
21. Field Trip	-
22. Role Playing	-
23. Peer Collaboration Learning	(A. Soria et al., 2012; A.H.W. Chun, 2004; Cubric, 2013; D. Lembo and M. Vacca, 2012; D. Monett, 2013; Dillard., 2012; Hagan, 2012; Hagan., 2012; J. C. Stewart et al., 2009; M. Tesar, 2010; Michael., 2007; Solomon., 2013)
24. Reciprocal Peer Tutoring	-
25. Podcast	-
26. Lecture and Tutorial	(A. Soria et al., 2012; A.H.W. Chun, 2004; Cubric, 2013; D. Lembo and M. Vacca, 2012; D. Monett, 2013; Dillard., 2012; Hagan, 2012; Hagan., 2012; J. C. Stewart et al., 2009; M. Tesar, 2010; Michael., 2007; Solomon., 2013)

5. CONCLUSION

From the above discussion, we can see how the agile manifesto and its values have greatly influenced and improved the variety of teaching and learning in university that promotes active learning. Consequently, those experiences have offered some points on how to exploit the opportunity to use learning environment to evaluate agile principles since both of software development and teaching and learning share almost similar values in its operation.

Research in this paper is generally conducted as motivation for our university research to explore the alternative teaching and learning model to support active learning environment by adopting agile concept.

At the moment, our university looks into the concept of flipped classroom and according to our preliminary research flipped classroom is also related with agile processes with regards to daily scrum meeting, sprint planning meeting, sprint and sprint review and lastly sprint retrospective meeting. This future work is similar with an article written by Sarah Dillard (Dillard., 2012). Our future research will look into this direction as part of teaching and learning improvement in the context of flipped classroom.

REFERENCES

Chun, A. H. W. (2004). *The Agile Teaching / Learning Methodology and its e-Learning Platform. In Lecture Notes in Computer Science-Advances in Web-Based Learning* (Vol. 3143, pp. 11–18). Springer-Verlag Heidelberg.

Cubric, M. (2013). An agile method for teaching agile in business schools. *The International Journal of Management Education, 11*(3), 119–131. doi:10.1016/j.ijme.2013.10.001

Dillard., S. (2012). Lean but agile: rethink workforce planning and gain a true competitive edge. *Choice Reviews Online, 49*(12). doi: 10.5860/choice.49-6982

Hagan, R. (2012). *Agile Performance Reviews*. Academic Press.

Hagan, R. (2012). Agile Performance Review. *Microform & Digitization Review, 41*(3-4). doi:10.1515/mir-2012-0026

Lembo, D., & Vacca, M. (2012). Project Based Learning + Agile Instructional Design = Extreme Programming based Instructional Design Methodology for Collaborative Learning. *Acta Informatica Medica, Depardemento di Informatica, Sapienza, Universita di Roma, Tech. Rep.N.8, 20*(1), 15. doi: 10.5455/aim.2012.20.15-17

Michael. (2007). *Agile Learning – an alternative model*. Academic Press.

Monett, D. (2013). *Agile Project-Based Teaching and Learning*. Paper presented at the 11th International Conference on Software Engineering Research and Practice.

Solomon, C. F. (2013). *Teaching in an Agile Manner*. Bloomsbury Academic.

Soria, A., Campo, M. R., & Rodriguez, G. (2012). *Improving Software Engineering Teaching by Introducing Agile Management*. Paper presented at the INCOSE International Symposium, 13th Argentine Symposium on Software Engineering, La Plata, Argentina.

Stewart, J. C., DeCusatis, C. S., Kidder, K., Massi, J. R., & Anne, K. M. (2009). Evaluating Agile Principles in Active and Cooperative Learning. *Toxicology Letters, 191*(2-3), 231–235. doi:10.1016/j.toxlet.2009.09.003 PMID:19748556

Tesar, M., & Sieber, S. (2010). Managing Blended Learning Scenarios by Using Agile e-Learning Development. *International Association for the Development of the Information Society, Freiburg, Germany, 26*(2), 124–129. doi:10.1177/0266666910368123

KEY TERMS AND DEFINITIONS

Acceptance Test-Driven Development: Acceptance Test-Driven Development (ATDD) is a development methodology based on communication between the business customers, the developers, and the testers. ATDD encompasses many of the same practices as Specification by Example, Behavior Driven Development (BDD), Example-Driven Development (EDD), and Story Test-Driven Development (SDD). All these processes aid developers and testers in understanding the customer's needs prior to implementation and allow customers to be able to converse in their own domain language.

Extreme Programming: Extreme Programming (XP) is an agile methodology that specifically emphasizes the use of agile technical practices (e.g. Test Driven Development) for the success of an agile project. Practical experience shows that XP complements Scrum well and both the methods work well together.

User Stories: User stories are part of an agile approach that helps shift the focus from writing about requirements to talking about them. All agile user stories include a written sentence or two and, more importantly, a series of conversations about the desired functionality.

User-Centered Design (UCD): User-centered design is a process (not restricted to interfaces or technologies) in which the needs, wants, and limitations of end users of a product, service or process are given extensive attention at each stage of the design process. User-centered design can be characterized as a multi-stage problem solving process that not only requires designers to analyse and foresee how users are likely to use a product, but also to test the validity of their assumptions with regard to user behaviour in real world tests with actual users. Such testing is necessary as it is often very difficult for the designers of a product to understand intuitively what a first-time user of their design experiences, and what each user's learning curve may look like.

Waterfall Model: A sequential design, used in software development processes, in which progress is seen as flowing steadily downwards (like a waterfall) through the phases of Conception, Initiation, Analysis, Design, Construction, Testing, Deployment, and Maintenance.

Compilation of References

Abrahamsson, P., Conboy, K., & Wang, X. (2009). 'Lots done, more to do': The current state of agile systems development research. *European Journal of Information Systems*, *18*(4), 281–284. doi:10.1057/ejis.2009.27

Adamopoulos, A. (2012). *Roadmap for Agile Success*. Retrieved from http://www.emergn.com/insights/blogs/roadmap-for-agile-success/

Adkins, L. (2010). *Coaching agile teams: a companion for ScrumMasters, agile coaches, and project managers in transition*. Addison-Wesley Professional.

Adolph, S. (2014). *Agile BA in Practice: Using Cadence to Leave Things to the Last Responsible Moment*. Retrieved from http://www.developmentknowledge.com/index.php/blog/141-agile-ba-in-practice-using-cadence-to-leave-things-to-the-last-responsible-moment

Adolph, S., Hall, W., & Kruchten, P. (2011). Using grounded theory to study the experience of software development. *Empirical Software Engineering*, *16*(4), 487–513. doi:10.1007/s10664-010-9152-6

Adzic, G. (2009). *Bridging the Communication Gap- Specification By Example and Agile Acceptance Testing*. Academic Press.

Adzic, G. (2011). Specification by Example: How successful teams deliver the right software. *Childhood Education*, *87*(4), 302–303. doi:10.1080/00094056.2011.10523198

Ågerfalk, J., Fitzgerald, B., & In, O. P. (2006). *Flexible and distributed software processes: old petunias in new bowls*. Paper presented at the Communications of the ACM.

Agile Manifesto. (2014, December 12). Retrieved from http://www.agilemanifesto.org

Agile Methodology in Fixed Price projects. Global Advanced Research Journal of Engineering, Technology and Innovation. (2013). *Systemic Foresight Methodology, 2*, 243-249.

Ahmed, E., & Sidky, A. (2009). 25 percent Ahead of Schedule and just at "Step 2" of the SAMI. In *Proceedings of the 2009 Agile Conference*. IEEE Computer Society. doi:10.1109/AGILE.2009.63

Aker, S., Audin, C., Lindy, E., Marcelli, L., Massart, J. P., & Okur, Y. (2013). Lessons Learned and Challenges of Developing the NATO Air Command and Control Information Services. In *Proceedings of International Systems Conference (SysCon 2013)*. Orlando, FL: IEEE. doi:10.1109/SysCon.2013.6549974

Ali Babar, M., Brown, A. W., & Mistrik, I. (2014). Agile Software Architecture. *Communication Design Quarterly Review*, *2*(2), 43–47. doi:10.1145/2597469.2597477

Ambler, S. (2002). Agile modeling: effective practices for extreme programming and the unified process. Academic Press.

Ambler, S. (2014). *Generalizing Specialists: Improving Your IT Career Skills*. Academic Press.

Ambler, S. W. (2008). Tailoring Usability into Agile Software Developement Projects. In E. Law, E. Hvannberg, & G. Cocklon (Eds.), Measuring Usability (pp. 75-95). London: Springer-Verlag.

Ambler, S. W. (2009a). *Ambysoft*. Retrieved 9 September, 2014, from http://www.ambysoft.com/surveys/stateOfI-TUnion200907.html

Ambler, S. W. (2010). *The Agile Maturity Model (AMM)*. Retrieved from http://www.drdobbs.com/architecture-and-design/the-agile-maturity-model-amm/224201005

Ambler, S. W. (2015, March 21). *Introduction to Agile Usability: User Experience (UX) Activities on Agile Development Projects*. Retrieved from Agile Modeling: http://agilemodeling.com/essays/agileUsability.htm

Ambler, S.W. (2013). *What Was Final Status*. Academic Press.

Ambler, S. W. (2002). *Agile modeling. In Effective Practices for Extreme Programming and the Unified Process*. New York: Wiley & Sons.

Ambler, S. W. (2003). Usage Scenarios. *An Agile Introduction, 2753*, 208.

Ambler, S. W. (2009b). *The Agile Scaling Model (ASM)*. Adapting Agile Methods for Complex Environments.

Ambler, S. W. (2010). *Agile Modeling*. Ambisoft.

Ambler, S. W. (2014). *2014 Agile Adoption Mini-Survey*. AmbySoft.

Ambler, S. W., & Lines, M. (2012). *Disciplined agile delivery: A practitioner's guide to agile software delivery in the enterprise*. IBM Press.

Anderson, D. (2004). *Feature-Driven Development: towards a TOC, Lean and Six Sigma solution for software engineering, Theory of Constraints*. International Certification Organization, Microsoft.

Anderson, L., Alleman, G. B., Beck, K., Blotner, J., Cunningham, W., Poppendieck, M., & Wirfs-Brock, R. (2003). *Agile management - an oxymoron?: who needs managers anyway?* Paper presented at the Companion of the 18th annual ACM SIGPLAN conference on Object-oriented programming, systems, languages, and applications, Anaheim, CA. doi:10.1145/949344.949410

Andrea, J. (2005). If the Shoe Doesn't Fit – Agile Requirements for Stepsister Projects. Better Software Magazine. *Molecular Pharmacology*. doi:10.1124/mol.105.020230

Andrzeevski, S. (2007). Experiencing Report 'Offshore XP for PDA development'. In *Proceedings of Agile Conference (Agile 2007)*. Washington, DC: IEEE

Aoyama, M. (1998). Web-based Agile software development. *IEEE Software, 15*(6), 56–65. doi:10.1109/52.730844

AS-22 BNL. (1968). *Brookhaven National Laboratory*. BNL 50106 (AS-22). T. Brookhaven National Laboratory.

Atlas, A. (2009). Accidental Adoption: The Story of Scrum at Amazon.com. In *Proceedings of Agile Conference (AGILE '09)*. Chicago, IL: IEEE. doi:10.1109/AGILE.2009.10

Atlassian. (2013). *Agile maturity – How agile is your organization?* Retrieved Nov. 2013, from http://blogs.atlassian.com/2013/11/agile-maturity-how-agile-is-your-organization/

Augustine, S. (2005). Managing agile projects. Prentice Hall.

Awad, M. A. (2005). *A comparison between agile and traditional software development methodologies.* University of Western Australia.

Babar, M. A. (2009). An Exploratory Study of Architectural Practices and Challenges inUsing Agile Software Development Approaches. In *Proceedings of Software Architecture, 2009 & European Conference on SoftwareArchitecture (WICSA/ECSA 2009). Joint Working IEEE/IFIP.* Cambridge: IEEE.

Babb, J., Hoda, R., & Norbjerg, J. (2014). Embedding reflection and learning into agile software development. *IEEE Software, 31*(4), 51–57. doi:10.1109/MS.2014.54

Babinet, E., & Ramanathan, R. (2008). *Dependency management in a large agile environment.* Paper presented at the Agile 2008 Conference. doi:10.1109/Agile.2008.58

Baker, S. W. (2005). Formalizing Agility: An Agile Organization's Journey toward CMMI Accreditation. In *Proceedings of the Agile Development Conference (ADC'05).* Denver, CO: IEEE. doi:10.1109/ADC.2005.27

Bass, J. M. (2013). Agile Method Tailoring in Distributed Enterprises: Product Owner Teams. In *Proceedings of 8th International Conference on Global Software Engineering (ICGSE 2013).* Bari: IEEE. doi:10.1109/ICGSE.2013.27

Bass, J. M. (2014). Scrum Master Activities: Process Tailoring in Large Enterprise Projects. In *Proceedings of 9th International Conference on Global Software Engineering (ICGSE 2014).* Shanghai: IEEE. doi:10.1109/ICGSE.2014.24

Bayona, S., Calvo-Manzano, J. A., & San Feliu, T. (2012). Critical success factors in software process improvement: A systematic review. In A. Mas, A. Mesquida, T. Rout, R. V. O'Connor, & A. Dorling (Eds.), *Vol. SPICE 2012, CCIS 290* (pp. 1–12). Palma. doi:10.1007/978-3-642-30439-2_1

Beck, K., Beedle, M., Van Bennekum, A., Cockburn, A., Cunningham, W., Fowler, M., & Jeffries, R. (2001). *Manifesto for agile software development.* Retrieved from http://agilemanifesto.org/

Beck, K., Beedle, M., van Bennekum, A., Cockburn, A., Cunningham, W., Fowler, M., . . . Sutherland, J. (2001). *Agile Manifesto.* Retrieved May 2014, from www.agilemanifesto.org

Beck, K., Cockburn, A., Jeffries, R., & Highsmith, J. (2001). *Agile manifesto.* Retrieved May 2014, from http://www.agilemanifesto.org

Beck, K. (2000). *Extreme programming explained: embrace change.* Addison-Wesley Professional.

Beck, K., & Andres, C. (2004). *Extreme Programming Explained: Embrace Change* (2nd ed.). Boston, MA: Addison-Wesley Professional.

Begel, A., & Nagappan, N. (2007). Usage and perceptions of agile software development in an industrial context: An exploratory study. In *Empirical Software Engineering and Measurement*, (pp. 255-264). doi: 10.1109/esem.2007.84

Begel, A., & Nagappan, N. (2007). Usage and Perceptions of Agile Software Development in an Industrial Context: An Exploratory Study. In *Proceedings of First International Symposium on Empirical Software Engineering and Measurement (ESEM 2007).* Madrid: IEEE. doi:10.1109/ESEM.2007.12

Bell, T. E., & Thayer, T. A. (1976). 2nd International Conference on Software Engineering. *Computer, 9*(8), 9–12. doi:10.1109/C-M.1976.218669

Benefield, G. (2008). Rolling out Agile in a Large Enterprise. In *Proceedings of the 41st Hawaii International Conference on System Sciences.* Waikoloa, HI: IEEE. doi:10.1109/HICSS.2008.382

Benington, H. D. (1983). Production of Large Computer Programs. *IEEE Annals of the History of Computing, 5* (4), 350–361. doi:10.1109/MAHC.1983.10102

Berger, B., & Rumpe, B. (2010). Supporting Agile Change Management by Scenario-BasedRegression Simulation. *IEEE Transactions on Intelligent Transportation Systems, 11*(2), 504–509. doi:10.1109/TITS.2010.2044571

Berger, J. (2013). *Contagious: Why things catch on.* Simon and Schuster.

Bhalerao, S., & Ingle, M. (2007). Mapping SDLC phase with Various Agile Methods. *International conference on Advances in Computer Vision and information Technology*, (pp. 318-325). Aurangabad.

Bhalerao, S., Puntambekar, D., & Ingle, M. (2009). Generalizing Agile Software Development Life Cycle. *International Journal on Computer Science and Engineering, 1* (3), 222–226.

Blank, S. (2013). *The four steps to the epiphany.* K&S Ranch.

Blank, S. (2013). Why the lean start-up changes everything. *Harvard Business Review, 91*(5), 63–72. doi:10.4324/9780203104569

Blocher, M., Blumberg, S., & Laartz, J. (2012). *Delivering Large-Scale IT Projects on Time, on Budget.* And on Value.

Boehm, B. (2006). A view of 20th and 21st century software engineering. In *Proceedings of the 28th international conference on Software engineering.*

Boehm, B., & Turner, R. (2004). *Balancing agility and discipline: Evaluating and integrating agile and plan-driven methods.* Paper presented at the Software Engineering. doi:10.1109/ICSE.2004.1317503

Boehm, B. (1986). A spiral model of software development and enhancement. *ACM SIGSOFT Software Engineering Notes, ACM, 11*(4), 22–42. doi:10.1145/12944.12948

Boehm, B. (2002). Get ready for agile methods, with care. *Computer, 35*(1), 64–69. doi:10.1109/2.976920

Boehm, B. W. (1988). A spiral model of software development and enhancement. *Computer, 21*(5), 61–72. doi:10.1109/2.59

Bogard, J. (2012). Why I'm done with Scrum. In Combining Kanban and Scrum -- Lessons from a Team of Sysadmins (pp. 99–102). LosTechieshoughtWorks.

Bogsnes, B. (2008). *Implementing beyond budgeting: unlocking the performance potential.* John Wiley & Sons.

Borland. (2009). *Borland agile assessment.* Retrieved Dec. 2013, from http://borland.typepad.com/agile_transformation/2009/03/borland-agile-assessment-2009.html

Brock, J., & Hobbs, P. E. (2010). *Agile Transformation – rethinking IT strategy in an uncertain world.* Retrieved from https://www-304.ibm.com/easyaccess/fileserve?contentid=208473

Brooks, F. (1995). The Mythical Man-Month. *IEEE Software, 12*(5), 57–60. doi:10.1109/MS.1995.10042

Brown, A. W., Ambler, S., & Royce, W. (2013). Agility at scale: Economic governance, measured improvement, and disciplined delivery. In *Proceedings 35th International Conference of Software Engineering (ICSE)*, San Francisco, CA: IEEE. doi:10.1109/ICSE.2013.6606636

Brown, T. (2009). *Change by design: how design thinking transforms organizations and inspires innovation.* New York: HarperBusiness.

Cantor, M., & Royce, W. (2013). Economic Governance of Software Delivery. *IEEE Software, 31*(1), 54–61. doi:10.1109/MS.2013.102

Cao, L., Mohan, K., Xu, P., & Balasubramaniam, R. (2004). How Extreme does Extreme Programming Have to be? Adapting XP Practices to Large-scale Projects. In *Proceedings of the 37th Hawaii International Conference on System Sciences*, Waikoloa, HI: IEEE.

Cao, L., & Ramesh, B. (2008). Agile requirements engineering practices: An empirical study. *Software, IEEE, 25*(1), 60–67. doi:10.1109/MS.2008.1

Chan, F. K., & Thong, J. Y. (2009). Acceptance of agile methodologies: A critical review and conceptual framework. *Decision Support Systems, 46*(4), 803–814. doi:10.1016/j.dss.2008.11.009

Chow, T., & Cao, D.-B. (2008). A survey study of critical success factors in agile software projects. *Journal of Systems and Software, 81*(6), 961–971. doi:10.1016/j.jss.2007.08.020

Chun, A. H. W. (2004). *The Agile Teaching / Learning Methodology and its e-Learning Platform. In Lecture Notes in Computer Science-Advances in Web-Based Learning* (Vol. 3143, pp. 11–18). Springer-Verlag Heidelberg.

Chung, M. W., & Drummond, B. (2009). *Agile @ yahoo! from the trenches*. Paper presented at the Agile Conference (AGILE 2009), Chicago, IL. doi:10.1109/AGILE.2009.41

Clarke, P., & O'Connor, R. V. (2012). The situational factors that affect the software development process: Towards a comprehensive reference framework. *Information and Software Technology, 54*(5), 433–447. doi:10.1016/j.infsof.2011.12.003

Cloke, G. (2007). GET YOUR AGILE FREAK ON! Agile Adoption at Yahoo! Music. In *Proceedings of Agile Conference (Agile 2007)*, Washington, DC: IEEE. doi:10.1109/AGILE.2007.30

Cockburn, A. (1999). A Methodology per project. Academic Press.

Cockburn, A. (2006). *Agile software development: the cooperative game*. Pearson Education.

Cockburn, A., & Highsmith, J. (2001). Agile software development: The people factor. *Computer, 34*(11), 131–133. doi:10.1109/2.963450

Cohen, D., Lindvall, M., & Costa, P. (2004). An introduction to Agile methods. *Advances in Computers, 62*, 1-66. doi: 10.1016/S0065-2458(03)62001-2

Cohen, B., & Thias, M. (2009). The Failure of the Off-shore Experiment: A Case for Collocated Agile Teams. *InProceedings of Agile 2009 Conference*. Chicago, IL: IEEE. doi:10.1109/AGILE.2009.8

Cohn, M. (2006). The Purpose of Planning. Journal of Planning Education and Research, 25(4), 446–448. doi:10.1177/0739456x0602500412

Cohn, M. (2010a). *ADAPTing to Agile for Continued Success*. Paper presented at the Agile 2010.

Cohn, M., & Ford, D. (2003). Introducing an Agile Process to an Organization. IEEE Computer Society, 74-78.

Cohn, M. (2005). *Agile estimating and planning*. Pearson Education.

Cohn, M. (2010b). *Succeeding with agile: software development using Scrum*. Pearson Education.

Coleman, G., & O'Connor, R. (2007). Using grounded theory to understand software process improvement: A study of Irish software product companies. *Information and Software Technology, 49*(6), 654–667. doi:10.1016/j.infsof.2007.02.011

Collier, M. J. (2009). CHAOS Summary 2009, The Standish Group. *Negotiation and Conflict Management Research, 2*(3), 285–306. doi:10.1111/j.1750-4716.2009.00041.x

Collins, J., & Porras, J. (2004). *Built to Last: Successful Habits of Visionary Companies.* HarperBusiness. doi: 10.1002/hrdq.1092

Collins, E., Macedo, G., Maia, N., & Dias-Neto, A. (2012). An Industrial Experience on the Application of Distributed Testing in an Agile Software Development Environment. In *Proceedings of Seventh International Conference on Global Software Engineering.* Porto Alegre: IEEE. doi:10.1109/ICGSE.2012.40

Conboy, K., Coyle, S., Wang, X., & Pikkarainen, M. (2011). People over process: Key challenges in agile development. *IEEE Software, 28*(4), 48–57. doi:10.1109/MS.2010.132

Constantine, L. L. (2001). Process Agility and Software Usability: Toward Lightweight Usage-Centered Design. *Information Age, 8* (2).

Construx. (2014). *The Cone of Uncertainty.* Retrieved from http://www.construx.com/Thought_Leadership/Books/The_Cone_of_Uncertainty/

Cooper, A. (2009). *An Insurgency of Quality.* Retrieved March 11, 2015, from http://www.cooper.com/journal/insurgency-of-quality.pdf

Coram, M., & Bohner, S. (2005). *The impact of agile methods on software project management.* Paper presented at the Engineering of Computer-Based Systems, 2005. ECBS'05. 12th IEEE International Conference and Workshops on the. doi:10.1109/ECBS.2005.68

Cottmeyer, M. (2008). The Good and Bad of Agile Offshore Development. *InProceedings of Agile 2008 Conference (AGILE '08).* Toronto, ON: IEEE. doi:10.1109/Agile.2008.18

Cubric, M. (2013). An agile method for teaching agile in business schools. *The International Journal of Management Education, 11*(3), 119–131. doi:10.1016/j.ijme.2013.10.001

Cummins, D. (2004). Using Competition to Build a Stronger Team. In *Proceedings of Agile Development Conference,* Salt Lake City, Utah: IEEE doi:10.1109/ADEVC.2004.25

Cunningham, J. (2005). Costs of Compliance: Agile in an Inelastic Organization. In *Proceedings of the Agile Development Conference (ADC'05).* 202-211. Denver, Colorado: IEEE. doi:10.1109/ADC.2005.18

Currim, I. S., Mintz, O., & Siddarth, S. (2015). Information Accessed or Information Available? The Impact on Consumer Preferences Inferred at a Durable Product E-commerce Website. *Journal of Interactive Marketing, 29,* 11–25. doi:10.1016/j.intmar.2014.09.003

da Silva, T., Martin, A., Maurer, F., & Silveira, M. (2011). User-centered design and Agile methods: a systematic review. *International Conference on Agile Methods in Software Development AGILE 2011.* doi:10.1109/AGILE.2011.24

Dannemiller, K. D., & Jacobs, R. W. (1992). Changing the way organizations change: A revolution of common sense. *The Journal of Applied Behavioral Science, 28*(4), 480–498. doi:10.1177/0021886392284003

Debois, P. (2008). Agile infrastructure and operations: how infra-gile are you? In *Proceedings of Agile Conference (AGILE '08).* Toronto, ON: IEEE. doi:10.1109/Agile.2008.42

DeMarco, T., & Boehm, B. (2002). The agile methods fray. *Computer, 35*(6), 90–92. doi:10.1109/MC.2002.1009175

Dillard., S. (2012). Lean but agile: rethink workforce planning and gain a true competitive edge. *Choice Reviews Online, 49*(12). doi: 10.5860/choice.49-6982

Dillon, R. (2015). *Ready.* Singapore: Springer Singapore.

Dingsøyr, T., Nerur, S., Balijepally, V. G., & Moe, N. B. (2012). A decade of agile methodologies: Towards explaining agile software development. *Journal of Systems and Software, 85*(6), 1213–1221. doi:10.1016/j.jss.2012.02.033

Dinwiddie, G. (2011). The three amigos. *StickyMinds Magazine.*

Dorairaj, S., Noble, J., & Malik, P. (2012, May 14-15). *Understanding lack of trust in distributed agile teams: A grounded theory study.* Paper presented at the 16th International Conference on Evaluation and Assessment in Software Engineering, EASE 2012, Ciudad Real, Spain. doi:10.1049/ic.2012.0011

Dorairaj, S., & Noble, J. (2013). Agile Software Development with Distributed Teams: Agility, Distribution and Trust. In *Proceedings of 35th International Conference on Software Engineering (ICSE).* San Francisco, CA: IEEE. doi:10.1109/AGILE.2013.7

Dorairaj, S., Noble, J., & Allan, G. (2013). Agile Software Development with Distributed Teams: Senior Management Support. In *Proceedings of 8th International Conference on Global Software Engineering (ICGSE 2013).* Bari: IEEE. doi:10.1109/ICGSE.2013.33

Doshi, C., & Doshi, D. (2009). A Peek into an Agile Infected Culture.*InProceedings of Agile 2009 Conference.* Chicago, IL: IEEE. doi:10.1109/AGILE.2009.65

Druckman, A. (2011). *Agile Transformation Strategy.* White Paper.

Drummond, B., & Unson, J. F. (2008). Yahoo! Distributed Agile: Notes from the World Over. In *Proceedings of Agile 2008 Conference (AGILE '08).* Toronto, ON: IEEE.

Duhigg, C. (2012). The Power of Habit: Why We Do What We Do in Life and Business, Random House. *Journal of Child and Family Studies, 22*(4), 582–584. doi:10.1007/s10826-012-9645-6

Duvall, P. M., Matyas, S., & Glover, A. (2007). *Continuous integration: improving software quality and reducing risk.* Pearson Education.

Dybå, T., Sjøberg, & Cruzes. (2012). *What works for whom, where, when, and why?: on the role of context in empirical software engineering* Paper presented at the ACM-IEEE international symposium on Empirical software engineering and measurement. doi:10.1145/2372251.2372256

Dybå, T. (2005). An empirical investigation of the key factors for success in software process improvement. *Software Engineering. IEEE Transactions on, 31*(5), 410–424.

Dyba, T. (2005). An empirical investigation of the key factors for success in software process improvement. *IEEE Transactions on Software Engineering, 31*(5), 410–424. doi:10.1109/TSE.2005.53

Dybå, T., & Dingsøyr, T. (2008). Empirical studies of agile software development: A systematic review. *Information and Software Technology, 50*(9-10), 833–859. doi:10.1016/j.infsof.2008.01.006

Dybå, T., & Dingsøyr, T. (2008). Strength of evidence in systematic reviews in software engineering. In *Proceedings of the Second ACM-IEEE international symposium on Empirical software engineering and measurement (ESEM '08),* Kaiserslautern, Germany: ACM. doi:10.1145/1414004.1414034

Edwards, M. (2008). Overhauling a Failed Project Using Out of the Box Scrum. In *Proceedings of Agile 2008 Conference.* Toronto: IEEE. doi:10.1109/Agile.2008.35

Eklund, J., & Levingston, C. (2008). Usability in Agile development. *UX Research,* 1-7.

Endres, A., & Rombach, H. D. (2003). *A handbook of software and systems engineering: Empirical observations, laws, and theories.* Pearson Education.

Eoyang, G. H. (2001). *Conditions for self-organizing in human systems.* The Union Institute.

Esfahani, H. C. (2012). *Transitioning to Agile: A Framework for Pre-Adoption Analysis using Empirical Knowledge and Strategic Modeling.* Canada: University of Toronto.

Exam Certification, I. S. T. Q. B. (2014, December 12). *What is waterfall model - advantages, disadvantages.* Retrieved from http://istqbexamcertification.com/what-is-waterfall-model-advantages-disadvantages-and-when-to-use-it/

Faegri, T. E., & Hanssen, G. K. (2007). Collaboration, Process Control, and Fragility in Evolutionary Product Development. *IEEE Software, 24*(3), 96–104. doi:10.1109/MS.2007.68

Farmer, M. (2004). DecisionSpace Infrastructure: Agile Development in a Large, Distributed Team. In *Proceedings of the Agile Development Conference (ADC'04).* Salt Lake City, Utah: IEEE. doi:10.1109/ADEVC.2004.11

Fenn, J. & Linden, A. (2005). *Gartner's Hype Cycle Special Report for 2005.* Gartner.

Fernandez, A., Insfran, E., & Abrahao, S. (2011). Usability evaluation methods for the web: A systematic mapping study. *Information and Software Technology, 53* (8), 789–817. doi:10.1016/j.infsof.2011.02.007

Ferneley, E., & Sobreperez, P. (2006). Resist, comply or workaround? An examination of different facets of user engagement with information systems. *European Journal of Information Systems, 15*(4), 345–356. doi:10.1057/palgrave.ejis.3000629

Fitzgerald, B., Hartnett, G., & Conboy, K. (2006). Customising agile methods to software practices at Intel Shannon. *European Journal of Information Systems, 15*(2), 200–213. doi:10.1057/palgrave.ejis.3000605

Fitzgerald, B., Stol, K.-J., O'Sullivan, R., & O'Brien, D. (2013). Scaling agile methods to regulated environments: an industry case study. In *Proceedings of the 2013 International Conference on Software Engineering.* doi:10.1109/ICSE.2013.6606635

Fowler, M. (2003). Bliki: FixedPrice. *Geochemistry, Geophysics, Geosystems, 4*(11). doi: 10.1029/2003gc000608

Fritscher, B., & Pigneur, Y. (2010). *Supporting Business Model Modelling: A Compromise between Creativity and Constraints.* Academic Press.

Fruhling, A., McDonald, P., & Dunbar, C. (2008). A Case Study: Introducing eXtreme Programming in a US Government System Development Project. In *Proceedings of the 41st Hawaii International Conference on System Sciences.* Waikoloa, HI: IEEE. doi:10.1109/HICSS.2008.4

Gamma, E., & Beck, K. (2006). *JUnit.* Academic Press.

Gandomani, T. J., Zulzalil, H., & Nafchi, M. Z. (2014). *Agile Transformation: What is it about?* Paper presented at the 8th Malaysian Software Engineering Conference (MySEC), Langkawi, Malaysia.

Gandomani, T. J., Zulzalil, H., Abdul Ghani, A. A., Sultan, A. B. M., & Sharif, K. Y. (2014). Exploring Facilitators of Transition and Adoption to Agile Methods: a Grounded Theory Study. *Journal of Software.*

Gandomani, T. J., Zulzalil, H., Abdul Ghani, A. A., Sultan, A. B. M., & Sharif, K. Y. (2014). How human aspects impress Agile software development transition and adoption. *International Journal of Software Engineering and its Applications, 8*(1), 129-148. doi: 10.14257/ijseia.2014.8.1.12

Gandomani, T. J., Zulzalil, H., Ghani, A. A. A., Sultan, A. B. M., & Sharif, K. Y. (2013). How Grounded Theory can facilitate research studies in context of Agile software development. *Science International-Lahore, 25*(4), 1131–1136.

Gandomani, T. J., & Nafchi, M. Z. (2014). Agility Assessment Model to Measure Agility Degree of Agile Software Companies. *Indian Journal of Science and Technology, 7*(7), 955–959.

Gandomani, T. J., Zulzalil, H., & Ghani, A. (2013). Obstacles to moving to agile software development; at a glance. *Journal of Computer Science*, 9(5), 620–625. doi:10.3844/jcssp.2013.620.625

Gandomani, T. J., Zulzalil, H., Ghani, A. A. A., & Sultan, A. B. M. (2013a). Important considerations for agile software development methods governance. *Journal of Theoretical and Applied Information Technology*, 55(3), 345–351.

Gandomani, T. J., Zulzalil, H., Ghani, A. A. A., & Sultan, A. B. M. (2013b). Towards comprehensive and disciplined change management strategy in agile transformation process. *Research Journal of Applied Sciences. Engineering and Technology*, 6(13), 2345–2351.

Gandomani, T. J., Zulzalil, H., Ghani, A. A. A., & Sultan, A. B. M., & Parizi, R. M. (2015). The impact of inadequate and dysfunctional training on Agile transformation process: A Grounded Theory study. *Information and Software Technology*, 57, 295–309. doi:10.1016/j.infsof.2014.05.011

Gandomani, T. J., Zulzalil, H., & Ghani, Abdul, A. A., Sultan, A. B. M., & Sharif, K. Y. (2014). Exploring Facilitators of Transition and Adoption to Agile Methods: A Grounded Theory Study. *Journal of Software*, 7(9), 1666–1678. doi:10.4304/jsw.9.7.1666-1678

Ganesh, N., & Thangasamy, S. (2012). Lessons learned in transforming from traditional to agile development. *Journal of Computer Science*, 8(3), 389–392. doi:10.3844/jcssp.2012.389.392

Gärtner, M. (2012). *ATDD by example: a practical guide to acceptance test-driven development*. Addison-Wesley.

Gat, I. (2006). How BMC is Scaling Agile Development. In *Proceedings of Agile Conference (AGILE'06)*. Minneapolis, MN: IEEE.

Ge, X., Paige, R., & McDermid, J. (2010). An Iterative Approach for Development of Safety-CriticalSoftware and Safety Arguments. In *Agile Conference (AGILE 2010)*. Orlando, FL: IEEE. doi:10.1109/AGILE.2010.10

Glaser, B. (1992). *Basics of Grounded Theory Analysis: Emergence Vs. Forcing*. Mill Valley, CA: Sociology Press.

Glaser, B. (1998). *Doing Grounded Theory: Issues and Discussions*. Mill Valley, CA: Sociology Press.

Glaser, B. G. (2005). *The Grounded Theory Perspective III: Theoretical Coding*. Mill Valley, CA: Sociology Press.

Glaser, B., & Strauss, A. (1967). *The Discovery of Grounded Theory, Strategies for Qualitative Research*. London: Weidenfeld and Nicolson.

Glaser, B., & Strauss, A. (1967). *The Discovery of Grounded Theory: Strategies for Qualitative Research*. Chicago: Aldine Transaction.

Glass, R. L. (2004). Matching methodology to problem domain. *Communications of the ACM*, 47(5), 19–21. doi:10.1145/986213.986228

Goebel, C. J. (2009). How Being Agile Changed Our Human Resources Policies. In *Proceedings of Agile 2009 Conference*. Chicago, IL: IEEE. doi:10.1109/AGILE.2009.49

Grapenthin, S., Book, M., Poggel, S., & Gruhn, V. (2014). Facilitating Task Breakdown in Sprint Planning Meeting 2 with an Interaction Room: An Experience Report. In *Proceeding of 40th Euromicro Conference Series on Software Engineering and Advanced Applications (SEAA 2014)*. Verona: IEEE. doi:10.1109/SEAA.2014.71

Greening, D. R. (2010). Scaling Scrum to the Executive Level. In *Proceedings of the 43rd Hawaii International Conference on System Sciences*. Honolulu, HI: IEEE.

Greenleaf, R. K. (1977). *Servant leadership*. New York: Paulist Press.

Gregorio, D. D. (2012). How the Business Analyst Supports and Encourages Collaboration on Agile Projects. In *Proceedings of International System Conference (SysCon 2012)*. Vancouver, BC: IEEE. doi:10.1109/SysCon.2012.6189437

Gren, L., Torkar, R., & Feldt, R. (2014). Work Motivational Challenges Regarding the Interface BetweenAgile Teams and a Non-Agile Surrounding Organization: A case study. In *Proceedings of Agile Conference (AGILE 2014)*. Kissimmee, FL: IEEE. doi:10.1109/AGILE.2014.13

Gualtieri, M. (2011). Agile Software is A Cop-Out; Here's What's Next. *Forrester*, *36*(6), 529–531. doi:10.1097/SHK.0b013e318239235a

Hadar, I., Sherman, S., Hadar, E., & Harrison, J. J. (2013). Less is More: Architecture Documentation for Agile Development. In *Proceedings of 6th International Workshop on Cooperative and Human Aspects of Software Engineering (CHASE)*. San Francisco, CA: IEEE. doi:10.1109/CHASE.2013.6614746

Hagan, R. (2012). *Agile Performance Reviews*. Academic Press.

Hagan, R. (2012). Agile Performance Review. *Microform & Digitization Review*, *41*(3-4). doi:10.1515/mir-2012-0026

Hajjdiab, H., & Taleb, A. S. (2011). *Agile adoption experience: A case study in the U.A.E.* Paper presented at the IEEE 2nd International Conference on Software Engineering and Service Science, ICSESS 2011, Beijing, China. doi:10.1109/ICSESS.2011.5982247

Hansen, M. T., & Baggesen, H. (2009). From CMMI and isolation to Scrum, Agile, Lean and collaboration.*InProceedings of Agile 2009 Conference*. Chicago, IL: IEEE. doi:10.1109/AGILE.2009.18

Harlow, M. (2014). Molecular biology: RNA retrieved from intact tissue. *Nature*, *505*(7483), 264. doi:10.1038/505264d

Hartmann Preuss, D. (2006). Interview: Jim Johnson of Standish Group. *Info*, *Q*(289), 253. doi:10.2307/20632978

Hasnain, E. (2010). An overview of published agile studies: a systematic literature review. In *Proceedings of the National Software Engineering Conference (NSEC '10)*. Rawalpindi, Pakistan: ACM. doi:10.1145/1890810.1890813

Hastie, S. (2014). *Knowing When to Stop – trim that tail ruthlessly*. Academic Press.

Heikkilä, V. T., Paasivaara, M., Lassenius, C., & Engblom, C. (2013). *Continuous release planning in a large-scale scrum development organization at Ericsson*. Springer. doi:10.1007/978-3-642-38314-4_14

Heimgartner, S., & Locke, M. (2006). A Tale of Two Writing Teams. In *Proceedings of Agile Conference (AGILE'06)*. Minneapolis, MN: IEEE.

Hiatt, J. M. (2006). *ADKAR: a model for change in business, government and our community*. Prosci Learning Center.

Highsmith, J. (2002). *Agile software development ecosystems*. Addison-Wesley Longman Publishing Co., Inc.

Highsmith, J. (2013). *Adaptive software development: a collaborative approach to managing complex systems*. Addison-Wesley.

Highsmith, J. A. (2002). *Agile software development ecosystems 13*. Addison-Wesley Professional.

Highsmith, J., & Cockburn, A. (2001). Agile software development: The business of innovation. *Computer*, *34*(9), 120–127. doi:10.1109/2.947100

Hoda, R. (2011). *Self-Organizing Agile Teams: A Grounded Theory*. (PhD Thesis). Victoria University of Wellington, New Zealand.

Hoda, R., Noble, J., & Marshall, S. (2010). *Organizing self-organizing teams.* Paper presented at the 32nd ACM/IEEE International Conference on Software Engineering, ICSE 2010, Cape Town, South Africa. doi:10.1145/1806799.1806843

Hoda, R., Kruchten, P., Noble, J., & Marshall, S. (2010). Agility in context. *ACM SIGPLAN Notices*, *45*(10), 74. doi:10.1145/1932682.1869467

Hoda, R., Noble, J., & Marshall, S. (2009). *Negotiating contracts for agile projects: A practical perspective. In Agile Processes in Software Engineering and Extreme Programming* (pp. 186–191). Springer. doi:10.1007/978-3-642-01853-4_25

Hoda, R., Noble, J., & Marshall, S. (2011a). Developing a grounded theory to explain the practices of self-organizing Agile teams. *Empirical Software Engineering*, *17*(6), 609–639. doi:10.1007/s10664-011-9161-0

Hoda, R., Noble, J., & Marshall, S. (2011b). The impact of inadequate customer collaboration on self-organizing Agile teams. *Information and Software Technology*, *53*(5), 521–534. doi:10.1016/j.infsof.2010.10.009

Hofmeister, C., Kruchten, P., Nord, R. L., Obbink, H., Ran, A., & America, P. (2007). A general model of software architecture design derived from five industrial approaches. *Journal of Systems and Software*, *80*(1), 106–126. doi:10.1016/j.jss.2006.05.024

Hogan, B. (2006). Lessons Learned from an eXtremely Distributed Project. In *Proceedings of Agile Conference (AGILE'06)*. Minneapolis, MN: IEEE. doi:10.1109/AGILE.2006.37

Hope, J., & Fraser, R. (2013). *Beyond budgeting: how managers can break free from the annual performance trap.* Harvard Business Press.

Hui, A. (2013). Lean Change: Enabling Agile Transformation through Lean Startup, Kanban, and Kotter: An Experience Report. In *Proceedings of Agile Conference (AGILE 2013)*, Nashville, TN: IEEE. doi:10.1109/AGILE.2013.22

Humble, J., & Russell, R. (2009). *The agile maturity model applied to building and releasing software.* ThoughtWorks White Paper, Web Publishing. Retrieved from http://www.thoughtworks-studios.com/sites/default/files/resource/the_agile_maturity_model.pdf

Hussain, Z., Lechner, M., Milchrahm, H., Shahzad, S., Slany, W., Umgeher, M., & Wolkerstorfer, P. (2008). *Agile User-Centered Design Applied to a Mobile Multimedia Streaming Application* (A. Holzinger, Ed.). Berlin: Springer-Verlag. doi:10.1007/978-3-540-89350-9_22

Iivari, J., & Iivari, N. (2011). The relationship between organizational culture and the deployment of agile methods. *Information and Software Technology*, *53*(5), 509–520. doi:10.1016/j.infsof.2010.10.008

ISO. IEC 9126. (2001). Software product evaluation—quality characteristics and guidelines for the user. Geneva: International Organization for Standardization.

Jackson, M. (2010). Engineering and Software Engineering. Academic Press.

Jackson, A., Tsang, S. L., Gray, A., Driver, C., & Clarke, S. (2004). Behind the Rules: XP Experiences. In *Proceedings of the Agile Development Conference (ADC'04)*. Salt Lake City, UT: IEEE. doi:10.1109/ADEVC.2004.9

Jacobson, M. S. (2014). Scrum Master Allocation: The Case for a Dedicated Scrum Master. Academic Press.

Jacobson, I., Ng, P.-W., McMahon, P. E., Spence, I., & Lidman, S. (2013). *The essence of software Engineering: applying the SEMAT kernel.* Addison-Wesley.

Jain, N. (2006). Offshore Agile Maintenance. In *Proceedings of Agile Conference (AGILE'06)*. Minneapolis, MN: IEEE.

Jakobsen, C. R., & Sutherland, J. (2009). Scrum and CMMI – Going from Good to Great Are you ready-ready to be done-done? In *Proceedings of Agile 2009 Conference*. Chicago, IL: IEEE. doi:10.1109/AGILE.2009.31

Jedlitschka, A., Ciolkowski, M., & Pfahl, D. (2008). Reporting experiments in software engineering. *Guide to Advanced Empirical Software Engineering*, *232*(3), 201–228. doi:10.1007/978-1-84800-044-5_8

Johnson, J., Boucher, K. D., Connors, K., & Robinson, J. (2001). *Collaborating on Project Success*. SOFTWAREMAG.

Kaisti, M., Rantala, V., Mujunen, T., Hyrynsalmi, S., Könnölä, K., Mäkilä, T., & Lehtonen, T. (2013). Agile methods for embedded systems development - a literature review and a mapping study. *EURASIP Journal on Embedded Systems*, *2013*(15).

Kalliney, M. (2009). Transitioning from Agile Development to Enterprise Product Management Agility. In *Proceedings of Agile 2009 Conference*. Chicago, IL: IEEE. doi:10.1109/AGILE.2009.64

Kettunen, P., & Laanti, M. (2008). Combining agile software projects and large-scale organizational agility. *Software Process Improvement and Practice*, *13*(2), 183–193. doi:10.1002/spip.354

Kiczales, G., Lamping, J., Mendhekar, A., Maeda, C., Videira Lopes, C., Loingtier, J., & Irwin, J. (1997). *Aspect-Oriented Programming*. Paper presented at the European Conference on Object-Oriented Programming ECOOP'97, Berlin, Germany. doi:10.1007/BFb0053381

Kim, G., Behr, K., & Spafford, G. (2013). The Phoenix Project: A Novel about IT, DevOps, and Helping Your Business Win. IT Revolution Press. doi:10.1524/hzhz.2013.0149

Kim, E., & Ryoo, S. (2012). Agile Adoption Story from NHN. In *Proceedings of 36th International Conference on Computer Software and Applications*. Izmir: IEEE.

Kim, G., Behr, K., & Spafford, G. (2014). *The phoenix project: A novel about IT, DevOps, and helping your business win*. IT Revolution.

Korkala, M., & Abrahamsson, P. (2007). Communication in Distributed Agile Development: A Case Study. In *Proceedings of 33rd EUROMICRO Conference on Software Engineering and Advanced Applications (SEAA 2007)*. Lubeck: IEEE. doi:10.1109/EUROMICRO.2007.23

Kornstädt, A., & Sauer, J. (2007). Tackling Offshore Communication Challenges with Agile Architecture-Centric Development. In *Proceedings of the Working IEEE/IFIP Conference on Software Architecture (WICSA'07)*. Mumbai: IEEE. doi:10.1109/WICSA.2007.39

Koskela, J. (2003). Software configuration management in agile methods. *ESPOO*, *514*, 1–54.

Kotter, J. P. (1995). Leading change: Why transformation efforts fail. *Harvard Business Review*, *73*(2), 59–67.

Kotter, J. P. (1996). *Leading change*. Harvard Business Press.

Kotter, J. P. (2013). *Leading Change, With a New Preface by the Author*. Harvard Business Press.

Krebs, W., Kroll, P., & Richard, E. (2008). Growing and Sustaining an Offshore Scrum Engagement, In *Proceedings of Agile 2008 Conference*. Toronto: IEEE.

Krigsman, M. (2006). *Management of Critical Success Factors*. ZDNet.

Krishnan, R. (2013). *Aditi Agile Transformation Maturity Model*. Retrieved from http://confengine.com/agile-india-2014/proposal/236/agile-transformation-maturity-model#comments

Kruchten, P. (2011). The Frog and the Octopus – A Conceptual Model of Software Development. Academic Press.

Kruchten, P. (2004). *The rational unified process: an introduction.* Addison-Wesley Professional.

Kruchten, P. (2007). Voyage in the agile memeplex. *Queue, 5*(5), 38. doi:10.1145/1281881.1281893

Kruchten, P. B. (1995). The 4+1 View Model of architecture. *IEEE Software, 12*(6), 42–50. doi:10.1109/52.469759

Kruchten, P. B. (2011). Agile's Teenage Crisis. *InfoQ, 10*(4), 363–364. doi:10.1080/15332691.2011.613313

Kum, W., & Law, A. (2006). *Learning effective test driven development: Software development projects in an energy company.* Paper presented at the 1st International Conference on Software and Data Technologies, ICSOFT 2006, Setubal, Portugal.

Kurtz, C. F., & Snowden, D. J. (2003). The new dynamics of strategy: Sense-making in a complex and complicated world. *IBM Systems Journal, 42*(3), 462–483. doi:10.1147/sj.423.0462

Laanti, M. (2008). Implementing Program Model with Agile Principles in a Large Software Development Organization. *InProceedings of 32nd Annual IEEE International Computer Software and Applications Conference (COMPSAC 2008).* Turku: IEEE. doi:10.1109/COMPSAC.2008.116

Laanti, M., Salo, O., & Abrahamsson, P. (2011). Agile methods rapidly replacing traditional methods at Nokia: A survey of opinions on agile transformation. *Information and Software Technology, 53*(3), 276–290. doi:10.1016/j.infsof.2010.11.010

Larman, C. (2003). *Agile and Iterative Development: A Manager's Guide.* Addison-Wesley.

Larman, C. (2003). *Agile and Iterative Development: A Manager's Guide.* Routledge.

Larman, C., & Basili, V. R. (2003). Iterative and incremental development: A brief history. *Computer, 36*(6), 47–56. doi:10.1109/MC.2003.1204375

Larman, C., & Vodde, B. (2013). Scaling Agile Development. *Crosstalk*, 9.

Lawrence, R. (2007). XP and Junior Developers: 7 Mistakes (and how to avoid them). In *Proceedings of Agile Conference (Agile 2007)*, Washington, DC: IEEE. doi:10.1109/AGILE.2007.67

Lee, E. C. (2008). Forming to Performing: Transitioning Large-Scale Project Into Agile. In *Proceedings of Agile 2008 Conference (AGILE '08).* Toronto, ON: IEEE. doi:10.1109/Agile.2008.75

Lee, J. C., & McCrickard, D. S. (2007). *Towards Extreme (ly) Usable Software: Exploring Tensions Between Usability and Agile Software Development.* IEEE Computer Society.

Leffingwell, D. (2013). *SAFe Glossary.* Retrieved from http://scaledagileframework.com/glossary/

Leffingwell, D. (2010). *Agile software requirements: lean requirements practices for teams, programs, and the enterprise.* Addison-Wesley Professional.

Lehtinen, T. O. A., Mäntylä, & Vanhanen. (2011). Development and evaluation of a lightweight root cause analysis method (ARCA method) – Field studies at four software companies. *Information and Software Technology, 53*(10), 1045–1061. doi: 10.1016/j.infsof.2011.05.005

Lehto, I., & Rautiainen, K. (2009). Software Development Governance Challenges of a Middle-Sized Company in Agile Transition. In *Proceedings of ICSE Workshop on Software Development Governance (SDG '09).* Vancouver, BC: IEEE. doi:10.1109/SDG.2009.5071335

Lembo, D., & Vacca, M. (2012). Project Based Learning + Agile Instructional Design = Extreme Programming based Instructional Design Methodology for Collaborative Learning. *Acta Informatica Medica, Depardemento di Informatica, Sapienza, Universita di Roma, Tech. Rep.N.8, 20*(1), 15. doi: 10.5455/aim.2012.20.15-17

Leszek, A., & Courage, C. (2008). The Doctor is "In" – Using the Office Hours Concept to Make Limited Resources Most Effective. In *Proceedings of Agile 2008 Conference (AGILE '08)*. Toronto, ON: IEEE. doi:10.1109/Agile.2008.46

Lethbridge, Diaz-Herrera, LeBlanc, & Thompson. (2007). Improving software practice through education: Challenges and future trends. *Future of Software Engineering*, 12–28. doi: 10.1109/fose.2007.13

Leusink, B. (2012). *Agile software development process improvement in large organizations*. Academic Press.

Lewin, K. (1946). Force field analysis. In *The 1973 Annual Handbook for Group Facilitators*, (pp. 111-113). Academic Press.

Lewin, K. (1951). Field theory in social science: selected theoretical papers (D. Cartwright, Ed.). Academic Press.

Lewin, K. (1989). *Changing as three steps: unfreezing, moving, and freezing of group standards. In Organizational Development. Theory, Practice, and Research* (3rd ed.; p. 87). Irwin.

Li, J., Moe, N. B., & Dybå, T. (2010). Transition from a plan-driven process to Scrum: a longitudinal case study on software quality. In *Proceedings of the 2010 ACM-IEEE international symposium on empirical software engineering and measurement*. doi:10.1145/1852786.1852804

Lindvall, M., Muthig, D., Dagnino, A., Wallin, C., Stupperich, M., Kiefer, D., & Kähkönen, T. et al. (2004). Agile Software Development in Large Organizations. *Computer*, *37*(12), 26–34. doi:10.1109/MC.2004.231

Little, J. (2014). *Joe's Unofficial Scrum Checklist*. Retrieved Dec. 2014, from http://agileconsortium.pbworks.com/w/file/66642311/Joe%E2%80%99s%20Unofficial%20Scrum%20CheckList%20V13.pdf

Lycett, M. (2001). Understanding 'variation' in component-based development: Case findings from practice. *Information and Software Technology*, *43*(3), 203–213. doi:10.1016/S0950-5849(00)00159-2

Lyon, R., & Evans, M. (2008). Scaling Up - pushing Scrum out of its Comfort Zone.*InProceedings of Agile 2008 Conference (AGILE '08)*. Toronto, ON: IEEE. doi:10.1109/Agile.2008.19

Maier, A. (2015, March 21). *Complete Beginner's Guide to Interaction Design*. Retrieved from UX Booth: http://www.uxbooth.com/articles/complete-beginners-guide-to-interaction-design/

Malan, R., & Bredemeyer, D. (2010). Software Architecture and Related Concerns. *Resources for Software Architects*, *6285*, 352–359.

Manuja, M., Manisha. (2014). Moving Agile based projects on Cloud. In *Proceedings of International Advance Computing Conference (IACC)*. Gurgaon: IEEE.

Marchenko, A., & Abrahamsson, P. (2008). Scrum in a Multiproject Environment: An Ethnographically-Inspired Case Study on the Adoption Challenges. In *Proceedings of Agile 2008 Conference (AGILE '08)*. Toronto, ON: IEEE. doi:10.1109/Agile.2008.77

Marshall, B. (2010). *The Marshall Model of Organisational Evolution (Dreyfus for the Organisation)*. Retrieved from http://fallingblossoms.com/opinion/content?id=1006

Martin, A., Biddle, R., & Noble, J. (2009). *The XP Customer Team: A Grounded Theory*. Paper presented at the 2009 Agile Conference. doi:10.1109/AGILE.2009.70

Martin, A., Biddle, R., & Noble, J. (2009). *XP customer practices: A grounded theory*. Paper presented at the Agile 2009 Conference, Chicago, IL.

Martin, A., Biddle, R., & Noble, J. (2004). The XP Customer Role in Practice: Three Studies. In *Proceedings of the Agile Development Conference (ADC'04)*. Salt Lake City, UT: IEEE. doi:10.1109/ADEVC.2004.23

Mathiassen, L., & Sandberg, A. B. (2014). Process Mass Customization in a Global Software Firm. *Software, IEEE*, *31*(6), 62–69. doi:10.1109/MS.2014.21

Maurer, F., & Melnik, G. (2007). *Agile methods: Crossing the chasm*. Paper presented at the Companion to the proceedings of the 29th International Conference on Software Engineering.

Maurya, A. (2012). *Running lean: iterate from plan A to a plan that works*. O'Reilly Media, Inc.

McAvoy, J., & Butler, T. (2009). *A failure to learn in a software development team: the unsuccessful introduction of an agile method*. In *Information Systems Development* (pp. 1–13). Springer.

McAvoy, J., & Butler, T. (2009). A Failure to Learn in a Software Development Team: The Unsuccessful Introduction of an Agile Method. *Information Systems Developmen*, *5*, 1–13. doi:10.1007/978-0-387-68772-8_1

McCall Smith, A. (2002). The No. 1 Ladies' Detective Agency. New York: Anchor Books.

McGovern, J., Ambler, S. W., Stevens, M. E., Linn, J., Sharan, V., & Jo, E. K. (2003). A Practical Guide To Enterprise Architecture. Upper Saddle River. *Business Communication Quarterly*, *66*(1), 108–111. doi:10.1177/108056990306600116

McHugh, O., Conboy, K., & Lang, M. (2012). Agile Practices: The Impact on Trust in Software Project Teams. *IEEE Software*, *29*(3), 71–76. doi:10.1109/MS.2011.118

McInerney, P., & Maurer, F. (2005). UCD in Agile Projects: Dream Team or Odd Couple? *Interaction*, *12*(6), 19–23. doi:10.1145/1096554.1096556

Mencke, R. (2008). Product Manager's Guide to Surviving the Big Bang Approach to Agile Transitions. *InProceedings of Agile 2008 Conference (AGILE '08)*. Toronto, ON: IEEE. doi:10.1109/Agile.2008.65

Michael, Chiosi, Paltiel, David, Sax, & Walensky. (2011). State of agile survey 2011. *Journal of General Internal Medicine*, *26*(6), 661–667. doi: 10.1007/s11606-011-1637-5

Michael. (2007). *Agile Learning – an alternative model*. Academic Press.

Middleton, P., & Joyce, D. (2012). Lean Software Management: BBC Worldwide Case Study. *IEEE Transactions on Engineering Management*, *59*(1), 20–32. doi:10.1109/TEM.2010.2081675

Miller, A., & Carter, E. (2007). Agility and the Inconceivably Large. In *Proceedings of Agile Conference (Agile 2007)*, Washington, DC: IEEE.

Miller, L. (2006). *Interaction Designers and Agile Development: A Partnership*. UPA.

Misra, S. C., Kumar, V., & Kumar, U. (2009). Identifying some important success factors in adopting agile software development practices. *Journal of Systems and Software*, *82*(11), 1869–1890. doi:10.1016/j.jss.2009.05.052

Miyazaki, K., & Suenaga, H. (2015). *Extradiol Dioxygenases*. Metagenome.

Moczar, L. (2013). *Why Agile Isn't Working: Bringing Common Sense To Agile Principles*. Academic Press.

Moe, N. B., Aurum, A., & Dybå, T. (2012). Challenges of shared decision-making: A multiple case study of agile software development. *Information and Software Technology*, *54*(8), 853–865. doi:10.1016/j.infsof.2011.11.006

Monett, D. (2013). *Agile Project-Based Teaching and Learning*. Paper presented at the 11th International Conference on Software Engineering Research and Practice.

Moniruzzaman, A. B. M., & Hossain, S. A. (2013). *Comparative Study on Agile software development methodologies.* arXiv preprint arXiv:1307.3356

Moore, E., & Spens, J. (2008). Scaling Agile: Finding your Agile Tribe. In *Proceedings of Agile 2008 Conference (AGILE '08)*. Toronto, ON: IEEE. doi:10.1109/Agile.2008.43

Moshref Razavi, A., & Ahmad, R. (2014). Agile development in large and distributed environments: A systematic literature review on organizational, managerial and cultural aspects. In *8th Malaysian Software Engineering Conference (MySEC)*, Langkawi, Malaysia: IEEE.

Murphy, B., Bird, C., Zimmermann, T., Williams, L., Nagappan, N., & Begel, A. (2013). Have Agile Techniques been the Silver Bullet for Software Development at Microsoft? In *Proceedings of International Symposium on Empirical Software Engineering and Measurement (ESEM 2013)*. Baltimore, MD: ACM/IEEE. doi:10.1109/ESEM.2013.21

Murphy, M. (2014). Agile Project Failure kills £15m Surrey Police System. *Computerworld UK, 283.* doi:10.1163/9789004266827_013

Nerur, S., Mahapatra, R., & Mangalaraj, G. (2005). Challenges of migrating to agile methodologies. *Communications of the ACM, 48*(5), 72–78. doi:10.1145/1060710.1060712

Ng, P-W., Huang, & Wu. (2013). On the value of essence to software engineering research: A preliminary study. *Software Engineering, 10*(3), 51-58. doi: 10.1002/rcs.1534

Ng, P. (2014). Software Process Improvement and Gaming using Essence: An Industrial Experience. *Journal of Industrial and Intelligent Information, 2*(1), 45–50. doi:10.12720/jiii.2.1.45-50

Ng, P.-W. (2013). Making Software Engineering Education Structured, Relevant and Engaging through Gaming and Simulation. *Journal of Communication and Computer, 10*, 1365–1373.

Ng, P.-W. (2014). Framework for Describing and Analyzing Context and Factors for Software Engineering Research. *Applying the SEMAT Kernel Lecture Notes on Software Engineering, 2*(4), 179–196. doi:10.1007/978-1-62703-721-1_10

Ng, P.-W. (2014). Theory based software engineering with the SEMAT kernel: preliminary investigation and experiences. In *Proceedings of the 3rd SEMAT Workshop on General Theories of Software Engineering*. doi:10.1145/2593752.2593756

Nielson, J. (1992). Usability Engineering Life Cycle. *IEEE Computer, 25* (3), 12–22. doi:10.1109/2.121503

Nielson, J. (2012). *Introduction to Usability engineering*. RMIT University.

Ning. (2014). . *BMJ (Clinical research ed.), 348*, g1585. doi: 10.1136/bmj.g1585

Norman, D. A. (2005). Do companies fail because their technology is unusable? *Interaction, 12* (4), 69. doi:10.1145/1070960.1070998

North, D. (2006). Introducing BDD. *Advances in Space Research, 37*(5), 958–962. doi:10.1016/j.asr.2005.12.009

Ntier Training. (2014, December 10). *Agile Software Development*. Retrieved from http://www.ntiercustomsolutions.com/training-courses/agile-software-development/

Olsen, G. (2005). The emperor has no lab coat. *Interaction, 9* (4), 13–17.

Osterweil, L. (1987). *Software processes are software too* Paper presented at the 9th international conference on Software Engineering.

Ozawa, H., & Zhang, L. (2013). Adapting Agile Methodology to Overcome Social Differences in Project Members. In *Proceedings of Agile Conference (AGILE 2013)*. Nashville, TN: IEEE. doi:10.1109/AGILE.2013.13

Paasivaara, M., & Lassenius, C. (2011). *Scaling scrum in a large distributed project.* Paper presented at the Empirical Software Engineering and Measurement (ESEM), 2011 International Symposium on. doi:10.1109/ESEM.2011.49

Paasivaara, M., Durasiewicz, S., & Lassenius, C. (2008). Distributed Agile Development: Using Scrum in a Large Project. In *Proceedings of International Conference on Global Software Engineering (ICGSE 2008)*, Bangalore: IEEE. doi:10.1109/ICGSE.2008.38

Packlick, J. (2007). *The agile maturity map a goal oriented approach to agile improvement.* Paper presented at the Agile Conference (AGILE). doi:10.1109/AGILE.2007.55

Pang, C. Y. (2012). *Improve Business Agility of Legacy IT System.* Paper presented at the Information Systems Reengineering for Modern Business Systems: ERP, SCM, CRM, E-Commerce Management Solutions, Hershey, PA.

Parcell, J., & Holden, S. H. (2013). Agile Policy Development for Digital Government: An Exploratory Case Study. In *Proceedings of the 14th Annual International Conference on Digital Government Research.* Quebec City, Canada: ACM.

Parnell-Klabo, E. (2006). Introducing Lean Principles with Agile Practices at a Fortune 500 Company. In *Proceedings of Agile Conference (AGILE'06).* Minneapolis, MN: IEEE. doi:10.1109/AGILE.2006.35

Patel, C., & Ramachandran, M. (2009). Agile Maturity Model (AMM): A Software Process Improvement framework for Agile Software Development Practices. *International Journal of Software Engineering, 2*(1), 3–28.

Patton, J. (2002). Hitting the target: adding interaction design to agile software development. *OOPSLA '02.*

Pichler, M., Rumetshofer, H., & Wahler, W. (2006). Agile Requirements Engineering for a Social Insurance for Occupational Risks Organization: A Case Study. In *Proceedings of 14th International Requirements Engineering Conference (RE'06).* Minneapolis/St. Paul, MN: IEEE. doi:10.1109/RE.2006.8

Pikkarainen, M., Salo, O., Kuusela, R., & Abrahamsson, P. (2012). Strengths and barriers behind the successful agile deployment-insights from the three software intensive companies in Finland. *Empirical Software Engineering, 17*(6), 675–702. doi:10.1007/s10664-011-9185-5

Pixton, P., Nickolaisen, N., Little, T., & McDonald, K. (2009). *Stand Back and Deliver, Accelerating Business Agility.* Boston: Addison-Wesley.

Popli, R., & Chauhan, N. (2013). A mapping model for transforming traditional software development methods to agile methodology. *International Journal of Software Engineering & Applications, 4*(4), 53–64. doi:10.5121/ijsea.2013.4405

Poppendieck, M., & Poppendieck, T. (2003). ixed-Price Contracts. In Lean software development: An agile toolkit. *Software Engineering Notes, 28*(6), 30. doi:10.1145/966221.966665

Power, K. (2010). *Stakeholder identification in agile software product development organizations: A model for understanding who and what really count.* Paper presented at the Agile conference. doi:10.1109/AGILE.2010.17

Power, K. (2011). *The Agile Office: Experience Report from Cisco's Unified Communications Business Unit.* Paper presented at the Agile Conference (AGILE). doi:10.1109/AGILE.2011.7

Pries-Heje, J., & Johansen, J. (2010). *Spi manifesto.* European System & Software Process Improvement and Innovation.

Prochaska, J. O., Velicer, W. F., Rossi, J. S., Goldstein, M. G., Marcus, B. H., Rakowski, W., & Rosenbloom, D. et al. (1994). Stages of change and decisional balance for 12 problem behaviors. *Health Psychology, 13*(1), 39–46. doi:10.1037/0278-6133.13.1.39 PMID:8168470

Programming, E. (2014). *Extreme Programming: A Gentle Introduction.* Retrieved from http://www.extremeprogramming.org

Qumer, A., & Henderson-Sellers, B. (2006). Measuring agility and adoptability of agile methods: a 4-dimensional analytical tool. In *Procs. IADIS International Conference Applied Computing 2006*, (pp. 503-507). IADIS.

Qumer, A. (2007). Defining an Integrated Agile Governance for Large Agile Software Development Environments. *Defining an Integrated Agile Governance for Large Agile Software Development Environments Agile Processes in Software Engineering and Extreme Programming, 4536*, 157–160. doi:10.1007/978-3-540-73101-6_23

Qumer, A., & Henderson-Sellers, B. (2008). A framework to support the evaluation, adoption and improvement of agile methods in practice. *Journal of Systems and Software, 81*(11), 1899–1919. doi:10.1016/j.jss.2007.12.806

Qumer, A., & Henderson-Sellers, B. (2008). An evaluation of the degree of agility in six agile methods and its applicability for method engineering. *Information and Software Technology, 50*(4), 280–295. doi:10.1016/j.infsof.2007.02.002

Qumer, A., Henderson-sellers, B., & Mcbride, T. (2007). Agile adoption and improvement model. In *Proceedings of European and Mediterranean Conference on Information Systems.*

Radoff, J. (2011). *Game on: energize your business with social media games.* John Wiley & Sons.

Rakitin, S. R. (2001). *Manifesto Elicits Cynicism: Reader's Letter to the Editor.* Paper presented at the IEEE.

Rao, K. N., Naidu, G. K., & Chakka, P. (2011). A study of the agile software development methods, applicability and implications in industry. *International Journal of Software Engineering and its Applications, 5*(2), 35-45.

Rasmussen, R., Hughes, T., Jenks, J., & Skach, J. (2009). Adopting Agile in an FDA Regulated Environment. In *Agile Conference (AGILE '09).* Chicago, IL: IEEE. doi:10.1109/AGILE.2009.50

Rayhan, H., & Haque, N. (2008). Incremental Adoption of Scrum for Successful Delivery of an IT Project in a Remote Setup. In *Proceedings of Agile 2008 Conference.* Toronto: IEEE. doi:10.1109/Agile.2008.98

Read, A., & Briggs, R. O. (2012). *The many lives of an agile story: Design processes, design products, and understandings in a large-scale agile development project.* Paper presented at the System Science (HICSS), 2012 45th Hawaii International Conference on. doi:10.1109/HICSS.2012.684

Reinertsen, D. G. (2009). The principles of product development flow. *Second Generation Lean Product Development, 62.* doi: 10.1787/dcr-2009-graph12-en

Reinertsen, D. G. (2009). *The principles of product development flow: second generation lean product development* (Vol. 62). Celeritas Redondo Beach.

Repenning, N. P., & Sterman, J. D. (2002). Capability traps and self-confirming attribution errors in the dynamics of process improvement. *Administrative Science Quarterly, 47*(2), 265–295. doi:10.2307/3094806

Ries, E. (2011). *The lean startup: How today's entrepreneurs use continuous innovation to create radically successful businesses.* Crown Business.

Rising, L., & Manns, M. L. (2004). *Fearless change: patterns for introducing new ideas.* Pearson Education.

Robarts, J. M. (2008). Practical Considerations for Distributed Agile Projects. In *Proceedings of Agile 2008 Conference (AGILE '08).* Toronto, ON: IEEE. doi:10.1109/Agile.2008.57

Roche, G., & Vaquez-McCall, B. (2009). The Amazing Team Race - A Team Based Agile Adoption. In *Proceedings of Agile 2009 Conference.* Chicago, IL: IEEE. doi:10.1109/AGILE.2009.67

Rodríguez, P., Partanen, J., Kuvaja, P., & Oivo, M. (2014). Combining Lean Thinking and Agile Methods for Software Development: A Case Study of a Finnish Provider of Wireless Embedded Systems. In *Proceedings of 47th Hawaii International Conference on System Science (HICSS)*. Waikoloa, HI: IEEE

Rogers, E. M. (2010). *Diffusion of innovations*. Simon and Schuster.

Rohunen, A., Rodriguez, P., Kuvaja, P., Krzanik, L., & Markkula, J. (2010). *Approaches to agile adoption in large settings: a comparison of the results from a literature analysis and an industrial inventory*. Paper presented at the 11th international conference on Product-Focused Software Process Improvement, Limerick, Ireland. doi:10.1007/978-3-642-13792-1_8

Rong, G., Shao, D., & Zhang, H. (2010). SCRUM-PSP: Embracing Process Agility and Discipline. In *Proceedings 17th Asia Pacific Software Engineering Conference (APSEC)*, Sydney, NSW: IEEE.

Royce, W. (1970). *Managing the Development of Large Software Systems*. Paper presented at the IEEE WESON.

Rubin, K. S. (2012). Essential Scrum: A practical guide to the most popular Agile process. *Journal of Functional Programming*, 22(03), 375–377. doi:10.1017/s0956796812000123

Sahota, M. (2012). An Agile Adoption and Transformation Survival Guide: Working with Organizational Culture. *InfoQ*. Retrieved from http://www.infoq.com/minibooks/agile-adoption-transformation

Salo, O., & Abrahamsson, P. (2008). Agile methods in European embedded software developmentorganisations: A survey on the actual use and usefulness of Extreme Programming and Scrum. *Software, IET*, 2(1), 58–64. doi:10.1049/iet-sen:20070038

Saravanan, G. (2013). Why Software Engineering Fails! (Most of the Time). *Software Engineering Notes*, 38(6), 1–4. doi:10.1145/2532780.2532802

Schatz, B., & Abdelshafi, I. (2005). Primavera gets Agile: A successful transition to Agile development. *IEEE Software*, 22(3), 36–42. doi:10.1109/MS.2005.74

Schein, E. H. (1996). Kurt Lewin's change theory in the field and in the classroom: Notes toward a model of managed learning. *Systems Practice*, 9(1), 27–47. doi:10.1007/BF02173417

Schneider, W. E. (1994). *The reengineering alternative: A plan for making your current culture work*. Richard D Irwin.

Schwaber, C, Laganza, G, & D'Silva, D. (2007). *The truth about agile processes: frank answers to frequently asked questions*. Forrester Report.

Schwaber, K. (2004). Fixed-rice, Fixed-Date Contracts. In Agile project management with Scrum. Academic Press.

Schwaber, K., & Sutherland, J. (2013). The Scrum Guide. Academic Press.

Schwaber, K. (1997). *Scrum development process. In Business Object Design and Implementation* (pp. 117–134). Springer. doi:10.1007/978-1-4471-0947-1_11

Scott, J., Johnson, R., & McCullough, M. (2008). Executing Agile in a Structured Organization: Government. In *Proceedings of Agile 2008 Conference (AGILE '08)*. Toronto, ON: IEEE. doi:10.1109/Agile.2008.40

Seffernick, T. R. (2007). Enabling Agile in a Large Organization Our Journey Down the Yellow Brick Road. In *Proceedings of Agile Conference (Agile 2007)*, Washington, DC: IEEE. doi:10.1109/AGILE.2007.23

Senapathi, M., & Srinivasan, A. (2012). Understanding post-adoptive agile usage: An exploratory cross-case analysis. *Journal of Systems and Software*, 85(6), 1255–1268. doi:10.1016/j.jss.2012.02.025

Sepulveda, C. (2003). Agile Development and Remote Teams: Learning to Love the Phone. In *Proceedings of the Agile Development Conference (ADC'03)*. Salt Lake City, Utah: IEEE. doi:10.1109/ADC.2003.1231464

Shah, V., & Nies, A. (2008). Agile with Fragile Large Legacy Applications. In *Proceedings of Agile 2008 Conference (AGILE '08)*. Toronto, ON: IEEE. doi:10.1109/Agile.2008.86

Shatil, A., Hazzan, O., & Dubinsky, Y. (2010). Agility in a Large-Scale System Engineering Project: A Case-Study of an Advanced Communication System Project. In *Proceedings of International Conference on Software Science, Technology & Engineering*. Herzlia, Israel: IEEE. doi:10.1109/SwSTE.2010.18

Sheard, S. (2001). Evolution of the frameworks quagmire. *Computer, 34*(7), 96–98. doi:10.1109/2.933516

Sheth, B. (2009). Scrum 911! Using Scrum to Overhaul a Support Organization. In *Proceedings of Agile 2009 Conference*. Chicago, IL: IEEE. doi:10.1109/AGILE.2009.23

Shrinivasavadhani, J. (2008). Remote Mentoring a Distributed Agile Team. In *Proceedings of Agile 2008 Conference (AGILE '08)*. Toronto, ON: IEEE. doi:10.1109/Agile.2008.89

Siddique, L., & Hussein, B. A. (2014). Practical insight about choice of methodology in large complex software projects in Norway. In *Proceedings of International Technology Management Conference (ITMC)*. Chicago, IL: IEEE. doi:10.1109/ITMC.2014.6918615

Sidky, A., & Arthur, J. D. (2007). *A Structured Approach to Adopting Agile Practices: The Agile Adoption Framework*. (Ph. D. Dissertation). Virginia Tech. doi: 10.2481/dsj.6.S70

Sidky, A., & Arthur, J. D. (2008). *Value-Driven Agile Adoption: Improving An Organization's Software Development Approach*. Paper presented at the New Trends in Software Methodologies, Tools and Techniques.

Sidky, A., Arthur, J., & Bohner, S. (2007). A disciplined approach to adopting agile practices: the agile adoption framework. *Innovations in Systems and Software Engineering, 3*(3), 203-216.

Sidky, A. S., Arthur, J. D., & Bohner, S. (2007). A Disciplined Approach to Adopting Agile Practices: The Agile Adoption Framework. *Journal of Innovations in Systems and Software Engineering, 3*. doi:10.1007/978-1-84628-821-0

Sidky, A., Arthur, J., & Bohner, S. (2007). A disciplined approach to adopting agile practices: The agile adoption framework. *Innovations in Systems and Software Engineering, 3*(3), 203–216. doi:10.1007/s11334-007-0026-z

Smith, C., & King, P. (2008). Agile Project Experiences – The Story of Three Little Pigs. *InProceedings of Agile 2008 Conference (AGILE '08)*. Toronto, ON: IEEE. doi:10.1109/Agile.2008.76

Smith, G., & Sidky, A. (2009). *Becoming agile: in an imperfect world*. Manning Publications.

Smits, H., & Pshigoda, G. (2007). Implementing Scrum in a Distributed Software Development Organization. In *Proceedings of Agile Conference (Agile 2007)*, Washington, DC: IEEE. doi:10.1109/AGILE.2007.34

Snapp, M. B., & Dagefoerde, D. (2008). The Accidental Agilists: One Team's Journey from Waterfall to Agile. In *Proceedings of Agile 2008 Conference (AGILE '08)*. Toronto, ON: IEEE. doi:10.1109/Agile.2008.68

Snowden, D. (1999). *Cynefin framework*. Retrieved from http://cognitive-edge.com/

Software Crisis. (2010). In *Wikipedia*. Retrieved July 26, 2010, from http://en.wikipedia.org/wiki/Software_crisis

Software Education. (2014). *Agile Product Ownership course*. Wellington, New Zealand: Author.

Sohaib, O., & Khan, K. (2010). Integrating Usability Engineering and Agile Software Development: A Litereture Review.*International Conference On Computer Design And Appliations (ICCDA 2010)* (pp. V2-32). IEEE. doi:10.1109/ICCDA.2010.5540916

Solomon, C. F. (2013). *Teaching in an Agile Manner*. Bloomsbury Academic.

Soria, A., Campo, M. R., & Rodriguez, G. (2012). *Improving Software Engineering Teaching by Introducing Agile Management*. Paper presented at the INCOSE International Symposium, 13th Argentine Symposium on Software Engineering, La Plata, Argentina.

Soundararajan, S., & Arthur, J. D. (2011). *A structured framework for assessing the "goodness" of agile methods*. Paper presented at the 18th IEEE International Conference and Workshops on Engineering of Computer-Based Systems, ECBS 2011, Las Vegas, NV.

Soundararajan, S., Arthur, J. D., & Balci, O. (2012). *A methodology for assessing agile software development methods*. Paper presented at the Agile Conference, Agile 2012, Dallas, TX. doi:10.1109/Agile.2012.24

Southwell, K. (2002). Agile process improvement. *TickIT International Journal*, 3-14.

Spayd, M. (2010). *Agile & Culture*. Retrieved from http://collectiveedgecoaching.com/2010/07/agile__culture/

Spinellis, D. (2012). Don't Install Software by Hand. *Software, IEEE*, 29(4), 86–87. doi:10.1109/MS.2012.85

Srinivasan, J., & Lundqvist, K. (2010). *Agile in India: Challenges and lessons learned*. Paper presented at the 3rd India Software Engineering Conference, ISEC'10, Mysore, India. doi:10.1145/1730874.1730898

Stapleton, J. (2003). *DSDM: Business focused development*. Pearson Education.

Stewart, J. C., DeCusatis, C. S., Kidder, K., Massi, J. R., & Anne, K. M. (2009). Evaluating Agile Principles in Active and Cooperative Learning. *Toxicology Letters*, 191(2-3), 231–235. doi:10.1016/j.toxlet.2009.09.003 PMID:19748556

Stray, V. G., Lindsjørn, Y., & Sjøberg, D. I. K. (2013). Obstacles to Efficient Daily Meetings in Agile Development Projects: A Case Study. In *Proceedings of International Symposium on Empirical Software Engineering and Measurement (ESEM 2013)*. Baltimore, MD: ACM/IEEE. doi:10.1109/ESEM.2013.30

Strydom, R. (2006). Time is money - agile fixed price. Academic Press.

Summers, M. (2008). Insights into an Agile Adventure with Offshore Partners. In *Proceedings of Agile 2008 Conference (AGILE '08)*. Toronto, ON: IEEE. doi:10.1109/Agile.2008.37

Sureshchandra, K., & Shrinivasavadhani, J. (2008). *Moving from waterfall to agile*. Paper presented at the Agile 2008 Conference, Toronto, Canada.

Sutherland, J., Schoonheim, G., Kumar, N., Pandey, V., & Vishal, S. (2009). Fully Distributed Scrum: Linear Scalability of Production between San Francisco and India.*InProceedings of Agile 2009 Conference*. Chicago, IL: IEEE. doi:10.1109/AGILE.2009.27

Sutherland, J., Schoonheim, G., Rustenburg, E., & Rijk, M. (2008). Fully Distributed Scrum: The Secret Sauce for Hyperproductive Offshored Development Teams. In *Proceedings of Agile 2008 Conference (AGILE '08)*. Toronto, ON: IEEE. doi:10.1109/Agile.2008.92

Sy, D. (2007). Adapting Usability Investigations for Agile User-centered Design. *Journal of Usability Studies, 2* (3), 112–132.

Takats, A., & Brewer, N. (2005). Improving Communication between Customers and Developers. In *Proceedings of the Agile Development Conference (ADC'05)*. Denver, CO: IEEE. doi:10.1109/ADC.2005.30

Takeuchi, H., & Nonaka, I. (1986). The new new product development game. *Harvard Business Review, 64*(1), 137–146.

Talby, D., & Dubinsky, Y. (2009). Governance of an Agile Software Project. In *Proceedings of ICSE Workshop on Software Development Governance (SDG '09)*. Vancouver, BC: IEEE.

Tartaglia, C. M., & Ramnath, P. (2005). Using Open Spaces to Resolve Cross Team Issue. In *Proceedings of the Agile Development Conference (ADC'05)*. Denver, CO: IEEE. doi:10.1109/ADC.2005.49

Tesar, M., & Sieber, S. (2010). Managing Blended Learning Scenarios by Using Agile e-Learning Development. *International Association for the Development of the Information Society, Freiburg, Germany, 26*(2), 124–129. doi:10.1177/0266666910368123

Thamhain, H. J. (2014). Can We Manage Agile in Traditional Project Environments? In *Proceeding of Portland International Conference on Management of Engineering & Technology (PICMET)*. Kanazawa: IEEE.

Therrien, I., & LeBel, E. (2009). From Anarchy to Sustainable Development: Scrum in Less Than Ideal Conditions. In *Proceedings of Agile 2009 Conference*. Chicago, IL: IEEE. doi:10.1109/AGILE.2009.73

Thomas, S. (2013). Specification by Example versus Behavior Driven Development. Academic Press.

Thomsett, R. (2001). *Radical Project Management*. Upper Saddle River, NJ: Prentice Hall.

Thoughtworks. (2010). *Agile assessments*. Retrieved June 2014, from http://www.agileassessments.com/

Treccani, P. J. F., & De Souza, C. R. B. (2011). *Collaborative refactoring: Results of an empirical study using grounded theory* (Vol. 6969). Paraty: LNCS.

Tsirakidis, P., Köbler, F., & Krcmar, H. (2009). *Identification of success and failure factors of two agile software development teams in an open source organization*. Paper presented at the 4th IEEE International Conference on Global Software Engineering, ICGSE 2009, Limerick. doi:10.1109/ICGSE.2009.42

Tudor, D., & Walter, G. A. (2006). Using an Agile Approach in a Large, Traditional Organization. In *Proceedings of Agile Conference (AGILE'06)*. Minneapolis, MN: IEEE. doi:10.1109/AGILE.2006.60

Unni, E. J., & Farris, K. B. (2015). Development of a new scale to measure self-reported medication nonadherence. *Research in Social & Administrative Pharmacy, 11*(3), e133-143. doi: 10.1016/j.sapharm.2009.06.005

Urdangarin, R., Fernandes, P., Avritzer, A., & Paulish, D. (2008). Experiences with Agile Practices in the Global Studio Project. In *Proceedings of International Conference on Global Software Engineering (ICGSE 2008)*. Bangalore: IEEE. doi:10.1109/ICGSE.2008.11

Urquhart, C. (2013). *Grounded Theory for Qualitative Research, A Practical Guide*. London: Sage Publications.

Uy, E., & Ioannou, N. (2008). Growing and Sustaining an Offshore Scrum Engagement. In *Proceedings of Agile Conference (AGILE '08)*. Toronto, ON: IEEE. doi:10.1109/Agile.2008.71

Valade, R. (2008). The Big Projects Always Fail: Taking an Enterprise Agile. In *Proceedings of Agile Conference (AGILE '08)*. Toronto, ON: IEEE. doi:10.1109/Agile.2008.63

van Cauwenberghe, P. (2015). *Agile Fixed Price Projects part 1: "The Price Is Right"*. Academic Press.

Van Vliet, H. (2007). *Software engineering: Principles and practice*. Wiley.

Vax, M., & Michaud, S. (2008). Distributed Agile: Growing a Practice Together. In *Proceedings of Agile Conference (AGILE '08)*. Toronto, ON: IEEE.

Vijayasarathy, L. E. O. R., & Turk. (2008). Agile Software Development: A survey of early adopters. *Journal of Information Technology Management, 19*(2), 1–8. doi:10.1080/1097198x.2008.10856469

Vijayasarathy, L., & Turk, D. (2008). Agile software development: A survey of early adopters. *Journal of Information Technology Management, 19*(2), 1–8.

Vijayasarathy, L., & Turk, D. (2012). Drivers of agile software development use: Dialectic interplay between benefits and hindrances. *Information and Software Technology, 54*(2), 137–148. doi:10.1016/j.infsof.2011.08.003

Vredenburg, K. S. I., & Righi. (2002). User-centered design: An integrated approach. Prentice Hall PTR.

Vriens, C., & Barto, R. (2008). 7 Years of Agile Management. In *Proceedings of Agile 2008 Conference (AGILE '08)*. Toronto, ON: IEEE. doi:10.1109/Agile.2008.97

Wake, W. C. (2003). *INVEST in Good Stories, and SMART Tasks*. Retrieved from www.xp123.com

Wegner, P. (1989). Concepts and Paradigms of Object-Oriented Programming. Academic Press.

Werbach, K., & Hunter, D. (2012). *For the win: How game thinking can revolutionize your business*. Wharton Digital Press.

West, D., & Grant, T., Gerush, M., & D'silva, D. (2010). Agile development: Mainstream adoption has changed agility. *Forrester Research, 2*, 41.

Weyrauch, K. (2006). What Are We Arguing About? A Framework for Defining Agile in our Organization. In *Proceedings of Agile Conference (AGILE'06)*. Minneapolis, MN: IEEE. doi:10.1109/AGILE.2006.62

Wikipedia. (2014). *Software Development Process*. Retrieved December 12, 2014, from http://en.wikipedia.org/wiki/Software_development_process

Williams, L., Rubin, K., & Cohn, M. (2010). *Driving Process Improvement via Comparative Agility Assessment*. Paper presented at the Agile Conference (AGILE). doi:10.1109/AGILE.2010.12

Williams, L. (2012). What agile teams think of agile principles. *Communications of the ACM, 55*(4), 71–76. doi:10.1145/2133806.2133823

Williams, M., Packlick, J., Bellubbi, R., & Coburn, S. (2007). How We Made Onsite Customer Work - An Extreme Success Story. In *Proceedings of Agile Conference (Agile 2007)*, Washington, DC: IEEE. doi:10.1109/AGILE.2007.33

Xiaofeng, W., Lane, M., Conboy, K., Pikkarainen, M. (2009). Where agile research goes: starting from a 7-year retrospective (report on agile research workshop at XP2009). *SIGSOFT Software Engineering Notes Archive, 34*(5), 28-30.

Yadgar, A., Grumberg, O., & Schuster, A. (2009). *Hybrid BDD and All-SAT Method for Model Checking*. Academic Press.

Yaju, Y., Kataoka, Y., Eto, H., Horiuchi, S., & Mori, R. (2013). Prophylactic interventions after delivery of placenta for reducing bleeding during the postnatal period. *Cochrane Database of Systematic Reviews, 11*, CD009328. doi:10.1002/14651858.CD009328.pub2 PMID:24277681

Yap, M. (2005).Follow the Sun: Distributed Extreme Programming Development. In *Proceedings of the Agile Development Conference (ADC'05)*. Denver, CO: IEEE. doi:10.1109/ADC.2005.26

Yi, L. (2011). Manager as Scrum Master, In *Proceedings of Agile 2011 Conference*. Salt Lake City, UT: IEEE. doi:10.1109/AGILE.2011.8

Young, C., & Terashima, H. (2008). How Did We Adapt Agile Processes to Our Distributed Development? In *Proceedings of Agile 2008 Conference (AGILE '08)*. Toronto, ON: IEEE. doi:10.1109/Agile.2008.7

Zeng, P., Rainforth, W. M., & Cook, R. B. (2015). Characterisation of the oxide film on the taper interface from retrieved large diameter metal on polymer modular total hip replacements. *Tribology International, 89*, 86–96. doi:10.1016/j.triboint.2014.12.012

Zhang, J.-G. (2008). *What is project management.* Method Study of Software Project Schedule Estimation Guide.

Zieris, F., & Salinger, S. (2013). Doing Scrum Rather Than Being Agile: A Case Study on Actual Nearshoring Practices. In *Proceedings of 8th International Conference on Global Software Engineering (ICGSE 2013)*. Bari: IEEE. doi:10.1109/ICGSE.2013.26

About the Contributors

Imran Ghani is a Senior Lecturer at Faculty of Computing, Universiti Teknologi Malaysia (UTM), Johor Campus. He received his Master of Information Technology Degree from UAAR (Pakistan), M.Sc. Computer Science from UTM (Malaysia) and Ph.D. from Kookmin University (South Korea). His research focus includes agile software development methods and practices, semantics techniques, secure software development life cycle, web services, software testing, enterprise architecture and software architecture.

Dayang Norhayati Abang Jawawi is an Associate Professor in Department of Software Engineering, Faculty of Computing, Universiti Teknologi Malaysia (UTM). She received her Ph.D. in the field of Software Engineering from Universiti Teknologi Malaysia. She has been an academic staff at Software Engineering Department since 1997 and she has served as the Head of Department from November 2009 till January 2015. She is a member of the Software Engineering Research Group (SERG), K-Economy Research Alliance, UTM.

Siva Dorairaj has a vast experience in coaching Agile teams and teaching Agile courses to practitioners. Siva has also taught software engineering courses at reputable universities in Malaysia and New Zealand. In his PhD research, Siva investigated a large number of Agile teams in the USA, India and Australia, and proposed "The Theory of One Team" which explains how a distributed team in Agile software development adopts explicit strategies for bridging spatial, temporal, and socio-cultural distances, while facing critical impact factors, in order to become one team. Siva has given talks at Agile conferences in the USA, Norway, Sweden, Italy, Spain and Australia. He also serves as a Program Committee Member (Reviewer) for international conferences such as AGILE, XP and ICGSE, and journals such as the Journal of Systems and Software (JSS), the Information and Software Technology (IST) and the Scientific World.

Ahmed Sidky, also known as Doctor Agile, is a well-known thought-leader in the Agile community. Ahmed combines over fifteen years of software development experience, with research from his Ph.D. in Agile transformation and agility assessment to help leaders and knowledge workers achieve measurable and sustainable organizational agility by being Agile not just doing Agile. Ahmed is the co-author of a top-rated Agile adoption book "Becoming Agile in an Imperfect World," and the Executive Director and co-founder of the International Consortium for Agile. Ahmed was selected to be on the steering committee of the PMI-ACP® Certification and the program chair for the Agile 2009 conference. He has been an invited speaker at numerous Agile Conferences around the world and divides his time between consulting, teaching, and writing. You can connect with Ahmed via his website AhmedSidky.com.

* * *

Aminu Onimisi Abdulsalami, is a Graduate Assistant in the Department of Mathematics at Ahmadu Bello University and a member of the University Software Development Committee. He is presently undergoing M.Sc. degree in Computer Science and also received a B.Sc. degree in Computer Science in 2011 at A.B.U, Zaria - Nigeria. His research interests lie in the area of web development, with a major focus on improving the World Wide Web in general. As a software developer with a 4 years experience he has participated in several software projects in the university. He has employed the agile technique in rapidly developing software projects and has recorded enormous success.

Rodina Ahmad is an Associate Professor in Software Engineering Department, Faculty of Computer Science and Information Technology, University of Malaya. She has been actively teaching and conducting research for the last twenty years in the area of information system management, software requirements engineering and software process improvement.

Jagadeesh Balakrishnan has around 15 years of experience in software development with a passion for Organizational Agile Transformation, Agile Delivery, Adaptive Leadership, Organizational Process Improvement and Change Management initiatives. He is a hands on Agile coach who has executed several projects as a Scrum Master with additional implementation experience in Feature Driven Development (FDD), Kanban, DSDM, Lean IT, etc. Teaching and Consulting in Agile and Software Engineering are his equal passions apart from Agile Delivery.

Deshinta Arrova Dewi Dewi is an active researcher and PhD cadidate who produces more than 10 international conference papers, two international journal article (JDCTA) and Science International Lahore (ISI Indexed), and training / seminar articles since year 2005. Practitioner in dynamic learning environment for Higher Education Learning Institution for more than 10 years of services in Malaysia and Indonesia, providing the best learning experiences to the learners including innovative methods of teaching and learning.

Anuradha Chaminda Gajanayaka is a graduate in production engineering and has 12+ years experience in software project management and implementation. His main expertise is on managing Agile offshore projects where he has engaged in management of agile offshore projects for last 9 years.

Taghi Javdani Gandomani received his PhD in Software Engineering from University of Putra Malaysia, Malaysia. His research interests in software engineering are Agile software development, development methodologies and empirical studies. He is an Assistant Professor in Islamic Azad University, Iran and has more than 15 years industry experience in software development.

Shane Hastie, MIM, CBAP, ICE-VM, has over 30 years of experience in software development across a wide range of roles from programmer to senior executive, and now has the role of Chief Knowledge Engineer for SoftEd (www.softed.com), a New Zealand based training, coaching, and consulting firm delivering classes around the world. He has a Master of Information Management degree from Victoria University of Wellington, New Zealand (2008). He is a Certified Business Analysis Professional, and is certified as an ICAgile Expert in Business Value Management. Shane has been actively involved in the global Business Analysis and Agile communities since 2008. He took a lead role in the joint Agile Alliance and IIBA™ (International Institute for Business Analysis) program that produced the Agile Extension to the Business Analysis Body of Knowledge™ (BANOK™) and was a member of the Core Team that led the production of Version 3 of the BABOK™ (published in April 2015). In 2011, Shane was elected to the Board of Directors of the Agile Alliance, and re-elected for a further term in 2013. He is the lead editor for all Agile topic on InfoQ.com.

Seung Ryul Jeong is a Professor in the Graduate School of Business IT at Kookmin University, Korea. He holds a B.A. in Economics from Sogang University, Korea, an M.S. in MIS from the University of Wisconsin, and a Ph.D. in MIS from the University of South Carolina. Professor Jeong has published extensively in the information systems field, with over 60 publications in refereed journals such as Journal of MIS, Communications of the ACM, Information and Management, Journal of Systems and Software, among others. Dr. Jeong has been the recipient of numerous awards such as the Merit Award for National Informatization from the Prime Minister's Office.

Murad Khan received His M.Sc. Information security from Universiti Teknologi Malaysia (UTM). He is now doing Ph.D. at faculty of computing, Universiti Teknologi Malaysia (UTM). His research interest include recommender systems, service-oriented architecture (SOA), cloud computing and agile processes.

Aliyu Muhammad Kufena, is presently a Master graduate student in computer science and holds a Bachelor degree in computer science in 2010 all in Ahmadu Bello University, Zaria, Nigeria. He is currently a Graduate Assistant in the department of Mathematics, Ahmadu Bello University and a member of the software development committee of the University since 2010. He has a high affinity to Software Engineering and Databases.

Praveen Ramachandra Menon holds a MBA degree in Information Systems from Delaware State University, USA and Bachelors in Computer Science Engineering from Madurai Kamaraj University, India. Praveen has more than 13 years of experience in Software Development with a passion for Organizational Agile Transformation, Agile Enterprise Framework Models (SAFe/LeSS/DAD), Agile Testing, Quality Engineering, DevOps. He has worn multiple hats and executed several projects as Scrum Developer, Scrum Master & Product Owner roles with additional implementation experience in Behavior Driven Development (BDD) & Test Driven Development (TDD). He is very passionate about Testing Automation Frameworks, Software Engineering best practices, Code Quality, Open Source Technologies, Continuous Build Integration and Deployment.

Mina Ziaei Nafchi received the MS in Software Engineering from University of Putra Malaysia. Currently, she is a PhD candidate in Software Engineering at University of Putra Malaysia. Her research area is Agile Software Development.

Pan-Wei Ng holds a Ph.D. from Nanyang Technological University. He has over 20 years working experience in the software industry. He is the author of "Aspect Oriented Software Development with Use Cases" and "Essence of Software Engineering: Applying the SEMAT Kernel" together with Ivar Jacobson. Since 2000, Dr Ng has been coaching software teams around the world including Singapore

Airlines, Sony, Samsung, Huawei Technologies in areas such as product line engineering, requirements, test, architecture, management, DevOps, gamification, agile and lean. Dr Ng is currently a lean and agile transformation coach with Ivar Jacobson International.

Naghmeh Niknejad received her M.Sc. Computer Science from Universiti Teknologi Malaysia (UTM). She is now doing her Ph.D. at faculty of computing, Universiti Teknologi Malaysia (UTM). Her research interest include service-oriented architecture (SOA), cloud computing and agile processes.

Chung-Yeung Pang received his Ph.D. degree from Cambridge University, England. He has over 25 years experience in software development in various areas, ranging from device driver to large enterprise IT systems. He has experience in many programming languages including low level languages like assembler and C, high level languages like COBOL, Java and Ada, and AI languages such as LISP and Prolog. For the past 20 years, he has been working as a consultant in different enterprise software projects. He has been engaged in architecture design, development, coaching and managing IT projects. At one time, he was one of the lead architects in a project with a budget for over 1 billion USD. In the last years, he has led many projects to completion within time and budgets despite the limited resources and high pressure in some of the projects.

Abbas Moshref Razavi is a researcher at FSKTM, University of Malaya.

Sheidu Salami Tenuche, has Bachelor and Master of Science degrees in Computer Sciences and currently undergoing his PhD programme in computer science at Ahmadu Bello University, Zaria Nigeria. He Lectures at the Mathematics Department, Computer Science Unit, and an Extension specialist and member of ICT Unit at National Agricultural Extension Research and Liaison Services (NAERLS), Ahmadu Bello University Zaria, Nigeria from 2011 till date. His research interest includes Expert systems, Databases and Cloud Computing.

Muhammad Aminu Umar holds a Bachelor of Science degree and Master degree both in Computer Science from Ahmadu Bello University, Zaria Nigeria and Universiti Teknologi Malaysia, Johor respectively. He presently works with Ahmadu Bello University as an Assistant Lecturer teaching Computer Science. His research interest include: Software Engineering, Human-Computer Interaction, Usability Engineering, Information Retrieval and ICT in Agriculture.

Sahabi Ali Yusuf holds a Master degree in 2013 and Bachelor degree in 2008 both in Computer Science from African University of Science and Technology, Abuja, Nigeria and Ahmadu Bello University, Zaria Nigeria respectively. He currently lectures at Department of Mathematics, Computer Science unit of Ahmadu Bello University, Zaria, Nigeria as an Assistant Lecturer. His research interest include: e-Learning and Software Engineering.

Index

T

teaching and learning 283-285, 287-288, 290

U

usability 71, 208-210, 212-219, 221
usability engineering 208-209, 212-214, 216, 218-219, 221
user stories 11, 22, 40, 43, 95, 98, 120, 158, 226-227, 232, 292

W

waterfall model 23, 50-55, 59, 70, 84, 102, 164, 208, 210, 213-215, 234, 292

X

XP 2, 26, 36, 39, 96, 126-127, 140, 142, 147, 152, 164, 168, 170, 174, 207, 210, 212, 217, 224, 236, 239-240, 272, 287, 291

Become an IRMA Member

Members of the **Information Resources Management Association (IRMA)** understand the importance of community within their field of study. The Information Resources Management Association is an ideal venue through which professionals, students, and academicians can convene and share the latest industry innovations and scholarly research that is changing the field of information science and technology. Become a member today and enjoy the benefits of membership as well as the opportunity to collaborate and network with fellow experts in the field.

IRMA Membership Benefits:

- **One FREE Journal Subscription**

- **30% Off Additional Journal Subscriptions**

- **20% Off Book Purchases**

- Updates on the latest events and research on Information Resources Management through the IRMA-L listserv.

- Updates on new open access and downloadable content added to Research IRM.

- A copy of the Information Technology Management Newsletter twice a year.

- A certificate of membership.

IRMA Membership $195

Scan code to visit irma-international.org and begin by selecting your free journal subscription.

Membership is good for one full year.

Printed in the United States
By Bookmasters